Network Programming in Python : The Basic

A Detailed Guide to Python 3 Network Programming and Management

John Galbraith

www.bpbonline.com

FIRST EDITION 2022

Copyright © BPB Publications, India

ISBN: 978-93-5551-257-4

To View Complete
BPB Publications Catalogue
Scan the QR Code:

www.bpbonline.com

Dedicated to

My family

About the Author

John Galbraith is an architect, designer, engineer, artist, playwright, and comedy writer. I've spent the last 14 years working with clients, vendors, service integrators In other life, I am student at MIT.

About the Reviewer

Jomny Carle is an Enterprise architecture, music critic, poet and software architect. He has successfully helped multiple customers in the design and execution of their corporate strategies, in ways that correspond with both security and business objectives, having over 22 years of industry expertise.

Acknowledgments

There are a few people I want to thank for the support they have given me during the writing of this book. First and foremost, I would like to thank my parents for continuously encouraging me to write the book. I could have never completed this book without their support.

My gratitude also goes to the team at BPB Publications for being supportive enough to provide me quite a long time to finish the book and also giving us the opportunity and providing us the necessary support in writing this book.

We would like to thank our family members for the support they have provided for us to focus on the book during our personal time.

Preface

Chapter 1: Introduction of Client-Server Networking: An Overview, you will learn Modern network gear is capable of transmitting small messages known as packets, which are typically no more than a few thousand bytes in size. How can these little individual messages be merged to make conversations between a web browser and a server, or an e-mail client and your ISP's mail server?

Chapter 2: in this section. It merely fixes the first of the two difficulties mentioned above. It assigns port numbers to packets destined for different services on a single system, as described in the next section. Nonetheless, when it comes to packet loss, duplication, and ordering, network programs employing UDP must fend for themselves.

Chapter 3: you will learn, It uses the same rules as UDP to incorporate port numbers and provides ordered and reliable data streams that mask the fact that the continuous stream of data has been cut into packets and then reassembled at the other end from applications.

Chapter 4: After understanding the fundamentals of UDP and TCP, the two major data transports accessible on IP networks, it's time for me to take a step back and discuss two larger challenges that must be addressed regardless of whatever data transport you use. In this chapter, I'll talk about network addresses and the distributed service that converts names to raw IP addresses.

Chapter 5: As you'll learn in Chapter 5, whenever your software has to seek for a DNS hostname, UDP is almost certainly participating in the background. Although TCP has practically become the universal default when two Internet programs need to interact, I'll go over a few situations where it's not the best choice, in case your application falls into one of these groups.

Chapter 6: This chapter will begin by defining TLS's goals and discussing the methods it employs to achieve them. Then you'll learn how to activate and configure TLS on a TCP socket using Python examples, both simple and complicated. Finally, you'll see how TLS is incorporated into the real-world protocols covered in the rest of the book.

Chapter 7: Before going on to the true issue of how network servers can be constructed as pieces of software, this chapter will spend only one part presenting the topic of deployment.

Chapter 8: Despite its briefness, this chapter may be one of the most important in the book. It examines two technologies—caches and message queues—that have evolved into essential building blocks for high-volume systems. The novel hits a turning point at this time.

Chapter 9: This is the first of three HTTP chapters. In this chapter, you'll learn how to use the protocol as a client application that wants to fetch and cache documents as well as maybe submit queries or data to the server. You will learn the protocol's rules as a result of this approach.

Chapter 10: After that, we'll look at the design and deployment of HTTP servers in this chapter. In both chapters, the protocol will be examined in its most basic conceptual form, that is, as a mechanism for retrieving or uploading documents.

Chapter 11: There, you'll learn about the programming patterns offered by template libraries, forms, and Ajax, as well as web frameworks that attempt to combine all of these patterns into a simple-to-program form.

Chapter 12: This chapter explains how e-mail messages are constructed, with a focus on proper multimedia inclusion and internationalization. The payload format for the protocols described in the following three chapters is established by this.

Chapter 13: The Simple Mail Transfer Protocol (SMTP) is described in this chapter, and it is used to transport e-mail messages from the machine on which they are composed to the server that retains the message, preparing it for reading by a specific recipient.

Chapter 14: you will learn about, illustrates how someone who is ready to read their e-mail can download and view fresh messages that are waiting in their in box on their e-mail server using the outdated, poorly built Post Office Protocol (POP).

Chapter 15: IMAP stands for Internet Message Access Protocol, and it is a better and more current choice for seeing e-mail that is hosted on your e-mail server locally. IMAP not only allows you to fetch and view messages, but it also allows you to mark them as read and store them in different folders on the server.

Chapter 16: The command line is the topic of this chapter. It describes how to connect to it via the network and provides enough information about its normal behaviour to assist you overcome any frustrating obstacles you may encounter while attempting to use it.

Chapter 17: FTP was originally used to fuel four basic activities. FTP was first and mostly used for file downloads. Second, FTP was frequently hacked to allow for anonymous uploads. Third, the protocol was frequently used to enable the synchronization of whole file trees between different computer accounts. Finally, FTP was utilized for what it was designed for: interactive, full-featured file management.

Chapter 18: In these chapter we'll learn about how to recover while having errors in the network and message queues,RPC's characters, and web frameworks.

Code Bundle and Coloured Images

Please follow the link to download the
Code Bundle and the *Coloured Images* of the book:

https://rebrand.ly/twfyjg1

The code bundle for the book is also hosted on GitHub at **https://github.com/ bpbpublications/Network-Programming-in-Python**. In case there's an update to the code, it will be updated on the existing GitHub repository.

We have code bundles from our rich catalogue of books and videos available at **https://github.com/bpbpublications**. Check them out!

Errata

We take immense pride in our work at BPB Publications and follow best practices to ensure the accuracy of our content to provide with an indulging reading experience to our subscribers. Our readers are our mirrors, and we use their inputs to reflect and improve upon human errors, if any, that may have occurred during the publishing processes involved. To let us maintain the quality and help us reach out to any readers who might be having difficulties due to any unforeseen errors, please write to us at :

errata@bpbonline.com

Your support, suggestions and feedbacks are highly appreciated by the BPB Publications' Family.

Did you know that BPB offers eBook versions of every book published, with PDF and ePub files available? You can upgrade to the eBook version at www.bpbonline.com and as a print book customer, you are entitled to a discount on the eBook copy. Get in touch with us at :

business@bpbonline.com for more details.

At **www.bpbonline.com**, you can also read a collection of free technical articles, sign up for a range of free newsletters, and receive exclusive discounts and offers on BPB books and eBooks.

Piracy

If you come across any illegal copies of our works in any form on the internet, we would be grateful if you would provide us with the location address or website name. Please contact us at **business@bpbonline.com** with a link to the material.

If you are interested in becoming an author

If there is a topic that you have expertise in, and you are interested in either writing or contributing to a book, please visit **www.bpbonline.com**. We have worked with thousands of developers and tech professionals, just like you, to help them share their insights with the global tech community. You can make a general application, apply for a specific hot topic that we are recruiting an author for, or submit your own idea.

Reviews

Please leave a review. Once you have read and used this book, why not leave a review on the site that you purchased it from? Potential readers can then see and use your unbiased opinion to make purchase decisions. We at BPB can understand what you think about our products, and our authors can see your feedback on their book. Thank you!

For more information about BPB, please visit **www.bpbonline.com**.

Table of Contents

CHAPTER 1

Client-Server Networking: An Overview

The Python language is used to explore network programming in this book. It covers the fundamental principles, modules, and third-party libraries that you'll need to communicate with remote machines via the Internet using the most common communication protocols.

The book does not have enough room to teach you how to write in Python if you have never seen the language or written a computer program before; instead, it assumes that you have already learned something about Python programming from the numerous great tutorials and books available. I hope the Python examples in this book provide you some ideas for structuring and writing your own code. But I'll use advanced Python capabilities without explanation or apologies—though I might point out how I'm utilizing a certain approach or construction when I believe it's particularly intriguing or brilliant.

This book, on the other hand, does not begin by presuming you are familiar with networking! You should be able to start reading this book at the beginning and learn about computer networking along the way if you've ever used a web browser or sent an e-mail. I'll approach networking from the perspective of an application programmer who is either creating a network-connected service—such as a web site, an e-mail server, or a networked computer game—or designing a client software to use one.

This book, on the other hand, will not teach you how to set up or configure networks. The disciplines of network architecture, server room administration, and automated provisioning are separate topics that do not intersect with the discipline of computer programming as it is described in this book. While Python is becoming a big part of the provisioning landscape thanks to projects like OpenStack, SaltStack, and Ansible, if you want to learn more about provisioning and its many technologies, you'll want to look for books and documentation that are specifically about provisioning and its many technologies.

Structure

- Layers of Application
- Talking a protocol
- A Network Conversation in its Natural State
- Turtles, Turtles, Turtles
- The Foundation: Stacks and Libraries
- The process of encoding and decoding
- The Internet Protocol (IP)
- Internet Protocol (IP Addresses)
- Routing
- Fragmentation of packets
- Learning More About internet protocol
- Conclusion

Objective:

In this chapter you will learn to use layer of application used in python like google geocoding, about internet protocol, how to encode and decode in python, many thing of python libraries, routing etc.

The Foundation: Stacks and Libraries

When you first start learning Python network programming, there are two notions that will come up repeatedly.

- The concept of a protocol stack, in which basic network services are utilized as the foundation for more complex services to be built.

- The fact that you'll frequently be utilizing Python libraries containing previously written code—whether modules from Python's built-in standard library or packages from third-party distributions you download and install—that already know how to communicate with the network protocol you want to utilize.

In many cases, network programming simply get in choosing and implementing a library that already implements the network functions you require. The main goals of this book are to introduce you to a number of important networking libraries for Python, as well as to teach you about the lower-level network services that those libraries are based on. Knowing the lower-level content is useful both for understanding how the libraries work and for understanding what happens when anything goes wrong at a lower level.

Let's start with a basic example. The following is a mailing address:

Taj mahal

Agra, Uttar Pradesh

This physical address's latitude and longitude are of importance to me. Google, fortunately, has a Geocoding API that can do such a conversion. What would you need to do in order to take advantage of Python's network service?

When considering a new network service, it's always a good idea to start by seeing if someone has already developed the protocol that your software will need to speak— in this example, the Google Geocoding protocol. Begin by going over the Python Standard Library's documentation for everything related to geocoding.

https://docs.python.org/3/library/

Is there any mention of geocoding? I don't think so, either. Even if you don't always find what you're searching for, it's necessary for a Python programmer to check through the Standard Library's table of contents on a regular basis because each read-through will help you get more comfortable with the Python services.

Doug Hellmann's "Python Module of the Week" blog is another excellent resource for learning about Python's possibilities thanks to its Standard Library.

Because the Standard Library does not offer a package to assist you in this scenario, you can look for general-purpose Python packages on the Python Package Index, which is a wonderful resource for locating packages provided by other programmers and organizations from all over the world. Of course, you may look on the website of the vendor whose service you'll be using to see if it has a Python library for accessing it. Alternatively, you may run a generic Google search for Python plus the name of whatever web service you wish to utilize and see if any of the first few results point to a package you should try.

In this example, I used the Python Package Index, which can be found at the following address:

https://pypi.org/

I typed in geocoding and found a package called pygeocoder, which provides a nice interface to Google's geocoding features (albeit, as its description indicates, it is not vendor-provided but rather was built by someone other than Google).

https://pypi.org/project/pygeocoder/

Because this is such a typical scenario—finding a Python package that sounds like it might already do precisely what you're looking for and wanting to try it out on your system—I thought I'd take a time to introduce you to the best Python technology for fast trying out new libraries: virtualenv!

Installing a Python package used to be a painful and irrevocable process that necessitated administrative intervention.

privileges on your machine, and as a result, your Python installation on your system has been permanently altered. After numerous months of preparation,

If you're doing a lot of Python work, your system Python installation could end up being a wasteland of dozens of packages, all installed at the same time.

by hand, and you may find that any new packages you try to install may fail due to incompatibility.

with the outdated packages from a project that ended months ago hanging on your hard drive

Python programmers who are cautious are no longer in this predicament. Many of us only ever install virtualenv as a system-wide Python package. Once virtualenv is installed, you can build as many small, self-contained "virtual Python environments" as you like, where you can install and uninstall packages and experiment without polluting your systemwide Python. When a project or experiment is completed, you just delete the virtual environment directory associated with it, and your system is clean.

You'll need to establish a virtual environment to test the pygeocoder package in this situation. If this is the first time you've installed virtualenv on your machine, go to this URL to download and install it:

https://pypi.org/project/virtualenv/

After you've installed virtualenv, use the following instructions to establish a new environment. (On Windows, the virtual environment's Python binary directory will be called Scripts rather than bin.)

```
$ virtualenv -p python3 geo_env
 $ cd geo_env
 $ ls
bin/ include/ lib/
 $ . bin/activate
$ python -c 'import pygeocoder'
 Traceback (most recent call last):
File "<string>", line 1, in
ImportError: No module named 'pygeocoder'
```

The pygeocoder package is not yet available, as you can see. To install it, use the pip command from within your virtual environment, which is now on your path as a result of the activate command you ran.

```
$ pip install pygeocoder
```

Downloading/unpacking pygeocoder

```
 Downloading pygeocoder-1.2.1.1.tar.gz
 Running setup.py egg_info for package pygeocoder
Downloading/unpacking requests>=1.0 (from pygeocoder)
 Downloading requests-2.0.1.tar.gz (412kB): 412kB downloaded
 Running setup.py egg_info for package requests
Installing collected packages: pygeocoder, requests
 Running setup.py install for pygeocoder
Running setup.py install for requests
Successfully installed pygeocoder requests
2
```

The pygeocoder package will now be available in the virtualenv's python binary.

```
$ python -c 'import pygeocoder'
```

Now that you've installed the pygeocoder package, you should be able to run the search1.py programme, as shown in Listing 1-1.

Listing1-1: Obtaining a Longitude and Latitude

```
#!/usr/bin/env python3
 # Network Programming in Python: The Basics
from pygeocoder import Geocoder
 if __name__ == '__main__':
address = taj mahal'
 print(Geocoder.geocode(address)[0].coordinates)
```

By running it at the command line, you should see a result like this:

```
 $ python3 search1.py (27.1751° N, 78.0421° E)
```

And there it is, right there on your computer screen, the answer to our inquiry concerning the latitude and longitude of the address! The information was obtained directly from Google's web site. The first sample software was a huge hit.

Are you frustrated that you opened a book on Python network programming only to be instructed to download and install a third-party package that turned a potentially intriguing networking challenge into a tedious three-line Python script? Relax and unwind! Ninety percent of the time, you'll discover that this is how programming problems are addressed—by locating other Python programmers who have already solved the problem you're encountering and then building smartly and succinctly on their solutions.

However, you are not quite finished with this example. You've seen how a complicated network service can be accessed with relative ease. But what lies beneath the attractive pygeocoder user interface? What is the procedure for using the service? You'll now learn more about how this complex service is actually just the top tier of a network stack with at least a half-dozen additional layers.

Layers of Application

To tackle a problem, the first application listed employed a third-party Python library acquired from the Python Package Index. It was well-versed in the Google Geocoding API and its usage guidelines. But what if that library didn't exist at all? What if you had to create your own client for Google's Maps API?

Look at search2.py, which is shown in Listing 1-2, for the answer. Instead of employing a geocoding-aware third-party library, it uses the popular requests library, which is the foundation for pygeocoding and, as you can see from the pip install line, is already installed in your virtual environment.

Listing 1-2. Using the Google Geocoding API to get a JSON Document

```python
#!/usr/bin/env python3
 # Network Programming in Python: The Basics
import requests

def geocode(address):
    base = 'https://nominatim.openstreetmap.org/search'
    parameters = {'q': address, 'format': 'json'}
    user_agent = ' Client-Server Networking: An Overview search2.py'
    headers = {'User-Agent': user_agent}
    response = requests.get(base, params=parameters, headers=headers)
    reply = response.json()
    print(reply[0]['lat'], reply[0]['lon'])


if __name__ == '__main__':
    geocode('taj mahal')
```

When you run this Python program, you'll get a result that's very similar to the first script.

```
$ python3 search2.py
{'lat': 27.1751° N, 'lng': - 78.0421° E }
```

The results aren't identical—for example, you can see that the JSON data encoded the result as a "object" that requests has handed to you as a Python dictionary. However, it is evident that this script achieves roughly the same result as the previous one.

The first thing you'll notice about this code is that the higher-level pygeocoder module's semantics are missing. If you don't look attentively at this code, you might not see that it's even asking for a mailing address! Unlike search1.py, which requested for an address to be converted to latitude and longitude, the second listing meticulously constructs both a base URL and a series of query parameters whose purpose may not be obvious unless you've read the Google documentation. By the way, if you want to read the documentation, the API is explained here:

https://developers.google.com/maps/documentation/geocoding/

If you look closely at the dictionary of query parameters in search2.py, you'll notice that the address parameter gives you the specific mailing address you're looking for. The other argument tells Google that you're not using a mobile device location sensor to pull data for this location query.

You manually call the response when you obtain a document as a result of looking for this URL. To convert it to JSON, use the json() method, and then dive into the resultant multilayered data structure to discover the correct element that holds the latitude and longitude.

The search2.py script then accomplishes the same thing as search1.py, but instead of using addresses and latitudes, it discusses the very gritty details of generating a URL, obtaining a response, and parsing it as JSON. When you go down a layer of a network stack to the layer behind it, there is a common difference: where the high-level code talked about what a request meant, the lower-level code can only see the specifics of how the request is produced.

Talking a protocol

As a result, the second example script generates a URL and retrieves the document associated with it. That action appears to be pretty straightforward, and your web browser does its best to make it appear so. Of fact, the real reason a URL may be used to download a document is that it is a kind of recipe that defines where to find—and how to fetch—a specific document on the Internet. The URL begins with the name of a protocol, then the name of the computer on which the document is stored, and finally the path that identifies a specific document on that machine. The URL offers instructions that inform a lower-level protocol how to find the document, which is why the search2.py Python application is able to resolve the URL and fetch the page at all.

The famous Hypertext Transfer Protocol (HTTP), which is the foundation of practically all modern web connections, is the lower-level protocol that the URL employs. In Chapters 9, 10, and 11 of this book, you'll learn more about it. HTTP offers the method that allows the Requests library to retrieve the result from Google.

What do you think it would look like if you removed the layer of magic—what if you just wanted to get the result through HTTP? As demonstrated in Listing 1-3, the result **is search3.py.**

Listing 1-3. Using Google Maps with a Raw HTTP Connection

```
#!/usr/bin/env python3
```

```python
# Network Programming in Python: The Basics
import http.client
import json
from urllib.parse import quote_plus


base = '/search'


def geocode(address):
    path = '{}?q={}&format=json'.format(base, quote_plus(address))
    user_agent = b' Client-Server Networking: An Overview.py'
    headers = {b'User-Agent': user_agent}
    connection=http.client.HTTPSConnection('nominatim.openstreetmap.
    org')
    connection.request('GET', path, None, headers)
    rawreply = connection.getresponse().read()
    reply = json.loads(rawreply.decode('utf-8'))
    print(reply[0]['lat'], reply[0]['lon'])


if __name__ == '__main__':
    geocode('taj mahal')
```

You're directly manipulating the HTTP protocol in this listing, asking it to connect to a specific computer, execute a GET request using a URL you've created by hand, and then receive the response directly from the HTTP connection. Instead of being able to provide your query parameters as individual keys and values, you may now do so in a more simple manner. You must insert them directly, by hand, in the path that you are seeking in a dictionary by first writing a The arguments in the format name=value separated by & characters are followed by a question mark (?)

The outcome of executing the program, on the other hand, is very similar to that of the prior programs.

```
$ python3 search2.py

{'lat': 27.1751° N, 'lng': - 78.0421° E }
```

HTTP is just one of many protocols for which the Python Standard Library has a built-in implementation, as you'll see throughout this book. Instead of having to worry about all of the specifics of how HTTP works, search3.py allows you to just ask for a request to be sent and then inspect the response. Because you have dropped down another level in the protocol stack, the protocol details that the script must deal with are, of course, more primitive than those of search2.py, but you can still rely on the Standard Library to handle the actual network data and ensure that you do it right.

A Network Conversation in its Natural State

Of course, HTTP can't only transport data between two devices in the air. Instead, the HTTP protocol must rely on a far more basic abstraction. In fact, it makes use of modern operating systems' capabilities to provide a plain-text network dialogue between two separate programmes over an IP network using the TCP protocol. In other words, the HTTP protocol works by specifying the exact text of messages that are sent back and forth between two hosts that can communicate using TCP.

When you proceed below HTTP to investigate what happens underneath it, you're descending to the lowest level of the network stack, which you can still readily reach from Python. Take a close look to search4.py, which can be found in Listings 1-4. It sends the identical networking request to Google Maps as the previous three applications, but it does so by sending a raw text message over the Internet and receives a bundle of text as a response.

Listing 1-4. Using a Bare Socket to Communicate with Google Maps

```python
#!/usr/bin/env python3
# Network Programming in Python: The Basics
import socket
from urllib.parse import quote_plus


request_text = """\
GET /maps/api/geocode/json?address={}&sensor=false HTTP/1.1\r\n\
Host: maps.google.com:80\r\n\
User-Agent: search4.py (Network Programming in Python: The Basics)\r\n\
Connection: close\r\n\
\r\n\
"""
```

```python
def geocode(address):
    sock = socket.socket()
    sock.connect(('maps.google.com', 80))
    request = request_text.format(quote_plus(address))
    sock.sendall(request.encode('ascii'))
    raw_reply = b''
    while True:
        more = sock.recv(4096)
        if not more:
            break
        raw_reply += more
    print(raw_reply.decode('utf-8'))

if __name__ == '__main__':
    geocode('taj mahal')
```

You've crossed a significant threshold by switching from search3.py to search4.py. You were utilizing a Python library—written in Python itself—in every prior program listing to speak a sophisticated network protocol on your behalf. But now you've reached the bottom: you're using the host operating system's raw socket() method to provide fundamental network communications over an IP network. In other words, when writing this network function in the C language, you're employing the same methods that a low-level system programmer would use.

Over the next few chapters, you'll learn more about sockets. For the time being, you can see that raw network communication in search4.py consists of sending and receiving byte strings. The request is one byte string, and the response is another huge byte string, which you simply print to the screen in order to experience it in all of its low-level beauty. (For more information on why you decode the string before printing it, see the section "Encoding and Decoding" later in this chapter.) The HTTP request, whose content you can see inside the sendall() function, consists of the term GET—the name of the operation you want to perform—followed by the location of the document you want fetched and the method you want to use to retrieve it the version of http you support.

GET/maps/api/geocode/json?address=taj+mahal+&sensor=false HTTP/1.1

Then there's a series of headers with a name, a colon, and a value, followed by a carriage-return/newline pair that closes the request.

Listing 1-5 shows the response, which will print as the script's output if you execute search4.py. Instead of writing the extensive text-manipulation code that would be able to comprehend the response, I elected to simply display the response to the screen in this example. I did this because I believed that viewing the HTTP response on your screen would give you a far better understanding of what it looks like than deciphering code designed to analyse it.

Listing 1-5. The Result of running search4.py

```
HTTP/1.1 200 OK
Server: nginx
Date: Tue, 25 Jan 2022 22:50:14 GMT
Content-Type: application/json; charset=UTF-8
Transfer-Encoding: chunked
Connection: close
Access-Control-Allow-Origin: *
Access-Control-Allow-Methods: OPTIONS,GET


37c
[{"place_id":188987579,"licence":"Data © OpenStreet-
Map contributors, ODbL 1.0. https://osm.org/copy-
right","osm_type":"way","osm_id":375257537,"boundingbox-
":["27.1745358","27.1754823","78.0415593","78.0426212"],"lat":"2
7.1750123","lon":"78.04209683661315","display_name":"Taj Mahal,
Taj Mahal Internal Path, Taj Ganj, Agra, Uttar Pradesh, 282001,
India","class":"tourism","type":"attraction","importance":1.0489
056883572618,"icon":"https://nominatim.openstreetmap.org/ui/mapi-
cons//poi_point_of_interest.p.20.png"},{"place_id":191576149,"li-
cence":"Data © OpenStreetMap contributors, ODbL 1.0. https://osm.
org/copyright","osm_type":"way","osm_id":382063175,"boundingbox-
":["27.1674585","27.1682576","78.0506999","78.0507466"],"lat":"27
.1682576","lon":"78.0507466","display_name":"gali no 1, Taj Ganj,
Agra, Uttar Pradesh, 282001, India","class":"highway","type":"resi-
dential","importance":0.5}]


0
```

The HTTP reply has a structure that is very similar to the HTTP request. It starts with a status line and then moves on to a series of headers. Following a blank line, the response content is displayed: a JavaScript data structure in the simple JSON format that answers your query by describing the geographic location supplied by the Google Geocoding API search.

Of course, all of these status lines and headers are the same low-level details that Python's httplib was handling in the previous listings. You can see how communication would look if that layer of software was removed.

Turtles, Turtles, Turtles

I hope you've liked these first glimpses into the world of Python network programming. Taking a step back, I can use this set of examples to illustrate a few points about Python network programming.

First, you may have a better understanding of what the term protocol stack means: it refers to the process of layering a high-level, semantically sophisticated conversation ("I want the geographic location of this mailing address") on top of simpler, and more rudimentary, conversations that are ultimately just text strings sent back and forth between two computers using their network hardware.

The protocol stack you just looked at is made up of four different protocols.

- On top of that, there's the Google Geocoding API, which explains how to express geographic inquiries as URLs that return JSON data with coordinates.
- URLs are unique identifiers for documents that may be retrieved over HTTP.
- HTTP uses raw TCP/IP sockets to support document-oriented operations like GET.
- TCP/IP sockets are only capable of sending and receiving byte strings.

Each layer of the stack, as you can see, makes use of the tools offered by the layer below it and, in turn, provides capabilities to the layer above it.

A second point brought up by these examples is how comprehensive Python support is for each of the network tiers you've just worked with. It was only necessary to use a third-party library when using a vendor-specific protocol and needing to format requests so that Google could understand them; I chose requests for the second listing not because the Standard Library lacks the urllib.request module, but because its API is overly clunky. . The Python Standard Library already had good support for all of the previous protocol levels you encountered. Python has functions and classes to help you get the job done, whether you needed to fetch a document at a specific URL or send and receive text over a raw network socket.

Third, when I forced myself to employ lower-level protocols, the quality of my programmes deteriorated significantly. For example, the search2.py and search3.py listings began to hard-code aspects like form structure and hostnames in a way that is inflexible and may be difficult to maintain later. Even worse, the code in search4.

py includes a handwritten, unparameterized HTTP request whose structure is utterly unknown to Python. Of course, it lacks the actual logic required to process and evaluate the HTTP response and comprehend any network error situations that may arise.

This shows a point that you should keep in mind throughout the rest of the book: correctly implementing network protocols is complex, and you should utilise the Standard Library or third-party libraries wherever possible. You will always be tempted to oversimplify your code, especially when writing a network client; you will tend to ignore many error conditions that may arise, to prepare only for the most likely responses, to avoid properly escaping parameters because you fondly believe that your query strings will only ever include simple alphabetic characters, and, in general, to write very brittle code that knows as little about the service it is talking to as is technical, and to write very brittle code that knows as little about the service it is talking to You will benefit from all of the edge cases and awkward corners that the library implementer has already discovered and learned how to handle properly by instead using a third-party library that has developed a thorough implementation of a protocol and has had to support many different Python developers who are using the library for a variety of tasks.

Fourth, it's worth noting that higher-level network protocols, such as Google's Geocoding API for resolving a street address, work by concealing the network layers behind them. You might not even realise that URLs and HTTP are the lower-level techniques that are utilised to generate and answer your queries if you've only ever used the pygeocoder library!

The right hiding of faults at those lower levels is a fascinating subject, the answer to which differs depending on how thoroughly a Python library has been constructed. Could a network issue that renders Google unreachable from your location cause a raw, low-level networking exception in the middle of code that's merely trying to find the coordinates of a street address trigger a raw, low-level networking exception? Or will all errors be reclassified as a higher-level geocoding exception? As you progress through this book, pay close attention to the topic of catching network problems, particularly in the chapters in this first section that focus on low-level networking.

Finally, we've arrived at the topic that will keep you busy for the rest of this first chapter: the socket() interface used in search4.py isn't the lowest protocol level in use when you send this request to Google! Just as there are network protocols functioning above raw sockets in the example, there are protocols working beneath the sockets abstraction that Python cannot see because your operating system maintains them.

The following layers operate behind the socket() API:

- The Transmission Control Protocol (TCP) facilitates two-way byte-stream conversations by transmitting (and perhaps re-sending), receiving, and re-ordering tiny network communications known as packets.

- The Internet Protocol (IP) is a protocol that allows packets to be sent between computers.

- At the absolute bottom, the "link layer" is made up of network hardware devices like Ethernet ports and wireless cards that can deliver physical communications between directly connected computers.

The rest of this chapter, as well as the two next chapters, will focus on the lowest protocol levels. You'll begin by looking at the IP level in this chapter, then move on to examine how two quite distinct protocols—UDP and TCP—support the two main types of conversations that can be had between applications on two Internet-connected hosts in the next chapters.

But first, some background on bytes and characters.

The process of encoding and decoding

The Python 3 language distinguishes between strings of characters and low-level bytes sequences. Bytes are the real binary numbers that computers send back and forth during network connection. They are made up of eight binary digits and range from 00000000 to 11111111, or 0 to 255 in decimal terms. . Unicode symbols such as a ("Latin tiny letter A," as defined by the Unicode standard) or a ("right curly bracket") or a ("right curly bracket") can be found in Python character strings (empty set). While each Unicode character does have a numeric identifier called a code point, you can ignore this as an internal implementation detail because Python 3 is careful to keep characters behaving like characters at all times, and only when you ask will Python convert characters to and from actual externally visible bytes.

Both of these operations have official names.

Decoding: When bytes are on their way into your application and you need to figure out what they mean, decoding is what you do. Consider your program as a traditional Cold War spy tasked with deciphering the transmission of raw bytes arriving from across a communications channel when it gets bytes from a file or over the network.

Encoding: Encoding is the process of converting character strings that are ready to be presented to the outside world into bytes using one of the several encodings that digital computers employ when they need to communicate or store symbols using their only real currency, bytes. Consider your spy having to convert their communication into numbers for transmission, or symbols into a code that can be delivered over the network.

These two operations are available in Python 3 as a decode() function for byte strings after reading them in and an encode() method for character strings when it's time to write them back out. Listings 1-6 show the techniques in action.

Listing 1-6. Encoding Characters for Output and Decoding Input Bytes

```
#!/usr/bin/env python3
# Network Programming in Python: The Basics
if __name__ == '__main__':
# Translating from the outside world of bytes to Unicode characters.
  input_bytes = b'\xff\xfe4\x001\x003\x00 \x00i\x00s\x00 \x00i\x00n\x00.\x00
input_characters = input_bytes.decode('utf-16')
 print(repr(input_characters))
 # Translating characters back into bytes before sending them.
 output_characters = 'We copy you down, Eagle.\n'
 output_bytes = output_characters.encode('utf-8')
 with open('eagle.txt', 'wb') as f:
 f.write(output_bytes)'
```

The examples in this book make a conscious effort to distinguish between bytes and characters. When you show their repr(), you'll notice that byte strings begin with the letter b and look like b'Hello,' whereas true full-fledged character strings have no first character and simply look like 'world.' To avoid misunderstanding between byte strings and character strings, Python 3 only supports character strings for most string functions.

The Internet Protocol (IP)

Both networking and internetworking are really just sophisticated schemes to allow resource sharing. Networking connects numerous computers with a physical link so that they may communicate, while internetworking connects adjacent physical networks to form a much bigger system like the Internet.

Disk drives, RAM, and the CPU are all carefully guarded by the operating system so that the separate programmes running on your computer can access those resources without stomping on each other's toes. The network is another another resource that the operating system must safeguard in order for applications to speak with one another without interfering with other discussions on the same network.

Physical networking equipment, such as Ethernet cards, wireless transmitters, and USB ports, that your computer uses to communicate are each designed with an elaborate ability to share a single physical medium among many distinct devices that want to interact. A DSL modem uses frequency-domain multiplexing, a fundamental concept in electrical engineering, to keep its own digital signals from interfering with the analogue signals sent down the line when you talk on the phone. A dozen Ethernet cards could be plugged into the same hub; 30 wireless cards could be sharing the same radio channel; and a DSL modem uses frequency-domain multiplexing, a fundamental concept in electrical engineering, to keep its own digital signals from interfering with the analogue signals sent down the line when you.

The packet is the fundamental unit of sharing across network devices—the currency in which they exchange, if you will. A packet is a byte string that can range in length from a few bytes to a few thousand bytes and is sent across network devices as a single unit. Although specialised networks exist, particularly in areas such as telecommunications, where each individual byte coming down a transmission line may be routed to a different destination, the more general-purpose technologies used to build digital networks for modern computers are all based on the packet.

At the physical level, a packet usually has only two properties: the byte-string data it contains and the address to which it is to be delivered. A physical packet's address is typically a unique identifier for one of the other network cards connected to the same Ethernet segment or wireless channel as the computer sending the packet. A network card's job is to send and receive such packets without requiring the computer's operating system to be concerned with the specifics of how the network operates with cables, voltages, and signals.

So, what exactly is the Internet Protocol (IP)?

The Internet Protocol is a protocol for assigning a standard address system to all Internet-connected computers throughout the world and allowing packets to go from one end of the Internet to the other. A web browser, for example, should be able to connect to a host from anywhere without ever knowing which maze of network devices each packet passes through on its way there. It's rare for a Python programme to function at such a low level that it sees the Internet Protocol in action, but understanding how it works is useful at the very least.

Internet Protocol (IP Addresses)

Every computer connecting to the global network is given a 4-byte address in the original version of the Internet Protocol. Such addresses are typically represented by four decimal integers separated by periods, each representing a single byte of the address. As a result, each number can vary from 0 to 255. So, here's how a conventional four-byte IP address looks:

130.207.244.244

People utilizing the Internet are typically provided hostnames rather than IP addresses because solely numeric addresses are difficult for humans to memorize. The user can just enter google.com and forget that this resolves to an address such as 74.125.67.103, to which their computer can send packets for transmission over the Internet.

Listing 1-7 shows a basic Python programme called getname.py that requests the operating system—Linux, Mac OS, Windows, or whichever system the programme is executing on—to resolve the hostname www.python.org. The Domain Name System, the network service that responds to hostname searches, is pretty sophisticated, and I'll go over it in more depth in Chapter 4.

Listing 1-7. Converting a Hostname to an IP Address

```
#!/usr/bin/env python3
 # Network Programming in Python: The Basics
import socket
if __name__ == '__main__':
 hostname = 'www.python.org'
 addr = socket.gethostbyname(hostname)
 print('The IP address of {} is {}'.format(hostname, addr))
```

For now, you just need to remember two things.

- For starters, no matter how complex an Internet application appears to be, the Internet Protocol always uses numeric IP addresses to direct packets to their intended destination.

- Second, the operating system normally handles the intricate intricacies of how hostnames are resolved to IP addresses

Your operating system, like other aspects of Internet Protocol operation, prefers to take care of them. Both you and your Python code are kept in the dark about the details.

Actually, nowadays, the addressing issue is a little more complicated than the simple 4-byte approach.

described. Because the world is running out of 4-byte IP addresses, an expanded address scheme known as IPv6 is being implemented, which allows for absolutely massive 16-byte addresses that should service humanity's needs for a very long time. They're written in a different way than 4-byte IP addresses, and look somewhat like this:

fe80::fcfd:4aff:fecf:ea4e

You won't need to worry about the difference between IPv4 and IPv6 as long as your code accepts IP addresses or hostnames from the user and delivers them directly to a networking library for processing. Your Python code's operating system will recognise which IP version it is using and will interpret addresses accordingly.

Traditional IP addresses are read from left to right, with the first one or two bytes indicating an organisation and the next byte indicating the subnet on which the target computer is located. The address is narrowed down to that specific machine or service by the last byte. There are also a few IP address ranges that have unique significance.

- 127.*.*.*: IP addresses that start with the byte 127 belong to a particular, reserved range that is specific to the machine where an application is operating. When your web browser, FTP client, or Python programme connects to an address in this range, it's requesting to communicate with another service or programme on the same machine. The IP address 127.0.0.1 is commonly used to represent "this computer itself that this software is running on," and may often be reached under the hostname localhost.

- 10.*.*.*, 172.16–31.*.*, and 192.168.*.*: These IP addresses are reserved for private subnets. The Internet's administrators have made a firm promise: no IP addresses in any of these three ranges will be given to legitimate enterprises putting up servers or services. As a result, these addresses are assured to have no relevance on the Internet at large; they designate no host to which you may desire to connect. As a result, you are free to utilise these addresses on any of your organization's internal networks if you want to be able to assign IP addresses internally without having to make those hosts publicly accessible.

Some of these private addresses are even likely to appear in your own home: your wireless router or DSL modem will frequently assign IP addresses from one of these private ranges to your home computers and laptops, masking all of your Internet traffic behind the single "real" IP address that your Internet service provider has assigned to you.

Routing

When an application requests that data be sent to a specific IP address, the operating system must determine how to transport that data through one of the physical networks to which the computer is connected. Routing is the process of deciding where to send each Internet Protocol packet based on the IP address that it specifies as its destination.

Most, if not all, of the Python code you create during your career will run on hosts at the edge of the Internet, connected to the rest of the world by a single network interface. Routing becomes an easy decision for such machines.

- If the IP address begins with 127.*.*.*, the operating system recognises the packet as being for another application on the same machine. It will be passed immediately to another programme via an internal data copy by the operating system, rather than being sent to a real network device for transmission.

- If the IP address belongs to the same subnet as the machine, the destination host can be discovered by checking the local Ethernet segment, wireless channel, or whatever local network is in use, and delivering the packet to a machine that is locally connected.

- If not, the packet is forwarded to a gateway machine that connects your local subnet to the rest of the Internet. After that, it will be up to the gateway machine to decide where the packet should be sent.

Routing is, of fact, only as straightforward at the Internet's edge, where the only decisions are whether to keep the packet on the local network or send it flying over the Internet. You can imagine that routing decisions for the specialised network devices that make up the Internet's backbone are significantly more complicated! Extensive routing tables must be constructed, consulted, and constantly updated on the switches that connect entire continents in order to know that packets destined for Google go in one direction, packets directed to an Amazon IP address go in another, and packets directed to your machine go in yet another. run on Internet backbone routers, thus you'll almost always see the simpler routing scenario described above in operation.

In the preceding paragraphs, I was a little hazy on how your computer determines whether an IP address belongs to a local subnet or should be transmitted through a gateway to the rest of the Internet. I've been writing the prefix followed by asterisks for the sections of the address that could vary to show the concept of a subnet, where all of the hosts have the same IP address prefix. . Of all, your operating system's network stack's binary logic does not actually insert little ASCII asterisks into its routing table! Subnets are defined instead by combining an IP address with a mask that specifies how many of the address's most significant bits must match in order for a host to belong to that subnet. You can readily read subnet numbers if you keep in mind that each byte in an IP address comprises eight bits of binary data. They appear as follows:

- 127.0.0.0/8: This pattern, which describes the previously discussed IP address range and is reserved for the local host, specifies that the first 8 bits (1 byte) must match the number 127, while the subsequent 24 bits (3 bytes) can have any value.

- 192.168.0.0/16: Because the first 16 bits must match properly, this pattern will match any IP address that belongs in the private 192.168 range. The last 16 bits of the 32-bit address can be set to any value.

- 192.168.5.0/24: This is a subnet address specification for a single subnet. This is most likely the most widely used subnet mask on the Internet. For an IP address to fall into this range, the first three bytes of the address must match. Only the last byte (the last eight bits) of each machine in this range is allowed to differ. This leaves a total of 256 distinct addresses. The.0 address is typically used as the subnet's name, and the.255 address is used as the destination for a "broadcast packet" that addresses all of the subnet's hosts (as you'll learn in the following chapter), leaving 254 addresses available for computer assignment. Although the address.1 is commonly used for the gateway that connects the subnet to the rest of the Internet, some businesses and schools choose to use a different number.

In almost all circumstances, your Python code will simply rely on its host operating system to make proper packet routing decisions, just as it does to resolve hostnames to IP addresses in the first place.

Fragmentation of packets

Packet fragmentation is a final Internet Protocol concept worth mentioning. While it's meant to be a minor element that your operating system's network stack cleverly hides from your programme, it's caused enough problems throughout the Internet's history that it needs at least a passing mention.

Because the Internet Protocol enables very big packets—up to 64KB in length—fragmentation is required because the actual network equipment from which IP networks are created often accept considerably smaller packet sizes. Ethernet networks, for example, can only handle packets of 1,500 bytes. As a result, Internet packets include a "don't fragment" (DF) flag that allows the sender to specify what should happen if the packet is too large to fit through one of the physical networks connecting the source and destination computers:

- If the DF flag is not set, fragmentation is allowed, and when a packet hits a network threshold beyond which it can no longer fit, the gateway can divide it into smaller packets and designate them for reassembling at the other end.
- If the DF flag is set, fragmentation is forbidden, and if the packet cannot fit, it will be discarded and an error message will be sent back to the machine that sent the packet—in the form of an Internet Control Message Protocol (ICMP) packet—so that it can try splitting the message into smaller pieces and re-sending it.

The DF flag is normally set by the operating system, and your Python programmes have no control over it. The logic that the system would normally utilise is roughly as follows: If you're conducting a UDP conversation (see Chapter 2) where individual datagrams are flying over the Internet, The operating system will leave DF unset so that each datagram arrives at its destination in as many pieces as are required; however, if you're having a TCP conversation (see Chapter 3) with a long stream of data that could be hundreds or thousands of packets long, the operating system will set the DF flag so that it can choose exactly the right packet size to keep the conversation flowing smoothly without fragmenting packets en route, which would make the conversation unreliable.

The maximum transmission unit (MTU) is the largest packet that an Internet subnet can accept, and there used to be a huge problem with MTU processing that created problems for a lot of Internet users. In the 1990s, Internet service providers (most notably phone companies selling DSL connections) began to use PPPoE, a protocol that encapsulates IP packets in a capsule with just 1,492 bytes of space instead of the full 1,500 bytes allowed over Ethernet. Because they employed 1,500-byte packets by default and had disabled all ICMP packets as a mistaken security measure, many Internet sites were unprepared for this. As a result, their servers were never notified of ICMP failures indicating that their big, 1,500-byte "don't fragment" packets were reaching consumers' DSL lines but were too large to fit over them.

The perplexing symptom of this condition was that little files or web pages could be browsed without issue, and interactive protocols like Telnet and SSH would work because both of these activities send small packets of less than 1,492 bytes in the first place. The connection would freeze and become unusable if the customer attempted to download a huge file or if a Telnet or SSH command produced many screens full of output at once.

This problem is uncommon nowadays, but it demonstrates how a low-level IP feature can cause user-visible symptoms and, as a result, why it's important to remember all of IP's characteristics while creating and troubleshooting network programs.

Learning More About internet protocol

In the following chapters, you'll look at the protocol layers above IP and learn how your Python applications can use the various services built on top of the Internet Protocol to have various types of network talks. But what if the preceding overview of how IP works has piqued your interest and you want to learn more?

The requests for comment (RFCs) released by the Internet Engineering Task Force (IETF) that describe how the protocol operates are the official resources that describe the Internet Protocol. They are meticulously written and, when combined with a strong cup of coffee and a few hours of uninterrupted reading time, will reveal every last detail of how the Internet Protocols work. The RFC that defines the Internet Protocol, for example, is as follows:

RFCs are frequently cited in RFCs that describe greater specifics of a protocol or addressing scheme, and RFCs will commonly cite other RFCs that describe further details of a protocol or addressing scheme.

If you want to understand everything there is to know about the Internet Protocol and the additional protocols that operate on top of it, TCP/IP Illustrated, Volume 1: The Protocols (2nd Edition) by Kevin R. Fall and W. Richard Stevens is a good place to start (Addison-Wesley Professional, 2011). It goes over all of the protocol processes in great depth, with only a few gestures in this book. Other good books on networking in general, and network configuration in particular, are available if setting up IP networks and routing is something you do at work or at home to connect your computers to the Internet.

Conclusion

Except for the most fundamental network functions, all network services are built on top of another, more basic network function.

In the first few sections of this chapter, you looked at such a "stack." The TCP/IP protocol (which will be discussed in Chapter 3) allows byte strings to be sent between a client and a server. The HTTP protocol (Chapter 9) shows how a client can utilise such a connection to request a specific document and the server can react by supplying it. When the document returned by the server has to offer structured data to the client, the World Wide Web (Chapter 11) encodes the instructions for retrieving an HTTP-hosted document into a particular address called a URL, and the standard JSON data format is common. And, on top of it all, Google provides a geocoding service, which allows programmers to create a URL that Google responds with a JSON document representing a geographic location.

Characters must be encoded as bytes whenever textual information is transmitted over the network—or, for that matter, saved to persistent byteoriented storage such as a disc. For expressing characters as bytes, there are various widely used systems. The simple and limited ASCII encoding and the powerful and general Unicode system, particularly its particular encoding known as UTF-8, are the most frequent on the current Internet. The decode() method in Python can be used to convert byte strings to real characters, while the encode() method can be used to convert byte strings back to normal character strings. . Python 3 strives to avoid immediately converting bytes to strings—an action that would require it to just guess at the encoding you want—so Python 3 code will often include more calls to decode() and encode() than Python 2 code.

In order for the IP network to send packets on behalf of an application, network administrators, appliance vendors, and operating system programmers must collaborate to assign IP addresses to individual machines, set up routing tables at the machine and router levels, and configure the Domain Name System (Chapter 4) to associate IP addresses with user-visible names. Python programmers should be aware that each IP packet follows its own path over the network to its destination, and that a packet may be fragmented if it is too large to fit through one of the "hops" between routers.

In most applications, there are two main ways to use IP. They can either utilise each packet as a standalone message or request a stream of data that is automatically split into packets. These protocols are known as UDP and TCP, and they are the subjects of Chapters 2 and 3 of this book.

CHAPTER 2
UDP(User Datagram Protocol)

In the previous chapter, we learned that modern network gear allows for the transfer of little messages known as packets, which are typically only a few thousand bytes in size. How can these little individual messages be merged to make conversations between a web browser and a server, or an e-mail client and your ISP's mail server?

The IP protocol's sole responsibility is to try to deliver each packet to the appropriate machine. If distinct apps are to sustain dialogues, two more capabilities are normally required, and it is the responsibility of the protocols constructed on top of IP to offer these features.

- The numerous packets that pass between two hosts must be labelled so that web packets can be recognised from e-mail packets, and both can be distinguished from any other network talks in which the computer is involved. This is referred to as multiplexing.

- Any damage that a stream of packets going separately from one host to another can sustain must be repaired. Missing packets must be resent until they are received. Packets that come out of order must be reassembled in the proper sequence. Finally, duplicate packets must be destroyed to ensure that no data in the data stream is duplicated. This is referred to as providing dependable transportation.

Each of the two major protocols utilised atop IP gets its own chapter in this book.

The User Datagram Protocol (UDP) is the first and is covered in this chapter. It merely fixes the first of the two difficulties mentioned above. It assigns port numbers to packets destined for different services on a single system, as described in the next section. However, when it comes to packet loss, duplication, and ordering, network programmes using UDP must fend for themselves.

The second, the Transmission Control Protocol (TCP), is a protocol that addresses both issues. It uses the same rules as UDP to incorporate port numbers and provides ordered and reliable data streams that mask the fact that the continuous stream of data has been split into packets and then reassembled at the other end from applications. In Chapter 3, you'll learn how to use TCP.

It's worth noting that a few specialised applications, such as multimedia sharing among all hosts on a LAN, choose neither protocol and instead construct an altogether new IP-based protocol that sits alongside TCP and UDP as a new way of holding talks across an IP network. . This is not just unique, but it is also unlikely to be developed in Python, hence protocol engineering will not be covered in this book. The "Building and Examining Packets" section near the conclusion of Chapter 1,which builds raw ICMP packets and receives an ICMP reply, is the closest approach to raw packet construction atop IP in this book.

I'll be the first to admit that you're unlikely to use UDP in your own applications. If you believe UDP is a good fit for your application, you should investigate message queues (see Chapter 8). Nonetheless, the exposure to raw packet multiplexing that UDP provides is a necessary step before you can be ready to learn about TCP in Chapter 3.

Structure

- Numbers of particular service on the particular system.
- communications connection point (Socket)
- Clients who are promiscuous and unwelcome responses
- Backoff, blocking, and timeouts are all examples of unreliability.
- UDP Socket Connection
- The Use of Request IDs Is a Good Idea
- From Binding till Interfaces
- Fragmentation of UDP
- Options for Sockets

- Broadcast
- When Should We Use UDP?

Objective:

In these chapter we will learn about UDP socket connection, communication connection point many methods of socket, ip address etc.

Numbers of particular service on the particular system.

In both computer networking and electromagnetic signal theory, the difficulty of discriminating between many signals using the same channel is a common one. A multiplexing scheme is a system that permits numerous talks to share a medium or mechanism. Radio signals can be distinguished from one another by employing different frequencies, as was notably discovered. The creators of UDP chose the crude method of marking each and every UDP packet with a pair of unsigned 16-bit port numbers in the range of 0 to 65,536 to distinguish different talks in the digital domain of packets. The source port identifies the process or programme that sent the packet from the source system, whereas the destination port indicates the application that should receive the message at the destination IP address.

At the IP network layer, all that can be seen are packets flying toward a certain host.

Source IP | Destination IP

The network stacks of the two interacting machines, on the other hand—which must, after all, corral and wrangle so many machines—are a different storey. distinct programmes that may be communicating—consider the interaction to be between an IP address and a computer. Each machine has an address and port number pair.

Source (IP: port number) | Destination (IP : port number)

The four values for these in arriving packets relating to a specific conversation will always be the same. The two IP numbers and two port numbers will simply be exchanged in the replies heading the other way. in the fields for source and destination

Consider setting up a DNS server (Chapter 4) with the IP address 192.168.1.9 on one of your workstations to illustrate this concept. The server will ask the operating system for permission to receive packets arriving at the UDP port with the usual DNS port number: port 53, so that other computers can find the service. Assuming that no other process is currently using that port number, the DNS server will be given that port.

Consider a client machine with the IP address 192.168.1.30 that wishes to send a query to the server. It will create a request in memory, then request that the operating system transfer that block of data as a UDP packet. Because the client must be identified when the packet returns, and because the client has not requested a port number, the operating system assigns it a random one, such as port 44137.

As a result, the packet will fly its way to port 53 with addresses like this:

Source (192.168.1.30:44137) | Destination (192.168.1.9:53)

Once it has constructed a response, the DNS server will request that the operating system transmit a UDP packet with these two addresses reversed so that the reply returns straight to the sender.

Source (192.168.1.9:53) | Destination (192.168.1.30:44137)

As a result, the UDP scheme is quite basic; all that is required to direct a packet to its destination is an IP address and a port.

But how can a client programme figure out which port it needs to connect to? There are three approaches in general.

- many port numbers have been approved by the Internet Assigned Numbers Authority (IANA) as the official, well-known ports for various services. That's why, in the preceding case, DNS was expected on UDP port 53.

- Automatic configuration: When a computer connects to a network using a protocol like DHCP, the IP addresses of key services like DNS are frequently learned. Programs can access these vital services by pairing these IP addresses with well-known port numbers.

- Manual configuration: For all situations not covered by the previous two scenarios, an administrator or user will need to manually give an IP address or a service's associated hostname. In this sense, manual configuration is taking place. For instance, every time you type the name of a web server into your browser.

  When deciding on port numbers, such as 53 for DNS, IANA considers them to fall into one of two categories. There are three possible ranges for both UDP and TCP port numbers.

- The most significant and extensively utilised services are served by well-known ports (0–1023). Normal user programmes cannot listen on these ports on many Unix-like operating systems. This used to keep unruly undergraduates on multiuser university PCs at bay. executing apps that pretended to be critical system services Today, the same caution applies. When hosting firms give out command-line Linux accounts, this rule applies.

- Operating systems don't normally treat registered ports (1024–49151) as special—anyone can use them. For example, a user may develop a software that listens on port 5432 and claims to be a PostgreSQL database. IANA, for example, can register them for specific services, and IANA encourages that you do so. You should not use them for anything other than their allocated service.

- All other port numbers (49152–65535) are available for use. They're the pool from which current operating systems generate arbitrary port numbers when a client doesn't care what port is given to its outgoing connection, as you'll see.

When writing applications that accept port numbers from user input, such as the command line or configuration files, it's a good idea to include human-readable names for well-known ports in addition to numeric port numbers. These names are standard and can be obtained using Python's standard socket module's getservbyname() method. You may find out the port for the Domain Name Service by using this method.

```
>>> import socket
>>> socket.getservbyname('domain')
53
```

The more sophisticated getaddrinfo() function, which is also provided by the socket module, may also decode port names, as you'll see in Chapter 4.

On Linux and Mac OS X devices, the database of well-known service names and port numbers is normally kept in the file /etc/services, which you can browse at your leisure. The first few pages of the file, in particular, are packed with old protocols with reserved numbers despite the fact that they haven't received a packet addressed to them anywhere in the world in many years. IANA also keeps an up-to-date (and usually far more thorough) copy online at t www.iana.org/assignments/port-numbers.

Communications connection point (Socket)

Python took an interesting option rather than trying to create its own network programming API. At its most basic level, Python's Standard Library merely provides an object-based interface to all of the low-level operating system calls that are commonly used to perform networking activities on POSIX-compliant operating systems. The calls are even named after the underlying processes that they encapsulate. One of the reasons Python was such a breath of new air to those of us working in lower-level languages in the early 1990s was its willingness to expose the classic system calls that everyone already understood before it came on the scene. Finally, a higher-level language existed that allowed us to make low-level operating system calls whenever we required them, rather than forcing us to utilise a cumbersome, underpowered, but apparently "prettier" language-specific API. A single set of calls that worked in both C and Python was much easier to remember.

On both Windows and POSIX systems (such as Linux and Mac OS X), the underlying system calls for networking revolve around the concept of a communications endpoint called a socket. Integers are used by the operating system to identify sockets, but Python delivers a more useful socket.socket object to your Python code. Internally, it saves the integer (you may peep at it by calling its fileno() method) and uses it automatically whenever you call one of its methods to request that a system call be done on the socket.

Observe The fileno() integer, which identifies a socket on POSIX systems, is also a file descriptor selected from a pool of integers representing open files. You might come across code that, in the case of a POSIX environment, obtains this integer and then uses it to execute non-networking operations on the file descriptor, such as os.read() and os.write(), to perform filelike operations on what is actually a network communications endpoint. You will, however, only conduct genuine socket actions on your sockets because the code in this book is designed to run on Windows as well.

What do sockets look like while they're in use? Look at Listing 2-1 for an example of a simple UDP server and client. You can see that it only uses the Python Standard Library for one call, to socket.socket(), and that the rest of the calls are to the methods of the socket object it returns.

Listing 2-1. On the Loopback Interface, there is a UDP server and a UDP client.

```python
#!/usr/bin/env python3
 # Network Programming in Python: The Basics
# UDP client and server on localhost
import argparse, socket
from datetime import datetime
MAX_BYTES = 65535
def server(port):
```

```
 sock = socket.socket(socket.AF_INET, socket.SOCK_DGRAM)
 sock.bind(('127.0.0.1', port))
 print('Listening at {}'.format(sock.getsockname()))
 while True:
 data, address = sock.recvfrom(MAX_BYTES)
       text = data.decode('ascii')
       print('The client at {} says {!r}'.format(address, text))
 text = 'Your data was {} bytes long'.format(len(data))
 data = text.encode('ascii')
       sock.sendto(data, address)
def client(port):
 sock = socket.socket(socket.AF_INET, socket.SOCK_DGRAM)
 text = 'The time is {}'.format(datetime.now())
 data = text.encode('ascii')
 sock.sendto(data, ('127.0.0.1', port))
print('The OS assigned me the address {}'.format(sock.getsockname()))
 data, address = sock.recvfrom(MAX_BYTES) # Danger!
 text = data.decode('ascii')
 print('The server {} replied {!r}'.format(address, text))
if __name__ == '__main__':
 choices = {'client': client, 'server': server}
 parser = argparse.ArgumentParser(description='Send and receive UDP
locally')
 parser.add_argument('role', choices=choices, help='which role to
play')
 parser.add_argument('-p', metavar='PORT', type=int, default=1060,
 help='UDP port (default 1060)')
 args = parser.parse_args()
 function = choices[args.role]
 function(args.p)
```

Because both the server and the client utilise only the localhost IP address, which should be available whether or not you are connected to a real network, you should be able to run this script right on your own computer, even if you are not currently in the range of a network. First, try launching the server

```
$ python udp_local.py server
```

Listening at ('127.0.0.1', 1060)

The server waits for an incoming message after printing this line of output.

The server was up and operating in three phases, as you can see in the source code.

It started by calling socket() to construct a simple socket. This new socket does not yet have an IP address or a port assigned to it.

If you try to communicate with it, it will throw an error because it is not yet connected to anything. The socket is, at the very least, identified as being of a specific type: its family is AF INET, which stands for "Internet Family of Sockets." It's of the SOCK DGRAM datagram type, which means it'll run on an IP network using UDP. (See the next section for details on why I insist on a one-to-one correlation between datagrams and packets in order to calculate the maximum transmission unit [MTU].)

The bind() instruction is then used to request a UDP network address, which is a basic Python tuple consisting of a str IP address (a hostname is also fine, as you'll see later) and an int UDP port number. If another programme is already utilising that UDP port and the server script is unable to access it, this step may fail with an error. If you run another copy of the server, you'll notice that it complains like this:

```
$ python udp_local.py server
 Traceback (most recent call last):
 ...
 OSError: [Errno 98] Address already in use
```

Of course, because UDP port 1060 is already in use on your PC, there's a chance you got this error the first time you started the server. When it came to choosing the port number for this first example, I was in a bit of a pickle. Of course, it had to be greater than 1023, because else you couldn't run the script without being a system administrator—and, as much as I like my little example scripts, I don't want anyone to run them as the system administrator! I could have let the operating system determine the port number (like I did for the client, as you'll see shortly), had the server print it out, and then required you to type it into the client as one of its command-line arguments. However, I would not have been able to demonstrate you the syntax for requesting a specific port number. Finally, I contemplated selecting a port from the previously specified high-numbered "ephemeral" range, but those are precisely the ports that might be in use by another application on your machine, such as your web browser or SSH client, at any given time.

As a result, it appeared that my only alternative was to use a port in the reserved-but-unknown range above 1023. I had a look at the list and figured you, gentle reader, weren't running SAP BusinessObjects Polestar on the laptop, desktop, or server where you're running my Python scripts. If that's the case, use the –p option to pick a new port number for the server.

The getsockname() method of a socket can always be used by a Python programme to retrieve a tuple that contains the current IP address and port to which the socket is attached.

The server is now ready to receive requests after the socket has been successfully bound! It enters a loop and calls recvfrom() repeatedly, telling the function that it will happily accept messages up to a maximum length of 65,535 bytes—the maximum length that a UDP datagram may have—so that you will always see the entire content of each datagram. Your recvfrom() method will wait indefinitely until you send a message with a client.

Recvfrom() returns the address of the client who sent you a datagram as well as the datagram's contents as bytes when a datagram arrives. . You print the message to the console and then send a reply datagram to the client using Python's ability to convert bytes directly to strings.

So, let's fire up our client and see what happens. Listing 2-1 also includes the client code.

(I hope it's not too confusing because this example, like others in the book, mixes the server and client code into a single listing that may be selected using command-line options.) This is the way I prefer since it keeps server and client logic near together on the page and makes it simpler to understand which server code snippets fit with which client code snippets.)

Open another command window on your machine while the server is still operating, and try running the client twice in a row like this:

```
$ python udp_local.py client
The OS assigned me the address ('0.0.0.0', 46056)
The server ('127.0.0.1', 1060) replied 'Your data was 46 bytes long'
$ python udp_local.py client
The OS assigned me the address ('0.0.0.0', 39288)
The server ('127.0.0.1', 1060) replied 'Your data was 46 bytes long'
```

Each connection that the server serves should be reported in the server's command window.

```
The client at ('127.0.0.1', 46056) says 'The time is 2014-06-05
10:34:53.448338'
The client at ('127.0.0.1', 39288) says 'The time is 2014-06-05
10:34:54.065836'
```

The client code is slightly simpler than the server code, with only three lines of networking code, but it does introduce two new concepts. The sendto() method takes a message and a destination address from the client. This one-time call is all that's required to send a datagram flying toward the server! However, if you're going to communicate, you'll need an IP address and port number on the client side. As you can see from the output of the call to getsockname, the operating system assigns one automatically (). The client port numbers are all within the IANA range for "ephemeral" port numbers, as promised. (At least they are on my laptop, running Linux; you might get a different outcome if you use a different operating system.)

When you're finished utilising the server, press Ctrl+C in the terminal where it's running to terminate it.

Clients who are promiscuous and unwelcome responses

Listing 2-1's client software is actually harmful! If you look at the source code, you'll notice that, while recvfrom() provides the incoming datagram's address, the function never validates the datagram's source address to make sure it's a reply from the server.

You can check for this issue by delaying the server's answer and seeing whether someone else can provide a response that this naive client will accept. On a less capable operating system, such as Windows, you'll almost certainly need to add a significant amount of time. To imitate a server that takes a long time to respond, use the sleep() function between receive and transmit on the server. However, once the server has established up its socket on Mac OS X and Linux, you can simply suspend it with Ctrl+Z to imitate a server that takes a long time to respond. As a result, start a new server and then suspend it using Ctrl+Z.

```
$ python udp_local.py server
Listening at ('127.0.0.1', 1060)
^Z
[1] + 9370 suspended python udp_local.py server
$
```

If you run the client now, it will send a datagram and then hang while waiting for a response.

$ python udp_local.py client

The OS assigned me the address ('0.0.0.0', 39692)

Assume you're an attacker who wants to fabricate a response from the server by jumping in and transmitting your datagram before the server can respond. Because the client has told the operating system that it is willing to receive any datagram and is not doing any sanity checks on the output, it should believe that your phoney reply came from the server. A fast session at the Python prompt can be used to send such a packet.

```
$ python3
Python 3.4.0 (default, jan 25 2021, 13:05:18)
[GCC 4.8.2] on linux
Type "help", "copyright", "credits" or "license" for more information.
>>> import socket
>>> sock = socket.socket(socket.AF_INET, socket.SOCK_DGRAM)
>>> sock.sendto('FAKE'.encode('ascii'), ('127.0.0.1', 39692))
4
```

The client will quit instantly and joyfully interpret this third-party response as the one it was expecting.

The server ('127.0.0.1', 37821) replied 'FAKE'

You can now stop the server by typing fg to unfreeze it and allow it to continue running (it will now see the client packet that has been queued and will respond to it via the now-closed client socket). To kill it, press Ctrl+C as usual.

It's worth noting that everyone who can send a UDP packet to the client is susceptible. This is not a circumstance in which a man-in-the-middle attacker has control of the network and may counterfeit packets from bogus addresses, which can only be avoided by utilising encryption (see Chapter 6). Rather, the data of an unprivileged sender who follows all of the requirements and sends a packet with a legal return address is allowed.

A promiscuous client is a network client that listens for packets and accepts or records every single one it sees, regardless of whether the packet is appropriately addressed. We write these on purpose sometimes, as when we're doing network monitoring and want to see all of the packets coming at a particular interface. Promiscuity, on the other hand, is a concern in this scenario.

Only solid, well-written encryption should persuade your code that it is communicating with the correct server. There are two short checks you can do in the meanwhile. To begin, create or use protocols that provide a unique identification or request ID in the request, which is then repeated in the response. If the reply has the ID you're seeking for, then someone who saw your request—as long as the range of IDs is broad enough that someone couldn't simply flood you with hundreds or millions of packets having every possible ID—someone who saw your request must at least have composed it. Second, use connect() to prevent other addresses from sending you packets by comparing the address of the reply packet to the address that you gave it to (remember that tuples in Python can simply be == compared). Consider the following: For more information, see the sections "Connecting UDP Sockets" and "Request IDs."

Backoff, blocking, and timeouts are all examples of unreliability.

There was no real way for packets to get lost because the client and server in the previous sections were both running on the same machine and communicating through its loopback interface—which is not a physical network card that could experience a signalling glitch—so there was no real way for packets to get lost in Listing 2-1. When packets can truly be lost, how does code become more complicated?

Look at **Listing 2-2** for an example. Rather than always responding to client requests, this server chooses to respond to only half of them at random, allowing you to learn how to implement reliability into your client code without having to wait hours for a genuine dropped packet to occur on your network!

Listing 2-2-UDP Server and Client on Different Machines.

```
#!/usr/bin/env python3

# Network Programming in Python: The Basics
# UDP client and server for talking over the network


import argparse, random, socket, sys
MAX_BYTES = 65535
```

```python
def server(interface, port):
    sock = socket.socket(socket.AF_INET, socket.SOCK_DGRAM)
    sock.bind((interface, port))
    print('Listening at', sock.getsockname())
    while True:
        data, address = sock.recvfrom(MAX_BYTES)
        if random.random() < 0.5:
            print('Pretending to drop packet from {}'.format(address))
            continue
    text = data.decode('ascii')
    print('The client at {} says {!r}'.format(address, text))
    message = 'Your data was {} bytes long'.format(len(data))
        sock.sendto(message.encode('ascii'), address)
def client(hostname, port):
    sock = socket.socket(socket.AF_INET, socket.SOCK_DGRAM)
    hostname = sys.argv[2]
    sock.connect((hostname, port))
    print('Client socket name is {}'.format(sock.getsockname()))
        delay = 0.1 # seconds
        text = 'This is another message'
        data = text.encode('ascii')
        while True:
            sock.send(data)
            print('Waiting up to {} seconds for a reply'.format(delay))
    sock.settimeout(delay)
    try:
    data = sock.recv(MAX_BYTES)
    except socket.timeout:
                delay *= 2 # wait even longer for the next request
                if delay > 2.0:
    raise RuntimeError('I think the server is down')
    else:
```

```
        break # we are done, and can stop looping
```

```
print('The server says {!r}'.format(data.decode('ascii')))
if __name__ == '__main__':
 choices = {'client': client, 'server': server}
     parser = argparse.ArgumentParser(description='Send and receive
UDP,' 'pretending packets are often dropped')
 parser.add_argument('role', choices=choices, help='which role to
 take')
 parser.add_argument('host', help='interface the server listens at;'
                     'host the client sends to')
 parser.add_argument('-p', metavar='PORT', type=int, default=1060,
                    help='UDP port (default 1060)')
 args = parser.parse_args()
 function = choices[args.role]
 function(args.host, args.p)
```

While the server in the previous example instructed the operating system that it only wanted packets arriving through the private 127.0.0.1 interface from other processes on the same machine, you can make this server more generous by defining the server IP address as an empty string. This implies "any local interface," which on my Linux laptop means requesting the IP address 0.0.0.0 from the operating system.

```
$ python udp_remote.py server ""

 Listening at ('0.0.0.0', 1060)
```

When a request is received, the server will utilise a random() coin flip to determine whether the request will be responded, so you don't have to keep the client running all day waiting for an actual packet to be dropped. Whatever decision it makes, it displays a message on the screen so you can keep track of what it's doing. How can we create a "true" UDP client that has to deal with the possibility of packet loss?

Because of UDP's instability, the client must perform its request in a loop. It must either be prepared to wait indefinitely for a response or be rather arbitrary in determining when it has waited "too long" for a response and must send another. This challenging decision is necessitated by the fact that most clients are unable to discriminate between these three distinct events:

- The response is taking a long time to arrive, but it will be here soon.

- The response, like the request, will never arrive because it was misplaced.

- The server is down and not responding to any requests.

As a result, a UDP client must decide on a timetable for sending duplicate requests if it does not receive a response after a suitable amount of time. Of course, doing so may waste the server's time because the initial response may be on its way, and the second copy of the request may lead the server to undertake unnecessary redundant work. However, at some time, the client must decide whether to retry the request or risk waiting indefinitely.

Rather than allowing the operating system to keep the socket paused indefinitely during the recv() operation, this client first calls settimeout() on the socket. This tells the system that the client does not want to be left waiting for more than delay seconds inside a socket action, and that the call should be interrupted with a socket. Once a call has been waiting for so long, a timeout exception is thrown.

A caller is considered to be blocked when it waits for a network activity to complete. The term "blocking" refers to a call like recv() that forces the client to wait for new data. The distinction between blocking and nonblocking network requests will loom large when you get to Chapter 7, where server architecture is explained!

This particular customer has a tenth-of-a-second delay to begin with. In my home network, where ping times are often a few dozen milliseconds, this rarely causes the client to issue a duplicate request merely because the response is late.

What happens if the timeout is reached is an important component of this client software. It doesn't simply start sending out repeat requests at a predetermined period! Because congestion is the most common source of packet loss—as anybody who has tried sending regular data upstream over a DSL modem while images or movies are downloading knows—the last thing you want to do is respond to a potentially dropped packet by sending even more of them.

As a result, this client employs an exponential backoff strategy, in which its attempts get less and less frequent. . This serves the critical benefit of surviving a few missed requests or responses while allowing a congested network to gradually recover as all active clients reduce their demands and send fewer packets. Although there are more sophisticated exponential backoff algorithms—for example, the Ethernet version of the algorithm includes some randomness to ensure that two competing network cards do not back off on the same schedule—the basic effect can be achieved quite simply by doubling the delay each time a response is not received.

Please keep in mind that if the requests are being sent to a server that is 200 milliseconds away, this naïve method will always send at least two copies of each request, because it will never learn that requests to this server take longer than 0.1 seconds. If you're developing a long-lived UDP client, consider letting it remember how long the previous several requests took to complete so that it can delay its first retry until the server has responded.

Give the hostname of the other machine on which you're running the server script to the **Listing 2-2** client, as stated previously. This client may get lucky and receive an immediate response.

```
$ python udp_remote.py client guinness
Client socket name is ('127.0.0.1', 45420)
Waiting up to 0.1 seconds for a reply
The server says 'Your data was 23 bytes long'
```

However, it will frequently discover that one or more of its queries never receive responses, forcing it to retry. You can even witness the exponential backoff happening in real time if you closely observe its repeated attempts, as the print statements that echo to the screen become more and more slowly as the delay timer ramps up.

```
$ python udp_remote.py client guinness
Client socket name is ('127.0.0.1', 58414)
Waiting up to 0.1 seconds for a reply
Waiting up to 0.2 seconds for a reply
Waiting up to 0.4 seconds for a reply
Waiting up to 0.8 seconds for a reply
The server says 'Your data was 23 bytes long'
```

You can check whether the requests are making it or whether you've experienced a real packet drop on your network in the terminal where you're executing the server. When I conducted the previous test, I was able to see that all of the packets had made it to the server's console.

```
Pretending to drop packet from ('192.168.5.10', 53322)
Pretending to drop packet from ('192.168.5.10', 53322)
Pretending to drop packet from ('192.168.5.10', 53322)
Pretending to drop packet from ('192.168.5.10', 53322)
The client at ('192.168.5.10', 53322) says, 'This is another message'
```

What if the server is completely unavailable? Unfortunately, UDP does not allow us to discriminate between a down server and a network that is simply in such bad shape that all of our packets and responses are being dropped. Of course, I don't think we can blame UDP for this issue. After all, the world itself has no means of distinguishing between something we can't detect and something that doesn't exist! As a result, the client's best option is to give up after making enough attempts. Restart the client after killing the server process.

```
$ python udp_remote.py client guinness
Client socket name is ('127.0.0.1', 58414)
Waiting up to 0.1 seconds for a reply
Waiting up to 0.2 seconds for a reply
Waiting up to 0.4 seconds for a reply
Waiting up to 0.8 seconds for a reply
Waiting up to 1.6 seconds for a reply
Traceback (most recent call last):
  ...
socket.timeout: timed out
The preceding exception resulted in the following exception:
Traceback (most recent call last):
  ...
RuntimeError: I think the server is down
```

Giving up makes sense only if your programme is attempting to complete a brief task that requires it to produce output or return a result to the user. It's fine to have code that keeps retrying "forever" if you're developing a daemon programme that runs all day, such as a weather symbol in the corner of the screen that displays the temperature and forecast obtained from a remote UDP service. After all, a desktop or laptop machine may be disconnected from the network for an extended length of time, and your code may have to wait hours or days for the forecast server to respond.

If you're writing daemon code that retries all day, don't use a strict exponential backoff, or you'll quickly ramp up the delay to something like two hours, and you'll likely miss the entire half-hour period when the laptop owner sits down in a coffee shop and you could have actually gotten to the network. Instead, pick a maximum delay—say, five minutes—and keep it there until the exponential backoff reaches it, ensuring that you always attempt an update whenever the user has been on the network for five minutes after being disconnected for a lengthy time.

You'll be able to do a lot better than playing with timers and guessing when the network will come back up if your operating system allows your process to be alerted for events like the network coming back up. Unfortunately, system-specific procedures like those are outside the scope of this book, so let's get back to UDP and a few more concerns it poses.

UDP Socket Connection

In the last section, you looked at **Listing 2-2**, which introduced another new notion that needs to be explained. I've already talked about binding, both the explicit bind() call that a server makes to get the address it wants to use and the implicit binding that occurs when a client first tries to use a socket and the operating system assigns it a random ephemeral port number.

The remote UDP client in **Listing 2-2**, on the other hand, makes use of a new method that I haven't covered yet: the connect() socket action. You can see what it does quite well. Instead of having to use sendto() with an explicit address tuple every time you want to send something to the server, the connect() call informs the operating system of the remote address to which you want to send packets ahead of time, allowing you to simply supply data to the send() call without having to repeat the server address.

But connect() accomplishes something else significant that you won't see just looking at Listing 2-2: it solves the problem of a promiscuous client! If you run the test you did in the "Promiscuity" section on this client, you'll see that it's not vulnerable to receiving packets. . This is due to the second, less visible result of using connect() to configure a UDP socket's preferred destination: once you've performed connect(), any incoming packets to your port whose return address does not match the address to which you've connected will be discarded by the operating system.

There are two techniques to create UDP clients that pay attention to the return addresses of packets that are returned.

- You may use sendto() to route each outgoing packet to a specified destination, then use recvfrom() to receive the replies and compare each return address to the list of servers to which you have outstanding requests.

- Alternatively, you can connect() your socket immediately after creating it and use send() and recv() to interact (). Unwanted packets will be filtered away by the operating system. Because connecting to the same socket again does not add a second destination address, this only works for communicating to one server at a time. Instead, it completely deletes the original address, ensuring that no additional correspondence from that address reaches your application.

You can use the getpeername() method of a UDP socket to remember the address to which it was connected after connecting it with connect(). If you call this on a socket that isn't connected yet, be careful. The call will raise socket.error instead of returning 0.0.0.0 or another wildcard response. There are two final points to be addressed concerning the connect() function.

To begin with, connecting to a UDP socket does not transfer any data across the network or do anything to alert the server that packets are on their way. It merely stores the address in the operating system's memory for eventual use in send() and recv() calls ().

Second, keep in mind that connecting to a server—or even filtering out undesired packets using the return address—is not a secure method! If there is a hostile user on the network, it is usually simple for their machine to create packets with the server's return address, allowing their forged responses to pass through your address filter.

Spoofing is the act of sending packets with the return address of another computer, and it is one of the first things protocol designers must consider when creating protocols that are supposed to be free of interference.

More information on this can be found in **Chapter 6**.

The Use of Request IDs Is a Good Idea

Both **Listings 2–1** and **2–2** had plain ASCII text messages. However, if you ever create your own UDP request and response scheme, you should strongly consider assigning a sequence number to each request and ensuring that the reply you accept has the same number. Simply copy the number from each request into the appropriate reply on the server. This offers at least two significant benefits.

For starters, it guards you against getting perplexed by duplicate responses to queries that have been replayed numerous times by a client in an exponential backoff loop.

It's simple to understand how duplication could occur. Request A is sent to you. You become bored while waiting for a response, so you submit Request A again. Then you eventually get a response, which is A. You suppose the first copy was misplaced, so you continue on your way.

What if, on the other hand, both requests were sent to the server and the responses were a little late in arriving?

Have you received one of the two responses, but are you waiting for the other? If you now send request B to the server and begin listening, you will almost quickly receive duplicate reply A, which you will mistakenly believe is the answer to the query you asked in request B. and you will become confused. . You can end up entirely out of step from then on, misinterpreting each response as referring to a different request than the one you think it does!

Request IDs shield you from this. If you give the request ID #42496 to every copy of request A and the request ID #42496 to every copy of request B, If the programme loop waiting for the answer to B has ID #16916, then it can simply keep deleting replies with IDs that don't match. until it finally receives one that matches #16916. This prevents duplicate responses, which can occur not just if you asked the same inquiry twice, but also in the rare instance where a redundancy in the network fabric generates two copies of the packet somewhere between the server and the client.

Another use of request IDs, as discussed in the section "Promiscuity," is to provide a barrier against spoofing, at least when the attackers are unable to read your packets. Of course, if they can, you're absolutely lost: they'll see the IP, port number, and request ID of every packet you transmit and can attempt sending phoney responses to any request they choose (hoping that their responses arrive before the server's, of course)! However, if the attackers are unable to examine your traffic and must fire UDP packets at your server blindly, a large request ID number can make it far less probable for your client to accept their response.

You'll notice that the request IDs I used in the article weren't in any particular order or were easy to predict. Because of these traits, an attacker will have no notion what sequence number is most likely. You make an attacker's task lot easy if you start with 0 or 1 and count upward from there. To create huge integers, consider using the random module instead. If your ID number is a random number between 0 and N, an attacker's likelihood of reaching you with a valid packet is at most $1/N$, and may be substantially lower if he or she needs to attempt all conceivable port numbers on your system.

Of course, none of this is true security; it only protects you from naive spoofing assaults by those who are unable to see your network traffic. Even if attackers can monitor your traffic and insert their own messages whenever they want, real security protects you. In Chapter 6, you'll learn about real-world security.

From Binding till Interfaces

So far, you've seen two alternatives for the IP address used in the server's bind() method. You can use '127.0.0.1' to specify that you only want packets from other programmes running on the same machine, or an empty string " as a wildcard to specify that you want packets arriving at the server via any of the server's network interfaces.

There is a choice. You can specify an IP address for one of the machine's external IP interfaces, such as its Ethernet or wireless card, and the server will only listen for packets destined for that IP address. You may have noted that **Listing 2-2** allows you to specify a server string for the bind() method, allowing you to conduct some tests.

What happens if you just bind to an external interface? Use whatever your operating system informs you is your system's external IP address to run the server:

```
$ python udp_remote.py server 192.168.5.130

Listening at ('192.168.5.130', 1060)
```

Connecting to this IP address from a different computer should function perfectly.

```
$ python udp_remote.py client guinness

Client socket name is ('192.168.5.10', 35084)

Waiting up to 0.1 seconds for a reply

The server says 'Your data was 23 bytes'
```

However, if you try to connect to the service via the loopback interface while running the client script on the same machine, the packets would never arrive.

```
$ python udp_remote.py client 127.0.0.1

Client socket name is ('127.0.0.1', 60251)

Waiting up to 0.1 seconds for a reply

Traceback (most recent call last):

  ...

socket.error: [Errno 111] Connection refused
```

Actually, the result is better than the packets never being delivered, at least on my operating system. Because the operating system can detect if one of its own ports is open without sending a packet over the network, a connection to that port is immediately denied! However, be aware that UDP's ability to return "Connection rejected" is a loopback superpower that you will never encounter on a real network. There, the packet must simply be transmitted with no indication of whether or not it will be received at a destination port. Restart the client on the same PC, but this time use the box's external IP address.

```
$ python udp_remote.py client 192.168.5.130

Client socket name is ('192.168.5.130', 34919)

Waiting up to 0.1 seconds for a reply

The server says 'Your data was 23 bytes'
```

Do you see what's going on? Locally running programmes are free to send requests to any of the computer's IP addresses, even if they're only utilising that IP address to communicate with another service on the same machine!

As a result, binding to an IP interface may restrict which external hosts can communicate with you. However, it will not prevent chats with other clients on the same workstation as long as they are aware of the IP address to which they should connect.

What happens if two servers are started at the same time? Stop any current scripts and try running two servers on the same machine. The loopback will be connected to one of them.

```
$ python udp_remote.py server 127.0.0.1

Listening at ('127.0.0.1', 1060)
```

You can't run a second server at that address now that it's occupied, because the operating system wouldn't know which process should receive any particular packet arriving at that address.

```
$ python udp_remote.py server 127.0.0.1
Traceback (most recent call last):
  ...
OSError: [Errno 98] Address already in use
```

But, perhaps even more shocking, you will not be able to run a server on the wildcard IP address.

```
$ python udp_remote.py server
Traceback (most recent call last):
  ...
OSError: [Errno 98] Address already in use
```

This fails because the wildcard address includes 127.0.0.1, which clashes with the address that the first server process already possesses. What if, instead of trying to run the second server against all IP interfaces, you just ran it against an external IP interface that the first server isn't listening to? Let us give it a shot.

```
$ python udp_remote.py server 192.168.5.130
Listening at ('192.168.5.130', 1060)
```

It was successful! Two servers with the same UDP port number are now running on this machine, one tethered to the loopback interface and the other peering outside for packets coming on the network to which my wireless card has connected. You can start up even more servers, one for each remote interface, if you chance to be on a system with many remote interfaces.

Once these servers are up and running, try sending them some packets using your UDP client. Only one server will get each request, and it will always be the server that has the IP address to which you have sent the UDP request packet.

The takeaway is that an IP network stack never considers a UDP port as a stand-alone object that is either completely available or in use at any given time. Instead, it thinks in terms of UDP "socket names," which are always a pair of IP interfaces (even the wildcard interface) and UDP port numbers. Rather than the raw UDP ports being used, these socket identifiers must not clash among the listening servers at any one time.

A final word of caution is in order. Given that binding your server to interface 127.0.0.1 protects you from potentially dangerous packets generated on the external network, you would believe that binding to one external interface will protect you from malicious packets generated by malcontents on other external networks. On a large server with several network cards, for example, you could be tempted to bind to a private subnet that faces your other servers, believing that this will prevent faked packets from reaching your public IP address.

Unfortunately, life is not that straightforward. Inbound packets directed to one interface may or may not be allowed to arrive at another interface, depending on your operating system and how it is configured. It's possible that if packets claiming to be from other servers on your network emerge through your public Internet connection, your system will cheerfully accept them! To learn more about your specific situation, consult your operating system documentation or your system administrator. If your operating system does not provide security, you can set up and run a firewall on your computer.

Fragmentation of UDP

So far in this chapter, I've assumed that UDP allows you to send raw datagrams that are simply packaged as IP packets with only a little extra information—a port for both the sender and receiver. However, you may already be sceptical because the preceding programme listings indicated that a UDP packet may be up to 64kB in size, whereas you are likely already aware that your Ethernet or wireless card can only handle packets of roughly 1,500 bytes.

While UDP sends small datagrams as single IP packets, it must break bigger UDP datagrams into numerous small IP packets in order for them to transit the network (as was briefly discussed in Chapter 1).

Large packets are more likely to be dropped as a result of this, because if one of their pieces fails to reach its destination, the entire packet cannot be reassembled and given to the listening operating system.

This process of fragmenting huge UDP packets so that they can fit on the wire should be unnoticeable to your application, save for the increased risk of failure. However, there are three scenarios in which it could be useful.

- If you're concerned about efficiency, you might want to keep your protocol to tiny packets to reduce the likelihood of retransmission and the time it takes the distant IP stack to reassemble your UDP packet and deliver it to the waiting application.

- If an ICMP packet is incorrectly denied by a firewall that would ordinarily allow your host to autodetect the MTU between you and the distant host (as was the case in the late 1990s), your larger UDP packets may vanish without your knowledge. The MTU (maximum transmission unit) or "biggest packet size" that all network devices between two hosts will support is the MTU.

If your protocol has complete control over how data is split across datagrams and you want to be able to auto-adjust the size based on the actual MTU between two hosts, some operating systems allow you to disable fragmentation and receive an exception if a UDP packet is too large. You could then build datagrams that are smaller than the minimum unit.

This last option is supported by some operating systems, including Linux. Consider **Listing 2-3,** which transmits a big datagram.

Listing 2-3:- Sending a Large UDP Packet.

```
#!/usr/bin/env python3

# Network Programming in Python: The Basics

# Send a big UDP datagram to learn the MTU of the network path.

import IN, argparse, socket

if not hasattr(IN, 'IP_MTU'):

        raise RuntimeError('cannot perform MTU discovery on this combination'
'
                        of operating system and Python distribution')
```

```python
def send_big_datagram(host, port):

    sock = socket.socket(socket.AF_INET, socket.SOCK_DGRAM)

    sock.setsockopt(socket.IPPROTO_IP, IN.IP_MTU_DISCOVER,
    IN.IP_PMTUDISC_DO)

    sock.connect((host, port))

try:

sock.send(b'#' * 65000)

except socket.error:

        print('Alas, the datagram did not make it')

        max_mtu = sock.getsockopt(socket.IPPROTO_IP, IN.IP_MTU)

        print('Actual MTU: {}'.format(max_mtu))

else:

        print('The big datagram was sent!')

if __name__ == '__main__':

parser = argparse.ArgumentParser(description='Send UDP packet to get
MTU')

parser.add_argument('host', help='the host to which to target the
packet')

        parser.add_argument('-p', metavar='PORT', type=int,
        default=1060,

help='UDP port (default 1060)')

args = parser.parse_args()

send_big_datagram(args.host, args.p)
```

When I run this application against a server on my home network, I notice that my wireless network supports physical packets no larger than the 1,500 bytes that Ethernet-style networks normally support.

```
$ python big_sender.py guinness

Alas, the datagram did not make it

Actual MTU: 1500
```

It's even more unexpected that my laptop's loopback interface, which could theoretically accommodate packets as large as my RAM, likewise imposes an MTU.

```
$ python big_sender.py 127.0.0.1
```

```
Alas, the datagram did not make it
```

```
Actual MTU: 65535
```

However, the ability to examine the MTU is not universal; consult your operating system documentation for more information.

Options for Sockets

The POSIX socket interface includes a variety of socket parameters that affect network socket behaviour. The IP MTU DISCOVER setting shown in Listing 2-3 is just the beginning. The options are obtained via Using the parameters listed in your operating system's documentation, use the Python socket functions getsockopt() and setsockopt(). For these two system calls, there are two lists. On Linux, look at the manual pages socket(7), udp(7), and—once you get to the end—https://manuals. sourceforge.net/manuals/https://manuals.sourceforge.nettcp is the next chapter (7).

When establishing socket options, you must first identify the option group in which they reside, and then name the actual option you want to set as a later argument. The names of these groups can be found in your operating system's handbook. The set call, like getattr() and setattr() in Python, merely accepts one extra argument than the get method.

```
value = s.getsockopt(socket.SOL_SOCKET, socket.SO_BROADCAST)
```

```
s.setsockopt(socket.SOL_SOCKET, socket.SO_BROADCAST, value)
```

Many options are unique to individual operating systems, and they may be picky about how they're presented. Here are a few of the most popular choices:

- **SO BROADCAST**: This allows you to send and receive broadcast UDP packets, which I'll go over in the following section.

- **SO DONTROUTE**: Only send packets that are addressed to hosts on subnets to which this computer is directly connected. If this socket option was set, my laptop, for example, would be willing to send packets to the networks 127.0.0.0/8 and 192.168.5.0/24 at this time, but not anywhere else because the packets would have to be routed through a gateway.

- **SO TYPE**: When supplied to getsockopt(), this determines whether a socket is of type SOCK DGRAM, which can be used for UDP, or of type SOCK STREAM, which supports TCP semantics (see Chapter 3).

Te following chapter will go over some more socket parameters that are exclusive to TCP sockets.

Broadcast

The ability to support broadcast is one of UDP's superpowers. Instead of sending a datagram to a single host, you can address it to the entire subnet to which your machine is connected and have the physical network card broadcast the datagram so that it is seen by all attached hosts without having to be duplicated to each one individually.

It should be noted right away that broadcast is now regarded obsolete due to the development of a more sophisticated technology known as multicast, which allows modern operating systems to better exploit the intelligence embedded into many networks and network interface devices. . Multicast can also work with hosts outside of the local subnet. However, if you want a simple way to keep something on the local LAN up to date, such as gaming clients or automated scoreboards, and each client can suffer the occasional missed packet, UDP broadcast is a good option.

A server that can receive broadcast packets and a client that can transmit them are shown in **Listing 2-4**. If you look closely, you'll notice that there's only one major variation between this listing and previous listings' tactics. To enable broadcast, invoke the socket object's setsockopt() method before using it. Aside from that, the socket is used by both the server and the client in a standard manner.

Listing 2-4. UDP Broadcast.

```python
#!/usr/bin/env python3
# Network Programming in Python: The Basics
# UDP client and server for broadcast messages on a local LAN
import argparse, socket
BUFSIZE = 65535
def server(interface, port):
 sock = socket.socket(socket.AF_INET, socket.SOCK_DGRAM)
 sock.bind((interface, port))
 print('Listening for datagrams at {}'.format(sock.getsockname()))
 while True:
 data, address = sock.recvfrom(BUFSIZE)
 text = data.decode('ascii')
```

```
print('The client at {} says: {!r}'.format(address, text))


def client(network, port):
 sock = socket.socket(socket.AF_INET, socket.SOCK_DGRAM)
 sock.setsockopt(socket.SOL_SOCKET, socket.SO_BROADCAST, 1)
 text = 'Broadcast datagram!'
 sock.sendto(text.encode('ascii'), (network, port))


if __name__ == '__main__':
 choices = {'client': client, 'server': server}
 parser = argparse.ArgumentParser(description='Send, receive UDP
broadcast')
 parser.add_argument('role', choices=choices, help='which role to
take')
 parser.add_argument('host', help='interface the server listens at;'
                            ' network the client sends to')
 parser.add_argument('-p', metavar='port', type=int, default=1060,
 help='UDP port (default 1060)')
 args = parser.parse_args()
 function = choices[args.role]
 function(args.host, args.p)
```

The first thing you should notice when using this server and client is that they work precisely like a normal client and server if you merely use the client to transmit packets to a specific server's IP address.

The ability to send and receive explicitly addressed packets is neither disabled or changed when a UDP socket is set to broadcast.

When you look at the settings for your local network and utilise its IP "broadcast address" as the client's destination, the magic happens. First, use instructions like these to bring up one or two servers on your network.

```
$ python udp_broadcast.py server ""
```

```
Listening for broadcasts at ('0.0.0.0', 1060)
```

Then, while those servers are up and running, send messages to each one using the client. You'll see that each message is delivered to only one server.

```
$ python udp_broadcast.py client 192.168.5.10
```

When you utilise the local network's broadcast address, however, you'll see that the packet arrives at all of the broadcast servers at the same time! (However, no normal servers will see it—to be convinced, run a few clones of the standard udp remote.py server while broadcasting.) The broadcast address on my local network right now, according to the ifconfig command, is:

```
$ python udp_broadcast.py client 192.168.5.255
```

And, sure enough, both servers indicate that they have received the message. If your operating system makes determining the broadcast address difficult, and you don't mind broadcasting from all of your host's network ports, Python lets you use the special hostname 'broadcast>' when sending with a UDP connection. When sending that name to your client, be sure to quote it because the & and > characters are unique to any POSIX shell.

$ python udp_broadcast.py client "<broadcast>"

I'd show you if there was a platform-independent way to figure out each connected subnet's broadcast address. If you wish to do anything more specific than use this unique 'broadcast>' string, you'll have to examine your individual operating system documentation.

When Should We Use UDP?

You could assume that sending short messages with UDP is a good idea. Actually, UDP is only effective if your server sends one message at a time and then waits for a response. If your application sends multiple messages in a burst, an intelligent message queue like MQ will be more efficient because it will set a short timer that allows it to bundle several small messages into a single transmission, most likely over a TCP connection that does a much better job of fragmenting the payload than you do!

However, there are a few compelling reasons to adopt UDP.

- Because you're using UDP to implement a protocol that already exists.
- Because you're constructing a time-critical media stream with redundancy that allows for occasional packet loss, and you don't want this second's data to get stuck waiting for old data that hasn't arrived yet (as happens with TCP).
- Why Because uncertain LAN subnet multicast is an excellent pattern for your application, and UDP properly supports it.

Outside of these three scenarios, you should definitely look to the book's later chapters for ideas on how to create your application's communication. There's an old adage that says if you can get a UDP protocol to work for your application, you've probably just bad-mouthed TCP.

Conclusion

The User Datagram Protocol allows individual packets to be sent across an IP network by user-level programmes. A client application typically transmits a packet to a server, which responds using the return address included in every UDP message.

The POSIX network stack provides access to UDP via the concept of a "socket," which is a communications endpoint that can transmit and receive datagrams by sitting at an IP address and UDP port number (the socket's name or address). The built-in socket module in Python provides some basic network activities.

Before it can receive incoming packets, the server must bind() to an address and port. Client UDP programmes can just start sending, and the operating system will assign them a port number.

UDP is unreliable since it is based on the actual behaviour of network packets. Packets might be dropped due to a network transmission medium fault or because a network segment becomes overburdened. Clients must compensate for this by agreeing to resend requests until they receive a response. Clients should utilise exponential backoff if they experience recurring failure to avoid making a crowded network worse, and they should also increase their initial wait time if round-trips to the server are taking longer than they were willing to wait.

Request IDs are essential for preventing reply duplication, which occurs when a reply you believed was lost turns up later and is misinterpreted for the answer to your current issue. Request IDs, if chosen at random, can also help protect against naive spoofing attempts.

When utilising sockets, it's vital to distinguish the process of binding—in which you take control of a specific UDP port for your own use—from the act of connecting, which limits all responses received to only those from the specific server with which you want to communicate.

The most powerful socket option for UDP sockets is broadcast, which allows you to transmit packets to every host on your subnet without having to send to each host separately. This is one of the few reasons why you would choose UDP for new applications when building local LAN games or other cooperative computation.

CHAPTER 3
Transmission control protocol (TCP)

The Internet's workhorse is the Transmission Control Protocol (technically TCP/IP, but referred simply as TCP for the rest of this book). It was first established in 1974, and it uses the Internet Protocol's (IP) packet transmission technology to allow programmes to communicate using continuous streams of data. TCP assures that the data stream will arrive intact, with no information lost, duplicated, or out of order, unless the connection dies or freezes due to a network fault.

TCP is almost always used by protocols that transport documents and files. This includes web page delivery to your browser, file transmission, and all main e-mail transmission protocols. TCP is also the foundation of choice for protocols like SSH terminal sessions and many popular chat protocols, which carry on long dialogues between people or computers.

It was once tempting to try to squeeze a little more speed out of a network by constructing an application on top of UDP (see Chapter 2) and carefully setting the size and timing of each individual datagram. Modern TCP implementations, on the other hand, are more sophisticated, having profited from almost 30 years of development, invention, and study. It's uncommon for anyone other than a protocol expert to improve on the performance of a current TCP stack. Even performance-critical applications such as message queues (Chapter 8) use TCP these days as their medium

Structure:

- How transmission control protocol works
- When to use transmission control protocol
- TCP Sockets Mean?
- TCP Client and Server
- Each conversation one socket
- Address that is in use
- From Binding to Interfaces
- Deadlock
- Half-Open Connections, Closed Connections
- TCP Streams as Files
- Conclusion

Objective:

In these chapter we will learn how to facilitate the transmission and receipt of data streams over the network between two sockets & learn about deadlock stream as files in TCP. Sometime about TCP client and server.

How transmission control protocol works

Networks are temperamental animals, as you learned in Chapters 1 and 2. They have a tendency to drop packets that you try to send through them. They make extra copies of a packet on occasion. Furthermore, they frequently deliver parcels out of sequence. When using a bare datagram facility like UDP, your application code must be concerned about whether each datagram arrives and have a mechanism in place to recover if it does not. TCP, on the other hand, hides the packets themselves beneath the protocol, allowing your application to simply stream data toward its destination, certain that any missed data will be retransmitted until it arrives successfully.

RFC 793 from 1981 is the original specification of TCP/IP, however numerous subsequent RFCs contain specified extensions and enhancements.

How does TCP ensure that a connection is secure? The following are its basic tenets:

- Instead of using sequential integers (1, 2, 3,...) to sequence packets, TCP uses a counter that counts the number of bytes transmitted. This allows the system on the receiving end to put them back together in the right order and to notice missing packets in the sequence and request that they be retransmitted. For example, a 1,024-byte packet with the sequence number 7,200 would be followed by a packet with the sequence number 8,224. This means that a busy network stack doesn't have to remember how a data stream was broken up into packets. If a retransmission is requested, it can split the stream into new packets in some other method (which may allow it to fit more data into a packet if more bytes are now waiting for transmission), and the receiver can still reassemble the packets.

- In good TCP implementations, the initial sequence number is selected at random so that villains cannot assume that every connection starts at byte zero.

- Rather than running very slowly in lock step, TCP sends complete bursts of packets at a time before expecting a response. The size of the TCP window refers to the amount of data a sender is willing to have on the wire at any given time.

- The TCP implementation on the receiving end can control the transmitting end's window size, slowing or pausing the connection. This is referred to as flow control.

- Finally, if TCP detects packets being dropped, it assumes the network is becoming crowded and limits the amount of data it transfers every second. On wireless networks and other media, where packets are lost merely due to noise, this can be a tragedy. It can even sabotage connections that were working properly until the router was rebooted. For example, the endpoints are unable to communicate for more than 20 seconds. When the network is restored, the two will be reunited. TCP peers will have determined that the network is severely overburdened with traffic, and they will take action. When they re-establish contact, they will initially refuse to send each other data at any other frequency.

Beyond the behaviours just described, TCP's design includes many more nuances and details, but hopefully this description gives you a good idea of how it works— even though, as you'll recall, all your application will see is a stream of data, with the actual packets and sequence numbers cleverly hidden away by your operating system network stack.

When to use transmission control protocol

If your network applications are anything like mine, TCP will be used for the majority of network connections. You could go your entire career without intentionally creating a UDP packet from your code. (However, as you'll see in Chapter 5, if your application has to search up a DNS hostname, UDP is very certainly engaged in the background.)

Although TCP has practically become the universal default when two Internet programmes need to interact, I'll go over a few situations where it's not the best choice, in case your application falls into one of these groups.

For starters, TCP is clunky for protocols in which clients want to send single, tiny requests to a server and then stop communicating with it. The famous SYN, SYN-ACK, and ACK sequence is used to establish a TCP connection between two hosts.

- SYN: "I'd want to speak; here's the packet sequence number with which I'll begin."
- SYN-ACK: "All right, here's the first sequence number I'll use in my direction."
- ACK: "All right!"

When the connection is complete, further three or four packets are required to close it down—either a short FIN, FIN-ACK, and ACK, or a slightly longer pair of distinct FIN and ACK packets in each direction. Just to deliver a single request, a minimum of six packets are required! In such instances, protocol designers quickly turn to UDP.

The question is whether a client would wish to start a TCP connection and then utilise it to make several requests to the same server over the course of several minutes or hours. Once the connection is established and the handshake fee has been paid, each request and answer will only require a single packet in each direction, taking advantage of all of TCP's retransmission, exponential backoff, and flow control capabilities.

When a long-term relationship between client and server is not required, UDP shines, particularly when there are so many clients that a standard TCP implementation would run out of memory if it had to keep up with a distinct data stream for each active client.

The second time TCP is ineffective is when an application can do something far more intelligent than merely retransmit data when a packet is lost. Take, for example, an audio chat conversation. If a second's worth of data is lost due to a failed packet, just resending the same second of music over and again until it arrives will be ineffective. Instead, the client should fill that awkward second with whatever audio it can cobble together from the packets that did arrive (a clever audio protocol will begin and end each packet with a bit of heavily compressed audio from the preceding and following moments of time to cover exactly this situation), and then continue on as if the interruption never happened. This is impossible with TCP, which will obstinately retransmit lost data even when it is far too old to be of any use. The cornerstone of live-streaming multimedia over the Internet is frequently UDP datagrams.

TCP Sockets Mean?

TCP employs port numbers to identify between various programmes operating at the same IP address, just as UDP did in Chapter 2, and it follows the same principles for well-known and ephemeral port numbers. If you wish to go through the information again, go back to the section "Port Numbers" in that chapter.

It only requires a single socket to speak UDP, as you saw in the last chapter: a server can establish a UDP port and subsequently receive datagrams from hundreds of different clients. While it is possible to connect() a datagram socket to a specific peer so that the socket will always send() and recv() packets sent back from that peer, the idea of a connection is merely for convenience. Connect() has the same effect as your programme selecting on its own to send to only one address using sendto() methods and then ignoring responses from everyone other than that address.

With a stateful stream protocol like TCP, however, the connect() call becomes the starting point for all subsequent network communication. It's the point at which your operating system's network stack initiates the handshake protocol described in the preceding section, which, if successful, makes both ends of the TCP stream available for usage.

This means that, unlike with a UDP socket, a TCP connect() call can fail. The remote host may or may not respond, or it may refuse to connect. n. More esoteric protocol faults, such as the immediate receipt of a RST ("reset") packet, may also occur. Because establishing a permanent connection between two hosts is required for a stream connection, the other host must be listening and ready to accept your connection.

An incoming connection generates an even more significant event for a Python application: the creation of a new socket! On the "server side," which is defined as the conversation partner not performing the connect() call but receiving the SYN packet that the connect call initiates, an incoming connection generates an even more significant event for a Python application: the creation of a new socket! This is due to the fact that the standard POSIX TCP interface uses two distinct types of sockets: "passive" listening sockets and active "connected" sockets.

- The passive socket, also known as a listening socket, keeps track of the server's "socket name"—the address and port number—at which it is ready to accept connections. This type of socket will never be able to receive or send data. It isn't a representation of a live network chat. Instead, it's how the server informs the operating system that it's willing to accept inbound connections at a specific TCP port number.

- A distant conversation partner with a certain IP address and port number is attached to an active, connected socket. It can only be used to communicate with that one partner, and it can be read and written to without having to worry about how the data will be broken up into packets. The stream resembles a pipe or file so closely that, on Unix systems, a connected TCP socket can be handed to another application that expects to read from a normal file and never realises it is communicating over the network.

While the interface address and port number at which a passive socket is listening make it unique—no one else is allowed to use those addresses and ports—there might be many active sockets with the same local socket name. A busy web server, for example, with a thousand HTTP connections, will have a thousand active sockets all tied to its public IP address at TCP port 80. The four-part coordinate, displayed here, is what distinguishes an active socket:

```
(remote ip, remote port, local ip, local port)
```

The operating system uses this four-tuple to identify each active TCP connection, and incoming TCP packets are checked to verify if their source and destination addresses match any of the system's currently active connections.

TCP Client and Server

Take a look at Listing 3-1 for an example. I've combined what may have been two independent programmes into a single listing, as I did in the last chapter, because they share some common code and so that the client and server code can be viewed together more simply.

Listing 3-1. Simple TCP Server and Client

```python
#!/usr/bin/env python3
# Network Programming in Python: The Basics
# Simple TCP client and server that send and receive 16 octets
import argparse, socket
def recvall(sock, length):
 data = b''
    while len(data) < length:
```

```
                more = sock.recv(length - len(data))
            if not more:
                raise EOFError('was  expecting  %d  bytes  but  only
                    received'
    ' %d bytes before the socket closed'
    % (length, len(data)))
    data += more
    return data
def server(interface, port):
        sock = socket.socket(socket.AF_INET, socket.SOCK_STREAM)
    sock.setsockopt(socket.SOL_SOCKET, socket.SO_REUSEADDR, 1)
        sock.bind((interface, port))
        sock.listen(1)
        print('Listening at', sock.getsockname())
while True:
            sc, sockname = sock.accept()
            print('We have accepted a connection from', sockname)
            print(' Socket name:', sc.getsockname())
    print(' Socket peer:', sc.getpeername())
message = recvall(sc, 16)
    print(' Incoming sixteen-octet message:', repr(message))
    sc.sendall(b'Farewell, client')
    sc.close()
            print(' Reply sent, socket closed')


def client(host, port):
sock = socket.socket(socket.AF_INET, socket.SOCK_STREAM)
    sock.connect((host, port))
    print('Client has been assigned socket name', sock.getsockname())
    sock.sendall(b'Hi there, server')
    reply = recvall(sock, 16)
    print('The server said', repr(reply))
```

```
sock.close()
if __name__ == '__main__':
        choices = {'client': client, 'server': server}
        parser = argparse.ArgumentParser(description='Send and receive
        over TCP')
        parser.add_argument('role', choices=choices, help='which role
        to play')
        parser.add_argument('host', help='interface the server listens
        at;'
' host the client sends to')
parser.add_argument('-p', metavar='PORT', type=int, default=1060,
                        help='TCP port (default 1060)')
args = parser.parse_args()
function = choices[args.role]
        function(args.host, args.p)
```

In Chapter 2, I went over bind() in great detail since the address you specify as its parameter controls whether distant hosts can try to connect to our server or whether your server can connect to them is secured from external connections and can only be contacted by other programmes operating on the same computer. As a result, Chapter 2 began with safe programme listings bound exclusively to the loopback interface and progressed from there. moved on to more risky application listings that accepted connections from other network hosts

However, in this case, I've integrated both options into a single listing. You can bind to 127.0.0.1 or one of your machine's external IP addresses using the host argument from the command line, or you can enter a blank string to indicate that you will accept connections from any of your machine's IP addresses. If you want to recall all of the rules, go back to Chapter 2 and go through them again. They apply to both TCP and UDP connections and sockets.

Your port number choice has the same weight as it did when you chose port numbers for UDP in Chapter 2, and the symmetry between TCP and UDP on the subject of port numbers is close enough that you can simply apply the rationale you used then to understand why the same choice was made here.

So, what's the difference between the earlier efforts with UDP and this new client and server, which are based on TCP instead?

The client has a similar appearance. It opens a socket, calls connect() with the address of the server it wishes to interact with, and then sends and receives data. But there are a few differences beyond that.

To begin with, the TCP connect() call is not the harmless bit of local socket setting that it is in UDP, where it just sets a default remote address to be used with any later send() or recv() operations, as I just mentioned. Connect() is a real-time network action that initiates a three-way handshake between the client and server machines to prepare them for communication. This means that connect() can fail, as you can see by running the client when the server isn't up and running.

```
$ python tcp_deadlock.py client localhost
Sending 16 bytes of data, in chunks of 16 bytes
Traceback (most recent call last):
  ...
ConnectionRefusedError: [Errno 111] Connection refused
```

Second, you'll see that this TCP client is significantly simpler than the UDP client in one respect: it doesn't need to account for missed packets. Because of the guarantees provided by TCP, it can send() data without even checking to see if the remote end has received it, and it can recv() without having to think about retransmitting its request. The client can be confident that the network stack will perform any necessary retransmissions to ensure that its data is delivered.

Third, this programme is more complicated in one direction than the comparable UDP code— which may surprise you because, with all of their guarantees, TCP streams appear to be uniformly simpler for programmers than UDP datagrams. TCP, on the other hand, considers your outgoing and incoming data to be nothing more than streams with no beginning or finish, so it feels free to divide them into packets anyway it sees fit. As a result, send() and recv() now have a different meaning than before. They simply meant "send this datagram" or "accept this datagram" in the case of UDP, and each datagram was atomic: it arrived or did not as a self-contained unit of data. Half-sent or half-received UDP datagrams will never be seen by an application. To a UDP application, only fully entire datagrams are ever transmitted.

TCP, on the other hand, may split its data stream into several packets of varying sizes during transmission and then reassemble them progressively on the receiving end. Despite the fact that this is extremely improbable with the little 16-octet messages in Listing 3-1, your code should be prepared in case it happens. What impact does TCP streaming have on the send() and recv() functions?

Consider sending first (). When you call TCP transmit(), one of three scenarios will occur in your operating system's networking stack.

- The data can be accepted right away by the local system's networking stack, either because the network card is free to transmit right away or because the system has enough room to copy the data to a temporary outgoing buffer so your programme can keep running. Because the entire string is being communicated, send() returns instantly in these circumstances and returns the length of your data string as its return value.

- Another option is that the network card is busy, and the socket's outgoing data buffer is full, and the system is unable to—or unwilling to—allocate any more space. In this scenario, send() will simply stall, putting your programme on hold until the data can be accepted for transmission.

- There's also the possibility that the outgoing buffers are almost full, but not quite, and that some of the data you're trying to send will be queued right away. The rest of the data block, though, will have to wait. Send() completes instantly in this situation, returning the amount of bytes taken from the beginning of your data string but leaving the rest of the data unprocessed.

You can't just call transmit() on a stream socket without inspecting the return value because of this last possibility. You must include a send() call within a loop that, if a partial transmission occurs, will continue to try to send the remaining data until the complete byte string has been sent. This is sometimes stated in networking code via a loop like the one below:

```
bytes_sent = 0
while bytes_sent < len(message):
 message_remaining = message[bytes_sent:]
 bytes_sent += s.send(message_remaining)
```

Fortunately, Python does not need you to perform this dance every time you need to transfer a block of data. The socket implementation in the Standard Library includes a friendly sendall() function(), which Listing 3-1 utilises instead. Because sendall() is written in C, it is not only faster than doing it yourself, but it also releases the Global Interpreter Lock during its loop, allowing other Python threads to run without interference until all of the data has been transferred.

Regrettably, there is no analogous Standard Library wrapper for the recv() method, despite the fact that it has the same risk of incomplete transmission. Recv() is implemented by the operating system using logic that is quite similar to that used while transmitting.

- If there is no data available, recv() will block and your programme will pause until data arrives.

- If there is enough data in the incoming buffer already, you will be given as many bytes as you gave recv() permission to deliver.

- If the buffer only contains some waiting data but not as much as you gave recv() permission to return, you will be returned what is there right away, even if it is not as much as you requested.

That's why the recv() method must be used within a loop. The operating system has no means of understanding that this simple client and server are sending messages with a fixed width of 16 octets. Because it can't predict when the incoming data will finally add up to what your programme will consider a full message, it offers you as much information as it can as soon as possible.

Why is there a sendall() method in the Python Standard Library but none for the recv() method? It's most likely due to the rarity of fixed-length communications these days. Most protocols have significantly more intricate rules for delimiting parts of an incoming stream than a simple "the message is always 16 bytes long" choice. The loop that performs recv() in most real-world applications is more complicated than the one in Listing 3-1, since a computer typically has to read or process part of the message before it can anticipate how much more is coming.

An HTTP response, for example, contains headers, a blank line, and whatever many additional bytes of data were supplied in the Content-Length header. You don't know how many times you should call recv() until you've at least received the headers and processed them to determine the content length, and this is something you should leave to your application rather than the Standard Library.

Each conversation one socket.

When you look at the server code in Listing 3-1, you'll notice that it follows a significantly different pattern from the one you saw earlier, and the difference is due to the definition of a TCP stream socket. Remember from earlier that there are two types of stream sockets: listening sockets, which are used by servers to make a port available for incoming connections, and connected sockets, which reflect a server's dialogue with a specific client.

You can see how this distinction is carried through in actual server code in Listing 3-1. The connection, which may seem strange at first, is that a listening socket provides a new, connected socket as the result returned by accept()!Let's look at the steps in the programme listing to see how the socket actions are performed.

To claim a certain port, the server first calls bind(). Note that this does not yet determine whether the programme will behave as a client or a server, i.e., whether it will actively make connections or passively wait for incoming connections. It simply reserves a certain port, either on a specific interface or across all interfaces, for usage by this software. Clients can use this method if they need to communicate with a server from a specific port on their system rather than the ephemeral port number that would otherwise be allocated to them.

The server announces that it wishes to use the socket to listen in the following method call, which is when the real decision is made (). Running this on a TCP socket completely changes its personality. The socket is irreversibly modified when listen() is invoked, and it can no longer be used to send or receive data. This socket object will no longer be attached to any particular client. Instead, the socket's accept() method—which you haven't seen until in this book because its sole purpose is to enable listening TCP sockets—can now only be used to receive incoming connections. and each of these calls waits for a new client to connect before returning a whole new socket that regulates the new dialogue with them that has just begun.

As you can see from the code, getsockname() works with both listening and connected sockets, and it tells you what local TCP port they're using in both cases. You can execute the getpeername() method at any time to learn the address of the client to which a connected socket is tied, or you can save the socket name returned as the second return value from accept (). You'll see that both values give you the same address when you run this server.

```
$ python tcp_sixteen.py server ""
Listening at ('0.0.0.0', 1060)
Waiting to accept a new connection
We have accepted a connection from ('127.0.0.1', 57971)
 Socket name: ('127.0.0.1', 1060)
 Socket peer: ('127.0.0.1', 57971)
 Incoming sixteen-octet message: b'Hi there, server'
 Reply sent, socket closed
Waiting to accept a new connection
```

The following output was obtained by having the client make only one connection to the server:

```
$ python3 tcp_sixteen.py client 127.0.0.1
Client has been assigned socket name ('127.0.0.1', 57971)
The server said b'Farewell, client'
```

The rest of the server code shows that once accept() has returned a connected socket, it behaves exactly like a client socket, with no more asymmetries in their communication pattern. Recv() returns data as it becomes available, while sendall() is the ideal way to send a large block of data and ensure that it all gets sent.

When listen() was called on the server socket, you'll notice that it was given an integer argument. This value specifies how many waiting connections should be allowed to stack up before the operating system starts rejecting new connections and deferring any further three-way handshakes. I'm using the extremely tiny value 1 in the examples since I only support one example client connecting at a time, but when I talk about network server design in Chapter 7, I'll explore greater values for this call.

Once the client and server have said everything they need to say, they close() their end of the connection, instructing the operating system to send any leftover data in their output buffer, and then end the TCP session using the FIN-packet shutdown method.

Address that is in use.

There is one last feature in Listing 3-1 that may pique your interest. Why does the server ensure that the socket option SO REUSEADDR is set before attempting to bind to a port?

If you comment out that line and then attempt starting the server, you can observe what happens if you don't set this option. At first glance, it may appear to be of no concern. You will see no effect if all you do is stop and start the server (here I am starting the server and then terminating it with a simple Ctrl+C at the terminal's prompt):

```
$ python tcp_sixteen.py server ""
Listening at ('127.0.0.1', 1060)
Waiting to accept a new connection
^C
Traceback (most recent call last):
  ...
KeyboardInterrupt
$ python tcp_sixteen.py server ""
Listening at ('127.0.0.1', 1060)
Waiting to accept a new connection
```

However, if you start the server, run the client against it, and then kill and restart the server, you'll see a significant change. When the server is restarted, you will see the following error:

```
$ python tcp_sixteen.py server

Traceback (most recent call last):

 ...

OSError: [Errno 98] Address already in use
```

What an enigma! Why should a bind() that can be repeated indefinitely become impossible just because a client has connected? If you continue to operate the server without using the SO REUSEADDR option, the address will not become available until several minutes after your last client connection.

The reason for this restriction is that your operating system's network stack is extremely cautious. A server socket that is only listening can be turned off and forgotten about right away. Even though both the client and the server have closed their connections and delivered FIN packets in both directions, a connected TCP socket that is currently communicating to a client cannot disappear quickly. Why? Because the network stack has no way of knowing whether or not the last packet, which closes the socket, was received. If it is dropped by the network, the remote end may wonder what is taking so long with the last packet and retransmit its FIN packet in the hopes of eventually receiving a response.

A trustworthy protocol like TCP must logically have a point where it stops talking; otherwise, systems would have to commit to an endless exchange of "Okay, we both agree that we are all done, right?" messages until the computers were ultimately shut down. Even the final packet may be lost and need to be retransmitted several times before reaching the other end. What is the answer?

The answer is that once a connected TCP connection is closed from your application's perspective, the operating system's network stack preserves a record of it in a waiting state for up to four minutes. These states are referred to as RFC states in the RFC. TIME-WAIT and CLOSE-WAIT Any final FIN packets can be correctly responded to while the closed socket is still in either of these phases. If the TCP implementation just forgot about the connection, it would be unable to respond to the FIN with an appropriate ACK.

So, a server attempting to claim a port on which a live connection was established within the last several minutes is actually attempting to claim a port that is currently in use in some way. That's why if you try to bind() to that address, you'll get an error.

By using the socket option SO REUSEADDR, you're telling your application that it's fine to hold a port whose former connections may still be shutting down on some network client. When writing server code, I always use SO REUSEADDR and have never had any issues.

From Binding to Interfaces

The IP address that you couple with a port number when you perform a bind() operation tells the operating system what network interfaces you are willing to receive connections from, as I outlined in Chapter 2 when discussing UDP. Listing 3-1's sample calls used the local IP address 127.0.0.1, which isolates your code from connections from other machines.

You may test this by running Listing 3-1 in server mode and connecting to a client from another machine, as shown earlier.

```
$ python tcp_sixteen.py client 192.168.5.130

Traceback (most recent call last):

  ...

ConnectionRefusedError: [Errno 111] Connection refused
```

You can see that the server does not even respond if it is running. Even if an inbound connection to its port is rejected, the operating system does not alert it. (Note that if your system has a firewall, the client may simply hang when it tries to connect, rather than receiving a polite "Connection rejected" exception to notify it what's wrong!)

However, if you start the server with an empty hostname, which tells the Python bind() procedure that you're willing to accept connections across any of your machine's active network interfaces, the server will accept connections. The client can then connect to another host successfully (the empty string is supplied by giving the shell these two double quotes at the end of the command line).

```
$ python tcp_sixteen.py server ""

Listening at ('0.0.0.0', 1060)
Waiting to accept a new connection
We have accepted a connection from ('127.0.0.1', 60359)
  Socket name: ('127.0.0.1', 1060)
  Socket peer: ('127.0.0.1', 60359)
  Incoming sixteen-octet message: b'Hi there, server'
```

```
 Reply sent, socket closed
Waiting to accept a new connection
```

As previously stated, my operating system uses the specific IP address 0.0.0.0 to mean "accept connections on any interface," but your operating system may use a different convention, which Python hides by allowing you to use the empty string instead.

Deadlock

Deadlock is a term used in computer science to describe a situation in which two programmes with limited resources are forced to wait on each other indefinitely due to bad planning. When utilising TCP, it turns out that this is a rather common occurrence.

As I previously indicated, standard TCP stacks use buffers to store incoming packet data until an application is ready to read it, as well as to gather outgoing data until the network hardware is ready to transmit an outgoing packet. . These buffers are usually relatively small, and the system is usually not willing to let programmes occupy all of RAM with unsent network data. After all, it's pointless to waste system resources generating more data if the remote end isn't ready to process it yet.

This limitation should not be a problem if you use the client-server pattern depicted in Listing 3-1, in which each end reads the entire message from its partner before turning around and delivering data in the opposite direction. However, if you create a client and server that leave too much data waiting without a plan in place to read it rapidly, you can quickly get into difficulties.

Look at Listing 3-2 for an example of a server and client attempting to be a little too clever without considering the repercussions. In this case, the server's author has done something rather clever. The server's task is to convert any amount of text into uppercase letters. Recognizing that client requests can be arbitrarily big and that reading an entire stream of information before processing it could cause the server to run out of memory, the server reads and processes tiny chunks of 1,024 bytes of data at a time.

Listing 3-2. TCP Server and Client That Can Deadlock

```
#!/usr/bin/env python3
# Network Programming in Python: The Basics
# TCP client and server that leave too much data waiting
import argparse, socket, sys
```

```
def server(host, port, bytecount):
 sock = socket.socket(socket.AF_INET, socket.SOCK_STREAM)
 sock.setsockopt(socket.SOL_SOCKET, socket.SO_REUSEADDR, 1)
 sock.bind((host, port))
 sock.listen(1)
 print('Listening at', sock.getsockname())
 while True:
 sc, sockname = sock.accept()
 print('Processing up to 1024 bytes at a time from', sockname)
 n = 0
 while True:
 data = sc.recv(1024)
 if not data:
 break
 output = data.decode('ascii').upper().encode('ascii')
 sc.sendall(output) # send it back uppercase
 n += len(data)
 print('\r %d bytes processed so far' % (n,), end=' ')
 sys.stdout.flush()
 print()
 sc.close()
 print(' Socket closed')
def client(host, port, bytecount):
 sock = socket.socket(socket.AF_INET, socket.SOCK_STREAM)
 bytecount = (bytecount + 15) // 16 * 16 # round up to a multiple
of 16
 message = b'capitalize this!' # 16-byte message to repeat over and
over
 print('Sending', bytecount, 'bytes of data, in chunks of 16 bytes')
 sock.connect((host, port))
 sent = 0
 while sent < bytecount:
```

```
  sock.sendall(message)
  sent += len(message)
  print('\r %d bytes sent' % (sent,), end=' ')
  sys.stdout.flush()
  print()
  sock.shutdown(socket.SHUT_WR)
  print('Receiving all the data the server sends back')
  received = 0
  while True:
  data = sock.recv(42)
  if not received:
  print(' The first data received says', repr(data))
  if not data:
  break
  received += len(data)
  print('\r %d bytes received' % (received,), end=' ')
  print()
  sock.close()
if __name__ == '__main__':
 choices = {'client': client, 'server': server}
 parser = argparse.ArgumentParser(description='Get deadlocked over TCP')
 parser.add_argument('role', choices=choices, help='which role to
play')
 parser.add_argument('host', help='interface the server listens at;'
 ' host the client sends to')
 parser.add_argument('bytecount', type=int, nargs='?', default=16,
 help='number of bytes for client to send (default 16)')
 parser.add_argument('-p', metavar='PORT', type=int, default=1060,
 help='TCP port (default 1060)')
 args = parser.parse_args()
 function = choices[args.role]
 function(args.host, args.p, args.bytecount)
```

Because it's just trying to use the upper() string method on plain ASCII characters, it can easily break the job off without needing to do any framing or analysis. This is a procedure that can be carried out separately on each computer. block of input, without regard for the blocks that preceded or followed it. Things would not be so straightforward if it weren't for the fact that If it were trying to do a more advanced string operation like title(), which capitalises a letter in the string, the server would crash. If a word is split over a block border without being correctly reconstructed, it will appear in the midst of the word. For If a data stream was split into 16-byte blocks, for example, mistakes would appear as follows:

```
>>> message = 'the tragedy of macbeth'
>>> blocks = message[:16], message[16:]
>>> ''.join( b.upper() for b in blocks ) # works fine
'THE TRAGEDY OF MACBETH'
>>> ''.join( b.title() for b in blocks ) # whoops
'The Tragedy Of MAcbeth'
```

For UTF-8 encoded Unicode data, processing text while splitting on fixed-length blocks would not work since a multibyte character could be divided across a boundary between two binary blocks. In such instances, the server would have to be more cautious than in this example and maintain some state between data blocks.

In any event, handling input one block at a time is a good idea for the server, even if the 1,024-byte block size employed here is actually fairly small for today's servers and networks. By breaking down the data and sending out responses as soon as possible, The server has a limit on how much data it can maintain in memory at any given time. This type of server could handle hundreds of clients at once, each transmitting gigabyte-sized streams, without putting a strain on memory or other hardware resources.

The client and server in Listing 3-2 also appear to perform well for tiny data streams. If you start the server and then execute the client with a command-line option providing a small amount of bytes—say, 32 bytes of data—it will receive all of its text in uppercase. It will round whatever value you pass up to a multiple of 16 bytes for simplicity.

```
$ python tcp_deadlock.py client 127.0.0.1 32
Sending 32 bytes of data, in chunks of 16 bytes
 32 bytes sent
Receiving all the data the server sends back
```

The first data received says b'CAPITALIZE THIS!CAPITALIZE THIS!'

```
32 bytes received
```

The server will acknowledge that it did indeed process 32 bytes for its most recent client. The server, by the way, must be operating on the same system as the client, and this script uses the localhost IP address to keep things easy.

```
Processing up to 1024 bytes at a time from ('127.0.0.1', 60461)
32 bytes processed so far
Socket closed
```

When tried with tiny quantities of data, this code looks to perform nicely. In fact, it may work for greater quantities as well. Attempt to run the client with hundreds of thousands of bytes and check if it still works.

By the way, this first data exchange demonstrates the behaviour of recv(), which I previously mentioned. Recv(1024) was glad to deliver only 16 bytes if that was the amount of data that became available and no more data had yet arrived from the client, even if the server had requested 1,024 bytes.

This client and server, on the other hand, can be pushed into dangerous terrain. If you try a large enough value, you'll end up with a disaster! Try sending a large stream of data using the client, say one that is a gigabit in size.

```
$ python tcp_deadlock.py client 127.0.0.1 1073741824
```

Both the client and the server will be frantically updating their terminal displays, informing you of the quantity of data they have transmitted and received. The numbers will continue to rise until, all of a sudden, both connections will freeze. Actually, if you pay attention, you'll see that the server comes to a halt first, followed by the client. On the Ubuntu laptop in which I'm writing this chapter, the amount of data processed before they seize up varies, but on the test run that I just finished on my laptop, the Python script processed a lot of data. The server came to a halt, saying:

```
$ python tcp_deadlock.py server ""
Listening at ('0.0.0.0', 1060)
Processing up to 1024 bytes at a time from ('127.0.0.1', 60482)
 4452624 bytes processed so far
```

In addition, the client is around 350,000 bytes ahead of schedule in sending its outgoing data stream.

```
$ python tcp_deadlock.py client "" 16000000
```

```
Sending 16000000 bytes of data, in chunks of 16 bytes
 8020912 bytes sent
```

Why have both the client and the server come to a halt?

The answer is that both the server's output and client's input buffers have finally filled, and TCP has utilised its window adjustment protocol to communicate this and prevent the connection from sending any more data that would have to be deleted and resent later.

Why is there a stalemate as a result of this? Consider what happens as each data block makes its way across the network. It is sent by the client using sendall (). The server then takes it using recv(), processes it, and sends it out again with a capitalised version via another sendall() call. What happens after that? Nothing, to be precise! The client never calls recv() while it still has data to communicate, so more and more data accumulates until the operating system buffers can no longer handle it.

During the last run, the operating system buffered around 4MB in the client's incoming queue before the network stack decided it was full. At that moment, the server's sendall() call becomes stuck, and the operating system pauses the server's operation until the logjam is cleared and it can send additional data. Now that the server isn't processing data or making any more recv() requests, it's up to the client to start backing up data. Because the client went nearly that far into creating data before being pulled to a standstill, the operating system appears to have set a limit of around 3.5MB on the amount of data it is willing to queue up in that direction.

You'll probably find that different limits are reached on your own system; the values above are arbitrary and based on the mood of my laptop at the time. They have nothing to do with the way TCP operates.

This example is intended to teach you two things, in addition to demonstrating that recv(1024) does indeed return less bytes than 1,024 when a smaller amount is readily available! These buffers can temporarily store data so that packets don't have to be discarded and resent if they come at a time when their reader isn't in the middle of a recv() call. However, the buffers are not infinite. A TCP routine attempting to write data that is never received or processed will eventually find itself unable to write, at least until some of the data is read and the buffer begins to empty.

Second, this illustration highlights the hazards of protocols that do not alternate lock step, with the client requesting a finite amount of data and then waiting for the server to respond or acknowledge. . If a protocol does not require the server to read a complete request until the client has finished sending it, and then send a complete response in the other direction, a situation like the one described here can cause both of them to freeze, leaving them with no choice but to kill the programme manually and rewrite it to improve its design.

But, if that's the case, how are network clients and servers intended to handle massive amounts of data without hitting a snag? In fact, there are two possible responses. To begin, they can utilise socket options to disable blocking, allowing functions like send() and recv() to return immediately if they are unable to deliver data. In Chapter 7, you'll learn more about this choice when you examine the many approaches to construct network server programmes in depth.

Alternatively, the programmes can process data from multiple inputs simultaneously by splitting into separate threads or processes (one tasked with sending data into a socket, for example, and another tasked with reading data back out), or by using operating system calls like select() or poll(), which allow them to wait on both busy outgoing and incoming sockets at the same time and respond to whichever is ready. Chapter 7 delves into these topics as well.

Finally, keep in mind that the preceding scenario is impossible to achieve when utilising UDP. This is due to the fact that UDP does not support flow control. If there are more datagrams coming than can be handled, UDP can simply discard some of them, leaving it up to the application to figure out what happened.

Half-Open Connections, Closed Connections

From the preceding example, there are two more arguments that need be stated on a separate subject.

To begin, Listing 3-2 demonstrates how a Python socket object responds to an end-of-file condition. When a socket is closed, it simply produces an empty string, just like when a Python file object gives an empty string when there is no more data to read.

In Listing 3-1, I never had to worry about this since I had placed a strong enough structure on the protocol—exchanging a pair of 16-byte messages—that I didn't need to close the connection to signal when communication was complete. The client and server could transmit a message while leaving the socket open and closing it later without worrying about anyone waiting for them to do so.

In Listing 3-2, however, the client sends—and the server processes and returns—an arbitrary amount of data, the length of which is determined solely by the number the user provides on the command line. As a result, the identical pattern can be seen twice in the code: a while loop that continues until it sees an empty string returned from recv (). Note that until you get to Chapter 7 and start looking at nonblocking sockets, recv() may throw an exception simply because no data is accessible right now. Other methods are employed to determine whether the socket has closed in this scenario.

Second, you'll see that after sending its transmission, the client calls shutdown() on the socket. This solves a significant issue. How will the client avoid having to conduct a full close() on the socket and so restrict itself from running the multiple recv() calls that it still needs to make to obtain the server's response if the server will read until it sees end-of-file? The solution is to "half-close" the connection, i.e., disable communication in one direction permanently without deleting the socket.

In a two-way socket, the shutdown() call can be used to halt communication in either direction, as demonstrated in Listing 3-2. One of three symbols can be used as its argument.

- **SHUT WR:** This is the most typical value, because most programmes know when their own output is complete, but not always when their conversation partner is. This value indicates that the caller will not be sending any more data into the socket, and that reads from the socket's opposite end should react with an end-of-file message.

- **SHUT RD:** This command is used to switch off the incoming socket stream, resulting in an end-of-file error if your peer tries to send you any further data through the socket.

- **SHUT RDWR:** This blocks communication on the socket in both directions. It may not appear beneficial at first because you can just close the socket with close(), and communication is terminated in both directions. The distinction between closing and shutting down a socket in both directions is somewhat complex. If your operating system allows many programmes to share a single socket, close() just terminates your process's relationship with the socket while keeping it open as long as another process is still utilising it. The shutdown() method, on the other hand, will always disable the socket for everyone who is currently using it.

Because you can't build unidirectional sockets using the regular socket() method, many programmers who only need to send data in one direction via a socket will construct it first and then execute shutdown() for the direction they don't need as soon as it's attached. This means that no operating system buffers will be filled unnecessarily if the peer with whom they are speaking sends data in an incorrect direction.

When you use shutdown() on sockets that should be unidirectional, you get a more apparent error message for a peer that gets confused and tries to communicate data.

Otherwise, the unexpected data will either be ignored or will fill a buffer, resulting in a deadlock because it will never be read.

TCP Streams as Files

TCP allows data streams, which may have reminded you of traditional files, which also support reading and writing sequential data as basic operations. Python does an excellent job of separating these ideas.While file objects can read and write, sockets can only send and receive data (). And no thing has the ability to do both.(This is a much cleaner and more portable conceptual separation than the underlying POSIX interface, which allows a C programmer to call read() and write() on a socket indiscriminately as if it were a normal file descriptor.)

However, there are occasions when you'll want to treat a socket like a standard Python file object, such as when you want to send it to code that can read and write data directly from a file, such as pickle, json, and zlib. Python provides a makefile() method on every socket for this purpose, which returns a Python file object that calls recv() and send() behind the scenes.

```
>>> import socket
>>> sock = socket.socket(socket.AF_INET, socket.SOCK_STREAM)
>>> hasattr(sock, 'read')
False
>>> f = sock.makefile()
>>> hasattr(f, 'read')
True
```

Sockets on Unix-based systems like Ubuntu and Mac OS X, like standard Python files, offer a fileno() method that helps you find out what file descriptor number they have in case you need to pass it to lower-level calls. This will come in handy when you look at select() and poll() in Chapter 7.

Conclusion

The TCP-powered "stream" socket does everything it can to facilitate the transmission and receipt of data streams over the network between two sockets, including retransmitting lost packets, reordering out-of-sequence packets, and breaking massive data streams into network-optimized packet sizes.

TCP, like UDP, uses port numbers to differentiate between multiple stream endpoints on a single system. A programme that wants to accept incoming TCP connections must bind() to a port, listen() on the socket, and then run accept() in a loop to receive a new socket for each incoming connection with which it can communicate with each individual client. To connect to an existing server port, all a programme needs to do is build a socket and connect() to an address.

Servers should commonly set the SO REUSEADDR option on the sockets they bind(), lest the operating system refuse to allow the binding due to old connections still closing on the same port from the last time the server was run.

With send() and recv(), data is really sent and received (). Some protocols that run on top of TCP will label their data in such a way that clients and servers will know when a communication is concluded automatically. Other protocols will interpret the TCP socket as a genuine stream, sending and receiving data until the file ends. The shutdown() socket method can be used to produce end-of-file in one direction (all sockets are bidirectional by default) while leaving the other open.

When two peers exchange data, the socket fills up with data that is never read, resulting in a deadlock. . One direction may eventually be unable to send() and may hang indefinitely while waiting for the backlog to clear.

If you wish to pass a socket to a Python procedure that knows how to read from or write to a regular file object, the makefile() socket method returns a Python object that executes recv() and send() behind the scenes when the caller wants to read or write.

CHAPTER 4
Domain name system & socket names

After understanding the fundamentals of UDP and TCP, the two major data transports accessible on IP networks, it's time for me to take a step back and discuss two larger challenges that must be addressed regardless of whatever data transport you use.

Structure

- Sockets and Hostnames
- Five Socket Coordinates
- IPv6
- Modern Address Resolution
- Bind Your Server to a Port Using getaddrinfo()
- To connect to a service, use getaddrinfo()
- Getting a Canonical Hostname with getaddrinfo()
- Other getaddrinfo() Flags
- Primitive Name Service Routines
- In Your Own Code, Use getsockaddr()
- DNS Protocol

- Why Shouldn't Use Raw DNS?
- Using Python to do a DNS query
- Getting Mail Domains Resolved
- Conclusion

Objective:

In this chapter, we'll talk about network addresses and the distributed service that converts names to raw IP addresses.

Sockets and Hostnames

Raw IP addresses are rarely typed into our browsers or e-mail clients. We type domain names instead. Some domain names, such as python.org and bbc.co.uk, are used to identify entire organisations. Some websites allow you to abbreviate a hostname by typing asaph, and they will fill in the rest of the name for you, presuming you mean the asaph machine on the same site. Regardless of any local customisation, specifying a fully qualified domain name that includes all elements up to and including the top-level domain is always proper.

A top-level domain (TLD) used to be as easy as.com,.net,.org,.gov,.mil, or a two-letter internationally recognised country code like.uk. However, many more, more frivolous top-level domains, such as.beer, are being introduced today, making it a little more difficult to tell the difference between fully qualified and partially qualified domain names at a glance (unless you try to memorise the entire list of top-level names!).

Each TLD often has its own set of servers, which are managed by an organisation in charge of awarding ownership to domains under the TLD. When you register a domain, they create an entry on their servers for it.

When a client from anywhere in the world tries to resolve a name within your domain, the top-level servers can direct the client to your own domain servers, which will allow your company to return the addresses it need for the various hostnames you generate. The Domain Name Service is a network of servers located all over the world that respond to name queries using this system of top-level names and referrals (DNS).

Sockets cannot be named with a single primitive Python value such as an integer or string, as you learned in the previous two chapters. Instead, both TCP and UDP employ integer port numbers to share a single machine's IP address among the many distinct applications that may be operating there, therefore the address and port number must be combined to create a socket name, such as this:

(115.114.148.6)

While you may have picked up a few tidbits about socket names from the previous chapters—for example, the knowledge that the first item can be either a hostname or a dotted IP address—time it's to go deeper into the issue.

Socket names are significant at various stages during the creation and use of sockets, as you will recall. Here are all of the key socket methods that require a socket name as an argument for your convenience:

- **mysocket.accept():** This function returns a tuple whose second item is the remote address that has connected (the first item in the tuple is the new socket connected to that remote address) each time it is called on a listening TCP stream socket that has incoming connections ready to hand off to the application.

- **mysocket.bind(address)**: This binds the socket to the supplied local address, giving outgoing packets an address from which to originate and incoming connections from other computers a name to which they can connect.

- **mysocket.connect(address):** This tells the socket that data supplied through it will be transmitted to the specified remote address. This just sets the default address for UDP sockets if the caller uses send() instead of sendto() or recv() instead of recvfrom() but does not execute any network communication right away. For TCP sockets, however, this really uses a three-way handshake to negotiate a new stream with another computer, raising a Python exception if the negotiation fails.

- **mysocket.getpeername():** This function returns the remote address of the socket.

- **getsockname()** returns the address of this socket's own local endpoint.

- **mysocket.recvfrom(...):** This method produces a tuple that contains a string of returned data and the address from which it was received for UDP sockets.

- **mysocket.sendto(data, address):** This function is used to send a data packet to a remote address from an unconnected UDP port.

That concludes the discussion. So that you have some context for the observations that follow, here are the important socket actions that care about socket addresses, all in one location. In general, any of the aforementioned methods can receive or return any of the addresses listed below, so they'll work whether you're using IPv4, IPv6, or one of the less popular address families that I won't be addressing in this book.

Five Socket Coordinates

You paid close attention to the hostnames and IP addresses that their sockets utilised when studying the sample programmes in Chapters 2 and 3. However, these are merely the final two coordinates of five critical decisions made during the design and deployment of each socket object. Remember that the steps are as follows:

```python
import socket

s = socket.socket(socket.AF_INET, socket.SOCK_DGRAM)

s.bind(('localhost', 1060))
```

You can see that you specify four values here: two for socket configuration and two for the bind() call address.Because socket() takes a third, optional argument, there is a fifth potential coordinate. I'll go over each one one by one, starting with the three possible socket parameters ().

First, the address family makes the most important decision: it specifies which type of network you wish to communicate with, out of the many that a given machine may be linked to.

Because I feel that writing about IP networking will best assist the vast majority of Python programmers while also offering you skills that will work on Linux, Mac OS, or even Windows, I will always use the value AF INET for the address family in this book. However, if you import the socket module, print dir(socket), and search for symbols that begin with AF_ ("Address Family"), you'll find more options with names you're familiar with, such as AppleTalk and Bluetooth. The AF UNIX address family is very prevalent on POSIX platforms. which provides connections similar to Internet sockets, but which run between applications on the same machine by "connecting" to filenames rather than hostnames and port numbers.

The socket type comes after the address family. It selects the type of communication strategy you want to utilise on the network you've selected. You may anticipate that each address family has its own set of socket types, which you'd have to check up for each one. After all, what other address family besides AF INET will support socket types such as UDP and TCP?

Fortunately, this suspicion is unfounded. Despite the fact that UDP and TCP are very specialised to the AF INET protocol family, , the socket interface designers chose to give the general concept of a packet-based socket a more generic moniker. This is known as SOCK DGRAM, and it refers to the general concept of a dependable flow-controlled data stream, also known as a SOCK STREAM. Because many address families support one or both of these techniques, only these two symbols are required to cover a wide range of protocols across several address families.

Because you have usually narrowed down the various protocols to only one major option after specifying the address family and socket type, the protocol field in the socket() method is rarely used. Typically, programmers leave this blank or offer the value 0 to force it to be chosen automatically. If you want a stream over IP, the system will automatically select TCP. It chooses UDP if you want datagrams. That's why there's no third argument in any of the socket() methods in this book: it's nearly never needed in practise. Some examples of protocols defined for the AF INET family can be found in the socket module under names beginning with IPPROTO. Under the titles IPPROTO TCP and IPPROTO UDP, you'll find the two protocols that this book focuses on.

Finally, the IP address and port number, which were discussed in the previous two chapters, are the fourth and fifth values used to establish a connection.

We need take a step back and realise that our socket names include two components: hostname and port, due to our precise choices for the first three coordinates. If you had picked AppleTalk, ATM, or Bluetooth as your address family instead, you might have needed a different data structure than a tuple with a string and an integer inside. So, the entire set of coordinates, which I've referred to as five throughout this section, is really just the three fixed coordinates required to create the socket, followed by however many extra coordinates your specific address family requires in order to establish a network connection.

IPv6

After explaining all of this, it turns out that this book will need to present one more address family beyond the AF INET used so far: the AF INET6 address family for IPv6, which is the path to a future in which the world will not run out of IP addresses.

When the old ARPANET truly took off, its 32-bit address names—which made perfect sense back when computer memory was measured in kilobytes—became a clear and concerning constraint. With only 4 billion potential addresses, there isn't enough IP addresses for everyone on the planet, which spells disaster once everyone has a computer and a smartphone!

Even though only a small percentage of computers on the Internet today use IPv6 to communicate with the global network through their Internet service providers (where "today" is June 2014), the steps to make your Python programmes IPv6 compatible are straightforward enough that you should try writing code that anticipates the future.

In Python, you can check the has ipv6 Boolean attribute inside the socket module to see if the underlying platform supports IPv6.

```
>>> import socket

>>> socket.has_ipv6

True
```

that this does not indicate if an IPv6 interface is currently operational and capable of sending packets anywhere! It's only a statement about whether IPv6 capability is included into the operating system, not about whether it's in use.

When enumerated one after the other, the alterations that IPv6 will bring for your Python code may appear to be pretty scary.

- If you're working on an IPv6 network, you'll need to make your sockets using the AF INET6 family.

- Socket names are no longer limited to just two components: an address and a port number. Additional coordinates that offer "flow" information and a "scope" identification can be used instead.

- IPv6 host addresses will sometimes replace the pretty IPv4 octets like 18.9.22.69 that you might already be reading from configuration files or command-line inputs, and you might not even have decent regular expressions for these just yet.

The benefits of the IPv6 transition include not only the availability of an enormous number of addresses, but also the protocol's more comprehensive support for things like link-level security than most IPv4 implementations.

However, if you're used to creating clumsy, old-fashioned code that scans or assembles IP addresses and hostnames using your own regular expressions, the adjustments just outlined may seem like a lot of work. . In other words, if you've ever done your own address interpretation, you're probably anticipating that the transition to IPv6 will require you to write even more complicated code than before. Don't worry: my true advice is to avoid address interpretation and scanning at all costs! The following section will demonstrate how to do so.

Modern Address Resolution

Getaddrinfo is one of the most powerful tools in the Python socket user's armoury for making your code simple, powerful, and resilient to the complications of the shift from IPv4 to IPv6 ().

The **getaddrinfo()** function, like most other actions involving addresses, is found in the socket module.

It's probably the only routine you'll ever need to use to convert the hostnames and port numbers that your users supply into addresses that socket methods can use, unless you're doing anything specialised.

It takes a straightforward approach. Rather than forcing you to approach the addressing problem piecemeal, as is required when utilising the socket module's older functions, It allows you to specify whatever you need to know about the connection in a single request. It responds by returning all of the coordinates I mentioned earlier, which you'll need to construct and connect a socket to the specified location.

Its fundamental functionality is as follows (notice that the pprint "pretty print" module has nothing to do with networking; it just improves the appearance of a list of tuples over the standard print function):

```
>>> from pprint import pprint
>>> infolist = socket.getaddrinfo('google.com', 'www')
>>> pprint(infolist)
[(2, 1, 6, '', ('142.250.67.174', 80))]
>>> info = infolist[0]
>>> info[0:3]
(2, 1, 6)
>>> s = socket.socket(*info[0:3])
>>> info[4]
('142.250.67.174', 80)
>>> s.connect(info[4])
```

Everything you need to construct a socket and use it to make a connection is in the info variable.

It gives you a family, a type, a protocol, a canonical name, and an address. What are the parameters for getaddrinfo()? The two-element list that was returned tells you that there are two ways to connect to the HTTP service of the host gatech.edu: either by creating a SOCK STREAM socket (socket type 1) that uses IPPROTO TCP (protocol number 6) or by using a SOCK DGRAM (socket type 2) socket with IPPROTO UDP (protocol number 2). (which is the protocol represented by the integer 17). Instead of leaving the response to chance, you will usually indicate which sort of socket you want when calling getaddrinfo() later from scripts.

If you use getaddrinfo() in your code, unlike the listings in Chapters 2 and 3, which used real symbols like AF INET to show how the low-level socket mechanisms worked, your production Python code will not use any symbols from the socket module except those that tell getaddrinfo() what kind of address you want. . Instead, use the first three things in the getaddrinfo() return value as parameters to the socket() function Object() { [native code] }, and the fifth item as the address to any of the address-aware functions described in the first section of this chapter, such as connect().

As you can see from the above code snippet, getaddrinfo() permits not just the hostname but also the port name to be a symbol rather than an integer, removing the need for older Python scripts to make extra calls if the user wants to use www or smtp instead of 80 or 25.

Before going over all of the options that getaddrinfo() has, it's a good idea to look at how it's used to support three common network tasks. I'll go over them in the order in which you might do socket operations: binding, connecting, and finally recognising a remote host who has sent you data.

Bind Your Server to a Port Using getaddrinfo()

If you wish to submit an address to bind(), either because you're constructing a server socket or because you want your client to connect to someone else but from a predictable address, use getaddrinfo() with None as the hostname but the port number and socket type filled in. Note that in this and subsequent getaddrinfo() calls, zeros are used as wildcards in fields that should include numbers:

```
>>> from socket import getaddrinfo
```

```
>>> getaddrinfo(None, 'smtp', 0, socket.SOCK_STREAM, 0, socket.
AI_PASSIVE)
```

```
[(2, 1, 6, '', ('0.0.0.0', 25)), (10, 1, 6, '', ('::', 25, 0, 0))]
```

```
>>> getaddrinfo(None, 53, 0, socket.SOCK_DGRAM, 0, socket.AI_PASSIVE)
```

```
[(2, 2, 6, '', ('0.0.0.0', 53)), (10, 2, 17, '', ('::', 53, 0, 0))]
```

I asked two distinct questions, one with a text port identifier and the other with a raw numeric port number. First, I wanted to know to which IP I should bind() a socket if I wanted to use TCP to serve SMTP traffic. Second, I inquired about using UDP to serve port 53 (DNS) traffic. The responses I received are the appropriate wildcard addresses that will allow you to bind to every IPv4 and IPv6 interface on the local machine using the correct socket family, socket type, and protocol settings in each case.

Instead, skip the AI PASSIVE parameter and merely enter the hostname if you wish to bind() to a specific IP address that you know is configured as a local address for the computer on which you are executing. Here are two examples of how you might try binding to localhost:

```
>>> getaddrinfo('127.0.0.1', 'smtp', 0, socket.SOCK_STREAM, 0)

[(2, 1, 6, '', ('127.0.0.1', 25))]

>>> getaddrinfo('localhost', 'smtp', 0, socket.SOCK_STREAM, 0)

[(10, 1, 6, '', ('::1', 25, 0, 0)), (2, 1, 6, '', ('127.0.0.1', 25))]
```

As you can see, providing the IPv4 address for the local host restricts you to receiving connections over IPv4, whereas using the symbolic name localhost (at least on my Linux laptop with a properly set /etc/hosts file) makes the machine available via both IPv4 and IPv6.

By the way, one thing you might be asking at this point is what you're supposed to do when you declare that you want to provide a simple service and getaddrinfo() offers you numerous addresses to use—you can't build a single socket and bind() it to multiple addresses! In Chapter 7, I'll go through some of the approaches you can use if you're creating server code and wish to run multiple bound server sockets at the same time.

To connect to a service, use getaddrinfo().

You'll use getaddrinfo() to learn about connecting to other services, unless you're binding to a local address to provide a service yourself. When looking up services, you can specify an empty string to link back to the local host through the loopback interface or a string containing an IPv4 address, IPv6 address, or a hostname to name your destination.

Call getaddrinfo() with the AI ADDRCONFIG flag when preparing to connect() or sendto() a service. This filters out any addresses that your computer cannot reach. For example, an organization's IP address range could include both IPv4 and IPv6 addresses. If your host only supports IPv4, you'll want the results filtered to only include addresses from that family. You'll also want to provide AI V4MAPPED to return the IPv4 addresses reencoded as IPv6 addresses that you can really use if your local machine only has an IPv6 network interface but the service to which you're connecting only supports IPv4.

When putting these components together, you'll most likely use getaddrinfo() before joining them.

```
>>> getaddrinfo('google.com', 'www', 0, socket.SOCK_STREAM, 0,
... socket.AI_ADDRCONFIG | socket.AI_V4MAPPED)
[(2, 1, 6, '', ('142.250.67.174', 80)),
 (2, 1, 6, '', ('142.250.67.174', 80))]
```

You've gotten exactly what you requested in return: a list of every technique to connect to ftp.kernel.org via a TCP connection to its FTP port. Because this service is located at numerous distinct addresses on the Internet to share load, several IP addresses were returned. When numerous addresses are returned in this manner, you should normally use the first one and only try the others if your connection attempt fails. You will provide the workload that the remote service managers intend if you follow the order in which they want you to try connecting their servers.

Another question concerns how I can connect from my laptop to the IANA's HTTP interface, which is responsible for assigning port numbers in the first place.

```
>>> getaddrinfo('google.com', 'www', 0, socket.SOCK_STREAM, 0,
... socket.AI_ADDRCONFIG | socket.AI_V4MAPPED)
[(2, 1, 6, '', ('142.250.67.174', 80))]
```

The IANA web site is an excellent example of the AI ADDRCONFIG flag's utility because, like any other decent Internet standards agency, it already supports IPv6. Because my laptop can only communicate with IPv4 on the wireless network to which it is now connected, the previous call was careful to only return an IPv4 address. If you remove the carefully specified flags in the sixth parameter, however, you can see their IPv6 address, which you are unable to utilize.

```
>>> getaddrinfo('google.com', 'www', 0, socket.SOCK_STREAM, 0)
[(2, 1, 6, '', ('142.250.67.174', 80)),
 (10, 1, 6, '', ('2001:4860:4860::8844', 80, 0, 0))]
```

This can be handy if you aren't planning on using the addresses yourself but are supplying directory information to other hosts or apps.

Getting a Canonical Hostname with getaddrinfo()

Last but not least, you may need to know the hostname that formally belongs to the IP address at the other end of your server socket if you are initiating a new connection or have just accepted an incoming connection on one of your own server sockets.

Although this wish is sensible, it comes with a serious risk: the owner of an IP address can have their DNS server return any name they want as the canonical name when your computer performs a reverse query! They can pretend to be google.com, python.org, or anyone else. When you ask them what hostname belongs to one of their IP addresses, they have complete control over the string of characters returned to you.

Before trusting a canonical name lookup—also known as a reverse DNS lookup because it maps an IP address to a hostname rather than the other way around—you should check the name that has been returned to determine if it really resolves to the original IP address. If not, the hostname is either intentionally misleading, or it was a well-intentioned response from a domain whose forward and reverse names, as well as IP addresses, were not appropriately configured to match.

Lookups for canonical names are expensive. Because they require an extra round-trip over the global DNS service, they are frequently omitted for logging. Services that pause to reverse-lookup every single IP address that makes a connection are slow and ponderous, therefore logging bare IP addresses is a common step by system administrators aiming to improve a system's response time. If one of them is causing a problem, you can always hunt it up in the log file later by hand.

However, if you need the canonical name of a host and wish to look it up, run getaddrinfo() with the AI CANONNAME flag enabled, and the fourth item of any of the tuples it returns—an item that was the empty string in the previous examples—will have the canonical name:

```
>>> getaddrinfo('google.com', 'www', 0, socket.SOCK_STREAM, 0,
... socket.AI_ADDRCONFIG | socket.AI_V4MAPPED | socket.AI_CANONNAME)
[(2, 1, 6, 'google.com', ('142.250.67.174', 80))]
```

Getaddrinfo() can also take the name of a socket that is already connected to a remote peer and return a canonical name.

```
>>> mysock = server_sock.accept()
>>> addr, port = mysock.getpeername()
>>> getaddrinfo(addr, port, mysock.family, mysock.type, mysock.proto,
... socket.AI_CANONNAME)
[(2, 1, 6, 'rr.pmtpa.wikimedia.org', ('103.102.166.226', 80))]
```

Once again, this will only work if the IP address's owner has a name assigned to it. Because many IP addresses on the Internet lack a suitable reverse name, you have no means of identifying who has contacted you unless you employ encryption to confirm the peer with whom you are interacting.

Other getaddrinfo() Flags

Three of the most essential getaddrinfo() flags are demonstrated in the preceding examples. The flags that are accessible differ by operating system, so if you're unsure about a value that your machine returns, you should always examine its documentation (not to mention its configuration). However, there are a few flags that are cross-platform. Here are a few of the most significant:

- **AI EVERYTHING:** The AI V4MAPPED option protects you from situations when you are on a purely IPv6-connected host but the host to which you want to connect advertises only IPv4 addresses, as I've already said. It overcomes this issue by converting IPv4 addresses to IPv6 equivalents. If any IPv6 addresses are accessible, these will be the only ones displayed, and none of the IPv4 addresses will be included in the return value. This is fixed by this option: if you wish to see all of the addresses from your IPv6-connected host, even if some perfectly fine IPv6 addresses are accessible, use the AI ALL flag in conjunction with AI V4MAPPED, and the list provided to you will include every address known for the target host.

- **AI NUMERICHOST:** This disables any effort to understand the hostname parameter—getaddrinfo(first)'s parameter—as a textual hostname like cern. ch, instead attempting to read the hostname string as a literal IPv4 or IPv6 hostname like 74.207.234.78 or fe80::fcfd:4aff:fecf:ea4e. This is much faster because the user or config file providing the address cannot force your programme to make a DNS round-trip to look up the name (see the next section), and it prevents potentially untrustworthy user input from forcing your system to issue a query to a name server controlled by someone else.

- AI NUMERICSERV: This disables symbolic port names such as 'www' and forces the use of port numbers such as 80 instead. Because port number databases are often maintained locally on IP-capable devices rather than requiring a distant query, you don't need to utilise this to protect your programmes from delayed DNS lookups. On POSIX systems, resolving a symbolic port name usually only involves a short scan of the /etc/services file (but double-check the services option in your /etc/nsswitch.conf file to be sure). Activating this flag, on the other hand, can be a handy sanity check if you know your port string should always be an integer.

Finally, you don't need to bother about the IDN-related flags that some operating systems provide, which instruct getaddrinfo() to resolve those fancy new domain names with Unicode letters.Instead, Python will identify whether a string requires special encoding and will apply the appropriate settings to convert it for you:

```
>>> getaddrinfo(' उदाहरण.परीक्षा ', 'www', 0, socket.SOCK_STREAM, 0,
... socket.AI_ADDRCONFIG | socket.AI_V4MAPPED)
[(2, 1, 6, '', ('199.7.85.13', 80))]
```

If you're interested in learning more about how this works behind the scenes, start with RFC 3492 and note that Python now contains a 'idna' codec that can translate to and from internationalised domain names.

```
>>> ' उदाहरण.परीक्षा '.encode('idna')
B'xn--11b5bs3a9aj6g '
```

When you input the hindi sample domain name shown in the previous example, it is this plain-ASCII string that is transmitted to the domain name service. Python will once again disguise this complexity for you.

Primitive Name Service Routines

Before getaddrinfo() became popular, socket-level programmers had to make do with a simpler set of name service methods provided by the operating system. Because most of them are built to only speak IPv4, they should be avoided today.

Their documentation may be found on the socket module's Standard Library page. To demonstrate each call, I'll give a few simple examples. The current machine's hostname is returned by two calls.

```
>>> socket.gethostname()
'bpbonline'
>>> socket.getfqdn()

'bpbonline'
```

Two more allow you to convert IPv4 hostnames to IP addresses.

```
>>> socket.gethostbyname('bpbonline.com')
'23.227.38.65'
>>> socket.gethostbyaddr('23.227.38.65')
('myshopify.com', [], ['23.227.38.65'])
```

Finally, three methods allow you to look for protocol numbers and ports by utilising symbolic names that your operating system understands.

```
>>> socket.getprotobyname('UDP')
17
>>> socket.getservbyname('www')
80
>>> socket.getservbyport(80)
'www'
```

You can try putting the fully qualified hostname of the system on which your Python programme is executing into a gethostbyname() call like this to obtain the primary IP address for the machine on which your Python programme is running.

In Your Own Code, Use getsockaddr()

To tie everything together, I've put up a small example of getaddrinfo() in action. Take a look at Table 4-1.

Listing 4-1. Using getaddrinfo() to Create and Connect a Socket

```python
#!/usr/bin/env python3
# Network Programming in Python: The Basics
# Find the WWW service of an arbitrary host using getaddrinfo().
import argparse, socket, sys
def connect_to(hostname_or_ip):
    try:
        infolist = socket.getaddrinfo(
 hostname_or_ip, 'www', 0, socket.SOCK_STREAM, 0,
            socket.AI_ADDRCONFIG   |   socket.AI_V4MAPPED   |
            socket.AI_CANONNAME,
 )
    except socket.gaierror as e:
        print('Name service failure:', e.args[1])
        sys.exit(1)
    info = infolist[0] # per standard recommendation, try the first one
    socket_args = info[0:3]
    address = info[4]
```

```
        s = socket.socket(*socket_args)
        try:
                s.connect(address)
        except socket.error as e:
                print('Network failure:', e.args[1])
        else:
                print('Success: host', info[3], 'is listening on port
80')
if __name__ == '__main__':
parser = argparse.ArgumentParser(description='Try connecting to port
80')
parser.add_argument('hostname', help='hostname that you want to
contact')
        connect_to(parser.parse_args().hostname)
```

This script attempts a rapid connection to port 80 with a streaming socket to do a simple "Are you there?" test of whichever web server you specify on the command line. The following is an example of how to use the script:

```
$ python www_ping.py bpbonline

Success: host bpbonline is listening on port 80

$ python www_ping.py smtp.google.com

Network failure: Connection timed out

$ python www_ping.py no-such-host.com

Name service failure: Name or service not known
```

Three points to note about the script:

- It is entirely generic, with no mention of IP as a protocol or TCP as a transport. If the user types a hostname that the system recognises as a host to which it is connected through AppleTalk (if you can believe that in this day and age), then getaddrinfo() is free to return the AppleTalk socket family, type, and protocol, and that is the type of socket that you would create and connect.

- Getaddrinfo() failures result in a specific name service problem, known as a gaierror in Python, rather than a standard socket error like the one found at the end of the script.

- You haven't sent a list of three distinct items to the socket() function Object() { [native code] }. Instead, an asterisk before the argument list, indicating that the three components of the socket args list are supplied to the function Object() { [native code] } as three independent parameters. This is in contrast to what you must do with the actual address returned, which is passed as a single unit to all socket procedures that require it.

DNS Protocol

The Domain Name System (DNS) is a system in which millions of Internet hosts collaborate to determine which hostnames correspond to which IP addresses. The DNS is responsible for the fact that you can type python.org into your web browser instead of needing to memorise 82.94.164.162 for IPv4 users or 2001:888:2000:d::a2 for IPv6 users.

THE DNS PROTOCOL

Purpose: Resolve hostnames by returning IP addresses

Standard: RFC 1034 and RFC 1035 (from 1987)

Runs atop: UDP/IP and TCP/IP

Port number: 53

Libraries: Third-party, including dnspython3

The communications that computers send to complete this resolution pass via a series of servers in a hierarchy. If your local computer and name server are unable to resolve a hostname because it is not local to your organisation or has not been seen recently enough to remain in the name server's cache, the next step is to query one of the world's top-level name servers to determine which machines are responsible for the domain in question. The domain name can then be queried using the DNS server IP addresses that have been returned.

Before delving into the intricacies, let's take a step back and look at how this surgery is often carried out.

Take, for example, the domain name www.python.org. If your web browser requires this address, it makes a call to getaddrinfo(), which asks the operating system to resolve the name. Your system will recognise whether it is running its own name server or whether the network to which it is connected provides name service. When your machine connects to the network—whether it's a LAN in a corporate office or an educational institution, a wireless network, or a home cable or DSL connection—it usually configures name server information automatically through DHCP. In other circumstances, when a system administrator set up your workstation, the DNS server IP addresses were manually setup. In either case, the DNS servers must be supplied using their raw IP addresses, as you won't be able to make any DNS queries unless you know how to get to them.

When users are dissatisfied with their ISP's DNS behaviour or performance, they can configure a third-party DNS server of their choice, such as Google's servers at 8.8.8.8 and 8.8.4.4. In certain rare circumstances, the local DNS domain name servers are identified by the computer's use of another set of names, such as the WINS Windows naming service. However, in order for name resolution to be possible, a DNS server must be identified in some way.

Some hostnames are known to your computer without the need to visit a domain name service. When you make a request like getaddrinfo, the first thing an operating system normally does is query DNS for a hostname (). In fact, because DNS queries are time-consuming, they are frequently the last option! Depending on the hosts item in your /etc/nsswitch.conf file if you're on a POSIX box, or the settings in your Windows Control Panel, the operating system may look in one or more different locations before resorting to DNS. On my Ubuntu laptop, for example, every hostname query starts with a check of the /etc/hosts file. If possible, a specific protocol known as multicast DNS is utilised. If that fails or is unavailable, full-fledged DNS is used to respond to the hostname inquiry.

Consider the case when the name www.python.org isn't defined locally on the machine and hasn't been searched recently enough to be in any local cache on the machine where your web browser is running.

In that situation, the computer will hunt up the local DNS server and send it a single UDP DNS request packet.

Now it's up to an actual DNS server to answer the question. For the remainder of this talk, I'll refer to it as "your DNS server," as in "the specific DNS server that is performing hostname lookups for you." Of course, the server itself most likely belongs to someone else, such as your work, ISP, or Google, and so is not yours in the sense that you own it.

Your DNS server's initial action will be to check its cache of previously requested domain names to see if www.python.org has already been checked by another computer served by the DNS server in the previous few minutes or hours. If an entry exists and has not yet expired (the owner of each domain name has control over the expiration timeout since some organisations prefer to change IP addresses rapidly if necessary), while some are content to let old IP addresses remain in DNS caches around the world for hours or days), it can be returned promptly. But say it's morning, and you're the first person in your office or coffee shop to try talking to www.python.org today; the DNS server will have to start from scratch to identify the hostname.

Your DNS server will now query for www.python.org at the top of the world's DNS server hierarchy, the "root-level" name servers, which know all of the top-level domains (TLDs) like.com,.org, and.net, as well as the groups of servers responsible for each. The IP addresses of these top-level servers are usually integrated into name server software to solve the bootstrapping problem of how to identify any domain name servers before connecting to the domain name system. Your DNS server will learn (assuming it didn't previously know from another recent query) which servers store the full index of the.org domain with this first UDP round-trip.

A second DNS request will now be sent, this time to one of the.org servers, inquiring about the python.org domain's owner.

A second DNS request will now be sent, this time to one of the.org servers, inquiring about the python.org domain's owner. Run the whois command-line programme on a POSIX system to see what those top-level servers know about a domain, or use one of the many "whois" web pages online if you don't have the command installed locally.

```
$ whois python.org
Domain Name:PYTHON.ORG
Created On:27-Mar-1995 05:00:00 UTC
Last Updated On:07-Sep-2006 20:50:54 UTC
Expiration Date:28-Mar-2016 05:00:00 UTC

...

Registrant Name:Python Software Foundation

...

Name Server:NS2.XS4ALL.NL
Name Server:NS.XS4ALL.NL
```

And with that, we have our answer! Any DNS request for any hostname within python.org must be sent to one of the two DNS servers listed in that entry, regardless of where you are in the globe. Of course, when your DNS server sends this request to a top-level domain name server, it does not receive only the two names listed above. Instead, it gets provided their IP addresses, allowing it to contact them immediately without having to go through another round of costly DNS lookups.

Your DNS server can now connect directly with NS2.XS4ALL.NL or NS.XS4ALL. NL to inquire about the python.org domain, as it has finished talking to both the root-level DNS server and the top-level.org DNS server. In reality, if the first one is unavailable, it will fall back to the second. This enhances your odds of receiving a response, but it also increases the amount of time you spend looking at your web browser waiting for the page to load.

Depending on how python.org's name servers are configured, the DNS server may only need one more query to return an answer, or it may need several more queries if the organisation is large and has multiple departments and subdepartments, each of which runs its own DNS server to which requests must be delegated. In this situation, either of the two servers previously mentioned can immediately respond to the www.python.org query, and your DNS server can now send a UDP packet to your browser notifying it which IP addresses correspond to that hostname.

This procedure necessitated four different network round-trips. Your machine performed a request and received a response from your own DNS server, and in order to respond, your DNS server had to perform a recursive query that required three round-trips to other servers. It's no surprise that your browser spins when you type in a domain name for the first time.

Why Shouldn't Use Raw DNS?

I hope that the preceding description of a typical DNS query has demonstrated that your operating system does a lot for you when you need a hostname searched up. As a result, unless you absolutely need to speak DNS for a specific purpose, I propose that you always rely on getaddrinfo() or another system-supported approach for resolving hostnames. Consider the following advantages of allowing your operating system to perform name searches for you:

- The DNS isn't always the only source of name information for a system. Users will notice that some computer names that work elsewhere on your system—in their browser, in file share paths, and so on—suddenly stop working when they use your application since you are not consulting mechanisms like WINS or /etc/hosts as the operating system does.

- The local machine's cache of previously queried domain names is likely to contain the host whose IP address you require. You will be duplicating work that has already been done if you try to answer your question via DNS.

- Thanks to manual setting by your system administrator or a network setup mechanism like DHCP, the system on which your Python script is running already knows about the local domain name servers. To use DNS in your

Python programme, you'll need to learn how to query your operating system for this information, which I won't discuss in this book because it's a system-specific action.

- If you don't use the local DNS server, you won't be able to take use of its cache, which prevents your app and other apps on the same network from making repeated requests for a hostname that is often used at your location.

- The world DNS infrastructure is updated from time to time, and operating system libraries and daemons are gradually updated to accommodate this. If your software makes its own DNS calls, you'll have to keep track of these changes and make sure your code is up to date with the newest changes in TLD server IP addresses, internationalisation conventions, and DNS protocol adjustments.

Finally, Python's Standard Library does not include any DNS functionality. If you want to use Python to talk about DNS, you'll need to pick and learn a third-party library.

Using Python to do a DNS query

There is, however, a good and valid reason to use Python to make a DNS request. It's because you're a mail server, or at the very least a client trying to send mail directly to your receivers without using a local mail relay, and you need to seek up the MX records associated with a domain in order to identify the correct mail server for your @example.com buddies.

As we near the end of this chapter, let's have a look at one of the third-party DNS libraries for Python. dnspython3, which you can install using the usual Python packaging tool, appears to be the best one currently available for Python 3.

```
$ pip install dnspython3
```

The library use its own methods to determine which domain name servers your Windows or POSIX operating system is currently utilising, and then requests that those servers perform recursive inquiries on its behalf. As a result, there isn't a single line of code in this chapter that doesn't require a properly configured host that has already been configured with working name servers by an administrator or network configuration service.

A basic and comprehensive lookup is shown in Listing 4-2.

Listing 4-2. A Simple DNS Query Doing Its Own Recursion

```
#!/usr/bin/env python3
```

```
# Network Programming in Python: The Basics
# Basic DNS query
import argparse, dns.resolver
def lookup(name):
 for qtype in 'A', 'AAAA', 'CNAME', 'MX', 'NS':
 answer = dns.resolver.query(name, qtype, raise_on_no_answer=False)
            if answer.rrset is not None:
                print(answer.rrset)
if __name__ == '__main__':
        parser = argparse.ArgumentParser(description='Resolve a name
        using DNS')
        parser.add_argument('name', help='name that you want to look
        up in DNS')
        lookup(parser.parse_args().name)
```

You can see that only one type of DNS query can be attempted at a time, so this small script runs in a loop asking for different types of records pertaining to the single hostname that has been given as its command-line argument. Running this against python.org will immediately teach you several things about DNS

```
$ python dns_basic.py python.org
python.org. 42945 IN A 140.211.10.69
python.org. 86140 IN MX 50 mail.python.org.
python.org. 86146 IN NS ns4.p11.dynect.net.
python.org. 86146 IN NS ns3.p11.dynect.net.
python.org. 86146 IN NS ns1.p11.dynect.net.
python.org. 86146 IN NS ns2.p11.dynect.net.
```

Each "response" in the reply that has been returned is represented as a sequence of objects, as you can see from the programme. The keys that are printed on each line in order are as follows:

- The name had been searched up.
- The number of seconds you have to cache the name before it expires in seconds.
- The "class" IN, which indicates that you are receiving responses with Internet addresses.

- The record's "type." A is for an IPv4 address, AAAA is for an IPv6 address, NS is for a record that identifies a name server, and MX is for a reply that specifies the mail server for a domain.

- Finally, the "data" section contains the information needed to connect to or contact a service.

Three things about the python.org domain are revealed in the query just quoted. First, the A record specifies that if you wish to connect to a real python.org system— to initiate an HTTP connection, start an SSH session, or do anything else because the user specified python.org as the machine to connect to—you should send your packets to IP address 140.211.10.69. Second, the NS records indicate that if you want to query the names of any hosts beneath python.org, you should ask the name servers ns1.p11.dynect.net through ns4.p11.dynect.net to resolve those names for you (ideally in the order indicated, rather than in numeric order). Finally, you'll need to seek up the hostname mail.python.org if you wish to send email to someone with the @python.org email domain.

A record type CNAME can be returned by a DNS query, indicating that the hostname you're looking for is actually an alias for another hostname that you'll have to look up separately! This record type is no longer popular because it often necessitates two round-trips, although you may still come across it.

Getting Mail Domains Resolved

In most Python projects, resolving an e-mail domain is a valid usage of raw DNS, as I previously stated.

The requirements for accomplishing this resolution were described most recently in RFC 5321. They are, in brief, that if MX records exist, you must attempt to contact those SMTP servers and, if none of them accept the message, you must return an error to the user (or place the message on a retry queue). If their priorities aren't equal, try them in sequence from lowest to greatest priority. If no MX records are present but the domain has an A or AAAA record, you may attempt an SMTP connection to that address. If neither record exists but a CNAME is requested, the domain name provided should be searched for MX or A records according to the same requirements.

Listing 4-3 explains how to put this method into practise. It works its way through the available destinations via a series of DNS requests, reporting its results as it goes. You could use a Python mail dispatcher to distribute e-mail to remote hosts by modifying a function like this to return addresses rather than just printing them.

Listing 4-3. Getting mail Domains resolved name.

```
#!/usr/bin/env python3
# Network Programming in Python: The Basics
# Looking up a mail domain - the part of an email address after the `@`

import argparse, dns.resolver
def resolve_hostname(hostname, indent=''):
        "Print an A or AAAA record for `hostname`; follow CNAMEs if
necessary."
 indent = indent + ' '
 answer = dns.resolver.query(hostname, 'A')
 if answer.rrset is not None:
            for record in answer:
 print(indent, hostname, 'has A address', record.address)
            return
 answer = dns.resolver.query(hostname, 'AAAA')
if answer.rrset is not None:
        for record in answer:
            print(indent, hostname, 'has AAAA address', record.
address)
return
 answer = dns.resolver.query(hostname, 'CNAME')
 if answer.rrset is not None:
        record = answer[0]
cname = record.address
        print(indent, hostname, 'is a CNAME alias for', cname) #?
        resolve_hostname(cname, indent)
        return
 print(indent, 'ERROR: no A, AAAA, or CNAME records for', hostname)
def resolve_email_domain(domain):
"For an email address `name@domain` find its mail server IP addresses."
```

```
try:

answer = dns.resolver.query(domain, 'MX', raise_on_no_answer=False)
except dns.resolver.NXDOMAIN:
            print('Error: No such domain', domain)
return

      if answer.rrset is not None:
            records = sorted(answer, key=lambda record: record.preference)
            for record in records:
name = record.exchange.to_text(omit_final_dot=True)
                  print('Priority', record.preference)
  resolve_hostname(name)
      else:
            print('This domain has no explicit MX records')
  print('Attempting to resolve it as an A, AAAA, or CNAME')
            resolve_hostname(domain)
if __name__ == '__main__':
      parser = argparse.ArgumentParser(description='Find mailserver
      IP address')
parser.add_argument('domain', help='domain that you want to send
mail to')
      resolve_email_domain(parser.parse_args().domain)
```

Of course, the implementation of resolve hostname() presented here is a little shaky, as it should should make a dynamic decision between A and AAAA records based on whether the current host is connected to an IPv4 or IPv6 network. In fact, instead of attempting to resolve the address, we should probably defer to our friend getsockaddr(). the hostname of the mail server! But, since Listing 4-3 is supposed to demonstrate how DNS works, I figured I'd give it a shot. Continue with the logic using pure DNS to see how the queries are resolved.

Instead of publishing the mail server addresses, a genuine mail server implementation would obviously try to deliver mail to them first and then cease. (If it kept running over the server list after the success, it would generate multiple copies of the e-mail, one for each server to which it was successfully sent.) Nonetheless, this straightforward script provides a solid overview of the procedure. As you can see, python.org currently only has one mail server IP address.

```
$ python dns_mx.py python.org
This domain has 1 MX records
Priority 50
 mail.python.org has A address 82.94.164.166
```

Of course, whether that IP belongs to a single machine or is shared by a group of hosts is something you can't see from the outside. Other companies are more aggressive in giving incoming e-mails many landing spots. The IANA now operates six e-mail servers (or, at the very least, six IP addresses through which you can connect, regardless of how many servers it actually operates).

```
$ python dns_mx.py iana.org
This domain has 6 MX records
Priority 10
 pechora7.icann.org has A address 192.0.46.73
Priority 10
 pechora5.icann.org has A address 192.0.46.71
Priority 10
 pechora8.icann.org has A address 192.0.46.74
Priority 10
 pechora1.icann.org has A address 192.0.33.71
Priority 10
 pechora4.icann.org has A address 192.0.33.74
Priority 10
 pechora3.icann.org has A address 192.0.33.73
```

By running this script against a variety of domains, you'll be able to see how large and small businesses handle inbound e-mail routing to IP addresses.

Conclusion.

Hostnames must frequently be converted into socket addresses so that Python programmes can connect to them.

The getsockaddr() function in the socket module should be used for most hostname lookups because its intelligence is usually provided by your operating system, and it will know not only how to look up domain names using all of the mechanisms available to it, but also what flavour of address (IPv4 or IPv6) the local IP stack is configured to support.

IPv4 addresses are still the most popular on the Internet, although IPv6 addresses are becoming more common. Your Python programme can regard addresses as opaque strings and not have to worry about parsing or interpreting them by deferring all hostname and port name search to getsockaddr().

The DNS, a globally distributed database that directs domain name inquiries to the servers of the domain owner, is at the heart of most name resolution. While it is not commonly used directly from Python, it can be useful for determining where to send e-mail based on the e-mail domain listed after the @ sign in an e-mail address.

After you've learned how to name the hosts to which you'll connect sockets, move on to Chapter 5 to learn about the various options for encrypting and delimiting the data payloads you'll send.

## CHAPTER 5

Data and Errors on the Internet

The first four chapters of this book demonstrated how IP hosts are called and how to set up and tear down TCP streams and UDP datagram connections between hosts. However, how should data be prepared for transmission?

Structure

- Strings and Bytes
- Character Strings
- Network Byte Order and Binary Numbers
- Quoting and framing
- Pickles and Self-delimiting Formats
- JSON And XML
- Compression
- Exceptions in the Network
- Raising More Specific Exceptions
- Network Exceptions: Detecting and Reporting
- Conclusion

Objectives:

What format and encoding should be used? What kinds of errors should Python applications be prepared for? Whether you're utilising streams or datagrams, these questions are all applicable, and this chapter gives all of the essential solutions.

Strings and Bytes

Both computer memory chips and network cards use the byte as their standard unit of measurement. This little 8-bit data payload has evolved into our worldwide unit of data storage. However, there is a distinction to be made between memory chips and network cards. Python may totally hide the decisions it takes as your programme runs regarding how to represent numbers, strings, lists, and dictionaries in memory. You can't view the bytes that these data structures are stored with unless you use special debugging tools; all you can see is how they act from the outside.

Because the socket interface exposes bytes and makes them available to both the programmer and the application, network communication is unique. When working with networks, you can't help but worry about how data will be represented on the wire, which introduces issues that a high-level language like Python would otherwise avoid.

Let's look at the qualities of bytes now.

- The smallest unit of information is a bit. It's a digit that might be zero or one. A bit is commonly implemented in electronics as a wire with a voltage that is either hot or linked to ground.

- A byte is made up of eight bits.

The bits must be arranged in a logical order so that you can determine which is which. When writing a binary number like 01100001, you order the digits in the same way you do when writing base-ten numbers, with the most significant bit first (just like in the decimal number 234, the 2 is the most significant and the 4 is the least significant, because the hundreds place makes a bigger difference in the number's magnitude than the tens or ones places).

A number between 00000000 and 11111111 can be used to represent a single byte. These are the decimal values 0 and 255, if you do the math.

Because you can wrap around backward from 0 to get to the greatest byte values in the 0 to 255 range, you may also interpret them as negative numbers. 10000000 through 11111111, which would ordinarily be 128 through 255, are sometimes interpreted as -128 through -1 instead, because the most important digit tells you whether the number is positive or negative. (Arithmetic with two's complement is known as two's complement arithmetic.) You can also use a variety of more intricate rules to interpret a byte, such as utilising a table to give a symbol or meaning to the byte, or combining the byte together with other bytes to construct even larger numbers.

Because a byte could have a range of different lengths on different systems in the past, network standards use the term octet to refer to the 8-bit byte.

Bytes are typically represented in Python in one of two ways: as an integer with a value between 0 and 255, or as a length-1 byte string with the byte being the sole value it contains. Any of the common bases allowed in Python source code—binary, octal, decimal, and hexadecimal—can be used to type a byte-valued number.

```
>>> 0b1100010
```

```
98
```

```
>>> 0b1100010 == 0o142 == 98 == 0x62
```

```
True
```

You can convert a list of such numbers to a byte string by using the bytes() type within a sequence, and you can convert back by iterating over the byte string.

```
>>> b = bytes([0, 1, 98, 99, 100])
>>> len(b)
5
>>> type(b)
<class 'bytes'>
>>> list(b)
[0, 1, 98, 99, 100]
```

The repr() method of a byte string object uses ASCII characters as a shorthand for array elements whose byte values happen to correspond to printable character codes, and it uses the explicit hexadecimal format xNN only for bytes that do not correspond to a printable ASCII character. This can be confusing.

```
>>> b
b'\x00\x01bcd'
```

But don't be fooled: byte strings aren't fundamentally ASCII in terms of semantics, and they're only meant to represent 8-bit byte sequences.

Character Strings

You'll need an encoding that assigns each symbol to a valid byte value if you truly want to send a string of symbols over a socket. The most widely used encoding is ASCII, which stands for American Standard Code for Information Interchange and defines character codes 0 to 127 that can be stored in 7 bits. As a result, the most significant bit in ASCII is always 0 when represented in bytes. Because codes 0 through 31 indicate control orders for an output display rather than real glyphs like letters, numbers, and punctuation, they are not visible in a fast chart like the one below. As you can see, the three consecutive 32-character tiers of ASCII characters that do represent glyphs are: a first tier of punctuation and digits, then an uppercase letter tier, and finally a lowercase letter tier:

```
>>> for i in range(32, 128, 32):
... print(' '.join(chr(j) for j in range(i, i+32)))
...
  ! " # $ % & ' ( ) * + , - . / 0 1 2 3 4 5 6 7 8 9 : ; < = > ?
@ A B C D E F G H I J K L M N O P Q R S T U V W X Y Z [ \ ] ^ _
` a b c d e f g h i j k l m n o p q r s t u v w x y z { | } ~
```

By the way, the character in the upper-left corner is the space, which has the code 32. (Oddly enough, the invisible character in the lower-right corner is one last control character: Delete at position 127.) In this 1960 encoding, there are two interesting tricks to notice. The digits are first sorted so that the mathematical value of any digit can be computed by subtracting the code for the digit zero. You can also switch between uppercase and lowercase letters by flipping the 32's bit, or force letters to one case or the other by setting or clearing the 32's bit on a full string of characters.

However, the character codes that Python 3 can contain in its strings go much beyond ASCII. We now have character code assignments for numbers that go beyond the 128 ASCII codes and into the thousands and even millions, thanks to a more modern standard known as Unicode. Python believes strings to be a sequence of Unicode characters, and the actual representation of Python strings in RAM, as with all Python data structures, is kept hidden from you while you interact with the language. However, while working with data in files or over a network, you'll need to consider external representation and two concepts that will help you distinguish between the meaning of your data and how it's transferred or stored:

> Encoding characters entails converting a string of Unicode characters into bytes that can be transferred outside of your Python programme.

Converting a byte string into real characters is known as decoding byte data.

If you imagine the outside world as bytes stored in a secret code that must be interpreted or cracked before your Python software can execute them correctly, it might help you recall which conversions these words refer to. Data must be encoded before it can be moved outside of your Python programme, and it must be decoded before it can be returned.

There are many different types of encodings in use around the world. They are divided into two groups.

The most basic encodings are one-byte encodings, which can only encode 256 distinct characters but guarantee that each character fits into a single byte. When writing network code, these are simple to use. You know that reading n bytes from a socket will produce n characters, and you also know that when a stream is broken into pieces, each byte is a stand-alone character that can be safely processed without knowing what byte will come after it. You can also look at the nth byte to find character n in your input right away.

Multibyte encodings are more complex, and each of these advantages is lost. Some, such as UTF-32, employ a fixed amount of bytes per character, which is inefficient when data contains largely ASCII characters but has the advantage of ensuring that each character is always the same length. Others, such as UTF-8, vary the number of bytes each character takes up, necessitating extreme caution; if the data stream is delivered in pieces, there is no way to know whether a character has been split across the boundary or not, and you can't find character n without starting at the beginning and reading until you've read that many characters.

The codecs module documentation in the Standard Library contains a list of all the encodings that Python supports.

The majority of Python's single-byte encodings are ASCII extensions that employ the remaining 128 values for region-specific letters and symbols:

```
>>> b'\x67\x68\x69\xe7\xe8\xe9'.decode('latin1')
'ghiçèé'
>>> b'\x67\x68\x69\xe7\xe8\xe9'.decode('latin2')
'ghiç
é'
>>> b'\x67\x68\x69\xe7\xe8\xe9'.decode('greek')
'ghihqi'
>>> b'\x67\x68\x69\xe7\xe8\xe9'.decode('hebrew')
```

'ghihqi'

The same may be said for the numerous Windows code pages mentioned in the Standard Library. A few single-byte encodings, on the other hand, have nothing in common with ASCII because they are based on obsolete IBM mainframe standards.

```
>>> b'\x67\x68\x69\xe7\xe8\xe9'.decode('EBCDIC-CP-BE')
```

'ÅÇÑXYZ'

The old UTF-16 scheme (which had a brief heyday back when Unicode was much smaller and could fit into 16 bits), the modern UTF-32 scheme, and the universally popular variable-width UTF-8 that looks like ASCII until you start including characters with codes greater than 127) are the multibyte encodings that you are most likely to encounter. Here's how a Unicode string looks when all three are used:

```
>>> len('Namárië!')
8
>>> 'Namárië!'.encode('UTF-16')
b'\xff\xfeN\x00a\x00m\x00\xe1\x00r\x00i\x00\xeb\x00!\x00'
>>> len(_)
18
>>> 'Namárië!'.encode('UTF-32')
b'\xff\xfe\x00\x00N\x00\x00\x00a\x00\x00\x00m\x00\x00\x00\xe1\x00\
x00\x00r\x00\x00\x00i\x00\x00\
x00\xeb\x00\x00\x00!\x00\x00\x00'
>>> len(_)
36
>>> 'Namárië!'.encode('UTF-8')
b'Nam\xc3\xa1ri\xc3\xab!'
>>> len(_)
10
```

You should be able to find the plain ASCII letters N, a, m, r, and I sprinkled among the byte values representing non-ASCII characters if you look closely at each encoding.

The multibyte encodings each have an extra character, bringing UTF-16 to a total of (8 2) + 2 bytes and UTF-32 to a total of (8 4) + 4 bytes. The byte order marker (BOM) is a special character that allows readers to automatically determine whether the many bytes of each Unicode character are stored with the most significant or least significant byte first. (For further information on byte order, see the following section.)

When working with encoded text, you'll run across two common errors: attempting to load from an encoded byte string that doesn't truly meet the encoding rules you're trying to decode, and attempting to encode characters that can't be represented in the encoding you're seeking.

```
>>> b'\x80'.decode('ascii')
Traceback (most recent call last):

 ...

UnicodeDecodeError: 'ascii' codec can't decode byte 0x80 in position
0: ordinal not in range(128)
>>> 'ghihqi'.encode('latin-1')
Traceback (most recent call last):

 ...

UnicodeEncodeError: 'latin-1' codec can't encode characters in
position 3-5: ordinal not in range(256)
```

You should usually remedy such issues by verifying whether you're using the incorrect encoding or figuring out why your data isn't adhering to the encoding you anticipate. If neither fix works, and you discover that your code has to deal with mismatches between specified encodings and actual strings and data on a regular basis, you should read the Standard Library documentation to learn about other ways to deal with problems instead of throwing exceptions.

```
>>> b'ab\x80def'.decode('ascii', 'replace')
'ab?def'
>>> b'ab\x80def'.decode('ascii', 'ignore')
'abdef'
>>> 'ghihqi'.encode('latin-1', 'replace')
b'ghi????'
>>> 'ghihqi'.encode('latin-1', 'ignore')
b'ghi'
```

These are explained in the codecs module's Standard Library documentation, and more examples may be found in Doug Hellman's Python Module of the Week section on codecs.

It's worth repeating that decoding a partially received message using an encoding that encodes some characters with several bytes is risky, because one of those characters may have been divided between the part of the message you've already received and the packets that haven't yet arrived. Some approaches to this issue can be found in the "Framing and Quoting" section later in this chapter.

Network Byte Order and Binary Numbers

If all you ever want to send across the network is text, the only issues you'll have to deal with are encoding and framing (which you'll learn about in the next section).

However, there may be occasions when you want to convey your facts in a more concise style than text allows.

Alternatively, you could be building Python code to communicate with a service that has already decided to use raw binary data. In any event, you'll have to start thinking about a new problem: network byte order.

Consider the procedure of sending an integer over the network to grasp the issue of byte order. Consider the number 4253 in particular.

Many protocols, however, will simply transmit this integer as the string '4253,' which consists of four different characters. In any of the common text encodings, the four numbers will require at least four bytes to convey. Because numbers are not stored in computers in base 10, using decimal digits will require repeated division—with inspection of the remainder—for the programme transmitting the value to realise that this number is in reality made up of 4 thousands, plus 2 hundreds, plus 5 tens, with 3 left over. When the four-digit string '4253' is received, it will take repeated addition and multiplication by powers of ten to turn the text into a number.

Despite its length, the method of utilising plain text for numbers may be the most widely used on the Internet today. When you request a web page, for example, the HTTP protocol communicates the result's Content-Length as a string of decimal digits like '4253.' Despite the cost, both the web server and the client perform the decimal conversion without hesitation. In reality, the replacement of dense binary formats with protocols that are clear, obvious, and human-readable—even if computationally expensive compared to their predecessors—has been a big part of networking's storey during the last 20 years.

Multiplication and division are, of course, less expensive on modern processors than they were when binary formats were more common—not only because processors have become much faster, but also because their designers have become much more clever about implementing integer math, so that the same operation takes far fewer cycles today than it did in the early 1980s.

In any case, your computer's representation of this number as an integer variable in Python is not the string '4253.'

Instead, it will save it as a binary integer, with the ones, twos, fours, and so on of a single huge number represented by the bits of numerous successive bytes. Using the hex() built-in function at the Python prompt, you can see how the integer is stored.

```
>>> hex(4253)
```

```
'0x109d'
```

Because each hex digit is four bits long, each pair of hex digits comprises a byte of data. The number is stored as a most significant byte 0x10 and a least significant byte 0x9d, adjacent to one another in memory, rather than four decimal digits (4, 4, 2, and 3), with the first 4 being the "most significant" digit (since changing its value would throw the number off by a thousand) and 3 being the least significant digit.

But what is the best sequence for these two bytes to appear? We've reached a point where the architectures of different computer processor brands diverge significantly. While they will all agree that bytes in memory have an order and that a string like Content-Length: 4253 should be stored in that order starting with C and ending with 3, they will not agree on the order in which binary numbers should be kept.

Some computers are "big-endian" (for example, older SPARC processors) and place the most significant byte first, just like we do when writing decimal digits; other computers (such as the nearly ubiquitous x86 architecture) place the least significant byte first (where "first" means "at the byte with the lower memory address").

Danny Cohen's paper IEN-137, "On Holy Wars and a Plea for Peace," which introduced the terms big-endian and little-endian in a parody of Jonathan Swift, is worth reading for a humorous historical perspective on this issue: www.ietf.org/rfc/ien/ien137.txt.

Python makes the distinction between the two endians obvious. Simply utilise the struct module, which has a number of procedures for translating data between binary forms. The number 4253 is represented in little-endian order first, then in big-endian order:

```
>>> import struct
```

```
>>> struct.pack('<i', 4253)
```

```
b'\x9d\x10\x00\x00'
```

```
>>> struct.pack('>i', 4253)
```

```
b'\x00\x00\x10\x9d'
```

For a little number like 4253, I used the struct formatting code I which uses four bytes to represent an integer and leaves the two top bytes zero. If it helps you remember which one to use, think of the struct endianness codes " and '>' for these two orders as small arrows pointing toward the least significant end of a string of bytes. The full list of data formats supported by the struct module may be found in the Standard Library's documentation. It also has an unpack() method for converting binary data to Python numbers.

```
>>> struct.unpack('>i', b'\x00\x00\x10\x9d')
```

```
(4253,)
```

If the big-endian format makes more intuitive sense to you, you'll be happy to know that it "won" the competition to choose which endianness would become the standard for network data. As a result, the struct module adds a new symbol, '!', to pack() and unpack() that communicates to other programmers (and, of course, to yourself as you read the code afterwards), "I am packing this data so that I may send it over the network."

In conclusion, here is my recommendation for preparing binary data for transmission over a network socket:

- Use the struct module to create binary data for network transmission and to unpack it when it arrives.

- If you have control over the data format, use the '!' prefix to select network byte order. If the protocol was designed by someone else and little-endian was specified, you must use " instead.

Always test struct to see how it organises your data in comparison to the protocol's standard; notice that the packing format string 'x' characters can be used to insert padding bytes.

In order to convert integers into byte strings in network order, older Python code might require a slew of oddly named functions from the socket module. These methods have names like ntohl() and htons(), and they match to POSIX networking library functions of the same name, which also include calls like socket() and bind() (). I recommend that you skip these inconvenient functions and instead use the struct module, which is more versatile, broad, and provides more understandable code.

Quoting and framing

If you're communicating with UDP datagrams, the protocol will transfer your data in discrete and identifiable pieces. If something goes wrong on the network, you'll have to reorganise and retransmit those pieces manually, as described in Chapter 2.

However, if you've selected the far more popular option of communicating via a TCP stream, you'll have to deal with the problem of framing—that is, how to delimit your messages so that the receiver knows where one message ends and the next one begins. Because the data you submit to sendall() may be split into many packets for real network delivery, Before the entire message is read, the application that gets it may have to make numerous recv() calls—or it may not, if all the packets arrive before the operating system has a chance to schedule the process again!

When is it safe for the receiver to cease running recv() since the entire message or data has arrived intact and complete, and it can now be interpreted or acted upon as a whole?

As you may expect, there are a variety of techniques.

For starters, there's a pattern that may be employed by very simple network protocols that merely entail data delivery—no response is needed, thus the receiver never has to say "Enough!" and turn around to give a response. The sender can loop until all of the outgoing data has been given to sendall() and then shut() the socket in this scenario. The receiver just needs to use recv() multiple times until the call returns an empty string, indicating that the sender has closed the socket. This pattern can be seen in Listing 5-1.

Listing 5-1: Simply send all of your data and then disconnect.

```
#!/usr/bin/env python3
# Network Programming in Python: The Basics
# Client that sends data then closes the socket, not expecting a
reply.
import socket
from argparse import ArgumentParser
def server(address):
 sock = socket.socket(socket.AF_INET, socket.SOCK_STREAM)
 sock.setsockopt(socket.SOL_SOCKET, socket.SO_REUSEADDR, 1)
 sock.bind(address)
 sock.listen(1)
```

```
print('Run this script in another window with "-c" to connect')
print('Listening at', sock.getsockname())
sc, sockname = sock.accept()
print('Accepted connection from', sockname)
sc.shutdown(socket.SHUT_WR)
message = b''
while True:
more = sc.recv(8192) # arbitrary value of 8k
if not more: # socket has closed when recv() returns ''
print('Received zero bytes - end of file')
break
print('Received {} bytes'.format(len(more)))
message += more
print('Message:\n')
print(message.decode('ascii'))
sc.close()
sock.close()
def client(address):
 sock = socket.socket(socket.AF_INET, socket.SOCK_STREAM)
 sock.connect(address)
 sock.shutdown(socket.SHUT_RD)
 sock.sendall(b'Beautiful is better than ugly.\n')
 sock.sendall(b'Explicit is better than implicit.\n')
 sock.sendall(b'Simple is better than complex.\n')
 sock.close()
if __name__ == '__main__':
  parser = ArgumentParser(description='Transmit & receive a data
stream')
 parser.add_argument('hostname', nargs='?', default='127.0.0.1',
 help='IP address or hostname (default: %(default)s)')
 parser.add_argument('-c', action='store_true', help='run as the client')
 parser.add_argument('-p', type=int, metavar='port', default=1060,
```

```
help='TCP port number (default: %(default)s)')
args = parser.parse_args()
function = client if args.c else server
function((args.hostname, args.p))
```

If you run this script as a server and then run the client version from a different command prompt, you'll notice that all of the client's data gets it to the server intact, with the only framing required being the end-of-file event triggered by the client closing the socket.

```
$ python streamer.py
Run this script in another window with "-c" to connect
Listening at ('127.0.0.1', 1060)
Accepted connection from ('127.0.0.1', 49057)
Received 96 bytes
Received zero bytes - end of file
Message:
Beautiful is better than ugly.
Explicit is better than implicit.
Simple is better than complex.
```

The client and server both go ahead and shut down communication in the direction they do not intend to use, which is a nicety because this socket is not supposed to receive any data. This avoids any unintentional use of the socket in the opposite direction, which could eventually result in a deadlock, as seen in Listing 3-2 in Chapter 3. Although only one of the client or server needs to call shutdown() on the socket, doing it from both directions gives symmetry and redundancy.

A second pattern is a variation on the first: it streams both ways. The socket is left open in both directions at first. Data is first transmitted in one direction (just as described in Listing 5-1), and then that direction is turned off. The socket is subsequently closed after data is streamed in the opposite direction. Listing 3-2 from Chapter 3 highlights an essential caution: always complete the data transfer in one direction before turning around to stream data back in the other, otherwise you risk creating a blocked client and server.

The usage of fixed-length messages, as shown in Listing 3-1, is a third pattern that was also demonstrated in Chapter 3. You can send your byte string using Python's sendall() method, and then use a custom recv() loop to ensure that you receive the entire message.

```
def recvall(sock, length):
 data = ''
 while len(data) < length:
 more = sock.recv(length - len(data))
 if not more:
 raise EOFError('socket closed {} bytes into a {}-byte'
 ' message'.format(len(data), length))
 data += more
 return data
```

Because so little data fits within static bounds these days, fixed-length messages are uncommon. However, it may be a suitable fit for certain cases when transferring binary data (think of a struct format that always outputs data blocks of the same length, for example).

A fourth pattern is to use special characters to delimit your messages. The receiver would stay in a recv() loop like the one above until the reply string it was accumulating eventually contained the delimiter signalling the end-of-message. If the message's bytes or characters are certain to fall within a certain range, the logical choice is to finish each message with a symbol from outside that range. If you were sending ASCII strings, for example, you might use the null character '0' or a character completely outside the ASCII range like 'xff' as the delimiter.

If the message can instead contain any data, using a delimiter becomes problematic: what if the character you're trying to use as a delimiter also appears in the data? Of course, quoting is the answer, just as representing a single-quote character as'in the middle of a Python string bounded by single-quote characters is.

```
'All\'s well that ends well.'
```

Nonetheless, I recommend employing a delimiter scheme only when your message alphabet is limited; accurate quoting and unquoting is frequently too difficult to accomplish when dealing with random data. For one thing, your check to see if the delimiter has come now must ensure that you aren't mixing up a quoted delimiter with a real one that closes the message. A second complication is that you must then go through the message again to remove the quotation characters that were safeguarding literal delimiter occurrences. Finally, it means that you can't tell how long a message is until you've decoded it; a message with a length of 400 could be 400 symbols long.

Prefixing each message with its length is a fifth pattern. Because blocks of binary data may be delivered verbatim without needing to be parsed, quoted, or interpolated, this is a popular choice for high-performance protocols. Of course, the length must be expressed using one of the approaches described previously—for example, the length is frequently expressed as a fixed-width binary integer or as a variable-length decimal string followed by a textual delimiter. Once the length has been read and decoded, the receiver can enter a loop and continuously call recv() until the entire message has arrived. The loop can look just like the one in Listing 3-1, except instead of the number 16, a length variable can be used.

Finally, what if you want the fifth pattern's simplicity and efficiency but don't know the length of each message ahead of time—perhaps because the sender is reading data from a source whose length they can't predict?

Do you have to give up elegance and trawl through the data looking for delimiters in such cases?

If you use the sixth and final pattern, you won't have any problems with unknown lengths. Rather than sending just one, consider sending many blocks of data, each prefixed with the length. This means that as fresh data becomes available to the sender, each chunk can be identified with its length and added to the outgoing stream. When the time comes to say good-bye, The sender can send an agreed-upon signal—for example, a length field with the number zero—informing the receiver that the sequence of blocks is finished.

Listing 5-2 is a simple illustration of this concept. This listing, like the previous one, sends data in only one direction—from the client to the server—but the data structure is far more fascinating than the previous one.

Each message is preceded by a struct containing a 4-byte length. Each frame can be up to 4GB in size because 'I' stands for a 32-bit unsigned integer. This sample code sends three blocks to the server, followed by a zero-length message (a length field with zeros within and no message contents following it), to the server the series of blocks is over.

Listing 5-2. Framing Each Data Block by Preceding It with Its Length.

```
#!/usr/bin/env python3
# Network Programming in Python: The Basics
# Sending data over a stream but delimited as length-prefixed blocks.

import socket, struct
```

```
from argparse import ArgumentParser
header_struct = struct.Struct('!I') # messages up to 2**32 - 1 in
length
def recvall(sock, length):
blocks = []
while length:
block = sock.recv(length)
if not block:
raise EOFError('socket closed with %d bytes left'
' in this block'.format(length))
length -= len(block)
blocks.append(block)
return b''.join(blocks)
def get_block(sock):
data = recvall(sock, header_struct.size)
(block_length,) = header_struct.unpack(data)
return recvall(sock, block_length)
def put_block(sock, message):
block_length = len(message)
sock.send(header_struct.pack(block_length))
sock.send(message)
def server(address):
sock = socket.socket(socket.AF_INET, socket.SOCK_STREAM)
sock.setsockopt(socket.SOL_SOCKET, socket.SO_REUSEADDR, 1)
sock.bind(address)
sock.listen(1)
print('Run this script in another window with "-c" to connect')
print('Listening at', sock.getsockname())
sc, sockname = sock.accept()
print('Accepted connection from', sockname)
sc.shutdown(socket.SHUT_WR)
while True:
```

```
block = get_block(sc)
if not block:
break
print('Block says:', repr(block))
sc.close()
sock.close()
def client(address):
sock = socket.socket(socket.AF_INET, socket.SOCK_STREAM)
sock.connect(address)
sock.shutdown(socket.SHUT_RD)
put_block(sock, b'Beautiful is better than ugly.')
put_block(sock, b'Explicit is better than implicit.')
put_block(sock, b'Simple is better than complex.')
put_block(sock, b'')
sock.close()
if __name__ == '__main__':
parser = ArgumentParser(description='Transmit & receive blocks over
TCP')
parser.add_argument('hostname', nargs='?', default='127.0.0.1',
help='IP address or hostname (default: %(default)s)')
parser.add_argument('-c', action='store_true', help='run as the
client')
parser.add_argument('-p', type=int, metavar='port', default=1060,
help='TCP port number (default: %(default)s)')
args = parser.parse_args()
function = client if args.c else server
function((args.hostname, args.p))
```

Take note of how cautious you must be! Even though the 4-byte length field is such a small amount of data that you might not think recv() could possibly return it all at once, the code is correct only if recv() is carefully wrapped in a loop. script will keep requesting more data until all four bytes have come (just in case). This is the type of warning that is required. When writing network programming, this is a must.

As a result, you have at least six possibilities for breaking down an endless stream of data into manageable bits. Clients and servers can turn around and respond when a message is complete. a lot of modern Protocols combine them, and you are allowed to do so as well.

The HTTP protocol, which you will study more about later in this book, is a nice example of a mashup of multiple framing approaches. It employs the blank line 'rnrn' as a delimiter to indicate when its headers are complete. Line endings can be safely regarded as special characters because the headers are text. However, because the actual payload can be pure binary data, such as an image or compressed file, the headers include a Content-Length parameter in bytes to determine how much more data to read off the socket once the headers have been read.

As a result, HTTP combines the fourth and fifth patterns you've seen thus far. It can, in fact, make advantage of the sixth option: If a server cannot estimate the duration of a response, HTTP can employ "chunked encoding," which delivers a sequence of blocks each prefixed with the length of the response. A zero-length field, as shown in Listing 5-2, indicates the end of the transmission.

Pickles and Self-delimiting Formats

It's worth noting that some types of data you might transfer over the network already have built-in delimiters. You may not need to impose your own framing on top of what the data is already doing if you are conveying such data.

Consider Python's native form of serialisation, "pickles," which comes with the Standard Library. A pickle preserves the contents of a Python data structure using a strange mix of text commands and data so that you can rebuild it later or on a different system.

```
>>> import pickle
>>> pickle.dumps([5, 6, 7])
b'\x80\x03]q\x94(K\x05K\x06K\x07e.'
```

The '.' character at the end of the preceding string is the most intriguing aspect of this output data. It's how the format marks the conclusion of a pickle. When the loader comes across it, it can stop and return the value without reading any further. As a result, you can take the preceding pickle and add some ugly stuff at the end, and loads() will disregard the extra data and return the original list.

```
>>> pickle.loads(b'\x80\x03]q\x94(K\x05K\x06K\x07e.blahblahblah')
[5, 6, 7]
```

Of course, this method is ineffective for network data since it does not indicate how many bytes were processed to reload the pickle; you still have no idea how much of the string is pickle data. If you use the pickle load() function to read from a file, the file pointer will stay at the end of the pickle data, and you can begin reading from there if you want to read what comes after the pickle.

```
>>> from io import BytesIO
>>> f = BytesIO(b'\x80\x03]q\x94(K\x05K\x06K\x07e.blahblahblah')
>>> pickle.load(f)
[5, 6, 7]
>>> f.tell()
14
>>> f.read()
b'blahblahblah'
```

You could also design a protocol that consisted solely of transmitting pickles back and forth between two Python applications. Because the pickle library knows all about reading from files and how it might have to make repeated reads until a full pickle has been read, you wouldn't require the kind of loop you put in the recvall() function in Listing 5-2. If you want to wrap a socket in a Python file object for consumption by a routine like the pickle load() function, use the makefile() socket method (described in Chapter 3).

Pickling huge data structures has many nuances, especially if they contain Python objects other than simple built-in types like integers, strings, lists, and dictionaries.

JSON And XML

The JSON and XML data formats are also common choices if your protocol needs to be readable from other programming languages or if you simply prefer universal standards than Python-specific forms. Because neither of these formats supports framing, you'll need to find out how to get a whole string of text from across the network before you can analyse it.

JSON is one of the most used options for transferring data between computer languages today. It has been included in the Standard Library as a module named json since Python 2.6. It provides a method for serialising simple data structures that is ubiquitous.

```
>>> import json
>>> json.dumps([49, 'hello!'])
```

```
'[49, "hello!]'
>>> json.dumps([49, 'hello!'], ensure_ascii=False)
'[49, "hello!"]'
>>> json.loads('{"name": "bob", "quest": "how are you?"}')
{'quest': 'how are you?', 'name': 'bob'}
```

Note that JSON not only supports Unicode characters in its strings, but it may also include Unicode characters inline in its payload if you inform the Python json module that its output does not have to be limited to ASCII characters. It's also worth noting that the JSON representation is defined as producing a string, which is why the json module's input and output are full strings rather than Python byte objects. Strings should be encoded as UTF-8 for transmission over the wire, as per the JSON standard.

Because its primary nature is to accept strings and mark them up by surrounding them in angle-bracketed components, the XML format is preferable for documents. For the time being, just remember that you don't have to limit your use of XML to when you're using the HTTP protocol. There may be times when you need text markup and find XML to be useful in conjunction with another standard.

Binary formats like Thrift and Google Protocol Buffers, which are a bit different from the formats previously outlined because both the client and the server need to have a code description of what each message will include, are among the many alternative formats that developers might wish to examine. These systems, on the other hand, have allowances for different protocol versions, allowing new servers to go into production while still communicating with machines running an older protocol version until they can all be updated to the new one. They're quick and easy to use, and they can handle binary data with ease.

Compression

Because the time it takes to send data over the network is typically greater than the time it takes for your CPU to prepare the data for transmission, compressing data before sending is sometimes worthwhile. As you'll see in Chapter 9, the popular HTTP protocol allows a client and server to determine whether they can both support compression.

The GNU zlib facility, which is available through the Python Standard Library and is one of the most widely used forms of compression on the Internet today, is self-framing, which is a noteworthy feature. If you start feeding it a compressed stream of data, it will tell you when it's finished and provide you access to the uncompressed payload that may follow.

Most protocols prefer to execute their own framing and then provide the resulting block to zlib for decompression if required. You might, however, make a promise to yourself that you'll always add a bit of uncompressed data to the end of each zlib compressed string (here, I'll use a single b'.' byte) and wait for your compression object to break out that "extra data" as a signal that you're done.

Consider the following pairing of compressed data streams:

```
>>> import zlib
>>> data = zlib.compress(b'Python') + b'.' + zlib.compress(b'zlib')
+ b'.'
>>> data
b'x\x9c\x0b\xa8,\xc9\xc8\xcf\x03\x00\x08\x97\x02\x83.x\x9c\xab\xca\
xc9L\x02\x00\x04d\x01\xb2.'
>>> len(data)
28
```

When given small payloads, most compression algorithms tend to make them longer rather than shorter since the overhead of the compression format overwhelms any small amount of compressibility in the payload. Assume that these 28 bytes arrive in 8-byte packets at their destination. After processing the first packet, the decompression object's unused data slot will still be empty, indicating that there is more data on the way.

```
>>> d = zlib.decompressobj()
>>> d.decompress(data[0:8]), d.unused_data
(b'Pytho', b'')
```

As a result, you'll need to recv() the socket once more. When you feed the second block of eight characters to the decompress object, it will both complete the compressed data you were waiting for and return a nonempty unused data value, indicating that you have finally received the b'.' byte:

```
>>> d.decompress(data[8:16]), d.unused_data
('n', '.x')
```

After the period, the next character must be the first byte of whatever payload follows this first bit of compressed data. Because you're expecting more compressed data here, you'll pass the 'x' to a new decompress object, and then feed the last 8-byte "packets" you're simulating to it.

```
>>> d = zlib.decompressobj()
>>> d.decompress(b'x'), d.unused_data
```

```
(b'', b'')
>>> d.decompress(data[16:24]), d.unused_data
(b'zlib', b'')
>>> d.decompress(data[24:]), d.unused_data
(b'', b'.')
```

unused data is now nonempty, indicating that you have read past the end of this second batch of compressed data and can study its content with confidence that it has arrived complete and intact. Most protocol designers, once again, make compression optional and conduct their own framing. However, if you know you'll always want to use zlib, a convention like this will allow you to take advantage of zlib's built-in stream termination and autodetect the end of each compressed stream.

Exceptions in the Network

The exceptions that are caught by the example scripts in this book are usually ones that are critical to the feature being presented. As a result, when I showed socket timeouts in Listing 2-2, I made sure to catch the exception socket.timeout because that's how timeouts are signalled. I ignored all of the other exceptions that will occur if the command line hostname is wrong, bind() is used with a remote IP, the port used with bind() is already busy, or the peer cannot be contacted or stops replying.

Working with sockets can lead to a variety of issues. Though the number of mistakes that can occur while using a network connection is extremely large—involving every conceivable misstep that can occur at every level of the complex TCP/IP protocol— the number of real exceptions that socket operations can impact your programmes is thankfully quite small. The following are exceptions that are particular to socket operations:

> **OSError:** This is the socket module's workhorse, and it will be raised for almost every problem that can occur during network transmission. This can happen at any time during a socket call, even when you don't expect it. When a previous send(), for example, evoked a reset (RST) packet from the remote host, the error caused by any socket operation you try next on that socket will be visible.

> **socket.gaierror:** Getaddrinfo() throws an exception because it can't find the name or service you're looking for, which is why the letters g, a, and I are in its name. It can be raised not just when you explicitly call getaddrinfo(), but also when you call bind() or connect() with a hostname instead of an IP address and the hostname lookup fails. If you catch this exception, you can search for the error number and message inside the exception object.

```
>>> import socket
>>> s = socket.socket(socket.AF_INET, socket.SOCK_STREAM)
>>> try:
... s.connect(('nonexistent.hostname.foo.bar', 80))
... except socket.gaierror as e:
... raise
...
Traceback (most recent call last):
  ...
socket.gaierror: [Errno -2] Name or service not known
>>> e.errno
-2
>>> e.strerror
'Name or service not known'
```

This exception is only thrown if you, or a library you're using, chooses to put a timeout on a socket rather than waiting indefinitely for a send() or recv() to complete. It means that the timeout ran out before the operation could finish normally.

An herror exception is also described in the Standard Library documentation for the socket module. Fortunately, it will only happen if you utilise specific old-fashioned address lookup calls rather than the procedures specified in Chapter 4.

When using Python's higher-level socket-based protocols, one of the most important questions is whether they allow raw socket errors to reach your code or if they catch them and transform them into their own type of error. The Python Standard Library contains examples of both ways! httplib, for example, deems itself low-level enough to display the raw socket error that occurs when connecting to an unrecognised hostname.

```
>>> import http.client
>>> h = http.client.HTTPConnection('nonexistent.hostname.boo.far')
>>> h.request('GET', '/')
Traceback (most recent call last):
  ...
socket.gaierror: [Errno -2] Name or service not known
```

However, urllib2 hides this problem and raises URLError instead, presumably to preserve the semantics of being a clean and neutral system for resolving URLs to documents.

```
>>> import urllib.request
>>> urllib.request.urlopen('http://nonexistent.hostname.boo.far/')
Traceback (most recent call last):
  ...
socket.gaierror: [Errno -2] Name or service not known
During handling of the above exception, another exception occurred:
Traceback (most recent call last):
  ...
urllib.error.URLError: <urlopen error [Errno -2] Name or service not known>
```

So, depending on the protocol implementation you're using, you may only have to deal with protocol-specific exceptions, or you may have to deal with both protocol-specific and raw socket problems. If you're unsure about a library's approach, read the documentation carefully. I've tried to give insets for the key packages that I cover in later chapters of this book that identify the possible exceptions to which each library can subject your code. Of course, you can always start the library, give it a non-existent hostname, or even run it while disconnected from the network to observe what kind of issue it throws.

How should you handle all of the possible errors while creating a network programme? Of course, this isn't a networking-specific question. Exceptions must be handled in all Python programmes, and the solutions I cover briefly in this chapter are relevant to a wide range of different programmes. Whether you're packaging up exceptions for processing by other programmers who contact your API or intercepting exceptions to report them appropriately to an end user, your method will be different.

Raising More Specific Exceptions

There are two methods for providing exceptions to users of an API you're developing. Of course, you will be the only customer of a module or procedure you create in many circumstances. However, consider your future self as a customer who will have forgotten almost everything about this module and will really appreciate its approach to exceptions for its simplicity and clarity.

One method is to just ignore network exceptions. They will then be visible to the caller, who will be able to catch or report them as they see fit. This method is well suited to low-level networking routines in which the caller can vividly imagine why you're putting up a socket and why its setup or use might have failed. The developer developing the calling code will only expect a network fault if the mapping between API callables and low-level networking actions is obvious.

The alternative option is to wrap the network failures in your own exception. This makes it much easier for authors who aren't familiar with how your routines are implemented, because their code may now catch exceptions relating to the actions your code performs without needing to understand how sockets work. Custom exceptions also allow you to create error messages that clarify exactly what your library was trying to do when it ran into network issues.

Whether you construct a little mycopy() method that copies a file from one remote system to another, for example, a socket.error will not tell the caller if the fault occurred with the source or destination machine, or if it was something else entirely. In this instance, it could be preferable to create your own exceptions, such as SourceError and DestinationError, that have a close semantic relationship with your API. If certain users of your API wish to dig deeper, you can always add the initial socket fault by using raise... from exception chaining.

```
class DestinationError(Exception):
 def __str__(self):
 return '%s: %s' % (self.args[0], self.__cause__.strerror)
# ...
try:
 host = sock.connect(address)
except socket.error as e:
 raise DestinationError('Error connecting to destination') from e
```

Of course, this code assumes that DestinationError will only ever wrap OSError descendants such as socket.error. Otherwise, to handle the circumstance where the cause exception's textual information is stored in an attribute other than strerror, the __str__() method would have to be more sophisticated. However, this does at least show the trend. After catching a DestinationError, the caller might investigate its

Network Exceptions: Detecting and Reporting

Granular exception handlers and blanket exception handlers are the two most common techniques of catching exceptions.

Wrapping a try...except clause around every single network call you ever make and printing out a pithy error message in its place is the granular approach to exceptions. While this is appropriate for short programmes, it can become tedious in longer ones without necessarily providing the user with more information. Ask yourself if you're really delivering additional information when you surround the hundredth network activity in your software with yet another try...except and specific error message. The alternative option is to use generic exception handlers. This entails taking a step back from your code and recognising large sections that do specific tasks, such as these:

- "The sole point of this procedure is to connect to the licence server."
- "This function's socket actions all retrieve a response from the database."
- "All of the cleanup and shutdown code is in this section."

Then the sections of your programme that collect input, command-line arguments, and configuration settings before starting big operations can wrap those huge actions in handlers like these:

```
import sys

...

try:

 deliver_updated_keyfiles(...)

except (socket.error, socket.gaierror) as e:

 print('cannot deliver remote keyfiles: {}'.format(e), file=sys.stderr)

 exit(1)
```

Better yet, have your code raise an error of your own devising that indicates an error that specifically needs to halt

```
the program and print error output for the user.
except:

 FatalError('cannot send replies: {}'.format(e))
```

Then, at the very start of your programme, catch all of the FatalError exceptions you throw and print out the error messages. When the time comes to add a command-line option that sends fatal errors to the system error logs rather than the screen, you'll only have to change one piece of code rather than a dozen!

There's one more reason why you might wish to include an exception handler in your network programme: you might want to intelligently retry a failed operation. This is frequent in long-running applications. Consider a utility that sent out e-mails with its status on a regular basis. If it suddenly becomes unable to send them, it is unlikely to shut down due to a temporary problem. Instead, the e-mail thread may log the problem, then wait a few minutes before trying again.

In such circumstances, you'll wrap exception handlers around specified sequences of network actions that you wish to treat as if they were a single combined operation that succeeded or failed. "If anything goes wrong in here, I'm just going to give up, wait ten minutes, and then try again to send that e-mail." Where you utilise try...except clauses will be determined by the structure and logic of the network operations you're executing, not by user or programmer convenience.

Conclusion

For machine data to be shared over the internet, it must be transformed so that, regardless of the private and idiosyncratic storage mechanisms employed within your machine, the data is presented in a public and reproducible format that can be read by other systems, programmes, and possibly even programming languages.

Because 8-bit octets are the common currency of an IP network, the key challenge for text will be which encoding to use so that the symbols you want to send can be converted into bytes. The Python struct module will assist you in ensuring that bytes are organised in a way that is compatible with multiple machines when dealing with binary data. Finally, data structures and documents are sometimes best communicated via JSON or XML, which provide a standard mechanism for machines to share structured data.

When working with TCP/IP streams, one of the most important considerations is framing: how will you know where a given message begins and finishes in a continuous stream of data? There are a variety of methods for accomplishing this, all of which should be used with caution because recv() may only return a portion of an incoming transmission with each call. Special delimiter characters or patterns, fixed-length messages, and chunked-encoding techniques are all possibilities for distinguishing blocks of data.

Python pickles will not only convert data structures into strings that can be sent over the network, but they will also tell the pickle module where an incoming pickle terminates. Pickles can now be used to frame individual messages in a stream, in addition to encoding data. The zlib compression module, which is commonly used with HTTP, can also detect when a compressed segment has reached its end, allowing for low-cost framing.

Sockets, as well as network protocols used by your programmes, can cause a variety of errors. If you're building a library for other developers or an utility for end users, you'll want to consider when to use try...except clauses. It also depends on semantics: you can wrap an entire portion of your programme in a try...unless all of that code is accomplishing one huge thing from the caller's or end user's perspective. Finally, you should encapsulate actions separately with a try...except that the call can be automatically retried if the error is transitory and the call may succeed later.

CHAPTER 6
SSL/TLS

Transport Layer Security (TLS), originally known as the Secure Sockets Layer (SSL) when initially introduced by Netscape in 1995, became an Internet standard in 1999 and may be the most extensively used form of encryption on the Internet today. It is used with many basic protocols on the modern Internet to verify server identification and protect data in transit, as you will see in this chapter.

The proper implementation and use of TLS is a shifting target. Each year, new assaults on its encryption algorithms are proposed, resulting in the development of new cyphers and methodologies. As of this Network Programming in Python: The Basics, TLS 1.2 is the most recent version, although further versions will undoubtedly be released in the future. As the state of the art evolves, I'll endeavour to keep the example scripts saved online in the book's source code repository up to date. As a result, be sure to go to the URL at the top of each script in this chapter and cut and paste from the version of the code found in version control.

Structure

- What TLS Fails to Secure
- What Is the Worst That Could Happen?
- Producing Certificates

- TLS Offloading
- Default Contexts in Python 3.4
- Wrapping Sockets in Different Ways
- Ciphers chosen by hand and perfect forward security
- Support for TLS Protocol
- Details of Studying
- Conclusion

Objectives:

This chapter will begin by defining TLS's goals and discussing the methods it employs to achieve them. Then you'll learn how to activate and configure TLS on a TCP socket using Python examples, both simple and complicated. Finally, you'll see how TLS is incorporated into the real-world protocols covered in the rest of the book.

What TLS Fails to Secure

Anyone observing data travelling across a properly configured TLS socket should see nonsense, as you'll see later in this chapter. Moreover, unless the inventors of TLS have failed mathematics, it will be nonsense that is astonishingly impenetrable even to a computer—and even to a government organisation with a vast budget. It should prevent eavesdroppers from knowing the URL you request, the content you receive, or any identifying information such as a password or cookie that might transit in either direction through the socket, for example. (For additional detail on HTTP features like passwords and cookies, see Chapter 9.)

Nonetheless, you should take a step back and remember that TLS does not encrypt everything about a connection, including its contents, and that any third party can see it.

- In every packet's IP header, the addresses of both your machine and the other host are available as plain bytes.
- Every TCP header also includes your client's and server's port numbers.
- The DNS request that your client made in the first place to discover the server's IP address most likely went unencrypted across the network.

The size of the data chunks that transit in each direction via the TLS-encrypted socket can be monitored by an observer. Even while TLS tries to obscure the actual number of bytes passed, the broad pattern of requests and responses may still be seen in roughly what sized chunks data flows.

I'll use an example to demonstrate the prior flaws. Consider fetching `https://pypi.python.org/pypi/skyfield/` over a coffee shop's wireless network using a secure HTTPS client (such as your favourite web browser).

What would an observer know—an "observer" being anyone else connected to the coffee shop's wireless network or in charge of one of the routers connecting it to the rest of the Internet? The observer will initially see your system perform a DNS query for pypi.python.org, and unless the IP address returned contains many other web sites, they will assume that your subsequent communications with that IP address at port 443 are for the purpose of reading `https://pypi.python.org` web pages. Because HTTP is a lock-step protocol in which each request is written out in its entirety before a response is written back, they will be able to tell the difference between your HTTP requests and the server's responses.

They will also know the approximate size of each returned document as well as the order in which they were retrieved.

Consider what the observer might discover! Different sizes will be found on different pages at `https://pypi.python.org`, which an observer may catalogue by scanning the site using a web scraper (see Chapter 11).Images and other resources that are referenced in the HTML and must be downloaded on first viewing or if they have expired from your browser's cache will vary by page genre. While an outside observer may not be aware of the particular searches you conduct or the packages you eventually view or download, They'll often be able to make an educated prediction based on the approximate sizes of the files you fetch.

The big question of how to keep your browsing habits private, or any other personal data that travels across the public Internet, is far beyond the scope of this book, and will require research into mechanisms like online anonymity networks (Tor, for example, has recently been in the news) and anonymous remailers. Even with such procedures in place, your system is still likely to send and receive data blocks whose size can be exploited to infer what you're doing. A sophisticated enough adversary might even notice that your request pattern correlates to payloads leaving the anonymous network to reach a certain location.

Instead, the remainder of this chapter will concentrate on the narrower subject of what TLS can accomplish and how your Python programmes can use it successfully.

What Is the Worst That Could Happen?

To understand about the key aspects of TLS, study the set of problems that the protocol faces when establishing a connection and how each one is addressed and overcome.

Let's say you want to start a TCP conversation with a specific hostname and port number on the Internet, and you've reluctantly accepted that your DNS lookup of the hostname, as well as the port number to which you're connecting (which will reveal the protocol you're using, unless you're connecting to a service whose owner has bound it to a nonstandard or misleading port number), will be public knowledge. You would connect to the IP address and port using a typical TCP connection. If the protocol you're talking about requires an introduction before enabling encryption, those first few bytes would be visible to everyone.

(Protocols differ in this regard—HTTPS sends nothing before enabling encryption, whereas SMTP sends multiple lines of text.) The behaviour of numerous significant protocols will be covered later in this chapter.)

Once you've got the socket up and running, and exchanged whatever pleasantries your protocol requires to prepare the way for encryption, it's time for TLS to take over and start constructing strong guarantees about who you're talking to and how you and the peer (the other party) will keep data safe from prying eyes.

The initial request of your TLS client will be for the remote server to give a binary document called a certificate, which includes a public key—an integer that can be used to encrypt data and can only be decrypted and understood by the owner of the associated private key integer. If the remote server is properly configured and has never been hacked, it will have a copy of the private key and will be the only server on the Internet (with the possible exception of the other machines in its cluster) to have one.

How can you ensure that the remote server has the private key in your TLS implementation? Simple! Your TLS library delivers data encrypted with the public key across the wire and requests that the remote server produce a checksum proving that the data was properly decrypted with the secret key.

Your TLS stack should also consider whether the remote certificate has been forged. After all, anyone with access to the openssl command-line tool (or any of a number of other tools) can create a certificate with a common name of cn=www.google.com, cn=pypi.python.org, or whatever they like. Why would you put your faith in such a claim? Your TLS session should preserve a list of certificate authorities (CAs) it trusts to validate Internet host identities as a solution. By default, your operating system's

TLS library or your web browser employs a few hundred certificates from around the world that represent organisations that provide trusted site verification.

If you are not satisfied with the defaults or wish to use a private CA that your company has generated for signing your own private host certificates for free, you can always give your own CA list. When no external clients are expected to connect and you only need to facilitate connections between your internal services, this is a popular choice.

A signature is a mathematical mark made by a CA on a certificate to show that it has been approved.

Before recognising that the certificate is legitimate, your TLS library will check the signature against the public key of the relevant CA certificate.

TLS will check the data fields of the certificate after confirming that the certificate's body was submitted to and signed by the trusted third party. There will be two types of fields that will be of particular importance. To begin with, certificates include a notBefore date and a notAfter date to bracket the time period in which they are valid, ensuring that certificates associated with stolen private keys do not remain valid indefinitely. Because your TLS stack checks these using your system clock, a poor or incorrect clock can actually prevent you from communicating over TLS!

Second, the certificate's common name should match the hostname you're trying to connect to—after all, if you're trying to connect to https://pypi.python.org, you're not going to be impressed if the site responds with a certificate for a completely different hostname!

A single certificate can be used for several hostnames. Modern certificates can store additional names in their subjectAltName field to supplement the single-value common name in the subject field. In addition, any of those names can contain wildcards, such as *.python.org, which match several hostnames instead than just one. Modern TLS algorithms will automatically conduct such matching for you, and the Python ssl module can do so as well.

Finally, the client and server TLS agents agree on a shared secret key and cypher to encrypt the data that goes through the connection. This is the last place where TLS can fail, because properly configured software will reject any cypher or key length it deems insufficient. TLS can fail on two levels: either the version of the TLS protocol that the other end wishes to use is too hopelessly out-of-date and insecure, or the cyphers that the other end provides are not regarded strong enough to trust.

Control is passed back to the application at each end once the cypher has been agreed upon and both peers have created the keys, both for encrypting and signing each block of data. Each chunk of data they send is encrypted with the encryption key, and the resulting block is signed with the signing key to verify to the other end that it was generated by the other peer and not by someone attempting a man-in-the-middle assault on the network. Data can flow freely in both directions, exactly like on a normal TCP socket, until TLS is off and the socket is closed or reverted to plain-text mode.

Because it makes all of the main decisions discussed earlier, you'll learn how to manipulate Python's ssl library in the parts that follow. Please refer to official references as well as sites such as Bruce Schneier's books, the Google Online Security blog, and blogs like Adam Langley's for more information. Hynek Schlawack's "The Sorry State Of SSL" keynote from PyCon 2014, which you can watch online, was quite useful to me. If more recent TLS lectures have been presented at conferences by the time you read this book, they may be an excellent source of up-to-date knowledge on the ever-changing field of cryptography.

Producing Certificates

The certs directory also contains various certificates that are used in the network playground (see Chapter 1), including those that you will use at the command line in the examples in this chapter. All of the other certificates have been signed by the ca.crt certificate, which is a small self-contained certificate authority that you'll instruct Python to trust when utilising the other certificates with TLS.

In a nutshell, certificate creation usually starts with two pieces of data: one generated by a human and the other by a machine. These are a textual description of the entity indicated by the certificate and a private key that has been carefully generated utilising the operating system's real randomness sources.

When prompted for the handwritten identity description, I normally save it to a version-controlled file for future reference; however, other administrators simply type the information into openssl when required. Listing 6-1 shows the www.cnf file for the network playground's www.example.com web server, which was used to generate the certificate.

Listing 6-1:. The OpenSSL Command Line Configuration for an X.509 Certificate

```
[ req ]
prompt = no
distinguished_name = req_distinguished_name
[ req_distinguished_name ]
countryName = India
```

```
stateOrProvinceName = New Delhi
localityName = New Delhi
0.organizationName = Example from Bpbonline
organizationalUnitName = Network Programming in Python: The Basics
commonName = www.example.com
emailAddress = root@example.com
[ ssl_client ]
basicConstraints = CA:FALSE
nsCertType = client
keyUsage = digitalSignature, keyEncipherment
extendedKeyUsage = clientAuth
```

Remember that TLS will compare the commonName and any subjectAltName elements (not present in this example) to the hostname to determine whether it is talking to the correct host.

Today, experts disagree over the length and kind of private key that should back up a certificate, with some administrators choosing RSA and others Diffie-Hellman. Without getting into that issue, here is a sample command line for establishing an RSA key with a key length that is currently regarded acceptable:

```
$ openssl genrsa -out www.key 4096

Generating RSA private key, 4096 bit long modulus

.........................................................
..............

.............++

.............++

e is 65537 (0x10001)
```

With these two components in place, the administrator can generate a certificate-signing request (CSR) to send to a certificate authority, whether it's the administrator's own or a third- party's.

```
$ openssl req -new -key www.key -config www.cnf -out www.csr
```

If you want to understand how the openssl tool creates a private CA and signs a CSR to build a www.crt file corresponding to the request generated before, look at the Makefile. If you deal with a public certificate authority instead, you might get your www.crt in an e-mail (don't worry, the certificate is designed to be public!) Alternatively, when the signed certificate is ready, you can download it from your account on the authority's website. In any event, combining the certificate and secret key into a single file for convenience is the final step to making your certificate easy to use with Python. If the files were created in the standard PEM format by the previous operations, combining them is as easy as using the Unix "concatenate" command.

```
$ cat www.crt www.key > www.pem
```

The finished file should include a textual explanation of the certificate's contents, followed by the certificate itself, and finally the private key. Use caution while working with this file! If either www.key or the PEM file www.pem holding the private key was leaked or made available to a third party, the third party may mimic your service for the months or years until the key expires.

More sophisticated configurations exist than a CA that signs certificates for server use directly. Some firms, for example, want their servers to only use certificates that are valid for a few days or weeks before expiring. If a server is hacked and the private key is stolen, the damage is reduced. Instead of having to contact (and pay) the CA organisation for a replacement every few days, such an organisation can have the CA sign a longer-lived intermediate certificate, whose private key the organisation keeps secret and uses to sign the user-visible certificates that are actually put on servers. The resulting certificate chain, or chain of trust, combines the flexibility of having your own CA (because you can sign new certificates whenever you want) with the convenience of using a publicly recognised CA (because you don't have to install a custom CA certificate in every browser or client that wants to communicate with you). Client software should have no trouble confirming their identity if your TLS-powered server gives them with both their own server certificate and the intermediate certificate that makes the cryptographic link back to the CA certificate that they trust.

If you're entrusted with establishing your organization's cryptographic identity and services, consult books or material on certificate signing.

TLS Offloading

Before I teach you how to utilise TLS from Python—especially if you're about to develop a server—I should point out that many experts would question why you'd want to use encryption in your Python application in the first place. After all, several tools exist that have carefully implemented TLS and can handle client connections on your behalf as well as delivering unencrypted data to your application if it is executed on a different port.

It may be easier to upgrade and tune a separate daemon or service that provides TLS termination for your Python application than the combination of your own server code, Python, and the underlying OpenSSL library. Furthermore, a third-party tool will frequently expose TLS functionality that the Python ssl module does not yet allow you to customise, even under Python 3.4. For example, using ECDSA elliptic curve signatures or fine-tuning session renegotiation appears to be unfeasible with the vanilla ssl module at the moment. Renegotiation of sessions is a particularly important problem. It can greatly lower the CPU cost of providing TLS, but if configured incorrectly, it can jeopardise your ability to guarantee Perfect Forward Security (see the section "Hand-Picked Ciphers and Perfect Forward Security"). "How to botch TLS forward secrecy," a 2013 blog entry at https://www.imperialviolet. org/2013/06/27/botchingpfs.html, is still one of the better introductions to the topic. Third-party daemons that provide TLS termination include front-end HTTPS servers. Because the HTTPS standard stipulates that the client and server should initially negotiate encryption before any protocol-specific messages transit across the channel, it is particularly simple for a third-party tool to wrap HTTP. TLS can disappear from your Python code and into the surrounding infrastructure, whether you deploy Apache, nginx, or another reverse proxy in front of your Python web service as an extra layer of defence or instead subscribe to a content delivery network like Fastly that tunnels requests through to your own servers.

However, even if you create your own raw socket protocol for which no third-party tools are accessible, If you decide to outsource TLS to another tool, you can probably just skim the rest of this chapter (to familiarise yourself with the knobs you'll be searching for) before diving into the tool's documentation. It is that tool, not Python, that will load your certificate and private key, and it must be configured appropriately to give the amount of security against weak cyphers that you require. The only concern is how your preferred front end will inform your Python service of the remote IP address and (if client certificates are used) the identity of each client that has connected. Additional headers can be added to HTTP requests to include information about the client. Extra information like the client IP address will have to be prepended as extra bytes in advance of the incoming data stream for more rudimentary technologies like stunnel or haproxy that may not truly be speaking HTTP. In any case, the tool will provide the TLS superpowers that will be demonstrated in the rest of this chapter using pure Python sockets.

Default Contexts in Python 3.4

There are several open source TLS implementations available. Despite multiple recent security incidents, the Python Standard Library chooses to wrap the most popular, the OpenSSL library, which appears to be the best option for most systems and languages. Some Python distributions include their own version of OpenSSL, while others just wrap the OpenSSL included with your operating system. ssl is the old and nostalgic moniker for the Standard Library module. Although this book will concentrate on ssl, other cryptography projects in the Python community are active, including the pyOpenSSL project, which exposes much more of the underlying library's API. Python 3.4 makes it more easier for Python applications to use TLS properly than previous versions of Python, thanks to the addition of the ssl.create default context() function. It's a great illustration of the kind of "opinionated API" that the majority of customers require. We owe it to Christian Heimes and Donald Stufft to introduce the concept of a default context to the Standard Library, as well as to advocate for strong and relevant feedback. Because they had already promised not to destroy backward compatibility when new versions of Python came out, the various procedures that the ssl module offers for setting up TLS connections are required to continue with older and less secure defaults. However, if the TLS cypher or key length you've been using is now considered insecure, create default context() is more than willing to throw an exception the next time you upgrade Python.

By abandoning the promise that you can upgrade Python without changing the behaviour of your application, create default context() can carefully select the cyphers it will support, freeing you from the need to become a TLS expert and read security blogs if you simply follow its advice and keep Python updated on your machine. After each upgrade, retest your applications to ensure that they can still connect to their TLS peers. If an application is unsuccessful,

Listing 6-2. In Python 3.4 or newer, securing a socket with TLS for both the client and the server

```python3
#!/usr/bin/env python3
# Network Programming in Python: The Basics
# Simple TLS client and server using safe configuration defaults
import argparse, socket, ssl
def client(host, port, cafile=None):
 purpose = ssl.Purpose.SERVER_AUTH
 context = ssl.create_default_context(purpose, cafile=cafile)
 raw_sock = socket.socket(socket.AF_INET, socket.SOCK_STREAM)
 raw_sock.connect((host, port))
 print('Connected to host {!r} and port {}'.format(host, port))
 ssl_sock = context.wrap_socket(raw_sock, server_hostname=host)
 while True:
```

```
    data = ssl_sock.recv(1024)
    if not data:
    break
    print(repr(data))
def server(host, port, certfile, cafile=None):
    purpose = ssl.Purpose.CLIENT_AUTH
    context = ssl.create_default_context(purpose, cafile=cafile)
    context.load_cert_chain(certfile)
    listener = socket.socket(socket.AF_INET, socket.SOCK_STREAM)
    listener.setsockopt(socket.SOL_SOCKET, socket.SO_REUSEADDR, 1)
    listener.bind((host, port))
    listener.listen(1)
    print('Listening at interface {!r} and port {}'.format(host, port))
    raw_sock, address = listener.accept()
    print('Connection from host {!r} and port {}'.format(*address))
    ssl_sock = context.wrap_socket(raw_sock, server_side=True)
    ssl_sock.sendall('Simple is better than complex.'.encode('ascii'))
    ssl_sock.close()
if __name__ == '__main__':
    parser = argparse.ArgumentParser(description='Safe TLS client and
server')
    parser.add_argument('host', help='hostname or IP address')
    parser.add_argument('port', type=int, help='TCP port number')
    parser.add_argument('-a', metavar='cafile', default=None,
    help='authority: path to CA certificate PEM file')
    parser.add_argument('-s', metavar='certfile', default=None,
    help='run as server: path to server PEM file')
    args = parser.parse_args()
    if args.s:
    server(args.host, args.port, args.s, args.a)
    else:
    client(args.host, args.port, args.a)
```

The listing shows that there are only three steps to fastening a socket. To begin, construct a TLS context object that contains all of your certificate validation and cypher options. Second, use the wrap_ socket() method of the context to allow the OpenSSL library control your TCP connection, exchange the proper pleasantries with the other end, and establish an encrypted channel. Finally, use the ssl sock that was returned to you for all subsequent communication so that the TLS layer may always encrypt your data before it reaches the wire. This wrapper, you'll see, has all of the same functions as a typical socket, including send(), recv(), and close(), which you learned about in Chapter 3 from your experience with normal TCP sockets.

Several options in the new context that is returned are affected by whether you are building context for a client trying to verify the server to which it connects (Purpose. SERVER AUTH) or a server requiring to accept client connections (Purpose.CLIENT AUTH). The logic behind having two different sets of settings is that you want TLS clients to be a little more forgiving of older cyphers because they will occasionally find themselves connecting to servers that are outside of your control and may be a little out-of-date. They believe, however, that you will want your own servers to use contemporary and secure cyphers! While the settings picked by create default context() will change with each new version of Python, below are some examples from Python 3.4:

- Because create default context() sets the protocol to PROTOCOL SSLv23 when constructing your new SSLContext object, both your client and server will be willing to negotiate the TLS version that is spoken.

- Both your client and server will refuse to communicate via the obsolete SSLv2 and SSLv3 protocols due to documented flaws in each of them. Instead, they'll demand that the peer with whom they're conversing use a dialect that's at least as modern as TLSv1. (The most common client that this choice eliminates is Internet Explorer 6 on Windows XP—a combination that is so outdated that Microsoft no longer supports it.)

- The first difference between the client and server settings is that TLS compression is disabled due to the assaults that it allows. Because the majority of TLS communications on the Internet involve a client (such as a standard web browser) communicating with a server (such as PyPI, Google, or your bank) that has a valid and signed certificate,

  Another distinction between clients and servers is the cyphers they use. The client settings allow for a wider range of cyphers, including the outdated RC4 stream encryption. The server settings are substantially tougher, with a strong preference for newer cyphers that enable Perfect Forward Security (PFS), ensuring that a compromised server key—whether obtained by criminals or disclosed by court order— does not result in the disclosure of prior chats.

The previous list was simple to put together: all I had to do was open ssl.py in the Standard Library and study the source code of create default context() to figure out what choices it makes. You can do it yourself, particularly as new Python versions are released and the preceding list becomes outdated. If you're curious, the ssl.py source code provides the raw list of cyphers for both client and server operations, which are currently labelled _DEFAULT CIPHERS and _RESTRICTED SERVER CIPHERS. To learn what the choices in each string signify, visit the most recent OpenSSL manual.

When constructing the context in Listing 6-2, the cafile option specifies which certificate authority your script will trust when verifying a remote certificate. Create default context() will execute the load default_ certs() method of your new context before returning it if its value is None, which is the default if you don't specify the cafile keyword. It should also be adequate to verify public web sites and other services that have purchased a certificate from a reputable public certificate authority. If cafile is a filename instead of a string, no certificates from the operating system are imported, and only CA certificates from that file are trusted to validate the remote end of your TLS connection. (Note that if you build the context with cafile set to None and then run load verify locations() to install any additional certificates, you can make both types of certificates available.)

Finally, wrap socket() in Listing 6-2 provides two important options: one for the server and the other for the client. Because one of the two ends must assume the server's obligations or the negotiation will fail with an error, the server is provided the option server side=True. The client call requires further information: the name of the host to which you believe you connected with connect(), so that it may be compared to the subject fields of the server's certificate. As long as you constantly provide the server hostname keyword to wrap socket(), as shown in the listing, this critical check is completed automatically.

Wrapping Sockets in Different Ways

All of the scripts in this chapter show how to use the ssl module to achieve TLS by creating a configured SSLContext object that describes your security requirements, making the client-server connection yourself with a plain socket, and then calling the context's wrap socket() method to perform actual TLS negotiation. This pattern is used in all of my examples since it is the most reliable, efficient, and versatile way to access the module's API. It's the pattern that you can always utilise successfully in a Python programme, and by doing so, you'll be able to write clients and servers that are easy to read since their approaches are consistent, and their code is easy to compare to the examples here and to each other. However, the ssl module in the

Standard Library includes a few other shortcuts that you might see in other scripts and that I should mention. Let me describe each of them, as well as their flaws.

The first option you'll come across is calling the module-level function ssl.wrap socket() without previously generating a context. This is especially common in older scripts because it was the only way to establish a TLS connection prior to the addition of context objects in Python 3.2! There are at least four flaws in it.

- It's inefficient because it creates a new context object with settings every time it's invoked. Instead, by generating and setting your own context, you can reuse it multiple times while only incurring the cost of doing so once.

- It lacks the flexibility of a true context—despite offering nine (!) distinct optional keyword arguments in a desperate attempt to provide enough knobs and buttons, it still manages to leave out features like allowing you to define the cyphers you want to employ. Because of the promise of backward compatibility with Python versions that are now a decade old, it is dreadfully liberal in terms of the weak cyphers that it will allow. • Finally, it fails to provide real security because it doesn't check hostnames! You won't know whether the certificate given by your peer is even for the same hostname to which you think you're connected until you remember to execute match hostname() after a "successful" connection.

For all of these reasons, you should avoid using ssl.wrap socket() and be prepared to transition away from it in any existing code. Instead, follow the guidelines outlined in Listing 6-2. Wrapping a socket before it is connected, either a client socket before it runs connect() or a server socket before it runs accept(), is another common shortcut ().The wrapped socket can't really negotiate TLS right away in either situation, so it'll have to wait till the socket is connected to do so. Obviously, this will only work for protocols that perform TLS activation as the initial step after connecting, such as HTTPS. Because a protocol like SMTP requires cleartext to begin the interaction, a keyword option do handshake on connect is provided when wrapping, which you may set to False if you want to delay TLS negotiation until later with the socket's do handshake() method. True, prewrapping a socket does not reduce security by itself, but I advise against it for the following three reasons involving code readability:

- For starters, it places the wrapping function somewhere other than where the actual TLS negotiation occurs, which can obscure the fact that the TLS protocol is even involved from someone reading your final connect() or accept() call.

- Connect() and accept() will now be able to fail not only with socket or DNS exceptions, but also with TLS failures if the negotiation goes wrong, which is related to the prior issue. Any try...except clause that wraps those calls will now have to worry about two distinct types of errors, as two distinct procedures will be buried beneath the hood of a single method call.

- Finally, you'll notice that you now have an SSLSocket object that may or may not be performing any encryption. The so-called SSLSocket will only provide genuine encryption once a connection is established or when an explicit do handshake() is invoked (if autonegotiation is disabled). The method described in the programme listings in this book, on the other hand, transitions to an SSLSocket only when encryption is enabled, resulting in a significantly more meaningful link between the class of your current socket object and the status of the underlying connection.

Prewrapping has only been useful in one situation: when trying to use an old, naive library that only allows cleartext communication. You can add TLS protection to the protocol without it even knowing by providing a prewrapped socket and setting the do handshake on_ connect keyword argument to its default value of True. This is a unique situation that should be addressed (if at all possible) by making the underlying library TLS-aware and capable of accepting a TLS context as an argument.

Ciphers chosen by hand and perfect forward security

If you're concerned about data security, you might wish to use the create default context() function to specify the exact cyphers that OpenSSL can use rather than relying on the defaults.

As the field of encryption develops, there will undoubtedly be issues, flaws, and solutions that we have yet to imagine. However, when this book goes to press, one crucial concern is Perfect Forward Security (PFS), or whether someone who acquires (or cracks) an old private key of yours in the future will be able to read past TLS chats that they captured and saved for future decryption. The most popular cyphers nowadays are those that defend against this risk by encrypting each new socket using an ephemeral (temporary) key. One of the most common reasons for wanting to hand-specify the characteristics of your context object is to ensure PFS.

Although the ssl module's default contexts do not require a PFS-capable cypher, if both your client and server are using recent-enough versions of OpenSSL, you will almost certainly get one. For example, if I run the safe tls.py script from Listing 6-2 in server mode and connect to it using the test tls.py script from Listing 6-4, then (given my laptop, operating system, and other factors),

```
$ python3.4 test_tls.py -a ca.crt localhost 1060
```

...

```
Cipher chosen for this connection... ECDHE-RSA-AES256-GCM-SHA384
Cipher defined in TLS version....... TLSv1/SSLv3
Cipher key has this many bits....... 256
Compression algorithm in use........ none
```

As a result, Python will often make smart decisions without you having to specify them. However, if you want to ensure that a specific protocol version or algorithm is used, simply restrict the context to your preferences. For example, when this book is being published, a good server setup (for a server that will not expect clients to give TLS certificates and hence can use CERT NONE as its verification mode) is:

```
context = ssl.SSLContext(ssl.PROTOCOL_TLSv1_2)
context.verify_mode = ssl.CERT_NONE
context.options |= ssl.OP_CIPHER_SERVER_PREFERENCE # choose *our* favorite cipher
context.options |= ssl.OP_NO_COMPRESSION # avoid CRIME exploit
context.options |= ssl.OP_SINGLE_DH_USE # for PFS
context.options |= ssl.OP_SINGLE_ECDH_USE # for PFS
context.set_ciphers('ECDH+AES128 ') # choose over AES256, says Schneier
```

These lines of code can be substituted into a programme like Listing 6-2 anytime a server socket is formed.

Only a few explicit parameters have been used to specify the specific TLS version and cypher. Any client attempting to connect that does not support these options will fail instead of establishing a successful connection. A client trying a connection with an even slightly older version of TLS (like 1.1) or a slightly weaker cypher (like 3DES) will be refused if the previous code is added to Listing 6-3 in place of the default context.

```
$ python3.4 test_tls.py -p TLSv1_1 -a ca.crt localhost 1060
Address we want to talk to.......... ('localhost', 1060)
Traceback (most recent call last):
  ...
ssl.SSLError: [SSL: TLSV1_ALERT_PROTOCOL_VERSION] tlsv1 alert protocol version (_ssl.c:598)
$ python3.4 test_tls.py -C 'ECDH+3DES' -a ca.crt localhost 1060
```

```
Address we want to talk to.......... ('localhost', 1060)
Traceback (most recent call last):

  ...

ssl.SSLError:  [SSL:  SSLV3_ALERT_HANDSHAKE_FAILURE]  sslv3  alert
handshake failure (_ssl.c:598)
```

In each of these circumstances, the server will additionally raise a Python exception, analysing the fault from its own perspective. As a result, if the connection succeeds, your data will be protected using the latest and most capable version of TLS (1.2) and one of the best cyphers available. The problem with switching from the ssl module's default contexts to hand-picked settings like this is that you must not only do the research to determine your needs and choose a TLS version and cypher when you first write an application, but you must also stay up-to-date in case your choices are later discovered to be vulnerable to a new exploit. Combining TLS 1.2 with an elliptic curve Diffie–Hellman appears to be in excellent shape, as least as far as this book is concerned. However, the option will most likely appear antiquated or even quaint in the future. Alternatively, you could appear utterly insecure. Will you be able to pick this up quickly and replace your manual decisions in your software projects with superior ones?

You'll be locked between these two possibilities unless create default context() gains an option that allows you to insist on Perfect Forward Security. Either trust the default context and accept that some clients (or servers) with whom you communicate may not be protected by PFS, or lock down the cypher and stay current with cryptography news. Keep in mind that PFS is only as good as your process for frequently discarding the server's session state or session ticket key. Simply restarting your server process every evening should ensure that new keys are issued, but if you have a full fleet of servers to deploy and want them to be able to handle a pool of TLS clients that take advantage of session restart, do more research. (However, in this case—wanting an entire cluster's session-restart keys to be coordinated without jeopardising PFS—it might make more sense to look at tools other than Python to handle TLS termination!) Last but not least, if you're developing, or at least configuring, both the client and server, as you may be if you're setting up encrypted communications within your own machine room or between your own servers, locking down the cypher option is significantly easier. When other pieces of software are involved, a less flexible cypher set may make it more difficult for others to interact with your services, especially if their tools use different TLS implementations. If you do limit things to just a few options, make sure to explain them clearly and publicly for individuals who create and setup the clients so they can figure out why older clients aren't connecting.

Support for TLS Protocol

TLS support has now been implemented to the majority of frequently used Internet protocols. When using these protocols from a Python Standard Library module or a third-party library, the key feature to look for is how to specify the TLS cypher and parameters to prevent peers from connecting with weak protocol versions, weak cyphers, or weakening features like compression. This setup can take the form of library-specific API calls or simply allowing you to send an SSLContext object along with your configuration options.The Python Standard Library includes the following TLS-aware protocols:

- **http.client:** You can use the constructor's context keyword to pass in an SSLContext with your own settings when creating an HTTPSConnection object (see Chapter 9). Unfortunately, neither urllib.request nor the Requests library described in Chapter 9 presently take an SSLContext argument in their APIs.

- **smtplib:** You can use the constructor's context keyword to pass in an SSLContext with your own settings when creating an SMTP SSL object (see Chapter 13). If you instead build a plain SMTP object and then call its starttls() method later, the context parameter is passed to that method call.

- **poplib:** You can use the context keyword in the function Object() { [native code] } of a POP3 SSL object (see Chapter 14) to pass in an SSLContext with your own settings. Instead, if you build a normal POP3 object and then call its stls() method later, the context parameter will be passed to that method call.

- **imaplib:** You can use the ssl context keyword in the function Object() { [native code] } of an IMAP4 SSL object (see Chapter 15) to pass in an SSLContext with your own settings. If you instead build a simple IMAP4 object and then call its starttls() method later, the ssl context parameter will be passed to that method call.

- **ftplib:** You can use the context keyword in the function Object() { [native code] } of an FTP TLS object (see Chapter 17) to send in an SSLContext with your own settings. Before you can turn on encryption, the first line or two of the FTP discussion will always flow in the clear (such as the "220" welcome message, which often reveals the server hostname). Before the login() method provides a username and password, an FTP TLS object will automatically enable encryption. If you are not logging in to the remote server but still want encryption enabled, you must manually execute the auth() method as the initial action after connecting.

- **nntplib:** While the NNTP network news (Usenet) protocol is not discussed in this book, it can be protected as well. When creating an NNTP SSL, you can use the ssl context keyword in the function Object() { [native code] } to pass in an SSLContext with your own settings. If you instead build a plain NNTP object and then call its starttls() method later, the context parameter will be passed to that method call.

It's worth noting that a common theme running through nearly all of these protocols is that TLS can be used to expand an older plain-text standard in one of two ways. One option is to introduce a new command to the protocol that enables for a TLS upgrade in the middle of a discussion. The other option is for the Internet standard to designate a second well-defined TCP port number for the TLS-protected version of the protocol, in which case TLS negotiation can happen automatically without the need to ask. Most of the previously stated protocols offer both options, but HTTP only supports the second because it is designed to be stateless.

If you're connecting to a server set up by another team or organisation that supports the TLS version of one of the previous protocols, you'll need to test (in the absence of any documentation) to see if they opened the protocol's new TLS port or just support TLS upgrades on top of the old plain-text protocol. If you're not using the Standard Library for network communication and instead utilising a third-party package that you learned about in this book or elsewhere, you'll want to look out how to provide your own SSLContext in its documentation. If no mechanism is provided—and, as I type, even popular third-party libraries for Python 3.4 and newer do not typically provide this ability—you will have to experiment with whatever knobs and settings the package does provide and test the result (perhaps using Listing 6-4, introduced in the next section) to see if the third-party library guarantees a strong enough protocol and cypher for the privacy required by your data.

Details of Studying

Listing 6-3 provides a Python 3.4 script that creates an encrypted connection and then reports on its features to help you learn more about the TLS protocol version and cypher choices that your clients and servers can make. To do so, it makes use of many new capabilities of the SSLSocket object in the Standard Library's ssl module, which now allow Python scripts to inspect the status of their OpenSSL-powered connections to determine how they're configured.

The following are the strategies it use to complete its reporting:

- **getpeercert()** is a function that returns a list of peer certificates. This method returns a Python dictionary of attributes selected from the X.509 certificate of the peer to which the TLS session is linked, a long-standing feature of SSLSocket that was accessible in multiple previous Python versions. However, subsequent Python versions have increased the number of certificate features available.

- **cypher():** Returns the name of the encryption that was finally agreed upon by OpenSSL and the peer's TLS implementation and is currently in use across the connection.

- **compression():** Returns the name of the compression algorithm being used, or None in Python.

The script in Listing 6-3 also tries a little of voodoo with ctypes in a desperate attempt to understand the TLS protocol in use (which will ideally be a native feature of the ssl module by the time Python 3.5 is published) in order to make its reporting as complete as feasible. Listing 6-3 allows you to connect to a client or server that you have built and understand what cyphers and protocols it will or will not negotiate by putting these components together.

Listing 6-3. Connect to Any TLS Endpoint and Report the Cipher Negotiated

```python
#!/usr/bin/env python3
# Network Programming in Python: The Basics
# Attempt a TLS connection and, if successful, report its properties
import argparse, socket, ssl, sys, textwrap
import ctypes
from pprint import pprint
def open_tls(context, address, server=False):
 raw_sock = socket.socket(socket.AF_INET, socket.SOCK_STREAM)
 if server:
 raw_sock.setsockopt(socket.SOL_SOCKET, socket.SO_REUSEADDR, 1)
 raw_sock.bind(address)
 raw_sock.listen(1)
 say('Interface where we are listening', address)
 raw_client_sock, address = raw_sock.accept()
 say('Client has connected from address', address)
 return context.wrap_socket(raw_client_sock, server_side=True)
 else:
 say('Address we want to talk to', address)
```

```
    raw_sock.connect(address)
    return context.wrap_socket(raw_sock)
def describe(ssl_sock, hostname, server=False, debug=False):
    cert = ssl_sock.getpeercert()
    if cert is None:
        say('Peer certificate', 'none')
    else:
        say('Peer certificate', 'provided')
        subject = cert.get('subject', [])
        names = [name for names in subject for (key, name) in names
                 if key == 'commonName']
        if 'subjectAltName' in cert:
            names.extend(name for (key, name) in cert['subjectAltName']
                         if key == 'DNS')
        say('Name(s) on peer certificate', *names or ['none'])
        if (not server) and names:
            try:
                ssl.match_hostname(cert, hostname)
            except ssl.CertificateError as e:
                message = str(e)
            else:
                message = 'Yes'
            say('Whether name(s) match the hostname', message)
        for category, count in sorted(context.cert_store_stats().items()):
            say('Certificates loaded of type {}'.format(category), count)
    try:
        protocol_version = SSL_get_version(ssl_sock)
    except Exception:
        if debug:
            raise
    else:
        say('Protocol version negotiated', protocol_version)
```

```python
    cipher, version, bits = ssl_sock.cipher()
    compression = ssl_sock.compression()
    say('Cipher chosen for this connection', cipher)
    say('Cipher defined in TLS version', version)
    say('Cipher key has this many bits', bits)
    say('Compression algorithm in use', compression or 'none')
    return cert
class PySSLSocket(ctypes.Structure):
    """The first few fields of a PySSLSocket (see Python's Modules/_
ssl.c)."""
    _fields_ = [('ob_refcnt', ctypes.c_ulong), ('ob_type', ctypes.c_
void_p),
    ('Socket', ctypes.c_void_p), ('ssl', ctypes.c_void_p)]
def SSL_get_version(ssl_sock):
    """Reach behind the scenes for a socket's TLS protocol version."""
    lib = ctypes.CDLL(ssl._ssl.__file__)
            lib.SSL_get_version.restype = ctypes.c_char_p
    address = id(ssl_sock._sslobj)
    struct = ctypes.cast(address, ctypes.POINTER(PySSLSocket)).contents
    version_bytestring = lib.SSL_get_version(struct.ssl)
    return version_bytestring.decode('ascii')
def lookup(prefix, name):
    if not name.startswith(prefix):
    name = prefix + name
    try:
    return getattr(ssl, name)
    except AttributeError:
    matching_names = (s for s in dir(ssl) if s.startswith(prefix))
    message = 'Error: {!r} is not one of the available names:\n {}'.
format(
    name, ' '.join(sorted(matching_names)))
    print(fill(message), file=sys.stderr)
    sys.exit(2)
```

```
def say(title, *words):
 print(fill(title.ljust(36, '.') + ' ' + ' '.join(str(w) for w in
words)))
def fill(text):
 return textwrap.fill(text, subsequent_indent=' ',
 break_long_words=False, break_on_hyphens=False)
if __name__ == '__main__':
 parser = argparse.ArgumentParser(description='Protect a socket with
TLS')
 parser.add_argument('host', help='hostname or IP address')
 parser.add_argument('port', type=int, help='TCP port number')
 parser.add_argument('-a', metavar='cafile', default=None,
 help='authority: path to CA certificate PEM file')
 parser.add_argument('-c', metavar='certfile', default=None,
 help='path to PEM file with client certificate')
 parser.add_argument('-C', metavar='ciphers', default='ALL',
 help='list of ciphers, formatted per OpenSSL')
 parser.add_argument('-p', metavar='PROTOCOL', default='SSLv23',
 help='protocol version (default: "SSLv23")')
 parser.add_argument('-s', metavar='certfile', default=None,
 help='run as server: path to certificate PEM file')
 parser.add_argument('-d', action='store_true', default=False,
 help='debug mode: do not hide "ctypes" exceptions')
 parser.add_argument('-v', action='store_true', default=False,
 help='verbose: print out remote certificate')
 args = parser.parse_args()
 address = (args.host, args.port)
 protocol = lookup('PROTOCOL_', args.p)
 context = ssl.SSLContext(protocol)
 context.set_ciphers(args.C)
 context.check_hostname = False
 if (args.s is not None) and (args.c is not None):
 parser.error('you cannot specify both -c and -s')
```

```
elif args.s is not None:
context.verify_mode = ssl.CERT_OPTIONAL
purpose = ssl.Purpose.CLIENT_AUTH
context.load_cert_chain(args.s)
else:
context.verify_mode = ssl.CERT_REQUIRED
purpose = ssl.Purpose.SERVER_AUTH
if args.c is not None:
context.load_cert_chain(args.c)
if args.a is None:
context.load_default_certs(purpose)
else:
context.load_verify_locations(args.a)
print()
ssl_sock = open_tls(context, address, args.s)
cert = describe(ssl_sock, args.host, args.s, args.d)
print()
if args.v:
pprint(cert)
```

The normal –h help option is the best way to learn about the command-line parameters offered by this tool. It tries to expose all of an SSLContext's primary features via command-line parameters so you can play with with them and see how they effect negotiation. You can look at how the default settings of a server using Python 3.4's create default context() are stricter than the settings of a client using it. Start the script from Listing 6-2 as a server in one terminal window. I'll assume you already have the certificate files ca.crt and localhost.pem from the book's source code repository's chapter06 directory.

```
$ /usr/bin/python3.4 safe_tls.py -s localhost.pem '' 1060
```

This server welcomes connections utilising the most modern protocol versions and cyphers; in fact, if given the chance, it will negotiate a strong configuration with Perfect Forward Security enabled. Using only Python's defaults, see what occurs if you connect as indicated in Listing 6-3:

```
$ /usr/bin/python3.4 test_tls.py -a ca.crt localhost 1060
Address we want to talk to.......... ('localhost', 1060)
```

```
Peer certificate.................. provided
Name(s) on peer certificate........ localhost
Whether name(s) match the hostname.. Yes
Certificates loaded of type crl..... 0
Certificates loaded of type x509.... 1
Certificates loaded of type x509_ca. 0
Protocol version negotiated........ TLSv1.2
Cipher chosen for this connection... ECDHE-RSA-AES128-GCM-SHA256
Cipher defined in TLS version....... TLSv1/SSLv3
Cipher key has this many bits....... 128
Compression algorithm in use....... none
```

The ECDHE-RSA-AES128-GCM-SHA256 combination is one of the greatest that OpenSSL has to offer right now! The safe tls.py server, on the other hand, will refuse to communicate with a client that only supports Windows XP encryption levels. Restart the safe tls.py server and connect with the following arguments this time:

```
$ /usr/bin/python3.4 test_tls.py -p SSLv3 -a ca.crt localhost 1060
Address we want to talk to.......... ('localhost', 1060)
Traceback (most recent call last):
  ...
ssl.SSLError: [SSL: SSLV3_ALERT_HANDSHAKE_FAILURE] sslv3 alert
handshake failure (_ssl.c:598)
```

The meticulous server settings offered by Python bluntly reject the obsolete SSLv3 protocol. Even when used in conjunction with contemporary protocols, old end-of-life cyphers such as RC4 will fail.

```
test tls.py /usr/bin/python3.4 -
localhost 1060 C 'RC4' -a ca.crt
('localhost', 1060) is the address we wish to talk to.
(Last call) Traceback (most recent call):
  ...
ssl.SSLError: [SSL: SSLV3_ALERT_HANDSHAKE_FAILURE] sslv3 alert
handshake failure (_ssl.c:598)
```

However, when you put the "safe" script in the role of a client, its behaviour changes dramatically. This is due to the theory, discussed earlier, that it is the server's responsibility to decide how secure the connection should be, whereas client authors generally just want things to work if they can do so without completely exposing the data. Remember that the safe server refused to speak RC4 when tested previously. Examine what happens if you use the tls safe.py client with RC4 instead. First, shut down any existing servers and execute the test script as the server, with the cypher set to -C.

```
$ /usr/bin/python3.4 test_tls.py -C 'RC4' -s localhost.pem '' 1060

Interface where we are listening.... ('', 1060)
```

Then try connecting with the safe tls.py script, which utilises Python 3.4's default context, in a new terminal window.

```
$ /usr/bin/python3.4 safe_tls.py -a ca.crt localhost 1060
```

The connection is successful even while using the safe default context! You can see that RC4 was selected as the streaming cypher in the server window. You may confirm that RC4 is as low as the safe script is willing to go by using the –C option with different strings. Ciphers or algorithms such as MD5 will be rejected outright as being unsuitable for a client attempting to ensure maximum compatibility with any server with which the user may wish to communicate.

To learn more about creating a custom protocol and cypher, consult the ssl module documentation and then the official OpenSSL documentation. If your system supports it, you can use the native OpenSSL command line to print out all of the cyphers that match a given cypher string—the same text that you could give to Listing 6-3 with the –C option or specify with the set cipher() method in your own code. Additionally, when cryptography advances and OpenSSL on your system is upgraded, the command line will allow you to evaluate how various cypher rules modify their effect over time. For the time being, here are the cyphers that match the ECDH+AES128 cypher string on the Ubuntu laptop on which I am typing this:

```
$ openssl ciphers -v 'ECDH+AES128'

ECDHE-RSA-AES128-GCM-SHA256 TLSv1.2 Kx=ECDH Au=RSA Enc=AESGCM(128)
Mac=AEAD

ECDHE-ECDSA-AES128-GCM-SHA256 TLSv1.2 Kx=ECDH Au=ECDSA Enc=AESGCM(128)
Mac=AEAD

ECDHE-RSA-AES128-SHA256    TLSv1.2   Kx=ECDH   Au=RSA   Enc=AES(128)
Mac=SHA256

ECDHE-ECDSA-AES128-SHA256  TLSv1.2   Kx=ECDH   Au=ECDSA  Enc=AES(128)
Mac=SHA256
```

ECDHE-RSA-AES128-SHA SSLv3 Kx=ECDH Au=RSA Enc=AES(128) Mac=SHA1

ECDHE-ECDSA-AES128-SHA SSLv3 Kx=ECDH Au=ECDSA Enc=AES(128) Mac=SHA1

AECDH-AES128-SHA SSLv3 Kx=ECDH Au=None Enc=AES(128) Mac=SHA1

ECDH-RSA-AES128-GCM-SHA256 TLSv1.2 Kx=ECDH/RSA Au=ECDH Enc=AESGCM(128) Mac=AEAD

ECDH-ECDSA-AES128-GCM-SHA256 TLSv1.2 Kx=ECDH/ECDSA Au=ECDH Enc=AESGCM(128) Mac=AEAD

ECDH-RSA-AES128-SHA256 TLSv1.2 Kx=ECDH/RSA Au=ECDH Enc=AES(128) Mac=SHA256

ECDH-ECDSA-AES128-SHA256 TLSv1.2 Kx=ECDH/ECDSA Au=ECDH Enc=AES(128) Mac=SHA256

ECDH-RSA-AES128-SHA SSLv3 Kx=ECDH/RSA Au=ECDH Enc=AES(128) Mac=SHA1

ECDH-ECDSA-AES128-SHA SSLv3 Kx=ECDH/ECDSA Au=ECDH Enc=AES(128) Mac=SHA1

Under the setting set_ cipher('ECDH+AES128'), the OpenSSL library will accept any of these combinations. Again, if at all feasible, use the default context; otherwise, test the exact client and server you intend to use, attempting to select one or two strong cyphers that they both support. However, if you find yourself doing more exploring and troubleshooting than that, I hope Listing 6-4 proves to be a valuable tool in narrowing down OpenSSL's behaviour. When you have a chance, download a new version of Listing 6-4 from the URL in the remark at the top of the page, as the version in the book will become out-of-date;

Conclusion

This chapter covers a subject on which few people are fully knowledgeable: the use of cryptography to safeguard data in transit via a TCP socket, with a focus on Python's TLS protocol (formerly known as SSL).

In a normal TLS transaction, the client asks the server for a certificate, which is a digital document that verifies an individual's identity. It must be signed by a trusted authority by both the client and the server, and it must include a public key, which the server must then show it has a copy of. The client should double-check that the certificate's identity matches the hostname it believes it is connected to. Finally, the client and server agree on cypher, compression, and key parameters, which are then used to safeguard data flowing in both directions across the socket.

Many administrators don't bother to support TLS in their applications at all. Instead, they conceal the apps behind industrial-strength front ends like Apache, nginx, or

HAProxy, which can handle TLS for them. Instead of implementing TLS in their own application, services that have content delivery networks in front of them must outsource TLS responsibility.

Though there are third-party libraries that can execute TLS in Python, the language's built-in capabilities come from the Standard Library's OpenSSL-powered ssl module. Basic encrypted channels can be set up with merely a server certificate if ssl is available and running properly on your operating system and version of Python.

Create a "context" object, open a connection, and then call the context's wrap socket() method to hand over control of the connection to the TLS protocol. Python applications written for Python 3.4 and newer (I strongly recommend using at least version 3.4 if your application is going to do its own TLS) will generally follow the pattern of creating a "context" object, opening a connection, and then calling the context's wrap socket() method to hand over The context-connect-wrap pattern is the most ubiquitous and versatile, despite the fact that the ssl module provides a few of shortcut functions that you'll notice in older programmes.

Many Python clients and servers can simply accept the default "context" object returned by ssl.create default context(), which tries to make servers slightly strict in the settings that they will accept while making clients slightly lenient so that they can connect to servers that only have older versions of TLS available. Other Python applications will wish to create their own SSLContext objects to customise the protocol and cypher to their needs. In either event, you can use either the test script from this chapter or another TLS tool to investigate the behaviours that occur from the settings. The Standard Library supports a number of protocols that can be protected with TLS if desired, the majority of which are covered in the book's later chapters. If you can give an SSLContext object, they will all work. Because Python 3.4 was only recently published, and most Python programmers are still using Python 2, third-party libraries currently provide inadequate support for contexts. Both circumstances should, in theory, improve over time.

Once you've implemented TLS in your application, it's always a good idea to put it through its paces with tools that will try a variety of connections with changing parameters. Outside of Python, there are third-party tools and online sites for testing TLS clients and servers, and the tool described in Listing 6-4 can be used with Python 3.4 directly on your own system if you want to experiment with different OpenSSL settings to see how it negotiates and acts.

CHAPTER 7

Architecture
of the Server

The author of a network service has two difficulties. The first is the fundamental difficulty of building code that will appropriately respond to incoming requests and craft acceptable answers. The second task is to embed this network code in a Windows service or a Unix daemon that starts automatically when the system boots, logs its activity to a persistent store, raises an alert if it can't connect to its database or back-end data store, and either completely protects itself against all possible failure modes or can be quickly restarted if it fails.

The first of these two challenges is the topic of this work. The second challenge, keeping a process running on your operating system of choice, is not only a topic worthy of a whole book, but it is also one that would take this book far away from its core theme of network programming. As a result, only one portion of this chapter will be dedicated to introducing the idea of deployment before going on to the main issue of how network servers might be created as software.

The way we deal with network servers will naturally fall into three categories. I'll start with a simple single-threaded server, comparable to the UDP and TCP servers discussed in Chapters 2 and 3, and concentrate on its drawbacks: It can only serve one client at a time, making any other clients wait, and it will almost certainly keep the system CPU almost fully idle even when talking to that client. Once you've grasped the problem, you'll look at the two competing solutions: duplicating the single-threaded server across several threads or processes, or taking the multiplexing responsibility away from the operating system and performing it yourself using asynchronous network activities.

Structure

- A Few Remarks on Deployment
- A Basic Protocol
- A single-threaded server.
- Multiprocess and Threaded Servers
- The SocketServer Framework of the Past
- Async Servers
- Callback-Style asyncio
- Coroutine-Style asyncio
- The asyncore Legacy Module
- The Best of Both Worlds
- Under the Influence of inetd
- Conclusion

Objectives:

You will first implement each pattern from the ground up while studying threaded versus asynchronous network programming, and then you will look at frameworks that implement each pattern on your behalf. All of the frameworks I show are from the Python Standard Library, but the text will also mention prominent third-party competitors when they exist. The majority of the scripts in this chapter can also be run in Python 2, but the most advanced framework introduced—the new asyncio module—is only available in Python 3, and it represents a significant step forward in standardisation that can only be appreciated by programmers willing to upgrade.

A Few Remarks on Deployment

A network service can be deployed to a single machine or a group of machines. Clients can connect to a service that is hosted on a single machine by entering its IP address. A service that runs on several machines necessitates a more complex strategy. You may give each client the address or hostname of a single instance of the service, such as one that is running in the same machine room as the client, but this will not provide any redundancy. Clients hardwired to its hostname or IP address will be unable to connect if that instance of the service goes down.

When a service's name is accessed, a more robust solution is to have your DNS server report every IP address where the service is located, and develop clients that fall back to the second or third IP address if the first one fails.

The most scalable strategy in the market today is to put your services behind a load balancer, which clients connect to directly and then directs each incoming connection to an actual server behind it. When a server goes down, the load balancer simply stops delivering requests to it until it comes back up, making server failures almost undetectable to a large client base. The largest Internet services combine these approaches: each machine room has a load balancer and server farm, as well as a public DNS name that delivers the IP addresses for the load balancer whose machine room appears to be physically nearest to you.

Regardless of how basic or grandiose your service architecture is, you'll need a mechanism to deploy your Python server code to a physical or virtual computer. When it comes to deployment, there are two schools of thinking. The traditional approach is to include all of the capabilities of a service in every server programme you write: double-forking to become a Unix daemon (or registering as a Windows service), system-level logging, a configuration file, and a way to start, stop, and restart it. You can do this by using a third-party library that has previously handled these issues or by starting from scratch with your own code.

Manifestos like The Twelve-Factor App have advocated a competing approach. They advocate for a minimalist approach in which each service is written as a regular programme that runs in the forefront and does not attempt to become a daemon. Instead of expecting a system-wide configuration file, such a software gets whatever configuration parameters it needs from its environment (the sys.environ dictionary in Python). It connects to any back-end services specified by the environment. It also writes its logging messages to the screen, using a technique as simple as Python's own print() function. Open and listen at whatever port the environment setup recommends to accept network requests.

Developers can easily test a service created in this simple approach by running it from a shell prompt. However, by simply surrounding the application with the appropriate scaffolding, it may be turned into a daemon or system service, or deployed to a web-scale server farm. For example, the scaffolding may get environment variable settings from a central configuration service, link the application's standard output and standard error to a remote logging server, and restart the service if it fails or appears to freeze. The programmer can be confident that the service code is executing in production exactly as it is in development because the programme itself is unaware of this and is simply outputting to standard output as usual.

Large platform-as-a-service providers now host such apps for you, spinning up dozens or even hundreds of clones of your application behind a single public-facing domain name and TCP load balancer, then aggregating all of the resulting logs for analysis. You can upload Python application code directly to some providers. Others prefer that you bundle your code, a Python interpreter, and any dependencies you need inside a container ("Docker" containers in particular are becoming a popular mechanism) that you can test on your own laptop before deploying, ensuring that your Python code will run in production from an image that is byte-for-byte identical to the one you used in testing. In either case, you are relieved of the responsibility of developing a service that spawns numerous processes; the platform will handle all redundancy and duplication for you.

In the Python community, there have long been modest efforts to pull programmers out of the business of writing stand-alone services. The widely used supervisord utility is a good example. It can execute several copies of your software, redirect standard output and errors to log files, restart a process if it fails, and even issue alarms if a service fails too often.

If you do decide to design a process that knows how to change itself into a daemon, despite all of these temptations, you should be able to discover decent methods for doing so in the Python community. PEP 3143 (available at http://python.org), whose section "Other daemon implementations" provides a well-curated collection of resources on the steps required, is a solid starting point. The supervisord source code, as well as the documentation for Python's Standard Library module logging, may be of interest.

The challenge of how to leverage an operating system network stack with an operating system process to serve network requests is the same whether you have a standalone Python process or a platform-powered web-scale service. For the rest of the chapter, you'll focus on this issue, with the goal of keeping the system as active as possible so that clients wait as little as possible for their network requests to be answered.

A Basic Protocol

The examples in this chapter use a simple TCP protocol in which the client asks one of three plain-text ASCII inquiries and then waits for the server to complete its response. This keeps your attention on the many alternatives given by server design. The client can ask as many questions as it likes while the socket is open, and then close the connection without warning when it runs out of questions, just like in HTTP. The ASCII question mark character is used to mark the end of each inquiry.

Beautiful is better than?

The response is then returned, separated by a period.

Ugly.

Each of the three question-and-answer pairings is based on an aphorism from the Zen of Python, a poem about the Python language's inner consistent architecture. Any time you need inspiration or want to reread the poetry, open Python and type import this.

A number of routines are defined in Listing 7-1 to build a client and numerous servers around this protocol, which you will see has no command-line interface of its own. The module exists purely for later listings to import as a support module so that they can utilise its patterns without having to repeat them.

Listing 7-1. Supporting Data and Routines for the Toy Zen-of-Python Protocol

```
#!/usr/bin/env python3
# Network Programming in Python: The Basics
# Constants and routines for supporting a certain network conversation.

import argparse, socket, time


aphorisms = {b'Beautiful is better than?': b'Ugly.',
b'Explicit is better than?': b'Implicit.',
b'Simple is better than?': b'Complex.'}
def get_answer(aphorism):
"""Return the string response to a particular Zen-of-Python aphorism."""
time.sleep(0.0) # increase to simulate an expensive operation
return aphorisms.get(aphorism, b'Error: unknown aphorism.')
def parse_command_line(description):
"""Parse command line and return a socket address."""
parser = argparse.ArgumentParser(description=description)
parser.add_argument('host', help='IP or hostname')
```

```python
parser.add_argument('-p', metavar='port', type=int, default=1060,
help='TCP port (default 1060)')
args = parser.parse_args()
address = (args.host, args.p)
return address
def create_srv_socket(address):
"""Build and return a listening server socket."""
listener = socket.socket(socket.AF_INET, socket.SOCK_STREAM)
listener.setsockopt(socket.SOL_SOCKET, socket.SO_REUSEADDR, 1)
listener.bind(address)
listener.listen(64)
print('Listening at {}'.format(address))
return listener
def accept_connections_forever(listener):
"""Forever answer incoming connections on a listening socket."""
while True:
sock, address = listener.accept()
print('Accepted connection from {}'.format(address))
handle_conversation(sock, address)
def handle_conversation(sock, address):
"""Converse with a client over `sock` until they are done talking."""
try:
while True:
handle_request(sock)
except EOFError:
print('Client socket to {} has closed'.format(address))
except Exception as e:
print('Client {} error: {}'.format(address, e))
finally:
sock.close()
def handle_request(sock):
"""Receive a single client request on `sock` and send the answer."""
```

```
aphorism = recv_until(sock, b'?')
answer = get_answer(aphorism)
sock.sendall(answer)
def recv_until(sock, suffix):
"""Receive bytes over socket `sock` until we receive the `suffix`."""
message = sock.recv(4096)
if not message:
raise EOFError('socket closed')
while not message.endswith(suffix):
data = sock.recv(4096)
if not data:
raise IOError('received {!r} then socket closed'.format(message))
message += data
return message
```

In the aphorisms dictionary, the three questions that a client can expect a server to comprehend are listed as keys, and their responses are stored as values. The get answer() function is a shorthand for performing a safe lookup for an answer in this dictionary, with a brief error message returned if the aphorism is not recognised. It's worth noting that client requests always end in a question mark, and that responses, including the fallback error message, always end in a period. The small protocol's framing is provided by these two punctuation marks.

The next two functions provide some shared startup code that will be used by all servers. Create srv socket() can generate the listening TCP socket that a server requires to handle incoming connections, while parse command line() provides a common technique for processing command-line parameters.

The listing begins to highlight the central patterns of a server operation in the last four procedures.

The cascade of four functions essentially replicates movements you learned in Chapters 3 and 5, which dealt with building a TCP server for a listening socket and framing data and handling errors, respectively.

- **accept connections forever()** is a simple listen() loop that uses print() to announce each joining client before passing the socket to the next function.

- **handle conversation()** is an error-catching procedure that wraps an endless number of request-response cycles in such a way that any difficulties with the client socket will not cause the programme to fail. The one exception is EOFError is trapped in its own world. because it is through this phrase that the innermost data-reception loop will indicate that a client has completed making requests and has now hung up—which, in this protocol (as in, HTTP), is a common occurrence rather than a truly unique one. All other exceptions, on the other hand, are handled as After being caught, mistakes are reported using print(). (Recall that all Python mistakes are normal.) inherit from Exception and, as a result, will be caught by this except clause!) Regardless of the code path by which this function terminates, the finally clause ensures that the client socket is always closed. Because already-closed file and socket objects in Python allow close() to be called as many times as a programme desires, running close() like this is always safe.

- **handle request()** conducts a single back-and-forth with the client, reading its question and then responding with a response. Because the send() method alone cannot guarantee the delivery of a whole payload, send all() is used with caution.

- The framing is done by **recv until()**, which follows the procedure mentioned in Chapter 5. The socket's recv() function is called repeatedly until the accumulated byte string qualifies as a complete question.

These procedures are the toolbox from which you'll construct a number of servers.

A client application is required to test the various servers in this chapter. One is offered as a basic command-line tool in Listing 7-2.

Listing 7-2:. Example Zen-of-Python Protocol Client Program.

```
#!/usr/bin/env python3
# Network Programming in Python: The Basics
# Simple Zen-of-Python client that asks three questions then
disconnects.

import argparse, random, socket, zen_utils
def client(address, cause_error=False):
sock = socket.socket(socket.AF_INET, socket.SOCK_STREAM)
sock.connect(address)
aphorisms = list(zen_utils.aphorisms)
if cause_error:
sock.sendall(aphorisms[0][:-1])
```

```
return

for aphorism in random.sample(aphorisms, 3):
sock.sendall(aphorism)
        print(aphorism, zen_utils.recv_until(sock, b'.'))
sock.close()
if __name__ == '__main__':
        parser = argparse.ArgumentParser(description='Example client')
        parser.add_argument('host', help='IP or hostname')
        parser.add_argument('-e', action='store_true', help='cause an
error')
        parser.add_argument('-p',       metavar='port',       type=int,
default=1060,
                        help='TCP port (default 1060)')
        args = parser.parse_args()
        address = (args.host, args.p)
        client(address, args.e
```

When cause error is False, this client starts a TCP socket and sends three aphorisms, waiting for the server to respond with a response after each one. However, if you want to test what any of the servers in this chapter do in the event of a mistake, you may use the -e option to make this client send an unfinished inquiry and then hang up on the server abruptly. If a server is up and running properly, you should see three questions and their answers.

```
$ python client.py 127.0.0.1
b'Beautiful is better than?' b'Ugly.'
b'Simple is better than?' b'Complex.'
b'Explicit is better than?' b'Implicit.'
```

This client and the servers in this chapter utilise port 1060, as do many other examples in this book, but accept the -p option to indicate an alternative if that port is not accessible on your system.

A single-threaded server.

The zen utils module of Listing 7-1 provides a rich set of utilities that lowers the job of constructing a simple single-threaded server—the simplest conceivable architecture, as you saw in Chapter 3—to just the three-line function of Listing 7-3.

Listing 7-3. The Simplest Possible Server Is Single-Threaded.

```
#!/usr/bin/env python3
# Network Programming in Python: The Basics
# Single-threaded server that serves one client at a time; others
must wait.
import zen_utils
if __name__ == '__main__':
address  =  zen_utils.parse_command_line('simple   single-threaded
server')
listener = zen_utils.create_srv_socket(address)
zen_utils.accept_connections_forever(listener)
```

This server, like the servers you developed in Chapters 2 and 3, requires only one command-line argument: the interface on which the server should wait for incoming connections. Specify the typical local host IP address to secure the server from other users on your LAN or network.

```
$ python srv_single.py 127.0.0.1
Listening at ('127.0.0.1', 1060)
```

Alternatively, you can be more brave and offer the service across all of your system's interfaces by specifying an empty string, which Python understands as "every interface on the current machine."

```
$ python srv_single.py ''
Listening at ('', 1060)
```

In either case, the server publishes a line indicating that it has successfully opened its server port and then waits for incoming connections. If you wish to play with those, the server also has a -h help option and a -p option to specify a port other than 1060. To test how the server works once it's up and running, run the client script described in the previous section. The server will report client activity in the terminal window where it is executing as your clients connect and disconnect.

```
Accepted connection from ('127.0.0.1', 40765)
Client socket to ('127.0.0.1', 1060) has closed
Accepted connection from ('127.0.0.1', 40768)
Client socket to ('127.0.0.1', 1060) has closed
```

This design is all you need if your network service only has a single customer making a single connection at a time. This server is ready for the next connection as soon as the last one ends. For as long as there is a connection, this server is either stuck in a recv() function, waiting for the operating system to wake it up when fresh data arrives, or it is putting together an answer as rapidly as it can and broadcasting it without additional delay. Only when the client is not ready to receive data can send() or sendall() block. When the client is ready, the data will be transferred and the server will be unlocked, allowing it to return to its recv() function. As a result, replies are provided to the client as rapidly as they can be computed and received in all conditions.

When a second client tries to join while the server is still conversing with the first, the single-threaded design's flaw becomes evident. If the integer parameter to listen() is bigger than zero, the operating system will at least attempt to establish a connection with the second incoming client using a three-way TCP handshake, saving time when the server is eventually ready to talk. . However, until the server's interaction with the first client is complete, that connection will sit in the operating system's listen queue. The second client's connection will be available to the server and its initial request over that socket will be able to be responded only after the first client discussion is completed and the server function has looped back to its next call to accept().

It's simple to launch a denial-of-service attack against this single-threaded server: connect and never disconnect. The server will be stuck in recv() indefinitely, waiting for your data. If the server author gets creative and uses sock to specify a timeout. To avoid waiting indefinitely, use settimeout(), then tweak your denial-of-service tool to issue requests frequently enough that the timeout is never reached. The server will never be accessible to any other clients.

Finally, the single-threaded design wastes server CPU and system resources by preventing the server from performing other tasks while waiting for the client to send the next request. Run the single-threaded server under the control of the trace module from the Standard Library to see how long each line takes.

$ python3.4 -m trace -tg --ignore-dir=/usr srv_single.py "

Each line of output indicates the time in seconds since the server was launched when a line of Python code began to execute. You'll notice that most lines begin executing as soon as the previous line completes, either in the same hundredth or the next hundredth of a second. However, whenever the server needs to wait for a response from the client, execution is halted and must wait. Here's an example of a test run:

```
3.02 zen_utils.py(40):  print('Accepted connection...'...)
3.02 zen_utils.py(41):  handle_conversation(sock, address)
☐
3.02 zen_utils.py(57):  aphorism = recv_until(sock, b'?')
3.03 zen_utils.py(63):  message = sock.recv(4096)
3.03 zen_utils.py(64):  if not message:
3.03 zen_utils.py(66):  while not message.endswith(suffix):
☐
3.03 zen_utils.py(57):  aphorism = recv_until(sock, b'?')
3.03 zen_utils.py(63):  message = sock.recv(4096)
3.08 zen_utils.py(64):  if not message:
3.08 zen_utils.py(66):  while not message.endswith(suffix):
☐
3.08 zen_utils.py(57):  aphorism = recv_until(sock, b'?')
3.08 zen_utils.py(63):  message = sock.recv(4096)
3.12 zen_utils.py(64):  if not message:
3.12 zen_utils.py(66):  while not message.endswith(suffix):
☐
3.12 zen_utils.py(57):  aphorism = recv_until(sock, b'?')
3.12 zen_utils.py(63):  message = sock.recv(4096)
3.16 zen_utils.py(64):  if not message:
3.16 zen_utils.py(65):  raise EOFError('socket closed')
☐
3.16 zen_utils.py(48):  except EOFError:
3.16 zen_utils.py(49):  print('Client socket...has closed'...)
3.16 zen_utils.py(53):  sock.close()
3.16 zen_utils.py(39):  sock, address = listener.accept()
```

This is a complete discussion with the client.py programme, including three requests and responses. It has to wait for the client three times during the 0.14 seconds of processing time between the first and last lines of this trace, for a total of about 0.05 + 0.04 + 0.04 = 0.13 seconds spent idle! This suggests that during this exchange, the CPU is only 0.01 / 0.14 = 7% occupied. Of course, this is just an estimate. The fact that we're operating under trace causes the server to slow down and use more

CPU, and the resolution of these values is already imprecise. However, if you use more powerful technologies, you will find that this finding is confirmed. Unless they're doing a lot of in-CPU work during each request, single-threaded servers are terrible at making the server machine operate to its maximum capability. While other customers wait in line to be served, the CPU remains idle.

There are two technical details that are worth mentioning. The first recv() call returns immediately; only the second and third recv() calls, as well as the final recv() call before learning that the connection has been closed, exhibit a delay before returning data. This is because the network stacks of the operating system smartly include the text of the initial request in the same three-way handshake that establishes the TCP connection. As a result, by the time the connection is properly established and accept() may return, data is already waiting to be returned from recv()!

Another point to note is that send() has no delay. This is due to the fact that on a POSIX system, it returns as soon as the outgoing data has been enrolled in the operating system's outgoing buffers. Just because send() has returned does not mean that the system has really transmitted any data! The application can only force the operating system to halt its progress and wait for the result of transmitting by turning around and listening for more client data.

Let's return to our original topic. How may a single-threaded server's constraints be overcome? The rest of this chapter looks at two competing strategies for preventing a single client from having complete control over a server. Both strategies allow the server to communicate with multiple clients at the same time. First, I'll go over threads (processes also work), which assign the task of transferring the server's attention between different clients to the operating system. Then I'll go on to asynchronous server architecture, where I'll teach you how to manage your own attention shifts so that you may speak with multiple clients at once in a single thread of control.

Multiprocess and Threaded Servers

If you want your server to communicate with multiple clients at the same time, one popular solution is to use your operating system's built-in support for allowing multiple threads of control to pass through the same section of code independently, either by creating threads with the same memory footprint or by creating processes that run independently of one another.

The benefit of this technique is its simplicity: you may launch many copies of the same code that operates your single-threaded server.

Its drawback is that the number of clients with whom you can communicate is restricted by the scaling of your operating system's concurrency features. Even an idle or slow client will demand the attention of an entire thread or process, which will consume both system RAM and a slot in the process table even if it is blocked in recv(). Operating systems rarely scale well when thousands or more threads are running at the same time, and the context switches necessary when the system's attention shifts from one client to the next will slow down your service as it grows more popular.

A multithreaded or multiprocess server can be expected to be made up of a master thread of control that performs a tight accept() loop before handing off incoming client sockets to a waiting queue of workers. . Fortunately, the operating system makes things a lot easier for you: each thread can have its own copy of the listening server socket and run its own accept() command. If all threads are currently busy, the operating system will assign each new client connection to the thread that is waiting for its accept() to complete, or it will queue the connection until one of them is available. An example can be found in Listing 7-4.

Listing 7-4. Multithreaded Server

```python
#!/usr/bin/env python3
# Network Programming in Python: The Basics
# Using multiple threads to serve several clients in parallel.
import zen_utils
from threading import Thread


def start_threads(listener, workers=4):
t = (listener,)
for i in range(workers):
Thread(target=zen_utils.accept_connections_forever, args=t).start()
if __name__ == '__main__':
address = zen_utils.parse_command_line('multi-threaded server')
listener = zen_utils.create_srv_socket(address)
start_threads(listener)
```

Note that this is simply one conceivable multithreaded programme design: the main thread spawns n server threads and then exits, certain that those n threads would keep the process alive indefinitely. Other possibilities exist. The main thread, for example, could live on and become a server thread. Alternatively, it may serve as a monitor, occasionally checking to see if the n server threads are still active and restarting replacement threads if any of them die. A change of pace from stitching.

To multiprocessing, add a thread. Each control thread would have its own memory image and file descriptor area, according to the process. Increasing the operating system's cost, but better isolating the threads and making it far more difficult for them to crash the main monitor thread.

All of these patterns, which you can learn about in the threading and multiprocessing module documentation as well as in books and guides on Python concurrency, have one thing in common: they all dedicate a relatively expensive operating system–visible thread of control to every connected client, whether or not that client is currently making requests. However, because your server code can remain unchanged while being controlled by multiple threads (assuming that each thread establishes its own database connection and opens files, removing the need for resource coordination between threads), it's simple to test the multithreaded approach on your server's workload. If it shows capable of handling your request load, its simplicity makes it an especially appealing strategy for internal services that aren't accessible to the public, where an adversary can't simply open idle connections until your pool of threads or processes is depleted.

The SocketServer Framework of the Past

The pattern of leveraging operating system–visible threads of control for handling numerous client interactions at the same time outlined in the previous section is common enough that a framework embodying the pattern is integrated into the Python Standard Library. With a 1990s design riddled with object orientation and several inherited mix-ins, it's worth a quick example both to show how the multithreaded pattern may be generalised and to familiarise you with the module in case you ever need to maintain old code that utilises it.

The socketserver module (known as SocketServer in Python 2) separates the server pattern, which understands how to open a listening socket and accept new client connections, from the handler pattern, which understands how to speak over an open socket. As shown in Listing 7-5, these two patterns are merged by creating a server object with a handler class as one of its arguments.

Listing 7-5:. Built on the Standard Library Server Pattern, a Threaded Server

```
#!/usr/bin/env python3
# Network Programming in Python: The Basics
# Uses the legacy "socketserver" Standard Library module to write a
server.
from socketserver import BaseRequestHandler, TCPServer, ThreadingMixIn
```

```
import zen_utils

class ZenHandler(BaseRequestHandler):
 def handle(self):
 zen_utils.handle_conversation(self.request, self.client_address)

class ZenServer(ThreadingMixIn, TCPServer):
      allow_reuse_address = 1
 # address_family = socket.AF_INET6 # uncomment if you need IPv6
if __name__ == '__main__':
      address = zen_utils.parse_command_line('legacy "SocketServer"
server')
 server = ZenServer(address, ZenHandler)
      server.serve_forever()
```

Instead of threads, the programmer can have entirely isolated processes service incoming clients by substituting ForkingMixIn for ThreadingMixIn.

When compared to the earlier Listing 7-4, which started a fixed number of threads that could be chosen by a server administrator based on how many threads of control a given server and operating system can easily manage without a significant degradation in performance, the vast weakness of this approach should be obvious. In contrast, Listing 7-5 allows the pool of connecting clients to decide how many threads are started, with no limit on how many threads end up operating on the server! An attacker can easily bring the server to its knees as a result of this. This Standard Library module, therefore, cannot be recommended for production and customer-facing services.

Async Servers

How can you keep the CPU busy between giving a response to a client and receiving its next request without having to pay for an operating system–visible thread of control per client? The answer is that you can create your server in an asynchronous pattern, which means that instead of blocking and waiting for data to come or depart from a single client, the code is willing to listen to a long list of client sockets and react whenever one of them is ready for more interaction.

Two aspects of modern operating system network stacks enable this pattern. The first is that they provide a system function that allows a process to block waiting on a full list of client sockets rather than just one, allowing a single thread to service hundreds or thousands of client sockets at once. The second feature is that a socket can be configured as nonblocking, which means that it will never, ever block the calling thread in a send() or recv() call, and will always return from the send() or recv() system call immediately regardless of whether or not more progress can be made in the conversation. If progress is slow, the caller must try again later when the client appears to be ready for more interaction.

The term asynchronous refers to the fact that the client code never waits for a specific client, and that the thread of control that runs the code is not synchronised, or made to wait in lockstep, with any one client's interaction. Instead, it distributes the work of servicing among all connected clients at will.

Operating systems enable asynchronous mode through a variety of calls. The POSIX call select() is the oldest, but it has various inefficiencies that have led to newer equivalents such as poll() on Linux and epoll() on BSD. W. Richard Stevens' book UNIX Network Programming (Prentice Hall, 2003) is the classic reference on the subject. Because the goal of this chapter isn't for you to create your own asynchronous control loop, I'll concentrate on poll() and skip the others. Instead, you're using a poll()-powered loop as an illustration of what happens behind the scenes of a full asynchronous framework, which is how you'll want to implement asynchrony in your projects. In the next sections, we'll look at a few different frameworks.

The complete internals of a raw asynchronous server for your small Zen protocol are shown in Listing 7-6.

Listing 7-6. A Raw Asynchronous Event Loop

```python
#!/usr/bin/env python3
# Network Programming in Python: The Basics
# Asynchronous I/O driven directly by the poll() system call.
import select, zen_utils
def all_events_forever(poll_object):
 while True:
 for fd, event in poll_object.poll():
 yield fd, event
def serve(listener):
 sockets = {listener.fileno(): listener}
 addresses = {}
```

```
bytes_received = {}
bytes_to_send = {}


poll_object = select.poll()
poll_object.register(listener, select.POLLIN)
        for fd, event in all_events_forever(poll_object):
             sock = sockets[fd]
# Socket closed: remove it from our data structures.
             if event & (select.POLLHUP | select.POLLERR | select.
POLLNVAL):
address = addresses.pop(sock)
rb = bytes_received.pop(sock, b'')
sb = bytes_to_send.pop(sock, b'')
if rb:
print('Client {} sent {} but then closed'.format(address, rb))
elif sb:
print('Client {} closed before we sent {}'.format(address, sb))
                else:
print('Client {} closed socket normally'.format(address))
poll_object.unregister(fd)
del sockets[fd]
 # New socket: add it to our data structures.
 elif sock is listener:
                sock, address = sock.accept()
print('Accepted connection from {}'.format(address))
sock.setblocking(False) # force socket.timeout if we blunder
                sockets[sock.fileno()] = sock
        addresses[sock] = address
                poll_object.register(sock, select.POLLIN)
                # Incoming data: keep receiving until we see the suffix.
                elif event & select.POLLIN:
        more_data = sock.recv(4096)
```

```
                            if not more_data: # end-of-file
sock.close() # next poll() will POLLNVAL, and thus clean up
                          continue
                 data = bytes_received.pop(sock, b'') + more_data
                 if data.endswith(b'?'):
                 bytes_to_send[sock] = zen_utils.get_answer(data)
                     poll_object.modify(sock, select.POLLOUT)
                     else:
                         bytes_received[sock] = data
         # Socket ready to send: keep sending until all bytes are
         delivered.
    elif event & select.POLLOUT:
    data = bytes_to_send.pop(sock)
    n = sock.send(data)
    if n < len(data):
    bytes_to_send[sock] = data[n:]
    else:
    poll_object.modify(sock, select.POLLIN)
if __name__ == '__main__':
    address = zen_utils.parse_command_line('low-level async server')
    listener = zen_utils.create_srv_socket(address)
    serve(listener)
```

Instead of relying on the operating system to swap contexts when activity shifts from one client to another, this event loop takes control of keeping the state of each client dialogue in its own data structures. Because poll() can yield several events per call, the server has two loops: a while loop for repeatedly calling poll() and an inner loop for processing each event returned by poll(). To avoid the main server loop being buried two levels of indentation deep, you hide these two levels of iteration behind a generator.

When poll() indicates that file descriptor n is ready for more action, a dictionary of sockets is maintained. The matching Python socket may be found here. Even when the socket has closed and the operating system no longer reminds you of the endpoint to which it was connected, you remember the addresses of your sockets so that you can print diagnostic messages with the right remote address.

The bytes received dictionary, where you stuff incoming data while waiting for a request to complete, and the bytes to send dictionary, where outgoing bytes wait until the operating system can schedule them for transmission, are the real heart of the asynchronous server.

These data structures, when combined with the event for which you inform poll() that you're waiting on each socket, constitute a complete state machine for handling a client dialogue one tiny step at a time.

1. A ready-to-connect client appears first as activity on the listening server socket, which you keep in the POLLIN ("poll input") state at all times. When this happens, you run accept(), save the socket and its address in your dictionaries, and tell the poll object that you're ready to receive data from the new client socket.

2. You **recv()** up to 4KB of data when the client socket is supplied to you with a POLLIN event. If the request does not include a terminating question mark, save the data to the bytes received dictionary and return to the top of the loop to poll() again. Otherwise, you've got a full question, and you can answer to the client's request by seeking up the appropriate response and adding it to your bytes to send dictionary. This necessitates a pivotal change: moving the socket from POLLIN mode, where you want to be notified when more data comes, to POLLOUT mode, where you want to be told as soon as the outgoing buffers are free, because you're now sending rather than receiving data.

3. When the outgoing buffers on the client socket can receive at least one byte, the poll() function now tells you with POLLOUT, and you respond by attempting a send() of everything you have left to transmit and keeping just the bytes that send() could not fit into the outgoing buffers.

4. Finally, a POLLOUT appears, and its send() function allows you to complete the transmission of all remaining outbound data. A request-response cycle is completed at this point, and you flip the socket back into POLLIN state to handle another request.

5. You dispose of a client socket and any outgoing or incoming buffers when it ultimately gives you an error or closes. That conversation, at the very least, is now finished out of all the others you're having.

The asynchronous approach's fundamental feature is that a single control thread can handle hundreds, if not thousands, of client conversations. As each client socket prepares for its next event, the code advances to the next action for that socket, receives or sends any data it can, and then returns to poll() to monitor for more activity. This single thread of control can handle a large number of clients by keeping all client-conversation states in one set of dictionaries, indexed by client socket, without requiring a single operating system context switch (aside from the privilege-mode escalations and de-escalations involved in entering the operating system itself for the poll(), recv(), send(), and close() system calls). Essentially, you replace the full-fledged operating system context-switch that a multithreaded or multiprocess server would require to switch its attention from one client to another with the key lookup offered by Python dictionaries.

Technically, the previous code can run without having to use sock to set each new client socket to nonblocking mode.

setblocking(False). Why? Because Listing 7-6 never calls recv() unless data is waiting to be received, and recv() never blocks if at least one byte of input is ready; and it never calls send() unless data can be sent, and send() never blocks if at least one byte can be written to the operating system's outgoing network buffers. However, doing setblocking() is prudent in case you make a mistake. In the absence of it, a misplaced call to send() or recv() would cause you to block and become unresponsive to all but the one client. A misstep on your side will raise socket with the setblocking() call in place. timeout and notify you that you have made a call that the operating system cannot handle right away.

If you run many clients against this server, you'll notice that its single thread manages all of the concurrent interactions with ease. With Listing 7-6, however, you had to delve into quite a few operating system internals. What if you want to concentrate on your client code and delegate the specifics of select(), poll(), and epoll() to someone else?

Callback-Style asyncio

Python 3.4 included the asyncio framework to the Standard Library, which was designed in part by Guido van Rossum, the creator of Python. It attempts to unify a field that had grown fragmented in the era of Python 2 by providing a standard interface for event loops based on select(), epoll(), and related technologies.

You can probably already imagine the duties that such a framework assumes after looking at Listing 7-6 and observing how little of its code is particular to the sample question-and-answer protocol that you are studying in this chapter. It keeps a central select-style loop going. It maintains a table of sockets where I/O activity is expected and adds or removes them from the select loop's attention as needed. Once the sockets are closed, it cleans up and abandons them. Finally, when actual data is received, user code is used to decide the appropriate response.

Two programming styles are supported by the asyncio framework. One, which reminds programmers of the old Twisted framework under Python 2, uses an object instance to keep track of each open client connection. The stages in Listing 7-6 that advanced a client dialogue become method calls on the object instance in this design pattern. Listing 7-7 shows the familiar stages of reading in a question and generating a response, written in a way that works with the asyncio framework.

Listing 7-7:. An asyncio Server in the Callback Style

```python3
#!/usr/bin/env python3
# Network Programming in Python: The Basics
# Asynchronous I/O inside "asyncio" callback methods.
import asyncio, zen_utils
class ZenServer(asyncio.Protocol):
 def connection_made(self, transport):
 self.transport = transport
 self.address = transport.get_extra_info('peername')
 self.data = b''
 print('Accepted connection from {}'.format(self.address))
 def data_received(self, data):
 self.data += data
 if self.data.endswith(b'?'):
 answer = zen_utils.get_answer(self.data)
 self.transport.write(answer)
 self.data = b''
 def connection_lost(self, exc):
 if exc:
 print('Client {} error: {}'.format(self.address, exc))
 elif self.data:
 print('Client {} sent {} but then closed'
 .format(self.address, self.data))
 else:
 print('Client {} closed socket'.format(self.address))
if __name__ == '__main__':
```

```
  address = zen_utils.parse_command_line('asyncio server using
callbacks')
 loop = asyncio.get_event_loop()
 coro = loop.create_server(ZenServer, *address)
 server = loop.run_until_complete(coro)
 print('Listening at {}'.format(address))
 try:
 loop.run_forever()
 finally:
 server.close()
 loop.close()
```

In Listing 7-7, you can see how the real socket object is properly isolated from the protocol code. The framework, not the socket, is consulted for the remote address. A method call is used to deliver data, and it merely displays the string that has arrived. With its transit, the answer you want to send is passed off to the framework. Your code will be out of the loop—literally—about when that data will be handed off to the operating system for transmission back to the client, thanks to the write() method call. The framework guarantees that it will happen as soon as possible, as long as it does not interfere with the progress of other client connections that require attention.

In most cases, asynchronous workers grow more sophisticated than this. When responses to clients can't be composed as quickly as they can here, but instead require reading from files on the file system or consulting back-end services like databases, this is a common example. In such instance, your client code will have to work in two directions: it will defer to the framework while sending and receiving data from the filesystem or database, as well as when sending and receiving data from the client. In such cases, your callback methods may create futures objects that give even more callbacks, which will be triggered after the database or disc I/O is complete.

Details can be found in the official asyncio documentation.

Coroutine-Style asyncio

Another way to write protocol code for the asyncio framework is to write a coroutine, which is a function that, instead of blocking in an I/O routine, stops and returns control to its caller when it needs to do I/O. The most common way in which the

Python language enables coroutines is through generators, which are functions that contain one or more yield statements and, as a result, reel off a sequence of objects rather than returning a single value when called.

If you've ever created generic generators with yield statements that merely offer stuff for consumption, you'll be astonished at how asyncio-targeted generators appear. They make use of the PEP 380-developed expanded yield syntax. With the enhanced syntax, a running generator can not only reel off all the items yielded by another generator with the yield from statement, but it can also return a value to the inside of the coroutine and even raise an exception if the consumer requires it. This allows a pattern in which the coroutine performs a result = yield of an object describing an operation it wants performed—read on another socket or access to the filesystem— and either receives the result of the successful operation in result or experiences an exception indicating that the operation failed right there in the coroutine.

The protocol is implemented as a coroutine in Listing 7-8.

Listing 7-8. An asyncio Server in the Coroutine Style

```
#!/usr/bin/env python3
# Programming in Python: The Basics
# Asynchronous I/O inside an "asyncio" coroutine.
import asyncio, zen_utils
@asyncio.coroutine
def handle_conversation(reader, writer):
 address = writer.get_extra_info('peername')
 print('Accepted connection from {}'.format(address))
 while True:
 data = b''
 while not data.endswith(b'?'):
 more_data = yield from reader.read(4096)

 if not more_data:
                        if data:
                            print('Client {} sent {!r} but
                            then closed'
                                .format(address, data))
                        else:
```

```
print('Client {} closed socket normally'.format(address))
                            return
                 data += more_data
            answer = zen_utils.get_answer(data)
            writer.write(answer)
if __name__ == '__main__':
            address = zen_utils.parse_command_line('asyncio server
using coroutine')
            loop = asyncio.get_event_loop()
            coro     =     asyncio.start_server(handle_conversation,
*address)
            server = loop.run_until_complete(coro)
            print('Listening at {}'.format(address))
            try:
                loop.run_forever()
            finally:
                server.close()
                loop.close()
```

You'll recognise all of the code in this list if you compare it to the earlier server attempts. The old framing operation of the while loop calling recv() repeatedly is followed by a write of the reply to the waiting client, all wrapped up in a while loop that is eager to keep responding to as many requests as the client wants to make. However, there is a key distinction that prevents you from just reusing previous implementations of the same logic. It takes the shape of a generator here, which performs a yield whenever the previous code had merely performed a blocking action and waited for the operating system to reply. This distinction allows this generator to connect to the asyncio subsystem without blocking it or prohibiting several workers from working at the same time.

This method is recommended for coroutines by PEP 380 since it makes it easier to see where your generator might be paused. Every time it executes a yield, it could cease running for an indefinite period of time. Some programmers dislike having explicit yield statements in their code, thus frameworks like gevent and eventlet in Python 2 take typical networking code with normal blocking I/O requests and intercept them to do what is essentially asynchronous I/O underneath the hood.

As of this writing, none of these frameworks have been converted to Python 3. If they ever arrive, programmers will have to choose between the verbose but explicit approach of an asyncio coroutine, where a "yield" can be seen everywhere a pause might occur, and the implicit but more compact code possible when calls like recv() return control to the asynchronous I/O loop while appearing to be innocent method calls in the code itself.

The asyncore Legacy Module

Listing 7-9 uses the asyncore Standard Library module to build the sample protocol, in case you come across any services written against it.

Listing 7-9. Using legacy asyncore Framework

```
#!/usr/bin/env python3
# Programming in Python: The Basics
# Uses the legacy "asyncore" Standard Library module to write a
server.
import asyncore, asynchat, zen_utils
class ZenRequestHandler(asynchat.async_chat):
 def __init__(self, sock):
 asynchat.async_chat.__init__(self, sock)
     self.set_terminator(b'?')
     self.data = b''
 def collect_incoming_data(self, more_data):
 self.data += more_data
 def found_terminator(self):
     answer = zen_utils.get_answer(self.data + b'?')
 self.push(answer)
     self.initiate_send()
     self.data = b''
class ZenServer(asyncore.dispatcher):
 def handle_accept(self):
     sock, address = self.accept()
     ZenRequestHandler(sock)
if __name__ == '__main__':
```

```
address = zen_utils.parse_command_line('legacy "asyncore" server')
listener = zen_utils.create_srv_socket(address)
server = ZenServer(listener)
server.accepting = True # we already called listen()
asyncore.loop()
```

If you're a seasoned Python coder, this listing will trigger red flags. Despite the fact that the ZenServer object is never explicitly passed to the asyncore.loop() method or registered in any way, the control loop appears to know that the service is available! Clearly, this module is using module-level globals or some other malicious means to construct ties between the main control loop, the server object, and the request handlers it generates, but in a way that you can't see.

However, you can see that many of the same actions are carried out behind the scenes that asyncio had exposed. Each each client connection creates a new instance of ZenRequestHandler, in which you can store any kind of state you need to keep track of how the client interaction is going in the instance variables.

Furthermore, there is an asymmetry between receiving and sending, which is typical of the asynchronous frameworks you've been looking at. Receiving data entails returning and passing control to the framework, as well as being called back for each fresh block of bytes received as input. However, sending data is a fire-and-forget operation in which you hand over management of the entire outgoing payload to the framework and trust that it will make as many send() calls as necessary to get the data transferred.

Finally, you can see that asynchronous frameworks, unless they use invisible magic like gevent or eventlet (both of which are currently Python 2 only), force you to write server code in idioms that are distinct from those used in a simple server like the one illustrated in Listing 7-3. While multithreading and multiprocessing merely ran your single-threaded code, an asynchronous approach compels you to break up your code into small chunks that can independently run without ever blocking. Each unblockable code snippet must be included within a method in a callback style; in a coroutine style, each basic unblockable operation must be wedged between yield or yield from instructions.

The Best of Both Worlds

By just looking from one protocol object to another (or, in the case of the more rudimentary Listing 7-6, between one dictionary entry and another), these asynchronous servers can switch nimbly between one client's traffic and another's. Clients can be served at a lower cost than when the operating system is involved in the context shifts.

An asynchronous server, on the other hand, has a fixed limit. Because it executes all of its work in a single operating system thread, it reaches a wall and can no longer process client work once the CPU is at 100% utilisation. It's a pattern that, in its purest form, is always confined to a single CPU, no matter how many cores your server has.

Fortunately, there is a solution at hand. When you need high performance, use an asynchronous callback object or coroutine to design your service and run it in an asynchronous framework. Then take a step back and configure your server's operating system to launch as many event loop processes as you have CPU cores!

(One item to discuss with your server administrator: should you leave one or two cores open for the operating system rather than using them all?) You'll be able to enjoy the best of both worlds. . The asynchronous framework can blaze away on a given CPU, cycling between active client sockets as often as it wants without having to move contexts into another process. New incoming connections, on the other hand, can be distributed among all active server processes by the operating system, optimally balancing the load over the entire server.

You'll probably want to corral these processes inside a daemon that can check their health and restart them, or warn staff, if they fail, as explained in the section "A Few Words About Deployment." From supervisord to full platform-as-a-service containerization, any of the technologies outlined there should work nicely for an asynchronous service.

Under the Influence of inetd

I'd be remiss if I didn't include the venerable inetd daemon, which is available for practically all BSD and Linux variants. It overcomes the problem of needing to launch n different daemons when the system boots if you wish to offer n different network services on a single server machine. It was invented in the early days of the Internet.

You just list every port that you want listening on the machine in the /etc/inetd. conf file.

Every one of them gets a bind() and listen() from the inetd daemon, but it only starts a server process if a client connects. Because inetd is the process that opens the low-numbered port, this technique makes it simple to handle low-port-number services that operate under a normal user account. The inetd daemon can either launch one process per client connection or expect your server to stay up and continue listening for new connections once it has accepted the first one for a TCP service like the one in this chapter (see your inetd(8) documentation for the more complicated case of a UDP datagram service).

It is more expensive and places a greater demand on the server to create one process per connection, but it is also easier. The string nowait in the fourth field of a service's inetd.conf entry designates single-shot services.

When such a service starts up, it will discover that the client socket is already connected to its standard input, output, and error. The service should only communicate with that one client before exiting. **Listing 7-10** shows an example that can be utilised with the inetd.conf line previously mentioned.

Listing 7-10. Answer a Single Client, Whose Socket Is the stdin/stdout/stderr

```python
#!/usr/bin/env python3
# Programming in Python: The Basics
# Single-shot server for the use of inetd(8).
import socket, sys, zen_utils
if __name__ == '__main__':
 sock = socket.fromfd(0, socket.AF_INET, socket.SOCK_STREAM)
 sys.stdin = open('/dev/null', 'r')
 sys.stdout = sys.stderr = open('log.txt', 'a', buffering=1)
 address = sock.getpeername()
 print('Accepted connection from {}'.format(address))
 zen_utils.handle_conversation(sock, address)
```

Because you rarely want raw tracebacks and status messages—that Python or one of its libraries might direct toward standard out or especially standard error—interrupting your conversation with the client, this script is careful to replace the Python standard input, output, and error objects with more appropriate open files. Because it only touches the file objects inside of sys and not the real file descriptors, this manoeuvre only fixes I/O attempted from within Python. Close the underlying file descriptors 0, 1, and 2 as well if your server calls any low-level C libraries that do their own standard I/O. However, in that scenario, you're starting to do the kind of sandboxing that's best done using supervisord, a daemonization module, or platform-style containerization, as mentioned in the previous section "A Few Words About Deployment."

So long as the port you've chosen isn't a low-numbered one, you may verify Listing 7-10 from your normal user command line by executing inetd -d inet.conf against a little configuration file that contains the line supplied earlier, and then connecting to the port as usual using client.py.

The alternate pattern is to use the string wait in the fourth field of your inetd.conf entry, which will provide your script access to the listener socket. This assigns the responsibility of running accept() for the client who is currently waiting to your script. The benefit of this is that your server can opt to stay alive and continue to run accept() to accept new client connections without using inetd. This is potentially more efficient than beginning a new process for each incoming connection. If clients cease connecting for a time, your server can exit() to save memory until a client requires the service again; inetd will detect that your service has exited and resume listening.

Listing 7-11 is intended to be used when in the waiting state. It can accept new connections indefinitely, but if several seconds pass without any new client connections, it will time out and leave, freeing the server from the need to retain it in memory.

Listing 7-11. Answer a few client calls, but eventually become bored and time out.

```
#!/usr/bin/env python3
# Programming in Python: The Basics
# Multi-shot server for the use of inetd(8).
import socket, sys, zen_utils
if __name__ == '__main__':
 listener = socket.fromfd(0, socket.AF_INET, socket.SOCK_STREAM)
     sys.stdin = open('/dev/null', 'r')
sys.stdout = sys.stderr = open('log.txt', 'a', buffering=1)
     listener.settimeout(8.0)
 try:
zen_utils.accept_connections_forever(listener)
 except socket.timeout:
 print('Waited 8 seconds with no further connections; shutting down')
```

Of course, this server is based on the same single-threaded approach that I used to begin this chapter.

You'll probably want a more robust design in production, and you can utilise any of the ideas mentioned in this chapter. The only criterion is that they be able to accept() an already-listening socket again and over again indefinitely. This is straightforward if you don't mind your server process never exiting once it's started by inetd. If you want the server to time out and shut down after a period of inactivity, it can get a little more involved (and outside the scope of this book), because timing out and shutting down a group of threads can be tricky. or processes to ensure that none of them are now talking to a client and that none of them have recently received enough client connections to justify keeping the server alive.

In some versions of inetd, there is also a simple access control mechanism based on IP address and hostname. The mechanism is a descendant of tcpd, an old software that used to work alongside inetd before being merged into the same process. Its /etc/ hosts.allow and /etc/hosts.ban files can be used to grant and deny access to specific hosts. Prevent some (or all!) IP addresses from connecting to one of your services, depending on its rules. If you're having trouble getting customers to connect to one of your inetd-powered services, check your system documentation and look at how your system administrator has set these files.

Conclusion

The network servers in Chapters 2 and 3 could only deal with one client at a time, and all others had to wait until the last client socket had closed before continuing. There are two methods for getting beyond this stumbling barrier.

From a programming standpoint, the most basic is multithreading (or multiprocessing), in which the server code is largely unaffected and the operating system is tasked with switching between workers discreetly so that waiting clients receive results promptly while idle clients require no server CPU. This method not only allows multiple client discussions to progress at the same time, but it also makes better use of a server CPU that would otherwise be idle waiting for further work from a single client.

The more difficult but powerful alternative is to use an asynchronous programming style, which allows a single thread of control to switch its attention between as many clients as it wants by providing the operating system with a complete list of sockets with whom it is now conversing. The issue is that this necessitates splitting the logic of processing a client request and creating a response into discrete, nonblocking bits of code that can transfer control back to the asynchronous framework when it's time to wait on the client once more. While an asynchronous server can be developed manually using select() or poll(), most programmers will prefer to use a framework, such as the asyncio framework included in Python 3.4 and newer's Standard Library.

Deployment is the process of arranging for a service you've built to be placed on a server and to begin running when the system boots, and it can be automated using a variety of current technologies, such as supervisord or passing control to a platform-as-a-service container. The ancient inetd daemon, which provides a bare-bones technique to ensure your service is launched when a client first needs it, may be the simplest feasible deployment for a baseline Linux server.

The subject of servers will come up again in this book. After Chapter 8 looks at a few basic network-based services that modern Python programmers rely on, Chapters 9 through 11 look at the design of the HTTP protocol and the Python tools for acting as both a client and a server, with the designs presented in this chapter available all over again in the choice between a forking web server like Gunicorn and an asynchronous framework like Tornado.

CHAPTER 8

Message Queues and Caches

Despite its briefness, this chapter may be one of the most important in the book. It examines two technologies—caches and message queues—that have evolved into essential building blocks for high-volume systems. The novel hits a turning point at this time. The sockets API and how Python can use primitive IP network operations to establish communication channels were covered in the previous chapters. As you'll find if you go ahead, the following chapters are all about specific protocols based on sockets—how to retrieve documents from the World Wide Web, send e-mail, and submit commands to remote servers.

What distinguishes the two tools you'll examine in this chapter? They have a lot of similarities.

- These technologies are popular because they are effective tools. The point of utilising Memcached, or a message queue, is that it is a well-written service that will solve a specific problem for you, not that it implements an intriguing protocol that will allow you to communicate with other tools.

- These tools are typically used to handle challenges that are internal to a company. You can't always identify whether caches, queues, or load-distribution mechanisms are being utilised to power a web site or network service from the outside.

- While protocols like HTTP and SMTP were designed with specific payloads in mind (hypertext documents and e-mail messages, respectively), caches and message queues are typically agnostic about the data they transport for you.

This chapter is not meant to provide a comprehensive guide to any of these technologies. There is extensive online documentation for each of the libraries mentioned, and for the most prominent ones, entire books have been published about them. Instead,

Structure

- Using Memcached (memory caching)
- Hashing and Sharding
- Message Queues
- Using Python's Message Queues
- Conclusion

Objectives:

the goal of this chapter is to introduce you to the problem that each tool addresses, explain how to use the service to solve that problem, and provide some tips on how to utilise the tool from Python. After all, apart from the basic, lifelong process of learning to programme, the greatest hurdle that a programmer often faces is recognising common problems for which rapid prebuilt solutions exist. Programmers have an unfortunate propensity of re-inventing the wheel over and over again. Consider this chapter as a gift of two completed wheels in the hopes that you will not have to make them yourself.

Using Memcached (memory caching)

The "memory cache daemon" is Memcached. It creates a single, massive least-recently used (LRU) cache from the free, idle RAM on the servers where it is installed. It had a revolutionary impact on several significant Internet services, according to all reports. Following a brief overview of how to utilise it from Python, I'll go into its implementation, which will teach you about a key modern network concept known as sharding.

The actual use of Memcached is supposed to be straightforward.

- Every server with some free memory has a Memcached daemon running.

- You create a list of your new Memcached daemons' IP addresses and port numbers and disseminate it to all of the clients who will be accessing the cache.

- Your client programmes now have access to an enterprise-wide, lightning-fast key-value cache that serves as a large Python dictionary that all of your servers can share. The cache works on an LRU basis, which means it deletes old things that haven't been accessed in a while to make place for new entries and records that are often visited.

There are presently enough Python clients available for Memcached that I'd rather point you to the page that lists them than try to review them here: http://code. google.com/p/memcached/wiki/Clients.

Because the first client is written entirely in Python, it will not need to compile against any libraries. Because it's on the Python Package Index, it should go together smoothly in a virtual environment (see Chapter 1). The Python 3 version can be installed with with one line.

```
$ pip install python3-memcached
```

This package's API is straightforward. Though you would expect a more closely related interface to a Python dictionary with native methods like __getitem__(), the creator of this API elected to utilise the same method names as other Memcached-supported languages. This was a wise option because it makes translating Memcached examples into Python much easier. If you have Memcached installed and operating on your machine at its default port of 11211, a simple interaction at the Python prompt might look like this:

```
>>> import memcache
>>> mc = memcache.Client(['127.0.0.1:11211'])
>>> mc.set('user:19', 'Simple is better than complex.')
True
>>> mc.get('user:19')
'Simple is better than complex.'
```

The interface is pretty similar to that of a Python dictionary, as you can see. When you submit a string as a value like this, it is directly written to Memcached as UTF-8 and then decoded when you fetch it later. Any Python object other than a basic string will cause the memcache module to auto-pickle the value and save the binary pickle in Memcached (see Chapter 5). If you ever create a Python application that shares a Memcached cache with clients written in other languages, keep this distinction in mind. Only the values you save as strings will be readable by clients who don't speak English.

Always keep in mind that Memcached data can be discarded at the server's discretion. The cache is intended to speed up processes by storing results that are time-consuming to recompute. It's not meant to store information that can't be reconstructed from other sources! If the previous instructions were executed against a busy enough Memcached, and enough time had passed between the set() and get() operations, the get() action could readily detect that the string had expired from the cache and was no longer there.

The fundamental approach for using Memcached from Python is shown in Listing 8-1. This code examines Memcached to determine if the answer is already saved in the cache before doing a (artificially) expensive integer-squaring operation. If this is the case, the solution can be returned right away without having to be recalculated. If it isn't already computed and saved in the cache, it is before being returned.

Listing 8-1. Using Memcached to Speed Up a Time-Intensive Process

```python
#!/usr/bin/env python3
# Programming in Python: The Basics
# Using memcached to cache expensive results.
import memcache, random, time, timeit
def compute_square(mc, n):
    value = mc.get('sq:%d' % n)
    if value is None:
        time.sleep(0.001) # pretend that computing a square is expensive
        value = n * n
        mc.set('sq:%d' % n, value)
    return value
def main():
    mc = memcache.Client(['127.0.0.1:11211'])
    def make_request():
        compute_square(mc, random.randint(0, 5000))
    print('Ten successive runs:')
    for i in range(1, 11):
        print(' %.2fs' % timeit.timeit(make_request, number=2000), end='')
    print()
if __name__ == '__main__':
    main()
```

For this example to work, the Memcached daemon must be running on your machine and listening on port 11211.

Of course, the programme will operate at its normal pace for the first few hundred requests; however, when it asks for the square of a certain number for the first time, it will find it absent from the RAM cache and will have to compute it instead. However, when the programme runs and encounters the same integers over and over, it will begin to speed faster as it discovers squares that are still in the cache from the last time it saw that integer.

The software should exhibit a significant speedup after a few thousand queries selected from the domain of 5,000 potential input integers. The tenth batch of 2,000 squares on my machine is more than six times faster than the first batch.

```
$ python squares.py
```

Ten successive runs:

```
2.89s 2.14s 1.55s 1.20s 0.97s 0.79s 0.64s 0.51s 0.49s 0.44s
```

This pattern is typical of caching in general. As the cache learns enough keys and values, the runtime improves progressively, but as Memcached fills and the % coverage of the input domain hits its maximum, the rate of improvement slows. What kind of data would you want to write to the cache in a real application?

Many programmers just cache the lowest level of expensive call, such as database searches, filesystem reads, or external service queries. It's frequently simple to figure out which items can be cached for how long without causing information to become out-of-date at this level And if the value of a database record changes, the cache may be purged ahead of time of any stale objects associated with the new value. However, caching intermediate outputs at higher levels of the application, such as data structures, snippets of HTML, or even full web pages, can have a lot of utility. A cache hit avoids not just the cost of accessing the database, but also the cost of converting the result into a data structure and finally into rendered HTML.

There are numerous nice introductions and in-depth instructions linked from the Memcached site, as well as a fairly extensive FAQ; it's as if the Memcached developers have learned that catechism is the most effective approach to teach people about their service.

To begin with, keys must be unique, thus developers frequently employ prefixes and encodings to distinguish between the various types of objects they are storing. User:19, mypage:/node/14, and even the full body of a SQL query are frequently used as keys. Although keys can only be 250 characters long, you can get away with lookups that support longer strings if you use a strong hash function. By the way, values in Memcached can be longer than keys but are restricted to 1MB in size.

Second, always keep in mind that Memcached is a cache. It's ephemeral, stores data in RAM, and if you restart it, it forgets everything you've ever saved! If the cache is lost, your application should always be able to restore and reconstruct all of its data.

Third, ensure that your cache does not return data that is too old to deliver to your users appropriately.

The definition of "too old" is largely dependent on the problem domain. A bank balance should probably be kept up to date, yet "today's top headline" on a news site's front page can be a few minutes old.

There are three techniques to dealing with stale data and ensuring that it is cleaned away and not returned indefinitely after its useful shelf life has passed.

- You can define an expiration date and time on each item you put in the cache, and Memcached will take care of silently dropping these objects when the time comes.

- If you have a means to map from the identification of a piece of information to all of the keys in the cache that could conceivably have included it, you can reach in and actively invalidate individual cache entries the instant they become invalid.

- Instead of eliminating incorrect entries, you can rewrite and replace them, which works well for entries that are struck dozens of times per second. Rather of all of those clients discovering the missing entry and attempting to recompute it at the same time, they discover the changed entry there instead.

Decorators are a common technique to add caching in Python since they surround function calls without affecting their names or signatures, as you might expect. There are various decorator cache libraries that can use Memcached that can be found in the Python Package Index.

Hashing and Sharding

Memcached's design exemplifies a key notion that may be found in a variety of other databases and that you might wish to incorporate into your own architecture. When a Memcached client is presented with a list of Memcached instances, it will shard the database by hashing each key's string value and allowing the hash determine which server in the Memcached cluster is used to store that key.

Consider a specific key-value combination, such as the key sq:42 and the value 1764, that Listing 8-1 might store. The Memcached cluster wants to store this key and value exactly once to make the most of the RAM it has available. However, in order to keep the service running quickly, it wants to avoid duplication by avoiding any coordination between the many servers or communication between all of the customers.

This means that without any more information beyond the key and the list of Memcached servers with which they are configured, all of the clients will need a scheme to figure out where that piece of information belongs. If they fail to make the same conclusion, the key and value may be replicated to many servers, reducing the overall memory available, and a client's attempt to remove an invalid item may leave other invalid copies elsewhere.

The answer is for all clients to use the same, stable process to convert a key into an integer n that selects one of the servers from their list. They accomplish this by employing a "hash" method, which combines the bits of a string while producing a number, obliterating any patterns in the string.

Consider Listing 8-2 to see why key value patterns must be eliminated. It loads an English dictionary (you may need to download your own dictionary or change the path to make the script work on your machine) and investigates how those words would be spread across four servers if they were used as keys.

Listing 8-2. There are two approaches of assigning data to servers: Bits from a Hash and Patterns in the Data

```python
#!/usr/bin/env python3
# Programming in Python: The Basics
# Hashes are a great way to divide work.
import hashlib
def alpha_shard(word):
    """Do a poor job of assigning data to servers by using first
letters."""
    if word[0] < 'g':          # abcdef
    return 'server0'
    elif word[0] < 'n':        # ghijklm
        return 'server1'
    elif word[0] < 't':        # nopqrs
    return 'server2'
    else:                      # tuvwxyz
        return 'server3'
```

```
def hash_shard(word):
 """Assign data to servers using Python's built-in hash() function."""
 return 'server%d' % (hash(word) % 4)
def md5_shard(word):
 """Assign data to servers using a public hash algorithm."""
 data = word.encode('utf-8')
 return 'server%d' % (hashlib.md5(data).digest()[-1] % 4)
if __name__ == '__main__':
 words = open('/usr/share/dict/words').read().split()
 for function in alpha_shard, hash_shard, md5_shard:
 d = {'server0': 0, 'server1': 0, 'server2': 0, 'server3': 0}
 for word in words:
 d[function(word.lower())] += 1
 print(function.__name__[:-6])
 for key, value in sorted(d.items()):
                print(' {} {} {:.2}'.format(key, value, value /
                len(words)))
           print()
```

The hash() function is Python's built-in hash procedure, which is optimised for speed because it is used to implement Python dictionary lookup internally. Because it was created as a cryptographic hash, the MD5 algorithm is far more advanced. Although it is no longer considered secure, it can be used to distribute load across servers (albeit it is slower than Python's built-in hash). The results clearly demonstrate the dangers of attempting to disperse load using any way that could directly disclose your data's patterns.

```
$ python hashing.py
alpha
 server0 35285 0.37
 server1 22674 0.28
 server2 29097 0.39
 server3 12115 0.15
hash
 server0 24768 0.25
```

```
 server1 25004 0.25
 server2 24713 0.25
 server3 24686 0.25
md5
 server0 24777 0.25
 server1 24820 0.25
 server2 24717 0.25
 server3 24857 0.25
```

You can see that dividing load by initial letters, with nearly equal numbers of letters assigned to each of four bins, results in server 0 receiving more than three times the load of server 3, but having only six letters instead of seven! The hash routines, on the other hand, were both champions. Despite the strong patterns that characterise not only the first letters of English words, but also their entire structure and endings, the hash functions evenly distributed the words over these four imaginary servers.

Though many data sets aren't as skewed as English word letter distributions, sharded databases like Memcached must always deal with the appearance of patterns in their input data.

The employment of keys that always began with a similar prefix and were followed by characters from a restricted alphabet: the decimal digits, for example, was not rare. Because of these clear patterns, sharding should always be done with a hash function.

Of course, when using a database system like Memcached, whose client libraries allow sharding internally, this is an implementation issue that you may easily overlook. However, if you ever need to create your own service that assigns work or data to nodes in a cluster in a way that is repeatable across multiple clients of the same data store, you'll find the same concept handy in your own code.

Message Queues

Because, as you saw in Chapter 2, the idea of a datagram is particular to unreliable services where data can be lost, duplicated, or reordered by the underlying network, message queue protocols allow you to deliver dependable pieces of data called messages instead of datagrams. A message queue often guarantees to send messages consistently and atomically: a message either comes entire and intact, or it does not arrive at all. The message queue protocol itself does the framing. Your message queue clients will never have to loop and keep calling recv() until the entire message has arrived.

The additional benefit of message queues is that, rather than providing solely point-to-point connections as is allowed with an IP transport like TCP, they allow you to create a variety of topologies between messaging clients. Message queues can be used for a variety of purposes.

- When you use your email address to sign up for an account on a new website, the site usually responds right away with a page that says "Thank you, please watch your inbox for a confirmation e-mail," rather than making you wait the several minutes it might take the site to reach your e-mail service provider to deliver it. The site usually does this by saving your email address in a message queue, from which back-end servers can retrieve it when they're ready to try a new outgoing SMTP connection (Chapter 13). If a delivery attempt fails for some reason, your e-mail address can simply be re-entered into the queue with a longer wait for a later retry attempt.

- **Message queues** can be the foundation for a custom remote procedure call (RPC) service (see Chapter 18), a design in which busy front-end servers offload onerous work by sending requests to a message queue containing dozens or hundreds of back-end servers After that, you'll have to wait for an answer.

- **High-volume event data** that needs to be aggregated or centrally stored and evaluated is frequently sent via a message queue as tiny efficient messages. This has completely replaced both on-machine logging to local hard drives and previous log transmission technologies such as syslog at some sites.

The capacity to mix and match entire populations of clients and servers, or publisher and subscriber processes, by having them all attach to the same messaging fabric, is the characteristic of a message queue application design.

Using message queues can result in a significant change in the way you create applications. A single thread of control might flow from reading HTTP data from a socket to authenticating and interpreting the request to using an API to do bespoke image processing and lastly to writing the result to disc in a typical monolithic programme. Every API utilised by that single control thread must be installed on a single system and loaded into a single Python runtime instance. However, once you have message queues in your toolset, you may wonder why something as intensive, specialised, and web-agnostic as image processing should share the CPU and disc drive with your front-end HTTP service. You start pivoting toward single-purpose machines organised into clusters that serve a single service, rather than constructing services from big machines with dozens of heterogeneous libraries installed. So long as operations understands the messaging topology and the protocol for detaching a server without losing messages, they can easily start taking down, upgrading, and reattaching the image processing servers, for example, without even touching the load-balanced pool of HTTP services that sit out in front of your message queue.

Message queues typically offer a variety of topologies.

- **A pipeline topology** is the structure that most closely resembles the image you have in your mind when you think of a queue: a producer creates messages and sends them to a queue, from which they can be received by a consumer. For example, the front-end web machines of a photo-sharing website might receive end-user image uploads and place them in an internal queue. The queue might then be read by a machine room full of thumbnail generators, with each agent receiving one message at a time carrying the image for which it should generate many thumbnails. The queue may grow long during peak hours when the site is busy, then shorten or empty during off-peak hours, but in either case, the front-end web servers are freed to respond quickly to the waiting customer, informing them that their upload was successful and that their image would appear in their photo stream shortly.

- **A publisher-subscriber** or **fanout topology** resembles a pipeline, but with one important distinction. While the pipeline ensures that each queued message is sent to only one consumer—it would be inefficient to allocate the same photograph to two thumbnail servers—subscribers often wish to get all of the messages queued by the publishers. Subscribers can also provide a filter that limits their interest to messages in a specific format. External services that need to push events to the outside world can use this type of queue. It can also be used to create a fabric that a server room can use to advertise which systems are up, which are down for maintenance, and which can even publish the addresses of other message queues as they are built and deleted.

- Finally, because communications must go round-trip, the request-reply pattern is the most complicated. Both of the previous designs gave the message producer relatively little responsibility: the producer connects to the queue and transmits its message, and that's all. A message queue client that sends a request, on the other hand, must stay connected and wait for the response. To accomplish this, the queue must have some form of addressing method that allows responses to be sent to the correct client, possibly among thousands of connected clients, who is still waiting for it. This is, however, the most potent pattern of all, despite its underlying intricacy. It distributes the burden of dozens or hundreds of clients across a huge number of servers with no work other than setting up the message queue. . Because a good message queue lets servers to attach and detach without losing messages, this topology also enables servers to be taken down for maintenance while being transparent to the client workstations.

Request-reply queues are an excellent method to connect lightweight workers that can run in the hundreds on a single machine—for example, the threads of a web server front end—to database clients or file servers that are occasionally called in to undertake heavier work on behalf of the front end. The request-reply pattern is a natural fit for RPC techniques, and it comes with a bonus that simpler RPC systems don't normally provide: That is, in a fan-in or fan-out work pattern, several consumers or producers can all be assigned to the same queue without either group of clients knowing.

Using Python's Message Queues

Stand-alone servers are used to implement the most popular message queues. All of the various activities you select to build your application from—producers, consumers, filters, and RPC services—can then connect to the message queue without having to learn each other's addresses or identities. The AMQP protocol is one of the most extensively used language-independent message queue protocols, and it is supported by a variety of open source servers, including RabbitMQ, the Apache Qpid server, and others.

Many programmers never learn how to use a message protocol. Instead, they rely on third-party libraries that bundle the benefits of a message queue into an API for easy consumption. Instead of learning AMQP, many Python programmers who use the Django web framework, for example, utilise the popular Celery distributed task queue. By supporting various back-end services, a library can also provide protocol independence. Instead of a dedicated messaging system, Celery allows you to use the simple Redis key-value store as your "message queue."

For the purposes of this book, however, an example that does not necessitate the installation of a full-fledged separate message queue server is more convenient, so I will cover MQ, the Zero Message Queue, which was created by the same company as AMQP but moves the messaging intelligence from a centralised broker into each of your message client programmes. To put it another way, embedding the MQ library in each of your programmes allows your code to establish a message fabric on its own, without the requirement for a centralised broker. This differs from an architecture based on a central broker that can provide reliability, redundancy, retransmission, and persistence to disc in a number of ways. On the MQ website, there is an excellent description of the benefits and drawbacks:

`www.zeromq.org/docs:welcome-from-amqp.`

Listing 8-3, to keep the example in this section self-contained, takes on a basic problem that doesn't require a message queue: determining the value of p using a straightforward, if inefficient, Monte Carlo method. Figure 8-1 depicts the message structure, which is the most significant aspect. A bitsource procedure generates 2n-character strings of ones and zeros. The odd bits will be used as an n-digit integer x coordinate, whereas the even bits will be used as an n-digit integer y coordinate. Is this point inside or outside the quarter-circle centred on the origin, the radius of which is the largest value that either of these numbers can take?

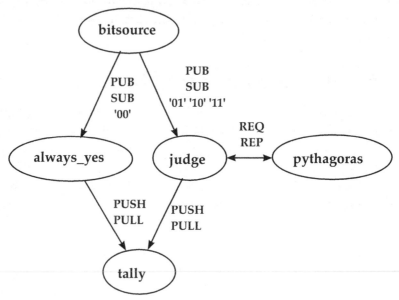

Figure 8.1 :- *The topology of the simple Monte Carlo estimate of pi.*

You create an audience of two listeners for these binary strings using a publish-subscribe topology. Because your two coordinates both start with the digit zero, the point must reside in the lower-left quadrant of the field and so fall safely inside the circle, the always yes listener will only receive digit strings starting with 00 and can thus always push the answer Y. The judge function that performs the genuine test, on the other hand, must process the other three possible patterns for the first two bits. It must ask Pythagoras to compute the sum-of-squares of the two integer coordinates to determine if the point they've named is within or outside the circle, and then send T or F to its outgoing queue.

The tally method at the bottom of the topology receives either the T or F created for each generated random bit pattern, and it estimates the value of p by comparing the number of T replies to the total number of T and F answers combined. If you're wondering about the arithmetic, look up monte carlo estimate of pi on the internet.

This five-worker architecture is implemented in Listing 8-3, which runs for 30 seconds before exiting the programme.

It necessitates MQ, which you can make available to Python by first creating a virtual environment and then typing:

```
$ pip install pyzmq
```

If you're using an operating system that comes with packaged Python or a standalone Python installation like Anaconda, this package may already be installed. In either instance, Listing 8-3 will be able to execute without an import error right out of the box.

Listing 8-3. A ØMQ Messaging Fabric connecting Five Different Workers

```python
#!/usr/bin/env python3
# Programming in Python: The Basics
# Small application that uses several different message queues
import random, threading, time, zmq
B = 32 # number of bits of precision in each random integer
def ones_and_zeros(digits):
  """Express `n` in at least `d` binary digits, with no special prefix."""
  return bin(random.getrandbits(digits)).lstrip('0b').zfill(digits)
def bitsource(zcontext, url):
  """Produce random points in the unit square."""
  zsock = zcontext.socket(zmq.PUB)
  zsock.bind(url)
  while True:
  zsock.send_string(ones_and_zeros(B * 2))
  time.sleep(0.01)
def always_yes(zcontext, in_url, out_url):
  """Coordinates in the lower-left quadrant are inside the unit circle."""
  isock = zcontext.socket(zmq.SUB)
  isock.connect(in_url)
  isock.setsockopt(zmq.SUBSCRIBE, b'00')
  osock = zcontext.socket(zmq.PUSH)
```

```
    osock.connect(out_url)
    while True:
    isock.recv_string()
    osock.send_string('Y')
def judge(zcontext, in_url, pythagoras_url, out_url):
    """Determine whether each input coordinate is inside the unit
circle."""
    isock = zcontext.socket(zmq.SUB)
    isock.connect(in_url)
    for prefix in b'01', b'10', b'11':
    isock.setsockopt(zmq.SUBSCRIBE, prefix)
    psock = zcontext.socket(zmq.REQ)
    psock.connect(pythagoras_url)
    osock = zcontext.socket(zmq.PUSH)
    osock.connect(out_url)
    unit = 2 ** (B * 2)
    while True:
    bits = isock.recv_string()
    n, m = int(bits[::2], 2), int(bits[1::2], 2)
    psock.send_json((n, m))
    sumsquares = psock.recv_json()
    osock.send_string('Y' if sumsquares < unit else 'N')
def pythagoras(zcontext, url):
    """Return the sum-of-squares of number sequences."""
    zsock = zcontext.socket(zmq.REP)
    zsock.bind(url)
    while True:
    numbers = zsock.recv_json()
    zsock.send_json(sum(n * n for n in numbers))
def tally(zcontext, url):
    """Tally how many points fall within the unit circle, and print
pi."""
```

```
zsock = zcontext.socket(zmq.PULL)
zsock.bind(url)
p = q = 0
while True:
decision = zsock.recv_string()
q += 1
if decision == 'Y':
p += 4
print(decision, p / q)
def start_thread(function, *args):
 thread = threading.Thread(target=function, args=args)
 thread.daemon = True # so you can easily Ctrl-C the whole program
 thread.start()
def main(zcontext):
 pubsub = 'tcp://127.0.0.1:6700'
 reqrep = 'tcp://127.0.0.1:6701'
 pushpull = 'tcp://127.0.0.1:6702'
 start_thread(bitsource, zcontext, pubsub)
 start_thread(always_yes, zcontext, pubsub, pushpull)
 start_thread(judge, zcontext, pubsub, reqrep, pushpull)
 start_thread(pythagoras, zcontext, reqrep)
 start_thread(tally, zcontext, pushpull)
 time.sleep(30)
if __name__ == '__main__':
 main(zmq.Context())
```

Because it is not safe for two threads to share a single message socket, each of these threads takes care to build its own socket or sockets for communication. The threads do, however, share a single context object, which ensures consistency. They're all contained within a shared arena of URLs, messages, and queues. Normally, you'll want to Per process, only one MQ context should be created.

Despite the fact that these sockets have methods with names that are similar to well-known socket operations like recv () Keep in mind that the meanings of send() and send() are not the same. Messages are always stored in chronological order and never duplicated, however Instead of becoming lost in a continuous stream, they are neatly demarcated as individual messages.

This example is obviously contrived so that you can use most of the primary messaging patterns supplied by a regular queue in only a few lines of code. Always yes and the judge establish connections to the bitsource, forming a publish-subscribe system in which each connected client receives a copy of every message issued by the publisher (minus, in this case, any messages that wind up being filtered out). By opting in to every message whose initial few digits match the filter string, each filter applied to a MQ socket adds, not subtracts, to the overall number of messages received. Because one of their four filters includes every possible combination of two leading binary digits, your pair of subscribers are guaranteed to receive every bit string produced by bitsource.

The judge-pythagoras relationship is a conventional RPC request-and-response relationship, in which the client holding the REQ socket must speak first in order to assign its message to one of the waiting agents tied to its socket. (Of course, just one agent is linked in this scenario.) Behind the scenes, the messaging fabric adds a return address to the request. When the agent is through with its task and responds, the return address can be used to send the response over the REP socket to the relevant client.

Finally, the tally worker shows how a push-pull arrangement ensures that each item pushed is received by one, and only one, of the agents connected to the socket; if you started up several tally workers, each new datum from upstream would arrive at only one of them, and they would all converge on p separately.

This listing, unlike all of the previous socket programming examples in this book, does not have to be concerned with whether bind() or connect() is called first! This is a MQ feature that uses timeouts and polling to keep retrying a failed connect() behind the scenes in the event that the endpoint represented by the URL becomes available later. This makes it resistant to agents entering and exiting an application while it is executing.

When run, the resulting system of workers can compute p to roughly three digits on my laptop by the time it exits.

```
$ python queuepi.py

...

Y 3.1406089633937735
```

This short example may make MQ programming appear unduly straightforward. In real life, you'll want more complicated patterns than the ones supplied here to ensure message delivery, persist them if they can't be processed yet, and perform flow management to ensure that a sluggish agent isn't overwhelmed by the quantity of messages queued and waiting for it. Extended talks of how to apply these patterns for a production service may be found in the official documentation. In the end, many programmers find that using a full-fledged message broker behind Celery, such as RabbitMQ, Qpid, or Redis, offers them the assurances they desire with the least amount of labour and risk of making mistakes.

Conclusion

In today's environment, serving thousands or millions of consumers has become a common task for application developers. Several essential technologies have arisen to assist them in achieving this size, and they are all easily accessible from Python.

Memcached is a popular service that combines all of the free RAM on all of the servers where it is deployed into a single huge LRU cache. Memcached can relieve a significant amount of strain from your database or other back-end storage if you have a system in place for invalidating or replacing entries that get out of date—or if you're dealing with data that can be expired on a fixed, predictable timetable. It can be inserted at a variety of points throughout your workflow. Instead of caching the result of a time-consuming database query, it may be preferable to merely cache the web widget that is eventually presented.

Message queues are another common mechanism for coordinating and integrating various portions of your application, which may require different hardware, load balancing strategies, platforms, or even programming languages. They can distribute messages to a large number of waiting consumers or servers in a way that is impossible with the single point-to-point links provided by standard TCP sockets, and they can also use a database or other persistent storage to ensure that messages are not lost if the server fails. Message queues also provide resilience and flexibility because, if a bottleneck occurs in one component of your system, the message queue can absorb the impact by allowing more messages to queue up for that service. The message queue design hides the population of servers or processes that serve a specific type of request, making it simple to disconnect, upgrade, reboot, and rejoin servers without disrupting the rest of your infrastructure.

Message queues are commonly used by programmers behind a more user-friendly API, such as the Celery project, which is popular in the Django community. Redis can also be used as a backend. Redis needs your attention, even though it isn't discussed in this chapter.

After you've gone through these basic and specific technologies built on top of IP/ TCP, you'll move on to the HTTP protocol, which implements the World Wide Web, in the next three chapters.

CHAPTER 9

HTTP Clients

This is the first of three HTTP chapters. The design and deployment of HTTP servers will be discussed in Chapter 10. In both chapters, the protocol will be examined in its most basic conceptual form, that is, as a mechanism for retrieving or uploading documents.

While HTTP can transport a variety of documents, including photos, PDFs, music, and video, Chapter 11 focuses on the type of document that has made HTTP and the Internet famous: the web page. The World Wide Web is a collection of hypertext texts that are connected together thanks to the creation of the URL, which is also covered in Chapter 11. There, you'll learn about template libraries, forms, and Ajax-enabled programming patterns, as well as web frameworks that strive to bring all of these patterns together in an easy-to-program manner.

RFCs 7230–7235 specify HTTP version 1.1, the most prevalent version in use today, to which you should refer if the wording of these chapters seems confused or leaves you wanting to know more. You can read Chapter 5 of Roy Thomas Fielding's famous PhD dissertation "Architectural Styles and the Design of Network-based Software Architectures" for a more technical introduction to the idea underlying the protocol's design.

For the time being, your adventure will begin here, where you will learn how to query a server and receive documents as a response.

Structure

- Python Client Libraries
- Framing, Encryption, and Ports
- Methods
- Hosts and Paths
- Status Codes
- Validation and Caching
- Encoding of Content
- Negotiation of Content
- Type of Content
- Authentication over HTTP
- Cookies
- Keep-Alive, Connections, and httplib
- Conclusion

Objectives:

In this chapter, you'll learn how to use the protocol as a client application that wants to fetch and cache documents as well as maybe submit queries or data to the server. You will learn the protocol's rules as a result of this approach.

Python Client Libraries

The HTTP protocol and the vast data resources it makes available are perennially attractive topics among Python programmers, as seen by a long line of third-party clients claiming to do a better job than the urllib included in the Standard Library.

Today, however, a single third-party solution stands alone, having not only swept the field of competitors but also supplanted urllib as the go-to tool for Python programmers who need to communicate over HTTP.

Requests, built by Kenneth Reitz and powered by Andrey Petrov's urllib3 connection pooling logic, is the library in question.

You'll return to both urllib and Requests as you learn about HTTP in this chapter to examine what they do well and what they don't when faced with each HTTP feature. Their basic interfaces are very similar: they give a callable that establishes an HTTP connection, sends a request, and waits for the response headers before delivering a response object that displays them to the programmer. The body of the answer is queued on the incoming socket and only read when the programmer requests it.

In most of the examples in this chapter, I'll be testing the two HTTP client libraries against http://httpbin.org, a small test web site built by Kenneth Reitz that you can run locally by installing it using pip and then running it inside a WSGI container like Gunicorn (see Chapter 10). Simply type the following to run it on localhost port 8000 so you may try the examples in this chapter on your own machine without having to go to httpbin.org's public version:

```
$ pip install gunicorn httpbin requests
$ gunicorn httpbin:app
```

You should then be able to use both urllib and Requests to fetch one of its pages to see how their interfaces are similar at first appearance.

```
>>> import requests
>>> r = requests.get('http://localhost:8000/headers')
>>> print(r.text)
{
  "headers": {
        "Accept": "*/*",
        "Accept-Encoding": "gzip, deflate",
        "Host": "localhost:8000",
    "User-Agent": "python-requests/2.3.0 CPython/3.4.1 Linux/3.13.0-
34-generic"
  }
}
>>> from urllib.request import urlopen
>>> import urllib.error
>>> r = urlopen('http://localhost:8000/headers')
>>> print(r.read().decode('ascii'))
{
  "headers": {
  "Accept-Encoding": "identity",
  "Connection": "close",
  "Host": "localhost:8000",
```

```
"User-Agent": "Python-urllib/3.4"
  }
}
```

Two distinctions can already be seen, and they serve as a good forecast of what is to come later in this chapter. Requests declares up front that it supports gzip and deflate-compressed HTTP responses, whereas urllib is completely unaware of these formats. Furthermore, although Requests was able to determine the proper decoding to convert this HTTP response from raw bytes to text, the urllib library just returned bytes and left you to decode them.

Other attempts at strong Python HTTP clients have been made, with many of them attempting to be more browser-like. These wanted to move beyond the HTTP protocol taught in this chapter and start talking about ideas you'll learn about in Chapter 11, combining the structure of HTML, the semantics of its forms, and the rules of what a browser should do when you submit a form. For example, the library mechanise was popular for a while.

Finally, web pages are frequently too sophisticated to interact with anything less than a full browser, as forms are frequently only valid today due to annotations or alterations done by JavaScript. Many current forms don't even have a physical Submit button, instead relying on a script to complete their tasks. Browser control technologies have proven to be more beneficial than mechanise, and I discuss a few of them in Chapter 11.

The purpose of this chapter is to help you understand HTTP and how many of its functions are accessible through Requests and urllib, as well as the restrictions within which you will work if you use the urllib package included in Standard Library instead. If you ever find yourself in a scenario where you can't install third-party libraries but still need to conduct complex HTTP operations, you should review not only the urllib library's documentation but also the following two resources: its entry for Python Module of the Week, as well as the HTTP chapter in the online Dive Into Python book.

http://pymotw.com/2/urllib2/index.html#module-urllib2

These materials were both produced in the days of Python 2, thus they refer to the library as urllib2 rather than urllib.request, but they should still serve as a basic introduction to urllib's clumsy and out-of-date object-oriented design.

Framing, Encryption, and Ports

For plain-text HTTP chats, port 80 is the standard port. Port 443 is the standard port for clients who want to start an encrypted TLS discussion first (see Chapter 6) and then speak HTTP only after the encryption is established—a variation of the protocol known as Hypertext Transfer Protocol Secure (HTTPS). HTTP is spoken just as it would be over an unencrypted socket inside the encrypted channel.

As you'll see in Chapter 11, the user's choice between HTTP and HTTPS, as well as between a standard and a nonstandard port, is usually expressed in the URLs that they create or are provided.

Remember that the goal of TLS is to verify the identity of the server to which the client is connecting (and, if a client certificate is supplied, to allow the server to validate the client's identity in return). Never use an HTTPS client that doesn't verify that the server's certificate matches the hostname to which the client is trying to connect. This is something that all of the clients in this chapter do.

The client talks first in HTTP, submitting a request that names a document. After the full request has been sent over the wire, the client waits for a complete response from the server, which either signals an error condition or offers information about the content the client has requested. The client is not allowed to send a second request over the same connection until the response is complete, at least in the HTTP/1.1 version of the protocol that is widely used today.

The request and answer employ the same formatting and framing standards, which is a key symmetry built into HTTP. Here's an example request and response that you may use as a guide as you read the protocol description that follows:

```
GET /ip HTTP/1.1
User-Agent: curl/7.35.0
Host: localhost:8000
Accept: */*

HTTP/1.1 200 OK
Server: gunicorn/19.1.1
Date: Sat, 21 Sep 2020 00:18:00 GMT
Connection: close
Content-Type: application/json
Content-Length: 27
Access-Control-Allow-Origin: *
```

Access-Control-Allow-Credentials: true

```
{
 "origin": "127.0.0.1"
}
```

The request is the text block that starts with GET. The response starts with the HTTP/1.1 version and continues with the three lines of JSON text below the headers on a blank line. The standard refers to both the request and the answer as HTTP messages, and each message is made up of three elements.

- A first line in the request that names a method and document, and a return code and description in the response. A carriage return and linefeed (CR-LF, ASCII codes 13 and 10) mark the end of the line.

- A name, a colon, and a value are contained in one or more headers. Because header names are case-insensitive, a client or server can uppercase them anyway they like. A CR-LF is at the conclusion of each header. The entire list of headers is then terminated by a blank line—the four bytes CR-LF-CR-LF that constitute a pair of end-of-line sequences with nothing in between.

- An optional body that immediately follows the blank line that ends the headers, regardless of whether any headers appear above it. As you shall see momentarily, there are numerous choices for framing the object.

The first line and headers are each framed by their CR-LF sequences at the conclusion, and the entire assembly is framed as a whole by the blank line at the end. So a server or client can find the end by executing recv() until the four-character sequence CR-LF-CR-LF appears. Because there is no indication of how lengthy the line and headers might be, many servers set reasonable length limits to avoid running out of RAM when a troublemaker connects and sends infinite-length headers.

If a body has been connected to the message, you have three possibilities for framing it.

The presence of a Content-Length header, whose value should be a decimal number indicating the length of the body in bytes, is the most frequent framing. This is simple enough to put into practise. The client can simply repeat the recv() operation until the total number of bytes equals the specified length. When data is generated dynamically, however, specifying a Content-Length is not always possible, because the length of the data cannot be determined until the process is complete.

If the headers provide "chunked" as the Transfer-Encoding, a more sophisticated technique is enabled. Instead than having the length of the body given up front, it is provided in a number of smaller sections, each of which is prefixed by its own length. Each chunk has at least a hexadecimal (as opposed to the decimal Content-Length header!) length field, the two characters CR-LF, and a block of data of exactly the given length, again the two characters CR-LF. The chunks come to a close with a final chunk that states it has zero length—at the very least, the digit zero, a CR-LF, and then another CR-LF.

The sender can put a semicolon after the chunk length but before the CR-LF, and then specify a "extension" option for that chunk. The sender can append a few final HTTP headers after the last chunk has supplied its length of zero and its CR-LF. If you're implementing HTTP yourself, you may look up these specifics in RFC 7230.

The server can also provide "Connection: close," send as much or as little body as it wishes, and then close the TCP socket as an alternative to Content-Length. This increases the risk that the client will not be able to tell whether the socket closed because the entire body was successfully delivered or because the socket closed prematurely due to a server or network error, and it also reduces the protocol's efficiency by requiring the client to reconnect for each request.

(According to the standard, the client cannot use the "Connection: close" trick since it will not be able to receive the server's response.) Hadn't they heard of a unidirectional shutdown() on the socket, which would allow the client to terminate its direction while still receiving data from the server?).

Methods

An HTTP request's first word indicates the action that the client wants the server to perform. For servers that want to expose a full document API to other computer programmes that may be accessing them (usually, JavaScript that they have supplied to a browser), there are two common ways, GET and POST, plus a number of less common methods described.

HTTP's basic "read" and "write" activities are provided through the two basic methods, GET and POST.

When you type an HTTP URL into your web browser, the GET method is used to request that the document named by the request path be sent as the server's response. It can't have a body in it. Servers cannot, under any circumstances, allow clients to edit data using this approach, according to the standard. Any path parameters (see Chapter 11 for more information on URLs) can only affect the document that is being returned, such as?q=python or?results=10, and cannot request that modifications be made on the server. The restriction that GET cannot modify data allows a client to safely retry a GET if the first attempt fails, allows GET responses to be cached (you'll learn more about caching later in this chapter), and allows web scraping programmes (see Chapter 11) to visit as many URLs as they want without fear of creating or deleting content on the sites they're traversing.

When a client wants to send fresh data to the server, they utilise POST. Traditional online forms normally use POST to deliver your request if they don't just copy your form fields into the URL. POST is also used by developer-oriented APIs to submit new documents, comments, and database rows. Because repeating the same POST may lead the server to conduct an action twice, such as making a second $100 payment to a merchant, the results of a POST cannot be cached for future repeats, nor can a POST be automatically retried if the response does not arrive.

The remaining HTTP methods can be divided into two groups: those that are similar to GET and those that are similar to POST. OPTIONS and HEAD are methods similar to GET. The OPTIONS method determines which header values are compatible with a given path, while the HEAD method instructs the server to begin the process of preparing to transmit the resource but then halt and only transmit the headers. This allows a client to validate things like ContentType without having to download the entire body.

PUT and DELETE are similar to POST in that they are anticipated to make potentially irreversible changes to the content stored on the server. As their names suggest, PUT requests the server to create a new document that will live at the path specified in the request, whereas DELETE requests the server to delete the path and any content associated with it. Interestingly, while requesting "writes" of the server content, these two methods are safe in a way that POST is not: they are idempotent and can be retried as many times as the client desires because the result of running either of them once should be the same as running them many times.

Finally, the standard specifies a debugging method TRACE as well as a method CONNECT for switching protocols to something other than HTTP (which, as you'll see in Chapter 11, is used to turn on WebSocket).

They are, however, infrequently utilised, and in neither case do they have anything to do with document delivery, which is HTTP's primary function, which you will learn about in this chapter. More information about them can be found in the standard.

It's worth noting that urlopen() in the Standard Library chooses its HTTP verb invisibly: POST if the caller specifies a data parameter, or GET otherwise. This is a regrettable decision because proper HTTP verb usage is critical for secure client and server design. For two essentially distinct methods, the Requests choice of get() and post() is considerably superior.

Hosts and Paths

The initial versions of HTTP allowed only a verb and a route to be included in the request.

`GET /html/rfc7230`

This worked fine in the early days when each server only housed one web site, but it broke down when administrators tried to build massive HTTP servers capable of serving dozens or hundreds of sites. How could the server predict which hostname the user had placed in the URL given only a path—especially for a path like /, which is seen on almost every website?

Making at least one header, the Host header, necessary was the solution. In modern versions of the protocol, the protocol version is also included in a minimally correct request, which would look like this:

`GET /html/rfc7230 HTTP/1.1`

`Host: tools.ietf.org`

Unless the client provides at least a Host header identifying which hostname was used in the URL, many HTTP servers may report a client error. In the absence of it, the consequence is frequently a 400 Bad Request. More information about error codes and their meanings can be found in the section below.

Status Codes

The response line, unlike the request line, begins with the protocol version rather than finishing with it, and then provides a standard status code before closing with an informal written explanation of the status for display to the user or entry into a log file. When everything goes smoothly, the status code is 200, and the response line looks something like this:

`HTTP/1.1 200 OK`

Because the text after the code is just informal, a server may substitute OK for Okay, Yippee, or It Worked, or even text that had been internationalised for the country in which the server was located.

RFC 7231, in instance, specifies almost two dozen return codes for both general and specific scenarios. If you need to learn the entire list, consult the standard. The 200s denote success, the 300s redirection, the 400s show that the client request is incoherent or illegal, and the 500s indicate that something unexpected has gone wrong that is solely the server's fault.

Only a few things in this chapter will affect you.

- **200 OK**: The request has been completed successfully. If it was a POST, it had the desired impact.

- **301; Permanently Moved**: While the path is legitimate, it is not the canonical path for the resource in question (though it may have been in the past), and the client should instead request the URL indicated in the response's Location header. If the client wants to cache it, all future requests can skip this old URL and go straight to the new one.

- **303; Other**: The client can learn the result of this specific, one-of-a-kind request by performing a GET against the URL indicated in the response's Location header. Any subsequent attempts to access this resource will have to be made from this location. This status is critical to the design of websites, as you'll see in Chapter 11—any form submitted correctly using POST should return 303, so the actual page the client views is obtained using the safe, idempotent GET operation instead.

- **304 Not Modified**: Because the request headers indicate that the client already has an up-to-date version of the document in its cache (see the "Caching and Validation" section), the document body does not need to be included in the response.

- **307 Temporary Redirect**: Any request made by the client, whether GET or POST, should be retried against the different URL indicated in the response's Location header. However, any subsequent attempts to access this resource must be made from this location. This permits forms to be delivered to a different address if a server is offline or unavailable, for example.

- **400 Bad Request:** The request appears to be an invalid HTTP request.

- **403 Forbidden:** There is no password, cookie, or other identifying data in the request that indicates to the server that the client has authorization to access it (for both, see later in this chapter).

- **404 Not Found:** The path does not refer to a resource that exists. This is the most well-known exception code since customers never see the 200 code on their screen; instead, they see a document.

- **405 Method Not Allowed**: Although the server recognises the method and path, this method does not make sense when used with this path.

- **500 Server Error**: This is a common error code. The server wishes to complete the request, but is currently unable to do so due to an internal problem.

- **501 Not Implemented:** Your HTTP verb was not recognised by the server.
- **502 Bad Gateway:** The server is a gateway or proxy (see Chapter 10), but it is unable to communicate with the server that should be providing the response for this path.

While responses with 3xx status codes are not intended to have a body, responses with 4xx and 5xx status codes are more likely to do so, providing a human-readable description of the mistake. Unmodified error pages for the language or framework in which the web server was created are often the least helpful examples. More informative pages have frequently been built by server authors to assist users or developers in resolving errors.

There are two crucial questions to ask about status codes when learning a certain Python HTTP client.

The first question is whether a library follows redirects automatically. If not, you'll have to hunt down 3xx status codes and follow their Location heading manually. While the Standard Library's low-level httplib module would force you to follow redirection manually, the urllib module will do it for you in accordance with the standard. The Requests library performs the same thing, but it also has a history attribute that details all of the redirects that led you to the final destination.

```
>>> r = urlopen('http://httpbin.org/status/301')
>>> r.status, r.url
(200, 'http://httpbin.org/get')
>>> r = requests.get('http://httpbin.org/status/301')
>>> (r.status, r.url)
(200, 'http://httpbin.org/get')
>>> r.history
[<Response [301]>, <Response [302]>]
```

If you wish, you can also turn off redirection with a simple keyword argument in the Requests library—a feat that is doable but considerably more difficult with urllib.

```
>> r = requests.get('http://httpbin.org/status/301',
... allow_redirects=False)
>>> r.raise_for_status()
>>> (r.status_code, r.url, r.headers['Location'])
(301, 'http://localhost:8000/status/301', '/redirect/1')
```

If your Python software spends the effort to discover 301 failures and try to avoid those URLs in the future, it will lessen the burden on the servers you query. If your software has a persistent state, it may be able to cache 301 failures to prevent having to visit those pages again, or it may be able to directly rewrite the URL wherever it is stored. If the URL was queried interactively, you could print a nice message telling the user of the page's changed location.

The prefix www belongs at the front of the hostname you use to contact a server is one of the most typical redirections.

```
>>> r = requests.get('http://google.com/')
>>> r.url
'http://www.google.com/'
>>> r = requests.get('http://www.twitter.com/')
>>> r.url
'https://twitter.com/'
```

Two well-known websites have taken opposing positions on whether or not the www prefix should be included in their official hostname. They are, however, willing to utilise a redirect in both circumstances to enforce their desire and to avoid the confusion of their site appearing to reside at two separate URLs. If your URLs are created from the wrong hostname, you'll end up executing two HTTP requests instead of one for every resource you get unless your application is careful to learn these redirections and prevent repeating them.

Another thing to look into with your HTTP client is how it notifies you if an attempt to fetch a URL with a 4xx or 5xx status code fails. The Standard Library urlopen() throws an exception for all such codes, making it impossible for your code to mistakenly process an error page received from the server as regular data.

```
>>> urlopen('http://localhost:8000/status/500')

Traceback (most recent call last):

...

urllib.error.HTTPError: HTTP Error 500: INTERNAL SERVER ERROR
```

When urlopen() throws an exception, it's unable to study the response's data. The answer can be found by looking at the exception object, which serves as both an exception and a response object containing headers and a body.

```
>>> try:

... urlopen('http://localhost:8000/status/500')
```

```
... except urllib.error.HTTPError as e:

... print(e.status, repr(e.headers['Content-Type']))

500 'text/html; charset=utf-8'
```

The Requests library presents an even more startling situation: even incorrect status codes result in a response object being sent to the caller without comment. The caller must either test the response's status code or volunteer to execute its raise for status() method, which will throw an exception if the status code is 4xx or 5xx.

```
>>> r = requests.get('http://localhost:8000/status/500')

>>> r.status_code

500

>>> r.raise_for_status()

Traceback (most recent call last):

...

requests.exceptions.HTTPError: 500 Server Error: INTERNAL SERVER
ERROR
```

If you're concerned about having to remember to do a status check every time you make a call request, don't worry. obtain, then you might want to consider building your own wrapper function that does the check for you.

Validation and Caching

HTTP has numerous well-designed techniques for allowing clients to avoid repeated GETs of resources they frequently use, but they only work if the server adds headers to the resource that allow them. Caching should be considered by server authors and enabled whenever practical, as it decreases network traffic and server stress while simultaneously allowing client applications to function faster. All of these processes are described in great detail in RFCs 7231 and 7232. This section merely tries to provide a general overview.

When adding headers to enable caching, the most crucial question a service architect may ask is whether two requests should actually return the same page just because their paths are identical. Is there anything else about a pair of requests that could lead to them returning two different resources? If this is the case, a service must provide a Vary header in every response that lists the other headers that the document's content is dependent on. If the designer is returning different documents to various users, Host, Accept-Encoding, and notably Cookie are common possibilities.

There are many levels of caching that can be engaged once the Vary header is set correctly.

Resources can be prohibited from being saved in a client cache at all, preventing the client from making any form of nonvolatile storage copy of the answer. The goal is to provide the user control over whether or not they choose "save" to save a copy of the resource to disc.

HTTP/1.1 200 OK

Cache-control: no-store

...

If the server chooses to enable caching instead, it will almost always wish to guard against the chance that the client will keep delivering the cached copy of the resource every time the user requests it until it is completely out-of-date. When a server is cautious to use a specific path only for a single permanent version of a document or picture, it does not need to worry about whether resources are cached indefinitely. If the version number or hash at the end of the URL is incremented or modified each time the designers release a new version of the corporate logo, for example, any version of the logo can be sent with permission to store it forever.

The server can restrict the client copy of the resource from being used indefinitely in two ways. For starters, it can define an expiration date and time after which the resource can no longer be reused without a server request.

HTTP/1.1 200 OK

Expires: Thu, 01 Dec 1999 16:00:00 GMT

...

However, using a date and time poses the risk that an erroneously set client clock will cause the cached copy of the resource to be consumed for an inordinate amount of time. The newer methodology of setting the number of seconds that the resource can be cached once it has been received is a far superior method, and it will function as long as the client clock is not just blocked.

HTTP/1.1 200 OK

Cache-control: max-age=3600

...

The two headers displayed here give the client the unilateral authority to keep utilising an old copy of a resource for a limited time without consulting the server.

But what if a server wants to keep the option of using a cached resource or fetching a new version? In that instance, the client will have to make an HTTP request to check back each time it wishes to utilise the resource. This will be more expensive than allowing the client to use the cached copy quietly and without a network activity, but it will save time because the server will have to transmit a new copy of the resource if the client's only old copy is actually out-of-date.

There are two ways for a server to force a client to check back after each use of a resource while allowing the client to reuse its cached copy of the resource if possible. The standard refers to them as conditional requests since they only result in the delivery of a body if the checks find that the client cache is out-of-date.

The first mechanism necessitates the server's knowledge of the most recent resource modification. If the resources are backed by a file on the file system, determining this is simple, but if the resources are taken from a database table without an audit log or a date of last modification, it can be difficult or impossible. The server can include the information in every response if it is accessible.

```
HTTP/1.1 200 OK

Last-Modified: Tue, 15 Nov 1999 12:45:26 GMT

...
```

If a client wants to reuse a cached copy of the resource, it can save the date and then send it back to the server the next time it needs it. If the server determines that the resource has not changed since the client last got it, the server can choose to provide only headers and the special status code 304 instead of a body.

```
GET / HTTP/1.1

If-Modified-Since: Tue, 15 Nov 1994 12:45:26 GMT

...

HTTP/1.1 304 Not Modified

...
```

Instead of modify time, the second approach deals with resource identity. In this situation, the server requires a means to establish a unique tag for each version of a resource that is guaranteed to change to a new unique value every time the resource changes—checksums or database UUIDs are two options. When the server constructs a response, it must include the tag in an ETag header.

```
HTTP/1.1 200 OK
```

```
ETag: "d41d8cd98f00b204e9800998ecf8427e"
```

...

When a client that has cached and owns this version of the resource wishes to reuse it to fulfil a user action, it can send a request to the server for the resource, including the cached tag if it still refers to the current version of the resource.

```
GET / HTTP/1.1
```

```
If-None-Match: "d41d8cd98f00b204e9800998ecf8427e"
```

...

```
HTTP/1.1 304 Not Modified
```

...

ETag and If-None-Match use quotation marks to indicate that the scheme can perform more powerful comparisons than merely comparing two strings for equality. If you want more information, see Section 3.2 of RFC 7232. It's worth noting that If-Modified-Since and If-None-Match both conserve bandwidth by avoiding the resource from being transferred twice, as well as time spent in transmission. Before the client may access the resource, they must first make a round-trip to the server and return.

Caching is a powerful tool that is critical to the current Web's performance. However, neither of the Python client libraries you're considering performs caching by default. Both urllib and Requests think that their duty is to perform a real-time network HTTP request when you need one, not to manage a cache that may prevent you from ever needing to talk over the network. If you want a wrapper that, when pointed to some sort of local persistent storage that you can provide, employs Expires and Cache-control headers, modification dates, and ETags to try to minimise latency and network traffic, you'll have to look for third-party libraries.

If you're configuring or operating a proxy, caching is another something to consider, which I'll go over in Chapter 10.

Encoding of Content

The distinction between an HTTP transport encoding and a content encoding is critical.

A transfer encoding is essentially a method of converting a resource into the body of an HTTP response. The choice of transfer encoding makes no difference in the end, by definition. For example, regardless of whether the response was framed with a Content-Length or a chunked encoding, the client should receive the same document or picture. Whether the bytes were delivered raw or compressed to speed up transmission, the resource should look the same.

A transfer encoding is merely a data transportation wrapper, not a change in the underlying data.

Despite the fact that modern web browsers accept a variety of transfer encodings, gzip is perhaps the most popular among programmers. A client capable of accepting this transfer encoding must declare it in an Accept-Encoding header and be prepared to read the response's Transfer-Encoding header to see if the server accepted it.

```
GET / HTTP/1.1

Accept-Encoding: gzip

...

HTTP/1.1 200 OK

Content-Length: 3913

Transfer-Encoding: gzip

...
```

Because the urllib library doesn't support this technique, you'll have to write your own code to generate and detect these headers, as well as uncompress the response body, if you want to use compressed transfer encodings.

If the server responds with an acceptable Transfer-Encoding, the Requests library immediately declares an Accept-Encoding of gzip,deflate and uncompresses the content. This enables compression both automated and invisible to Requests users when servers support it.

Negotiation of Content

In contrast to transfer encoding, content type and content encoding are completely visible to the end user or client software making an HTTP request. They define which file format will be used to represent a specific resource, as well as what encoding will be used to convert text code points into bytes if the format is text.

These headers allow an older browser that can't show new-fangled PNG images to indicate that it prefers GIF and JPG instead, and they allow resources to be delivered in the language that the user has specified. Here's an example of how such headers may seem when created by a contemporary browser:

```
GET / HTTP/1.1
Accept: text/html;q=0.9,text/plain,image/jpg,*/*;q=0.8
Accept-Charset: unicode-1-1;q=0.8
Accept-Language: en-US,en;q=0.8,ru;q=0.6
User-Agent: Mozilla/5.0 (X11; Linux i686) AppleWebKit/537.36 (KHTML)
...
```

The kinds and languages listed first in the header have the strongest preference value of 1.0, however those listed later in the header are frequently degraded to q=0.9 or q=0.8 to ensure that the server understands they are not favoured over the best options. Many simple HTTP services and sites ignore these headers entirely, opting instead to use a different URL for each version of a resource they have. If a site supports both English and French, the front page might be available in two versions: /en/index.html and /fr/index.html. When viewing the corporation's press kit, the identical corporate logo could be found at both /logo.png and /logo.gif, and the user could be given both for download. Different URL query parameters, such as?f=json and?f=xml, are frequently specified in the documentation for a RESTful web service (see Chapter 10) to pick the representation that is delivered.

That, however, is not how HTTP was intended to work.

The goal of HTTP was for a resource to have only one path to follow, regardless of how many different machine formats—or human languages—might be used to render it, and for the server to select that resource using content negotiation headers.

Why is it that content negotiation is so often overlooked?

For starters, content negotiation may provide the user minimal control over their experience. Consider a website that has pages in both English and French. The server has no control over the issue if it displays a language based on the Accept-Language header and the user wants to see the other language—it would have to propose to the user that they open their web browser's control panel and change their default language. What if the user is unable to locate that option? What if they're using a public computer and don't have permission to set preferences to begin with?

Rather than entrusting language selection to a browser that may or may not be well-written, consistent, or simple to configure, many websites create multiple redundant sets of pathways, one for each human language they wish to serve. They may evaluate the Accept-Language header when the user first enters in order to autodirect the browser to the language that is most likely to be appropriate. They do, however, want the user to be allowed to browse in the opposite way if the choice was incorrect.

Second, because HTTP client APIs (whether used by JavaScript in a browser or offered by other languages in their own runtimes) often make it difficult to control the Accepts headers, content negotiation is often ignored (or sits alongside a URL-based mechanism for forcing the return of the correct version of the content). The advantage of putting control components in the path within the URL is that anyone with even the most basic tool for getting a URL may twiddle the knob by modifying the URL.

Finally, content negotiation requires HTTP servers to generate or select content based on a variety of axes. You might think that server logic always has access to the Accepts headers, but this isn't necessarily the case. When content negotiation is removed from the equation, server programming becomes much easier. Information negotiation, on the other hand, can help complex services reduce the number of available URLs while still providing a way for an intelligent HTTP client to obtain content that has been rendered with its data formatting or human reader's needs in mind. If you intend to use it, review RFC 7231 for information on the syntax of the various Accept headers.

The User-Agent string is one last irritation.

The User-Agent was never designed to be used in content negotiation; it was only supposed to be used as a temporary workaround for browser constraints. In other words, it was a means for targeting specific clients with carefully prepared updates while allowing all other clients to access the page without issue.

However, developers of applications supported by customer call centres quickly realised that prohibiting any browser other than a single version of Internet Explorer from accessing their site could eliminate compatibility issues and reduce the number of support calls up front, reducing the number of support calls. As a result of the arms race between clients and browsers, you now have incredibly large User-Agent strings, as reported rather fancifully at

http://webaim.org/blog/user-agent-string-history/.

Both the client libraries you're looking at, urllib and Requests, allow you to include any Accept headers you like in your request. They also both support patterns for designing a client that automatically uses your preferred headers. This feature is included straight into Requests' concept of a Session.

```
>>> s = requests.Session()

>>> s.headers.update({'Accept-Language': 'en-US,en;q=0.8'})
```

Unless overridden with a different value, all subsequent calls to methods like s.get() will use this default value for the header. The urllib library has its own techniques for configuring default handlers that can inject default headers, but they're a bit confusing and object-oriented, so I'll recommend you to the documentation.

Type of Content

After inspecting the multiple Accepts headers from the client and deciding the representation of a resource to offer, the server modifies the Content-Type header of the outgoing response.

Content types are chosen from a list of MIME types that have already been developed for multimedia that is sent in e-mail communications (see Chapter 12). Text/plain and text/html, as well as image formats like image/gif, image/jpg, and image/png, are all widespread. Documents can be sent in a variety of formats, such as application/pdf. The content type application/octet-stream is assigned to a plain series of bytes for which the server can guarantee no more particular interpretation. When dealing with a Content-Type header delivered through HTTP, there is one issue to be aware of. If text is the major type (the term to the left of the slash), the server has several possibilities for encoding text characters for transmission to the client. It declares its preference by attaching a semicolon and a statement of the character encoding used to convert the text to bytes to the Content-Type header.

```
Content-Type: text/html; charset=utf-8
```

This implies you can't just compare the Content-Type header to a list of MIME types without first looking for the semicolon and breaking it in two. The majority of libraries will be unable to assist you in this area. If you build code that needs to inspect the content type, you'll have to split on the semicolon whether you use urllib or Requests (although Requests will at least use, if not tell you about, the content type's charset setting if you ask its Response object for its already-decoded text attribute).

Ian Bicking's WebOb library (Chapter 10) is the only one in this book that allows you to manipulate the content type and character set separately by default. Its Response objects have separate attributes called content type and charset that are combined with a semicolon in the Content-Type header as per the standard.

Authentication over HTTP

Authentication specifies any procedures for detecting whether a request originates from someone who is authorised to make it, just as the word authentic suggests something that is genuine, real, actual, or true. Just as a phone call to a bank or airline will be prefaced with questions about your address and personal information to ensure that the person calling is the account holder, an HTTP request will frequently require built-in proof of the identity of the machine or person making it.

Servers that want to announce formally, through the protocol itself, that they can't authenticate your identity or that your identity is fine but you're not authorized to view this particular resource it use the error code 401 Not Authorized.

Because they are built solely for human users, many real-world HTTP servers never bother to return 401. An attempt to fetch a resource without the necessary identifier will most likely result in a 303 See Other to their login page on these servers. This is useful for humans, but not so much for your Python software, which will have to learn to discern between a 303 See Other that actually indicates a failure to authenticate and a harmless redirection that is simply attempting to get you to the resource. Because each HTTP request is distinct from all others, including those that follow soon after it, Any authenticating information must be carried separately in each request before and after it on the same socket. This independence is what allows proxy servers and load balancers to distribute HTTP requests to as many servers as they choose, even if they originate from the same socket. To learn about the most modern HTTP authentication techniques, read RFC 7235. The first steps were not encouraging in the beginning.

Basic Authentication (also known as "Basic Auth") required the server to include a string called a realm in its 401 Not Authorized headers. Because the browser can keep track of which user password goes with which realm, a single server can encrypt different sections of its document tree with separate passwords. The client then sends another request with an Authorization header that includes the username and password (base-64 encoded, as if that matters), and it expects a 200 response.

```
GET / HTTP/1.1

...

HTTP/1.1 401 Unauthorized
WWW-Authenticate: Basic realm="engineering team"

...

GET / HTTP/1.1

Authorization: Basic YnJhbmRvbjphdGlnZG5nbmF0d3dhbA==
```

...

```
HTTP/1.1 200 OK
```

...

Passing the login and password in plain sight may seem unethical now, but there were no wireless networks back then, and switching equipment tended to be solid-state rather than running software that could be hacked. As protocol designers began to consider the risks, a new "Digest access authentication" approach was developed, in which the server sends a challenge and the client instead responds with an MD5 hash of the challenge-plus-password. However, the end effect is still a tragedy. Your username is still visible in the clear, even if Digest authentication is used. All form data is visible in the open, as are all resources returned from the website. r. An astute attacker can then execute a man-in-the-middle attack, convincing you to sign a challenge that they have just received from the server and can then use to impersonate you. If banks wanted to show you your balance and Amazon wanted you to fill in your credit card information, websites needed true security. As a result, SSL was created in order to develop HTTPS, and it was followed by the many versions of TLS that you use today, as described in Chapter 6.

In theory, the adoption of TLS meant that there was no longer any issue with Basic Auth. It's used in a lot of simple HTTPS-protected APIs and web applications today. Requests supports Basic Auth with a single keyword parameter, but urllib only supports it if you generate a sequence of objects to install in your URL opener (see the manual for details).

```
>>> r = requests.get('http://example.com/api/',

... auth=('bpbonline'))
```

You may also create a Requests Session for authentication so you don't have to do it every time you get() or post().

```
>>> s = requests.Session()

>>> s.auth = 'bpbonline'

>>> s.get('http://httpbin.org/basic-auth/bpbonline')

<Response [200]>
```

Please keep in mind that this method, as implemented by Requests or other current libraries, is not the whole protocol! The previously given username and password are not related to any specific world. Because the username and password are supplied unilaterally with the request without checking whether the server even needs them, there is no 401 response that may provide a realm. The auth keyword argument, or the analogous Session setting, is just a shortcut for establishing the Authorization header without having to do any base-64 encoding.

This simplicity is preferred by modern developers over the complete realm-based protocol. Their sole purpose is to authenticate GET or POST queries to a programmer-targeted API independent of the identity of the user or application making the request. This is when a unilateral Authorization header comes in handy. It also has another benefit: time and bandwidth are not wasted obtaining an initial 401 when the client has reason to assume the password would be required.

Requests will not help you if you end yourself talking to a true legacy system that requires you to use various passwords for different realms on the same server. It will be your responsibility to use the correct password with the correct URLs. This is a rare instance where urllib can perform the right thing whereas Requests can't! However, I've never heard anyone complain about this flaw in Requests, which shows how uncommon real Basic Auth negotiation has become.

Cookies

Today, HTTP-mediated authentication is uncommon. In the end, HTTP resources designed to be browsed by users using a web browser were a losing proposition.

What was the issue with users and HTTP authentication? Typically, web site designers want to do their own authentication in their own way. They want a personalised, user-friendly login page that adheres to their own set of user interaction rules. When web browsers are asked for in-protocol HTTP authentication, they display a sad little pop-up box. Even at their best, they aren't really informative. They entirely remove the user from the site's experience. Furthermore, any failure to fill in the correct username and password can result in the pop-up displaying repeatedly, with the user having no idea what is wrong or how to fix it.

As a result, cookies were created.

From the client's perspective, a cookie is an opaque key-value pair. It can be included in every successful server response that the client receives.

```
GET /login HTTP/1.1

...

HTTP/1.1 200 OK

Set-Cookie: session-id=d41d8cd98f00b204e9800998ecf8427e; Path=/
```

...

The client adds that name and value in a Cookie header in all subsequent requests to that particular server.

```
GET /login HTTP/1.1

Cookie: session-id=d41d8cd98f00b204e9800998ecf8427e
```

...

This enabled the creation of login pages generated by the site. When an invalid login form is submitted, the server can re-present it with as many helpful hints or support links as it wants, all formatted to match the rest of the site. Once the form has been successfully submitted, the client may be given a cookie that has been specially constructed to convince the site of the user's identity during all subsequent requests.

A login page that isn't a true web form but uses Ajax to stay on the same page (see Chapter 11) can still benefit from cookies if the API is hosted on the same hostname. When the login API call confirms the username and password and returns 200 OK with a Cookie header, it enables all subsequent requests to the same site—not just API calls, but also page, image, and data requests—to deliver the cookie and be recognised as coming from an authenticated user.

It's worth noting that cookies should be opaque. They should either be random UUID strings that direct the server to a database record containing the genuine username or encrypted strings that only the server can decrypt in order to learn the user's identity. If they were user-parsable—for example, if a cookie held the value THIS-USER-IS-bpbonline—a savvy user could change it to make a fabricated value and send it with their next request to impersonate another user whose username they knew or could estimate.

Real-world Set-Cookie headers can be even more complex than the example given, as RFC 6265 explains in detail. I'd like to bring up the secure attribute. When sending unencrypted requests to the site, it directs the HTTP client not to present the cookie. Without this characteristic, a cookie could be revealed, allowing anyone else using the coffee shop's wi-fi to learn the cookie's value and impersonate the user. Some websites will place a cookie on your computer just for visiting. This allows them to keep track of your visit as you navigate the site. The information gathered can already be used to target advertisements as you browse, and it can even be copied into your permanent account history if you check in with a username later.

Without cookies to keep track of your identification and prove that you have authenticated, many user-directed HTTP services will not work. Cookie tracking with urllib necessitates object orientation; please read the manual for more information.

Cookies are automatically tracked in Requests if a Session object is created and used consistently.

Keep-Alive, Connections, and httplib

If a connection is already open, the three-way handshake that initiates a TCP connection (see Chapter 3) can be skipped, which gave the impetus for HTTP to allow connections to stay open as a browser received an HTTP resource, then its JavaScript, and finally its CSS and images. The cost of establishing up a new connection has increased due to the development of TLS (see Chapter 6) as a best practise for all HTTP connections, increasing the value of connection reuse.

It is now the default for an HTTP connection to stay open after a request in protocol version HTTP/1.1. Connection: can be specified by either the client or the server. If they intend to hang up once a request is completed, close the connection; otherwise, a single TCP connection can be used to fetch as many resources from the server as the client desires. Web browsers frequently establish four or more simultaneous TCP connections per site in order to download a page and all of its supporting data and pictures in simultaneously in order to get them in front of the user as rapidly as feasible. If you are an implementer who is interested in the details, you should examine Section 6 of RFC 7230 to learn about the comprehensive connection control mechanism.

The urllib module does not allow for connection reuse, which is disappointing. Only the lower-level httplib module in the Standard Library allows you to make two requests on the same connection.

```
>>> import http.client
>>> h = http.client.HTTPConnection('localhost:8000')
>>> h.request('GET', '/ip')
>>> r = h.getresponse()
>>> r.status
200
>>> h.request('GET', '/user-agent')
>>> r = h.getresponse()
>>> r.status
200
```

When you ask it to conduct another request, an HTTPConnection object that has become stuck will not return an error, but it will discreetly construct a new TCP connection to replace the previous one. A TLS-protected version of the same object is provided by the HTTPSConnection class. The Session object in the Requests library, on the other hand, is supported by urllib3, a third-party package that keeps track of open connections to HTTP servers with which you've recently communicated so that it can try to reuse them automatically when you ask for another resource from the same site.

Conclusion

The HTTP protocol is used to retrieve resources that have a hostname and a path. The urllib client in the Standard Library will work in simple scenarios, but it is underpowered and lacks the functionality of Requests, a Python library that has become an Internet sensation and is the go-to tool for programmers who wish to get information from the Web.

HTTP employs the same basic layout on the wire for the client request and the server response: a line of information followed by name-value headers, then a blank line, and then, optionally, a body that can be encoded and delimited in a variety of ways. The client always talks first, submitting a request, and then waits for a response from the server. The most frequent HTTP methods are GET, which is used to retrieve a resource, and POST, which is used to deliver updated data to a server. There are a few different methods, but they all seem to be either GET or POST. Each answer from the server includes a status code that indicates whether the request was successful or unsuccessful, or whether the client has to be forwarded to another resource to complete it. HTTP is made up of numerous concentric layers of design. Caching headers could allow a resource to be cached and reused on a client without having to reload it, or they could allow the server to forgo redelivering a resource that hasn't changed. Both adjustments can make a big difference in the performance of a busy website.

Content negotiation has the potential to adjust data formats and human languages to the specific desires of the client and the user, but it has issues in practise that make it less often used. Although built-in HTTP authentication was a bad design for interactive use and was replaced with custom login pages and cookies, Basic Auth is still used to authenticate calls to TLS-secured APIs on occasion. By default, HTTP/1.1 connections can persist and be reused, and the Requests library makes every effort to do so. In the next chapter, you'll take what you've learned so far and apply it to the task of programming by looking at it from the perspective of constructing a server.

CHAPTER 10

Servers that handle HTTP

How can a Python programme reply to HTTP requests as a server? For constructing a TCP-based network server, you learnt various essential socket and concurrency patterns in Chapter 7. Because HTTP's popularity has led in off-the-shelf solutions for all of the key server patterns that you could require, it's doubtful that you'll ever need to create anything that low-level with it.

While It's even possible to use it from the command line.

```
$ python3 -m http.server
Serving HTTP on 0.0.0.0 port 8000 ...
```

For serving files from the filesystem, this server adheres to the old conventions established in the 1990s. The path in the HTTP request is converted to a path on the local filesystem to search. Only files in or beneath the current working directory are served by the server. Files are served as usual. When a directory is mentioned, the server either sends the contents of its index.html file, if one exists, or a dynamically created listing of the files contained within. When I've needed to transfer data between machines and none of the more particular file transfer protocols were accessible, having a small web server available wherever Python is installed has gotten me out of a lot of tight spots. But, if you need anything more—if you need to put your own programme in charge of responding to HTTP requests—what steps should you take?

This question is addressed in two chapters of this book. Whether your code produces documents or a programmerfacing API,. The World Wide Web will subsequently be described in Chapter 11, as well as methods for returning HTML pages and communicating with a user's browser.

Structure:

- Web Server Gateway Interface (WSGI)
- Server-Frameworks that are asynchronous
- Proxies (Forward and Reverse)
- four architecture style.
- Python on Apache
- Pure-Python HTTP Servers on the Rise
- The Advantages of Reverse Proxies
- Platforms as a Service (PaaS)
- The REST Question and GET and POST Patterns
- Web Server Gateway Interface (WSGI)Without a Framework
- Conclusion

Objectives:

the focus of this chapter is on third-party tools, the Standard Library includes an HTTP server implementation & will look at server architecture and deployment, answering the questions that need to be answered.

Web Server Gateway Interface (WSGI)

Many Python services were created as basic CGI scripts that were invoked once per incoming request in the early days of HTTP programming. The server broke up the HTTP request into chunks and stored them in the environment variables of the CGI script. Python programmers may inspect them directly and print an HTTP response to standard output, or they could use the Standard Library's cgi module for assistance. Because launching a new process for each incoming HTTP request slowed server performance significantly, language runtimes began to create their own HTTP servers.

Python now has the http.server Standard Library module, which allows programmers to create their own services by adding do_GET() and do_POST() methods to their own BaseHTTPRequestHandler subclasses.

Other programmers desired dynamic pages to be served through a web server that could also provide static material like images and stylesheets. Mod python was created as a result: an Apache module that allowed correctly registered Python functions to provide bespoke Apache handlers for authentication, logging, and content. Apache's API was one-of-a-kind. Python handlers were given a specific Apache request object as an argument and could use the apache module's special functions to interface with the web server. Applications created with mod python looked nothing like those written using CGI or http.server.

As a result, each HTTP application designed in Python tended to be tethered to a single method of communicating with the web server. To work with http.server, a service created for CGI would need at least a partial rewriting, and both would need to be modified before they could run under Apache. This makes it difficult to transfer Python web services to new platforms. PEP 333, Web Server Gateway Interface, was created as a result of the community's response (WSGI).

"All difficulties in computer science may be solved by another level of indirection," as David Wheeler famously observed, and the WSGI standard provided the extra level of indirection required for a Python HTTP service to work with any web server. It defined a calling convention that, if adopted by all major web servers, would allow low-level services and whole web frameworks to be plugged into any web server. The attempt to deploy WSGI everywhere was immediately successful, and it is currently the default mechanism for Python to communicate with HTTP.

A WSGI application is defined by the standard as a callable with two arguments. Listing 10-1 shows an example where the callable is a basic Python function. (A Python class, which is another type of callable, or even a class instance with a __ call__() method are alternative options.) The first parameter, environ, is given a dictionary that contains a more comprehensive version of the previous CGI set of environment variables. The second parameter is a callable named start_response() that the WSGI application should use to declare its response headers. The app can either start giving byte strings (if it is a generator) or return an iterable that yields byte strings when iterated across after being called (returning a simple Python list is sufficient, for example).

Listing 10-1. A Straightforward HTTP Service As a WSGI client, it's been written.

```
#!/usr/bin/env python3

# Programming in Python: The Basics

# A simple HTTP service built directly against the low-level WSGI spec.

from pprint import pformat
```

```
from wsgiref.simple_server import make_server

def app(environ, start_response):

 headers = {'Content-Type': 'text/plain; charset=utf-8'}

 start_response('200 OK', list(headers.items()))

 yield 'Here is the WSGI environment:\r\n\r\n'.encode('utf-8')

 yield pformat(environ).encode('utf-8')

if __name__ == '__main__':

 httpd = make_server('', 8000, app)

 host, port = httpd.socket.getsockname()

 print('Serving on', host, 'port', port)

       httpd.serve_forever()
```

Listing 10-1 may make WSGI appear straightforward, but that is only because it has chosen to operate in a simplistic manner rather than fully utilising the standard. When implementing the server side of the specification, the level of complexity is higher since the code must be prepared for applications that take full advantage of the standard's many caveats and edge cases. If you want a better grasp of what's involved, check PEP 3333, the contemporary Python 3 version of WSGI.

Following the release of WSGI, the idea of WSGI middleware—the idea that future Python HTTP services may be built from a series of concentric WSGI wrappers—gained popularity. Authentication could be provided by a single wrapper. Before returning a 500 Internal Server Error page, another might catch exceptions and log them. Another might reverse-proxy legacy URLs to an outdated CMS still in use in an organisation and re-theme it to fit the organization's more current pages using Diazo (a project that still exists). Although some developers continue to design and utilise WSGI middleware, most Python programmers now use it solely for the pluggability it provides between an application or framework and the web server that listens for incoming HTTP requests.

Server-Frameworks that are asynchronous

However, there is one application design that has remained unaffected by the WSGI revolution: asynchronous servers that allow coroutines or green threads.

Because the WSGI callable is designed to work with a standard multithreaded or multiprocess server, it is anticipated to block during any I/O operations. WSGI does not provide a way for the callable to return control to the main server thread so that other callables can take turns progressing. (Review how an asynchronous service separates its logic into short, nonblocking bits of code in Chapter 7's explanation of asynchrony.) As a result, each asynchronous server framework has had to develop its own set of rules for writing web services. While these patterns differ in terms of simplicity and convenience, they often handle parsing incoming HTTP requests and may provide conveniences such as automatic URL dispatch and database connection commit (see Chapter 11).

This is why "Server-Frameworks" is included in the section's title. Projects experimenting with async in Python must first create an HTTP web server on top of their engine, then devise a calling convention for passing the request information they've parsed to your own code. You can't choose an async HTTP server and web framework individually, unlike in the WSGI ecosystem. Both are most likely to be included in the same package. For more than a decade, the Twisted server, which supports a variety of protocol handlers, has provided its own set of rules for developing web services. Facebook recently built and released its Tornado engine, which, rather than supporting a wide range of protocols, focuses solely on HTTP performance. Twisted does not support the same set of callback conventions. The Eventlet project, whose green threads are implicitly asynchronous rather than explicitly handing control back at each I/O transaction, allows you to write callables that appear to be conventional WSGI but silently give control when they attempt blocking activities.

In the future, Guido van Rossum, the creator of Python, has pushed for the new asyncio engine in Python 3.4 (see Chapter 7) to provide a standardised interface for different event-loop implementations to integrate into different asynchronous protocol frameworks. While this may help to unify the diverse world of low-level event loops, it does not appear to have any immediate impact on authors who want to develop asynchronous HTTP services because it does not specify an API that speaks the HTTP request and response language. If you're developing an HTTP service using an async engine like asyncio, Tornado, or Twisted, keep in mind that you get to choose both your HTTP server and the framework that will help you parse requests and compose responses. Servers and frameworks will not be able to be mixed and matched.

Proxies (Forward and Reverse)

An HTTP proxy, whether forward or reverse, is an HTTP server that receives incoming requests and, in some cases, transforms into a client making an outbound HTTP request to a server behind it, before returning the response to the original client. For an introduction to proxies and how the design of HTTP anticipates their demands, see RFC 7230 Section 2.3: https://tools.ietf.org/html/rfc7230#section-2.3.

Forward proxies appear to have been the most popular proxying pattern in early accounts of the Web. Instead than directly communicating with remote servers, an employer can provide an HTTP proxy that employees' web browsers request. If a hundred employees request the Google logo first thing in the morning, the proxy might only make one request to Google for the logo, which could then be cached and used to meet all later employee requests. The employer would suffer less bandwidth and the employees would experience a speedier Web if Google was generous with its Expires and Cache-Control headers. Forward proxies are no longer possible due to the adoption of TLS as a universal best practise for protecting user privacy and credentials. A proxy can't inspect or cache a request it doesn't understand.

Reverse proxies, on the other hand, have become commonplace in major HTTP services. A reverse proxy is used as part of a web service and is completely hidden from HTTP clients. Clients who believe they are talking to python.org are actually communicating through a reverse proxy. If the core python.org servers were careful to include Expires or Cache-Control headers, the proxy can provide many static and dynamic pages directly from its cache. Because HTTP requests are only delivered to the core servers if a resource is either uncacheable or has expired from the proxy's cache, a reverse proxy can typically bear the majority of the load of maintaining a service.

TLS termination must be performed by a reverse proxy, and it must be the service that owns the certificate and private key for the service it proxies. A proxy cannot conduct caching or forwarding unless it can examine each incoming HTTP request.

When using a reverse proxy, whether it's a front-end web server like Apache or nginx or a dedicated daemon like Varnish, caching-related headers like Expires and Cache-Control become even more critical than usual. They become vital signals between tiers of your own service design, rather than being significant simply to the end user's browser.

Reverse proxies can also help with data that you don't think should be cached, such as a headline page or an event log that requires up-to-the-second accuracy, as long as you can live with the findings being a few seconds old. After all, retrieving a resource takes just a fraction of a second in most cases. Is it really so bad if the resource is one second older? Consider setting the Cache-Control header of a vital feed or event log that receives a hundred requests per second to a one-second maximum age. Your reverse proxy will kick in and potentially lower your server load by a factor of a hundred: it will only need to fetch the resource once every second at the start of the second, and it will be able to reuse that cached result for all other clients who ask.

If you're planning on creating and implementing a large HTTP service behind a proxy, RFC 7234 with its extensive discussion of HTTP caching's design and expected benefits is a good place to start. You'll find options and parameters like proxy-revalidate and s-maxage that are explicitly targeted at intermediary caches like Varnish rather than the end user's HTTP client, which you should have in your toolkit when you approach a service design.

The content of a page is frequently determined by factors other than its path and method, such as the Host header, the identity of the user making the request, and sometimes headers defining what content types their client can support. Examine the Vary header description in RFC 7231 section 7.1.4, as well as the Vary header description in Chapter 9. The value Vary: Cookie is frequently required to ensure accurate behaviour for reasons that will become evident.

four architecture style.

While architects appear to be capable of devising an infinite number of complex methods for putting together an HTTP service from smaller elements, the Python community has settled on four major approaches (see Figure 10-1). What are your alternatives for deploying an HTTP service if you've created Python code to generate dynamic content and choose a WSGI-aware API or framework?

- Create a server that is written in Python and can call your WSGI endpoint from within its own code. Although the Green Unicorn ("gunicorn") server is now the most popular, there are several production-ready, pure-Python servers available. For example, the battle-tested CherryPy server is still in use in projects today, while Flup continues to gain users. (Unless your service is modest load and internal to an organisation, prototype servers like wsgiref should be avoided.) If you use an async server engine, you'll have to run both the server and the framework in the same process.

- Use Apache with mod wsgi configured to run your Python code in a separate WSGIDaemonProcess, resulting in a hybrid solution in which two distinct languages are used on the same server. Static resources are served straight from Apache's C-language engine, whereas dynamic paths are passed to mod wsgi, which then calls the Python interpreter to execute your application code. (This option is not accessible for async web frameworks since WSGI does not provide a means for an application to momentarily relinquish control and then complete its work later.)

- Behind a web server, run a Python HTTP server like Gunicorn (or whatever server your async framework requires) that can serve static files directly while simultaneously acting as a reverse proxy for the dynamic resources you've developed in Python. For this role, both Apache and nginx are popular front-end servers. If your Python application outgrows a single computer, they may load-balance requests across multiple back-end servers.

- Create a third layer that faces the actual world by running a Python HTTP server behind Apache or nginx, which is then behind a pure reverse proxy like Varnish. These reverse proxies can be dispersed globally, allowing cached resources to be provided from sites close to client machines rather than all from the same continent. Fastly and other content delivery networks function by deploying armies of Varnish servers to machine rooms across the globe and then leveraging them to provide you with a turnkey service that terminates your externally facing TLS certificates and routes requests to your central servers.

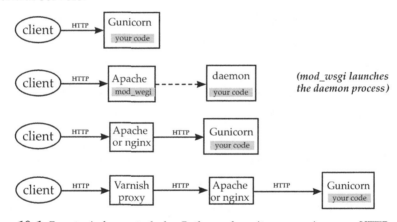

Figure 10-1. *Four typical ways to deploy Python code on its own or via reverse HTTP proxies.*

The interpreter is large, slow, and its Global Interpret Lock prevents more than one thread from executing Python bytecode at the same time, so the choice between these four architectures has historically been driven by three features of the C Python runtime: the interpreter is large, slow, and its Global Interpret Lock prevents more than one thread from executing Python bytecode at the same time.

Because of the interpreter lock's constraints, it was decided to employ distinct Python processes rather than numerous Python threads sharing the same process. However, the interpreter's size pushed the other way: only a limited number of Python instances can fit in RAM, limiting the number of processes.

Python on Apache

Imagine an early Python-powered web site running on Apache with the old mod python. This will help you understand the issues outlined before. The majority of queries to a normal web site (see Chapter 11) are for static resources: for every request to have Python dynamically build a page, there may be a dozen requests for CSS, JavaScript, and pictures. Despite this, mod python installed a copy of the Python interpreter runtime on each Apache worker, the majority of which sat idle. At any given time, only one worker out of a dozen might be running Python, while the rest spooled out files using Apache's core C code. This deadlock can be broken by separating Python interpreters from web server workers who shovel static content from disc onto waiting sockets. As a result, two conflicting methods arose.

The first option is to utilise the modern mod wsgi module with the "daemon process" capability enabled to prevent burdening each Apache thread with a Python interpreter. Apache workers, whether threads or processes, are spared the cost of loading or running Python in this mode, incurring just the cost of dynamically linking to mod wsgi. Mod wsgi, on the other hand, generates and manages a separate pool of Python worker processes to which it can send requests and where the WSGI application is really run. For each enormous Python interpreter that sits slowly developing a dynamic website, dozens of tiny Apache workers may be busy churning out static files.

Pure-Python HTTP Servers on the Rise

However, after you've accepted the fact that Python will not run in the primary server process and that HTTP requests will need to be serialised and forwarded from an Apache process to a Python process, why not just use HTTP? Why not set up Apache to forward each dynamic request to Gunicorn, where your service is running?

True, you'll now have to start and manage two separate daemons (Apache and Gunicorn), when previously you only had to start Apache and let mod wsgi handle generating your Python interpreters. However, you will acquire a tremendous degree of versatility in exchange. To begin with, there is no longer any rationale for Apache and Gunicorn to share a single box. You can run Apache on a server that is optimised for a large number of concurrent connections and expansive disc access, and Gunicorn on a second server that is tuned for dynamic language runtimes performing database back-end requests.

You have the option of changing Apache once it has been lowered from your application container to a static file server with reverse-proxy capabilities. After all, nginx, like many other modern web servers, can serve files while also reverse-proxying other paths.

In the end, the mod wsgi option is a limited and proprietary version of true reverse proxying: When you could be speaking real HTTP and having the choice of running Python on the same machine or on a different one as your needs develop, you're speaking its own internal protocol between processes that must reside on the same machine.

The Advantages of Reverse Proxies

What about HTTP apps that exclusively offer dynamic content generated by Python code, with no static resources involved? In such instances, Apache or nginx may appear to have little work to perform, and you may be tempted to disregard them and expose Gunicorn or another pure Python web server to the world directly.

Consider the security that a reverse proxy can give in such situations. Simply connect to your n-worker service with n sockets, deliver a few initial desultory bytes of request data, and then freeze to bring your web service to a standstill. All of your employees will be waiting for a comprehensive request that may or may not arrive.

Requests that take a long time to arrive with Apache or nginx in front of your service, on the other hand, are slowly collected by the reverse proxy's buffers, which will typically not forward the request to you until it has been received in its entirety, whether through malice or because some of your clients run on mobile devices or are otherwise suffering from low bandwidth.

Of course, a proxy that collects full requests before delivering them isn't impenetrable to a real denial-of-service attack—nothing is, unfortunately—but it does save your dynamic language runtime from freezing when data from a client isn't yet available. It also protects Python from a variety of other types of erroneous input, such as megabyte-long header names and completely malformed requests, because Apache or nginx would simply reject them with 4xx errors, leaving your back-end application code in the dark.

On the above list of architectures, I currently tend toward three sweet spots.

Gunicorn under nginx or, if a system administrator likes, Apache is my default.

If I'm operating a service that's basically just an API with no static components, I'll sometimes try to run Gunicorn by itself or directly behind Varnish if I want my dynamic resources to benefit from its first-class caching logic as well. Only when designing huge web services do I go all-in with three tiers: Gunicorn-based Python, nginx or Apache, and a local or geographically dispersed Varnish cluster.

Many additional configurations are, of course, possible, and I hope that the preceding discussion provided enough caveats and trade-offs to enable you to make informed decisions when the topic arises in your own projects and organisations.

The advent of Python runtimes like PyPy that can operate at machine speed is one key question that lurks on the horizon. Why not have Python serve both static and dynamic material once Python code can run as quickly as Apache? It will be fascinating to watch if servers based on fast Python runtimes put old and trustworthy solutions like Apache and nginx to the test. When the industry favourites are so well documented, known, and liked by system administrators, what incentives can Python servers give for migration?

Variations on any of the previous designs are, of course, possible. If no static files need to be served or you're okay for Python to pull them from the disc itself, Gunicorn can run immediately behind Varnish. Another alternative is to use nginx or Apache with reverse-caching enabled to give rudimentary Varnish-style caching without the requirement for a third tier. Some websites explore with alternate front-end server-to-Python communication protocols, such as those offered by the Flup and uwsgi projects. The four patterns presented in this section are only a few of the most popular. There are other additional designs that may be used, the most of which are now in use.

Platforms as a Service (PaaS)

Many of the previous section's topics—load balancing, multiple tiers of proxy server, and application deployment—start to wander into system administration and operations planning territory. Python isn't the only language that has to deal with issues like choosing a front-end load balancer or deciding how to make an HTTP service physically and geographically redundant. They would take you far away from the subject of Python network programming if they were discussed in this chapter.

As you include Python into your network service plan, I recommend reading about automated deployment, continuous integration, and high-performance scaling to learn about technologies that may be useful to your service and company. There isn't enough room to include them all here. However, there is one aspect worth mentioning: the rise of platform-as-a-service (PaaS) providers and the challenge of how to package your apps for deployment on these platforms.

Much of the drudgery of setting up and running an HTTP service is automated—or, at the very least, devolved upon your PaaS provider rather than yourself—with PaaS. You are not required to rent servers, provide them with storage and IP addresses, configure root access to administer and reboot them, install the correct version of Python, and copy your application to each server, along with the system scripts required to start your service up automatically after a reboot or power outage. Instead, these responsibilities are taken on by the PaaS provider, who may install or rent thousands of computers, hundreds of database servers, and dozens of load balancers to serve its customer base. After you've automated all of these steps, all that's left is for you to send the provider a configuration file. After that, your provider may add your domain name to its DNS, point it to one of its load balancers, install the correct version of Python and all of your Python dependencies inside an operating system image, and your application will be up and running. The procedure can make it simple to publish fresh source code to them, as well as roll back if the new version of your software appears to cause problems when used by real consumers. Heroku is a popular PaaS platform that includes first-class support for Python apps as part of its ecosystem. Small businesses who lack the skills or time in-house to set up and operate products like load balancers would benefit from Heroku and its competitors.

The emerging Docker ecosystem could be a Heroku competitor because it allows you to create and run Heroku-style containers on your own Linux machine, making it much easier to test and debug them than when every line of configuration you want to tweak requires a long and slow push and rebuild on Heroku. If you simply have a rudimentary understanding of PaaS, you might expect it to accept your WSGI-ready Python programme and execute it for you without any more effort.

This is not the case, as it turns out. You will still be responsible for selecting a web server whether you are using Heroku or a Docker instance.

While PaaS providers offer load balancing, containerization, version-controlled configuration, container image caching, and database administration, they still expect your application to provide the gold standard in HTTP interoperability: an open port to which the PaaS load balancer can connect and send HTTP requests. And, of course, you'll need a server to turn your WSGI application or framework into a listening network port.

Some developers, confident that the PaaS service would handle load balancing, choose a simple single-threaded server and delegate the task of spinning up as many instances of their application as they require to the PaaS provider.

However, many developers use Gunicorn or one of its competitors because each of its containers can have several workers running at the same time. This allows a single container to accept multiple requests if the PaaS load balancer's roundrobin logic returns it to the same container before the first request is completed—which is a problem if some of your service's resources take several seconds to render, causing subsequent requests to be queued until the first is completed.

It's worth noting that most PaaS providers don't allow you to serve static content unless you use Python or install Apache or nginx to your container. While you could build your URL space so that static resources have a different hostname than dynamic pages and host those static resources somewhere else, many architects want to be able to combine static and dynamic resources in one namespace.

The REST Question and GET and POST Patterns

One of the principal authors of the present HTTP standards, Dr. Roy Fielding, wrote his Ph.D. dissertation on its design. He coined the term Representational State Transfer (REST) to describe the architecture that develops when all of the functionalities of a hypertext system, like as HTTP, are turned on. If you wish to look at his dissertation, you can do so online.

He builds develops the concept of REST from a series of basic principles in Chapter 5.

www.ics.uci.edu/~fielding/pubs/dissertation/rest_arch_style.htm

"REST is defined by four interface constraints," says Dr. Fielding, who enumerates them quickly at the end of section 5.1.5 of his dissertation.

- Identifying resources
- Using representations to manipulate resources
- Messages that are self-descriptive
- Hypermedia as an application state engine

Many service designers have sought to create services that can truly merit the moniker "RESTful," because they desire their ideas to flow with the grain of HTTP's design rather than against it. Dr. Fielding is quick to point out that the majority of them don't. Where do they make a mistake?

The first constraint, "resource identification," eliminates practically all traditional kinds of RPC. At the HTTP protocol level, neither JSON-RPC nor XML-RPC (see Chapter 18) disclose resource identities. Consider a client who wants to retrieve a blog post, change the title, and then retrieve the post again to compare the two. If these stages were implemented as RPC method calls, the following methods and pathways would be available to HTTP:

```
POST /rpc-endpoint/ ® 200 OK
```

```
POST /rpc-endpoint/ ® 200 OK
```

```
POST /rpc-endpoint/ ® 200 OK
```

Each of these requests presumably mentions something like "post 1022" as the specific resource that the client wants to fetch or change somewhere inside the body of each POST. However, RPC hides this from the HTTP protocol. Instead, a RESTful interface would use the resource path to describe which post was being changed, for example, /post/1022/.

The second limitation, "Manipulation of resources through representations," prevents the designer from defining an ad-hoc mechanism for updating the title that is exclusive to their service. After all, every time a client author wanted to understand how to conduct an update, they'd have to sift through service-specific documentation. Because the representation of a post—whether it uses HTML, JSON, XML, or another format—is the sole form in which either reads or writes may be expressed in REST, there is no need to learn a specific strategy to change a post's title. A client simply obtains the current representation, updates the title, and submits the new representation back to the service to update the title of a blog post.

```
GET /post/1022/ ® 200 OK
```

```
PUT /post/1022/ ® 200 OK
```

```
GET /post/1022/ ® 200 OK
```

Many designers despise the idea that requesting or updating a dozen resources necessitates a dozen round-trips to the service, and there's a strong urge to make pragmatic exceptions to the architecture. However, symmetry between the activities of reading and writing a resource, as well as the exposure of meaningful semantics in the HTTP protocol, are advantages of REST properly followed. Because the protocol can now tell which requests are reads and which are writes, and if GET answers include the correct headers, caching and conditional requests are now allowed even when programmes communicate without using a browser.

The final restriction, "self-descriptive messages," is triggered by explicit caching headers, which make communications self-documenting. A client developer does not need to consult API documentation to learn that /post/1022/ is in JSON format or that it can only be cached if conditional requests are used to ensure that the cached copy is up-to-date, whereas a search like /post/?q=news can be served directly from cache for up to 60 seconds after retrieval. Instead, this knowledge is disclosed again in the headers of each HTTP response that is sent. If the first three REST criteria are met, a service becomes completely transparent to the HTTP protocol and, as a result, to the entire suite of proxies, caches, and clients built to exploit its semantics.

They can do so regardless of whether the service is designed for human consumption, producing HTML pages with forms and JavaScript (see Chapter 11), or for machine consumption, delivering short URLs that lead to JSON or XML representations.

The last constraint, on the other hand, is significantly less frequently met. The phrase "hypermedia as the engine of application state" has gotten so controversial that it now has an acronym! Despite the fact that it was not mentioned in Dr. Fielding's thesis, it has since been shortened to "HATEOAS" in following publications and arguments. He attracted attention to the restriction in a blog post titled "REST APIs Must Be Hypertextdriven," in which he lamented the announcement of a so-called REST API that failed this final constraint.

`http://roy.gbiv.com/untangled/2008/rest-apis-must-be-hypertext-driven`

There, he breaks out the HATEOAS limitation into six independent bullet points, the final of which is likely the most comprehensive. "A REST API should be entered with no prior information beyond the first URI (bookmark) and a set of standardised media types that are appropriate for the target audience," it says at the outset.

Almost all HTTP-driven APIs would be disqualified as a result. Whether it's from Google or GitHub, their documentation almost always begins with, "Each post lives at a URL like / post / 1022 / that names the post's unique ID." With this move, an API has moved away from total RESTfulness and into a murky world where specific rules hidden in documentation, rather than hypertext links, guide the client to the relevant resource.

A fully RESTful API, on the other hand, would only have one entry point. Perhaps a succession of forms would be returned, one of which could be used to input a blog post ID to learn its URL. Instead of human-readable documentation, the service would dynamically link the concept of "the post with ID 1022" to a specific location. According to Dr. Fielding, this inclusive concept of hypertext is a critical requirement for services aiming for decades of use, as it will be capable of supporting multiple generations of HTTP clients and, subsequently, data archaeology when the initial users of an old service have all passed away. However, because the first three aspects of HTTP provide the majority of the benefits—statelessness, redundancy, and cache acceleration—it appears that few services have yet to up to the challenge of full REST compliance.

Web Server Gateway Interface (WSGI) Without a Framework

Several techniques for constructing a network service were demonstrated in Chapter 7, all of which can be used to respond to HTTP requests.

However, writing your own low-level socket code to speak the protocol is rarely necessary. Many protocol specifics can be delegated to your web server and, if applicable, your web framework. What exactly is the distinction between the two?

The web server is the programme that keeps a listening socket open, calls accept() to accept new connections, and parses each HTTP request that comes in. A server will handle instances like a client that connects but never completes its request and a client whose request cannot be processed as HTTP without needing to call your code. Some servers will also time out and shut a client socket that is idle, as well as reject requests with excessively long path or headers.

By invoking the WSGI callable that you have registered with the server, only well-formed, full requests are given to your framework or code. The server will often issue HTTP response codes like these on its own authority (see Chapter 9):

- 400 words If the incoming HTTP request is incomprehensible or exceeds the size limit you've set, it's considered a bad request.

- **500 Server Error:** If your WSGI callable throws an exception rather than completing correctly.

There are two methods for creating a WSGI callable that your web server will use when HTTP requests arrive and are correctly parsed. You can create code that plugs into a web framework that provides its own WSGI callable, or you can write code that plugs into a web framework that provides its own WSGI callable. What is the distinction?

The most important function of a web framework is to handle dispatch. In the space of possible methods, hostnames, and pathways, each HTTP request name coordinates. You're probably only using one or two hostnames for your service, rather than all of them. You may be ready to execute GET or POST requests, but a request can specify any method it wants—even one it hasn't invented yet. You may be able to produce in a variety of ways. There are possibly many more for which you will not be able to provide helpful responses. The framework will allow you to declare which paths and methods you support, so it can take care of automatically responding to those that don't with status codes like these:

- **Not Found (404)**
- **405 Method Isn't Acceptable**
- **501 Not Initiated**

Chapter 11 examines how both traditional and asynchronous frameworks handle dispatch, as well as the other key capabilities they provide to programmers. But what would your code look like if they weren't there?

What if your own code communicates directly with WSGI and handles the dispatching?

There are two approaches to developing such an application: either by understanding the WSGI standard and learning to read its environment dictionary for yourself, or by utilising a wrapper such as that offered by the competing WebOb and Werkzeug toolkits, both of which are accessible via the Python Package Index. Working in the raw WSGI environment necessitates a verbose coding style, as shown in Listing 10-2.

Listing 10-2. WSGI Callable for Returning the Current Time in Raw Form

```python
#!/usr/bin/env python3
# Programming in Python: The Basics
# A simple HTTP service built directly against the low-level WSGI
spec.
import time
def app(environ, start_response):
 host = environ.get('HTTP_HOST', '127.0.0.1')
 path = environ.get('PATH_INFO', '/')
 if ':' in host:
 host, port = host.split(':', 1)
 if '?' in path:
 path, query = path.split('?', 1)
 headers = [('Content-Type', 'text/plain; charset=utf-8')]
 if environ['REQUEST_METHOD'] != 'GET':
 start_response('501 Not Implemented', headers)
 yield b'501 Not Implemented'
 elif host != '127.0.0.1' or path != '/':
 start_response('404 Not Found', headers)
 yield b'404 Not Found'
```

```
else:
start_response('200 OK', headers)
yield time.ctime().encode('ascii')
```

Without a framework, your code will have to do all of the negative work of figuring out which hostnames, routes, and methods don't match the services you want to deliver. You must return an error for every deviation from that combination of request parameters that you are able to identify while offering a GET of the path / at the hostname 127.0.0.1. Of all, for such a little service, it may seem stupid not to take any hostname. However, we're pretending to be a large service with a variety of material available at dozens of distinct hostnames, so we're paying close attention to them. If the client provides a Host header like 127.0.0.1:8000, you are responsible for splitting apart the hostname and port. In addition, if the URL has a query string like /?name=value dangling off the end, you must divide the path on the character? (The listing assumes that you wish to disregard unnecessary query strings rather than returning 404 Not Found, as is standard practise.)

The following two listings show how third-party libraries, which can be added using the normal "pip" installation tool, can make these bare WSGI patterns easier (see Chapter 1).

```
$ pip install WebOb
```

```
$ pip install Werkzeug
```

WebOb is a lightweight object interface that covers a conventional WSGI dictionary to provide more accessible access to its information. It was originally designed by Ian Bicking. Listing 10-3 demonstrates how it avoids several of the preceding example's typical patterns.

Listing 10-3. Callable WSGI WebOb was used to return the current time.

```
#!/usr/bin/env python3
# Programming in Python: The Basics
# A WSGI callable built using webob.
import time, webob
def app(environ, start_response):
 request = webob.Request(environ)
 if environ['REQUEST_METHOD'] != 'GET':
 response = webob.Response('501 Not Implemented', status=501)
 elif request.domain != '127.0.0.1' or request.path != '/':
```

```
response = webob.Response('404 Not Found', status=404)
else:
response = webob.Response(time.ctime())
return response(environ, start_response)
```

WebOb already supports the two frequent patterns of examining the hostname from the Host header separately from any optional port numbers, and looking at the path without the query string at the end. It also comes with a Response object that knows all there is to know about content types and encodings (it defaults to plain text), so all you have to do is provide a string for the response body and WebOb will handle the rest.

Among the many Python HTTP response object implementations, WebOb offers a characteristic that makes it practically unique. The WebOb Response class allows you to consider the two elements of a Content-Type header, such as text/plain; charset=utf-8, as two different values, which it exposes as the content type and charset attributes.

Armin Ronacher's Werkzeug library, which is also the backbone of his Flask framework, is less popular than WebOb for pure WSGI code but has a devoted following (discussed in Chapter 11). Instead of allowing changes to the underlying WSGI environment, its request and response objects are immutable. In this scenario, Listing 10-4 explains how it differs from WebOb in terms of ease.

Listing 10-4. Callable WSGI Returning the Current Time was written with Werkzeug.

```
#!/usr/bin/env python3
# Programming in Python: The Basics
# A WSGI callable built using Werkzeug.
import time
from werkzeug.wrappers import Request, Response
@Request.application
def app(request):
 host = request.host
 if ':' in host:
 host, port = host.split(':', 1)
 if request.method != 'GET':
```

```
return Response('501 Not Implemented', status=501)

elif host != '127.0.0.1' or request.path != '/':

return Response('404 Not Found', status=404)

else:

return Response(time.ctime())
```

Werkzeug has spared you the trouble of remembering the correct WSGI callable signature, instead providing a decorator that converts your function to a more simpler calling convention. You'll get a Werkzeug Request object as your only argument, and you'll have the option of only returning a Response object—the library will take care of the rest.

The only small reversal from WebOb code is that you must divide hostnames like 127.0.0.1:8000 in half yourself rather than having a convenience method do it for you. Despite this little difference, the two libraries perform the same thing in terms of allowing you to speak about HTTP requests and answers at a higher level than the WSGI convention allows. Working at this low level instead of using a web framework is usually not worth your time as a developer. However, when you need to make certain transformations on incoming HTTP requests before passing them on to your web framework for processing, writing in raw WSGI comes in useful. If you're developing a bespoke reverse proxy or another pure HTTP service in Python, a plain WSGI application may be ideal.

Raw WSGI callables can be regarded of as having the same place in Python programming as forward and reverse proxies do in the larger HTTP ecosystem. They're better at low-level activities like filtering, normalising, and dispatching requests than they are at offering resources at specific hostnames and URLs like an HTTP service. Read the specification or reference the patterns provided in either the WebOb or Werkzeug documentation for creating middleware for more information on how a WSGI callable can change a request before passing it on to another callable.

Conclusion

When launched from the command line, the http.server module in Python serves files from beneath the current working directory. While useful in an emergency or when inspecting a web site stored on disc, the module is rarely used to create new HTTP services these days.

In Python, the WSGI standard is frequently used to mediate normal, synchronous HTTP. Servers scan incoming requests to create an information dictionary, which applications evaluate before delivering HTTP headers and an optional response content. This allows you to use any mainstream Python web framework with any web server. The WSGI ecosystem does not include asynchronous web servers. Because WSGI callables aren't entire coroutines, each async HTTP server must establish its own pattern for writing services in its own framework. In this situation, the server and framework are packaged together, with little chance of greater compatibility. There are four main architectures for providing HTTP from Python. Gunicorn or other pure-Python server implementations like CherryPy can be used to run a standalone server. Other architects prefer to use mod wsgi to run their Python under Apache's control. Many architects, however, find it easier to use Gunicorn or another pure now that the concept of a reverse proxy is a go-to pattern for web services of all kinds. Python server running directly behind nginx or Apache as a separate HTTP service to which requests for routes with dynamically produced resources can be forwarded. Varnish or another reverse proxy can then be placed in front of any of these patterns to provide a caching layer. Cache instances can be located in the same machine room (or even on the same machine), but they are frequently geographically spread to serve certain populations of HTTP clients. When you use a PaaS provider to host your service, you'll often get caching, reverse proxying, and load balancing as part of the package. Your application's sole responsibility will be to respond to HTTP requests, which is typically accomplished through the use of a simple container such as Gunicorn. The question of whether a service is RESTful, or whether it has the properties that standards author Dr. Roy Fielding describes as being intended by the design of HTTP, is a common one. While many services have moved away from opaque method and path choices that obscured what the service was doing, few have fully adopted Fielding's vision of using hypertext instead of programmer-directed documentation to power semantics. Small services, especially those that filter or transform an HTTP request, can be written as a WSGI callable. WebOb or Werkzeug, two competing solutions, can reduce the raw WSGI environment to an easier-to-consume Request object, as well as assist you in building your answer with their Response classes.

The World Wide Web—the massive collection of interconnected documents that has made the Internet world famous—will be covered in the next chapter, taking you beyond both general HTTP services and low-level WSGI programming. You'll learn how to retrieve and handle hypertext documents, as well as how to build websites using common web frameworks

CHAPTER 11
www (world wide web)

The Hypertext Transfer Protocol (HTTP) was introduced in Chapters 9 and 10 as a universal way for clients to request documents and servers to reply by supplying them.

However, something remained inexplicable. Why does the protocol's name begin with the word hypertext? The truth is that HTTP was not created just as a new method of file transport. It's not just a clever caching system. FTP and other outdated file transfer protocols are no longer supported (see Chapter 17). While it is unquestionably capable of doing so, The World Wide Web was designed with HTTP in mind.

Structure:

- URLs and hypermedia
- Creating and Parsing URLs
- URLs that are relative
- HTML(Hypertext Markup language)
- Using a Database to Read and Write
- A Horrible Internet Program (in Flask)
- The HTTP Methods and Forms Of Dance

- When Forms Use Inappropriate Methods
- Cookies that are safe and those that are not
- Cross-Site Scripting that isn't persistent
- Cross-Site Scripting that Remains Persistent
- Forgery of Cross-Site Requests
- The Enhanced Software
- Django's Payments Application
- Choosing a Framework for a Website
- WebSockets
- Scraping the Internet
- Obtaining Pages
- Pages for Scraping
- Recursive Scraping
- Conclusion

Objectives:

We will learn about HTTP's goal is significantly more ambitious than that of stand-alone documents like books, photos, and video: to allow servers all over the world to publish papers that become an one interconnected fabric of knowledge through mutual cross-references.

URLs and hypermedia

For thousands of years, books have referred to other books. A human, on the other hand, must perform each reference by retrieving the other book and flipping the pages until the cited paragraph is located. The World Wide Web (WWW, or simply "the Web") has realised the dream of delegating the responsibility of resolving the reference to the computer.

A hyperlink is created when idle text, such as "the discussion of cookies in Chapter 9," becomes underlined and clickable on a computer screen, and a click sends you to the material it refers to. Hypertext documents are whole documents with hyperlinks incorporated in the text. A printed book's words "see page 103" does not have the power to transport you to the destination it depicts. The browser displaying a hyperlink, on the other hand, has this capability.

The universal resource location (URL) was created to power hypermedia. It provides a uniform mechanism for referencing not only modern hypertext documents, but also ancient FTP files and Telnet servers. Many of these instances can be found in the address bar of your web browser.

```
# Some sample URLs

https://www.python.org/

http://en.wikipedia.org/wiki/Python_(programming_language)

http://localhost:8000/headers

ftp://ssd.jpl.nasa.gov/pub/eph/planets/README.txt

telnet://rainmaker.wunderground.com
```

The scheme, which names the protocol via which a page can be obtained, is the first label, such as https or http. The hostname and optional port number appear after the colon and two slashes:/. Finally, a path chooses one document from among all those that might be available on a service. This syntax can be used for more than only describing material that has to be retrieved from a network.

A uniform resource identifier (URI) is a more general concept that can be used to identify physical network-accessible documents or as a generic unique identifier for giving computer-readable names to conceptual things, such as labels called uniform resource names (URNs). Everything in this book will be a hyperlink.

By the way, the pronunciation of URL is you-are-ell. An "earl" is a member of the British aristocracy whose position is not exactly that of a marquis but is higher than that of a viscount—in other words, an earl is the continental counterpart of a count (not, in other words, a network document address). The URL is extended with a query string that starts with a question mark (?) and utilises the ampersand character (&) to delimit each further parameter when a page is automatically created based on parameters given by the user. A name, an equals sign, and a value are all included in each parameter.

```
https://www.google.com/search?q=apod&btnI=yes
```

Finally, a URL might be suffixed with a fragment that identifies the specific spot on the page to which the link points.

```
http://tools.ietf.org/html/rfc2324#section-2.3.2
```

The fragment is distinct from the rest of the URL's components. Because a web browser assumes it needs to fetch the complete page specified by the route in order to find the element named by the fragment, the fragment is not actually sent in the HTTP request! When a browser downloads an HTTP URL, all the server can learn from it is the hostname, path, and query. The path and query are concatenated to produce the full path that follows the HTTP method on the first line of the request, as you recall from Chapter 9. The hostname is delivered as the Host header, and the path and query are concatenated to produce the full path that follows the HTTP method on the first line of the request.

If you look over RFC 3986 closely, you'll see a few extra features that are rarely used. It is the definitive reference to consult when you come across unusual features you want to learn more about, such as the ability to include a user@password authentication string directly in the URL.

Creating and Parsing URLs

The built-in urllib.parse module in the Python Standard Library gives you the tools you'll need to both interpret and construct URLs. A single function call is all it takes to break down a URL into its constituent parts. It returns a tuple, which you may still view and access via integer indexing—or tuple unpacking in an assignment statement—in earlier versions of Python.

```
>>> from urllib.parse import urlsplit
```

```
>>> u = urlsplit('https://www.google.com/search?q=apod&btnI=yes')
```

```
>>> tuple(u)
```

```
('https', 'www.google.com', '/search', 'q=apod&btnI=yes', '')
```

But the tuple also supports named attribute access to its items to help make your code more readable when you

are inspecting a URL.

```
>>> u.scheme
```

```
'https'
```

```
>>> u.netloc
```

```
'www.google.com'
```

```
>>> u.path
```

```
'/search'
```

```
>>> u.query
```

```
'q=apod&btnI=yes'
```

```
>>> u.fragment
```

`''`

Netloc, the "network location," can have numerous subordinate components, but they're uncommon enough that urlsplit() doesn't divide them as separate items in its tuple. They are only available as properties of the result.

```
>>> u = urlsplit('https://bpb:online@localhost:8000/')
>>> u.netloc
'bpb:online@localhost:8000'
>>> u.username
'bpb'
>>> u.password
'online'
>>> u.hostname
'localhost'
>>> u.port
8000
```

Only half of the parsing process involves breaking down a URL into parts. Characters that had to be escaped before becoming part of the URL can appear in both the path and query components. & and #, for example, cannot be used literally because they delimit the URL. The character / must also be escaped if it appears within a path component, as the slash is used to divide path components.

The query portion of a URL has its own set of encoding requirements. Because query values frequently contain spaces (consider all of the Google searches that include a space), the plus symbol + is specified as an alternative way of encoding spaces in queries. Otherwise, the query string would only have the option of encoding spaces as a percent 20 hexadecimal escape code, just like the remainder of the URL.

The only correct way to parse a URL that accesses your site's "Q&A" section in order to access the "TCP/IP" part and search for information regarding "packet loss" is to do it as follows:

```
>>> from urllib.parse import parse_qs, parse_qsl, unquote
>>> u = urlsplit('http://example.com/Q%26A/TCP%2FIP?q=packet+loss')
```

```
>>> path = [unquote(s) for s in u.path.split('/')]
```

```
>>> query = parse_qsl(u.query)
```

```
>>> path
```

```
['', 'Q&A', 'TCP/IP']
```

```
>>> query
```

```
[('q', 'packet loss')]
```

Because this path is an absolute path that starts with a slash, my splitting of the path with split() yields an initial empty string.

Because a URL query string permits a query parameter to be specified several times, the query is presented as a list of tuples rather than a simple dictionary. You can feed the list of tuples to dict() and only see the last value given for each parameter if you're building code that doesn't care about this possibility. If you want a dictionary but also want to allow multiple values for a parameter, go from parse qsl() to parse qs() and you'll receive a dictionary with lists as values.

```
>>> parse_qs(u.query)
```

```
{'q': ['packet loss']}
```

The Standard Library contains all of the essential procedures to reverse the process. By quoting each path component, connecting them back together with slashes, encoding the query, and giving the result to the "unsplit" procedure, which is the inverse of the urlsplit() function called earlier, Python can reconstruct the URL from its pieces.

```
>>> from urllib.parse import quote, urlencode, urlunsplit
```

```
>>> urlunsplit(('http', 'example.com',
```

```
... '/'.join(quote(p, safe='') for p in path),
```

```
... urlencode(query), ''))
```

```
'http://example.com/Q%26A/TCP%2FIP?q=packet+loss'
```

If you carefully delegate all URL parsing to these Standard Library methods, you should discover that all of the finer points of the whole specification are handled for you.

Some programmers could even describe the code in the previous examples as fussy, because it is so flawless. or perhaps exaggerated. When it comes to path components, how often do they have slashes in them? The majority of websites are Path elements, sometimes known as slugs by developers, should be carefully designed so that they never require unattractive escaping to appear in a document. URL. If a site only permits letters, digits, dashes, and underscores in URL slugs, there's a risk that a slug will be mistyped. It's clear that could include a slash is out of place. If you're positive you're working with routes that don't include any escaped slashes inside individual path components, you can just expose the entire path to quote() and unquote() without dividing it.

```
>>> quote('Q&A/TCP IP')
```

'Q%26A/TCP%20IP'

```
>>> unquote('Q%26A/TCP%20IP')
```

'Q&A/TCP IP'

In reality, the quote() method anticipates this to be the case, since its default option is safe='/', which ignores slashes in most cases. That was overridden in the picky version of the code by safe=".

The urllib.parse module in the Standard Library offers a few more specialised procedures than the ones listed above, such as urldefrag(), which splits the URL apart from its fragment at the # character. Read the documentation to learn more about this and other functions that can help with a few unique situations.

URLs that are relative

The "change working directory" command in your filesystem command line defines the position where the system will begin exploring relative paths without a leading slash. Paths that begin with a slash expressly declare that they will begin their search at the filesystem's root. They're absolute pathways, meaning they always refer to the same location, regardless of where you're working.

```
$ wc -l /var/log/dmesg
977 dmesg
$ wc -l dmesg
wc: dmesg: No such file or directory
$ cd /var/log
$ wc -l dmesg
977 dmesg
```

The concept of hypertext is the same. If all of the links in a document are absolute URLs, such as the ones in the previous section, the resource to which each of them links is clear. If the document contains relative URLs, however, the document's own location must be taken into consideration.

Python has a urljoin() function that comprehends the full standard in its entirety. You can use urljoin() to fill in any missing information from a URL that you've recovered from inside a hypertext document, which can be relative or absolute. No problem if the URL was absolute to begin with; it will be returned unaltered. urljoin() uses the same argument order as os.path.join() (). Provide the basic URL of the document you're looking at first, followed by the URL you discovered within it. A relative URL can rewrite elements of its base in numerous distinct ways.

```
>>> from urllib.parse import urljoin
>>> base = 'http://tools.ietf.org/html/rfc3986'
>>> urljoin(base, 'rfc7320')
'http://tools.ietf.org/html/rfc7320'
>>> urljoin(base, '.')
'http://tools.ietf.org/html/'
>>> urljoin(base, '..')
'http://tools.ietf.org/'
>>> urljoin(base, '/dailydose/')
'http://tools.ietf.org/dailydose/'
>>> urljoin(base, '?version=1.0')
'http://tools.ietf.org/html/rfc3986?version=1.0'
>>> urljoin(base, '#section-5.4')
'http://tools.ietf.org/html/rfc3986#section-5.4'
```

Again, providing an absolute URL to urljoin() is perfectly safe because it will determine that it is completely self-contained and return it unchanged from the original URL.

```
>>> urljoin(base, 'https://www.google.com/search?q=apod&btnI=yes')

'https://www.google.com/search?q=apod&btnI=yes'
```

Because a relative URL can omit the scheme but describe everything else, it's straightforward to create web pages that are agnostic about whether they're served via HTTP or HTTPS, even on static parts of a website. Only the scheme is replicated from the base URL in this situation.

```
>>> urljoin(base, '//www.google.com/search?q=apod')
```

`'http://www.google.com/search?q=apod'`

If you're going to use relative URLs on your site, you'll need to be very careful about whether or not your pages have a trailing slash, because a relative URL might signify two different things depending on whether or not the following slash is there.

```
>>> urljoin('http://tools.ietf.org/html/rfc3986', 'rfc7320')
```

`'http://tools.ietf.org/html/rfc7320'`

```
>>> urljoin('http://tools.ietf.org/html/rfc3986/', 'rfc7320')
```

`'http://tools.ietf.org/html/rfc3986/rfc7320'`

What appears to be a minor distinction between these two base URLs is critical to the meaning of any relative links! The first URL is equivalent to accessing the html directory in order to show the rfc3986 file that it finds there, leaving the html directory as the "current working directory." Because only directories can take a trailing slash in a real filesystem, the second URL treats rfc3986 as the directory it is accessing.

As a result, the relative link formed on top of the second URL begins at the rfc3986 component rather than the parent html component. Always build your site so that a user who enters a URL that is incorrectly written is quickly redirected.

to the right track For example, if you try to visit the second URL from the previous example, you will be redirected to the IETF website. The web server will notice the erroneous trailing slash and respond with a Location: header containing the proper URL.

If you ever create a web client, remember that relative URLs are not always relative to the path that you specify. as part of your HTTP request! Relative URLs should be used if the site wishes to respond with a Location header. built in relation to the alternate location.

HTML(Hypertext Markup language)

There are entire libraries dedicated to the essential document formats that fuel the Internet. There are also active standards that describe the hypertext document format, the mechanisms for styling them with Cascading Style Sheets (CSS), and the API through which a browser-embedded language like JavaScript (JS) can make live changes to a document as the user interacts with it or as more data is retrieved from the server. The following are the basic standards and resources:

Because this is a book about network programming, I'll focus on how these technologies interact with the network.

The Hypertext Markup Language (HTML) is a method of embellishing ordinary text with an almost absurd amount of angle brackets—that is, the less-than and greater-than marks reimagined as opening and closing brackets. Each pair of angle brackets creates a tag that either opens a new element in the document or closes an element that was already opened, as indicated by the initial slash. A basic paragraph containing a bolded word and an italicised word can look like this:

<p>This is a paragraph with <b>bold</b> and <i>italic</i> words.</p>

Some tags, such as the br> tag that generates a mid-paragraph line break, are self-contained and do not require a corresponding closing tag to occur afterwards. Authors who be more conscientious type this as the self-closing tag br/>instead, a habit they picked up from the Extensible Markup Language (XML), however HTML makes this optional.

Many things, including proper closing tags, are optional in HTML. Whether or not an actual /li> tag was encountered, when an ul> unordered list element finishes, a conforming parser will also recognise that the particular list element li> that it has been reading is now closed and ended.

HTML is concentric, as evidenced by the preceding example paragraph. A designer can arrange pieces in several ways. As they build a complete web page out of boxes, they nest items inside of other elements. As the creator, They nearly always end up recycling elements from the limited set defined by HTML for multiple different projects. on the page's goals Despite the fact that the new HTML5 standard allows for the creation of new elements on the fly in the middle of a page, designers tend to stick with the conventional ones. A huge page might employ a generic tag like <div> (the most generic type of box) or <span> (the most generic type of box). for a dozen different functions each) as a generic way to mark flowing text. When all div> elements are the same tag, how can CSS style each element appropriately and JavaScript allow the user to interact with them differently?

The answer is that the HTML author can give each element a class that serves as a more particular label with which it can be addressed. When it comes to employing classes, there are two general techniques.

The designer's blanket strategy is to assign a unique class to each and every HTML element in their design.

```
<div class="weather">
 <h5 class="city">Provo</h5>
```

```
<p class="temperature">61°F</p>
```

```
</div>
```

Their CSS and JavaScript might then refer to these components with selectors like.city and.temperature, or h5.city and p.temperature if they wanted to be more particular. The most basic CSS selector consists of a tag name followed by a period-prefixed class name, with any of these options. Alternatively, the designer may believe that a <h5> can only serve one purpose inside one of their weather symbols, and that a paragraph can only serve one purpose, and thus choose to decorate only the outside element with a class.

```
<div class="weather"><h5>Provo</h5><p>61°F</p></div>
```

They'd have to use more complicated patterns now to express that they want the <h5> and <p> that exist inside a div> with the class that distinguishes its type of <div>. Whitespace-concatenating the pattern that matches the outer tag with the pattern for the inner tag creates patterns.

```
.weather h5
```

```
.weather p
```

To understand about all of the options accessible beyond these basic possibilities, consult the CSS standard or an introduction to CSS. If you want to discover how selectors can be used to target components from live code running in the browser, you can read an introduction to JavaScript or a strong document manipulation library like jQuery.

With two characteristics of a modern browser like Google Chrome or Firefox, you can look at how your favourite websites package information. If you press Ctrl+U, they'll show you the HTML code for the page you're looking at, complete with syntax highlights. As illustrated in Figure 11-1, you can right-click any element and select Inspect Element to bring up debugging tools that help you study how each document element interacts to the material on the page.

You may also move to the Network tab while in the inspector to see all of the other resources that were downloaded and displayed as a result of visiting the page.

It's worth noting that the Network pane (shown in Figure 11-2), by default, is empty. Once you've got it up and running, click Reload to watch it fill up with data.

Be aware that depending on whether JavaScript has gone to work and added or removed elements from the page after the first page load, the live document you study with Inspect Element may have little or no similarity to the HTML that was originally supplied as the page's source. If an element in the inspector piques your attention but you can't find it in the original code, you'll need to use the debugger's Network tab to figure out which extra resources JavaScript is retrieving and how it might have been used to create those extra page items. As you begin to play with little web applications in the following programme listings, you should utilise your browser's Inspect Element capability to inspect the pages that the programmes return as much as possible.

Using a Database to Read and Write

Consider a simple bank application that allows account holders to transmit payments to one another using a web application. At the absolute least, such an application will require a table of payments, a method of inserting a new payment, and a method of retrieving and displaying all payments associated with the currently logged-in user's account.

Listing 11-1 shows a small library that uses the SQLite database included with the Python Standard Library to demonstrate all three of these functionalities. As a result, the listing should function anywhere Python is installed!

Listing 11-1. A Procedure for Creating and Communicating with a Database

```
#!/usr/bin/env python3
# Programming in Python: The Basics
# A small library of database routines to power a payments application.
import os, pprint, sqlite3
from collections import namedtuple
def open_database(path='bank.db'):
 new = not os.path.exists(path)
 db = sqlite3.connect(path)
 if new:
 c = db.cursor()
 c.execute('CREATE TABLE payment (id INTEGER PRIMARY KEY,'
 ` debit TEXT, credit TEXT, dollars INTEGER, memo TEXT)')
 add_payment(db, 'john', 'psf', 125, 'Registration for PyCon')
 add_payment(db, 'john', 'liz', 200, 'Payment for writing that code')
 add_payment(db, 'jason', 'john', 25, 'Gas money-thanks for the ride!')
 db.commit()
```

```
   return db
def add_payment(db, debit, credit, dollars, memo):
 db.cursor().execute('INSERT INTO payment (debit, credit, dollars,
memo)'
 ' VALUES (?, ?, ?, ?)', (debit, credit, dollars, memo))
def get_payments_of(db, account):
 c = db.cursor()
 c.execute('SELECT * FROM payment WHERE credit = ? or debit = ?'
 ' ORDER BY id', (account, account))
 Row = namedtuple('Row', [tup[0] for tup in c.description])
 return [Row(*row) for row in c.fetchall()]
if __name__ == '__main__':
db = open_database()
 pprint.pprint(get_payments_of(db, 'john'))
```

Because the SQLite engine stores each database in a single file on disc, the open database() function can identify whether the database is being created or merely reopened by checking for the file's existence. When you create the database, it creates a single payment table and populates it with three sample payments so that your web application doesn't just display an empty list of payments. The schema is overly simplistic, but it's all that's required to get this application up and running. A users' table for usernames and safe password hashes, as well as an official table of bank accounts where money may come from and be stored to, would be required in real life. This programme allows the user to create example account names as they type, rather than being realistic.

The fact that all of the inputs to the SQL calls in this example are appropriately escaped is an important point to note. Programmer failure to correctly escape special characters while submitting them to an interpreted language like SQL is a key source of security issues today. What if a malicious user of your web front end figures out a method to insert specific SQL code into the memo field? To cite data correctly, the greatest protection is to rely on the database itself, rather than your own logic.

Instead of trying to do any escaping or interpolation on its own, Listing 11-1 handles it right by sending SQLite a question mark (?) anywhere the code wants a value interpolated.

Another important step is to combine the raw database entries into something more intelligible. The fetchall() method is part of the DB-API 2.0, which all recent Python database connectors provide for compatibility. Furthermore, for each row returned from the database, it does not return an object or even a dictionary. For each returned row, it returns a tuple.

```
(1, 'john', 'psf', 125, 'Registration for PyCon')
```

Handling these raw tuples could have unfavourable consequences. Row[2] or row[3] in your code may show as "the account credited" or "the quantity of dollars paid," making it tough to interpret. As a result, bank.py creates a named-tuple class that responds to attribute names like row.credit and row.dollars. Although creating a new class each time SELECT is called is inefficient, it does give the semantics that online application code requires with one or two lines of code, allowing you to focus more on the web application code itself.

A Horrible Internet Program (in Flask)

App insecure.py, which is presented in Listing 11-2, is the first file you should review. Before answering these questions, it's a good idea to read over the code carefully: Is it the kind of dreadful, untrustworthy code that leads to security breaches and public humiliation? Does it even appear to be dangerous?

Listing 11-2. (Not Flask's fault!) An insecure web application

```python
#!/usr/bin/env python3
# Programming in Python: The Basics
# A poorly-written and profoundly insecure payments application.
# (Not the fault of Flask, but of how we are choosing to use it!)
import bank
from flask import Flask, redirect, request, url_for
from jinja2 import Environment, PackageLoader
app = Flask(__name__)
get = Environment(loader=PackageLoader(__name__, 'templates')).get_
template
@app.route('/login', methods=['GET', 'POST'])
def login():
 username = request.form.get('username', '')
 password = request.form.get('password', '')
 if request.method == 'POST':
 if (username, password) in [('john', 12345678), ('sam', 'abcde')]:
```

```
 response = redirect(url_for('index'))
 response.set_cookie('username', username)
 return response
 return get('login.html').render(username=username)
@app.route('/logout')
def logout():
 response = redirect(url_for('login'))
 response.set_cookie('username', '')
      return response
@app.route('/')
def index():
 username = request.cookies.get('username')
 if not username:
 return redirect(url_for('login'))
 payments = bank.get_payments_of(bank.open_database(), username)
 return get('index.html').render(payments=payments, username=username,
 flash_messages=request.args.getlist('flash'))
@app.route('/pay', methods=['GET', 'POST'])
def pay():
 username = request.cookies.get('username')
 if not username:
 return redirect(url_for('login'))
 account = request.form.get('account', '').strip()
 dollars = request.form.get('dollars', '').strip()
 memo = request.form.get('memo', '').strip()
 complaint = None
 if request.method == 'POST':
 if account and dollars and dollars.isdigit() and memo:
 db = bank.open_database()
 bank.add_payment(db, username, account, dollars, memo)
 db.commit()
 return redirect(url_for('index', flash='Payment successful'))
```

```
complaint = ('Dollars must be an integer' if not dollars.isdigit()
else 'Please fill in all three fields')
return get('pay.html').render(complaint=complaint, account=account,
dollars=dollars, memo=memo)
if __name__ == '__main__':
 app.debug = True
 app.run()
```

The listing is not only harmful, but it is also vulnerable to many of the most common attack vectors on the modern Internet! You will understand the minimal armour that an application requires to live by researching its flaws in the following sections of this chapter. These flaws are all due to errors in the site's data processing, and are unrelated to the question of whether the site was effectively protected against prying eyes with TLS in the first place. You Let's pretend it's encrypted, perhaps with the help of a reverse proxy sitting in front of the server. server (see Chapter 10) since I'll be thinking about what an attacker could do even if they couldn't view the data. transferring data between a certain user and the programme

The programme makes use of the Flask web framework to handle the essentials of running a Python online application: processing input from HTML forms (as you will learn in the next section), and answering 404 for pages that the application does not define next sections), as well as making it simple to create valid HTTP answers containing either HTML content from one source or HTML text from another a redirect to another URL or one of its templates. Visit the Flask documentation at http://flask.pocoo.org/ to learn a lot more about it than what will be covered in this chapter.

Assume that this list was compiled by programmers who were unfamiliar with the Internet. They'd heard about template languages that make it simple to add custom text to HTML, so they figured out how to load and run Jinja2. They also discovered that the Flask micro-framework is second only to Django in popularity, and they decided to give it a try because a Flask application can fit in a single file.

A login() page and a logout() page can be found by reading from top to bottom. The login screen hard-codes two possible user accounts and passwords because this app has no real user database. In a moment, you'll learn more about form logic, but you can already see that logging in and out creates and deletes a cookie (see Chapters 9 and 10) that, when present in subsequent requests, identifies them as belonging to a certain authenticated user.

The other two pages on the site defend themselves from unauthorised visitors by looking for this cookie and routing them back to the login page if there isn't one. Beyond the check for a logged-in user, the login() view includes only two lines of code (well, three because of line length): it takes the current user's payments from the database and combines them with some other information to present to the HTML page template.

It seems obvious that the page would want to know the username, but why does the code look for a message named 'flash' in the URL parameters (which Flask makes available as a request.args dictionary)?

If you read the pay() page, the answer is obvious. The user will be routed to the index page after a successful payment, but they will most likely want some indicator that the form had the desired result. A flash message, as web frameworks call them, is displayed at the top of the page to offer this. (The name relates to the fact that the message is "flashed" in front of the viewer when a page is next viewed and then disappears. It has nothing to do with the previous Adobe Flash system for authoring adverts.) The flash message is simply conveyed as a query string in the URL in this first iteration of the web application.

```
http://example.com/?flash=Payment+successful
```

The rest of the pay() procedure is a familiar dance to web application readers: it checks whether a form has been submitted successfully and, if it has, takes some action. Because the user or browser may have provided or omitted any of the form arguments, the code uses the request's get() method to sensitively and cautiously check for them. If a key is absent, the form dictionary can return a default (here, the empty string ").

If the request is approved, the payment is saved in the database indefinitely. Otherwise, the user will be given with the form. Instead of presenting users with a blank form and an error notice that discards their effort, the code sends the values they have input back into the template so that they can be redisplayed if they have already done the work of entering in some information.

Reviewing the three HTML templates listed in Listing 11-2 will be critical for the discussion of forms and methods in the following section. Because the common design features of HTML have been factored out into a base template, which is the most popular pattern utilised by designers developing multipage sites, there are actually four templates. The template in Listing 11-3 specifies a page skeleton with insertion points for a page title and a page body that may be added by other templates. Because of how beautifully structured the Jinja2 template language is—written by Armin Ronacher, who also invented Werkzeug (see Chapter 10) and Flask—the title can be used twice, once in the title> element and once in the h1> element.

Listing 11-3. Jinja2 Page Jinja2 Template base.html

```
<html>

  <head>

    <title>{% block title %}{% endblock %}</title>

    <link rel="stylesheet" type="text/css" href="/static/style.css">

  </head>

 <body>

   <h1>{{ self.title() }}</h1>

    {% block body %}{% endblock %}

  </body>

</html>
```

The Jinja2 template language determines, for example, that you can ask for a value to be substituted into a template using a double-brace syntax, as in username, and that brace-percent techniques like percent for percent can be used to loop and again output the same HTML pattern. For more information on its syntax and features, visit http://jinja.pocoo.org/.

The only elements on the login page shown in Listing 11-4 are the title and the form itself. For the first time, you can see a pattern that will arise again: a form element with an initial value="..." that should already be present in the editable element when it first shows on the screen.

Listing 11-4. Jinja2 Template login.html

```
{% extends "base.html" %}
{% block title %}Please log in{% endblock %}
{% block body %}
<form method="post">
 <label>User: <input name="username" value="{{ username }}"></label>
 <label>Password: <input name="password" type="password"></label>
 <button type="submit">Log in</button>
</form>
{% endblock %}
```

This form will allow the user avoid having to retype their username if they mistype the password and obtain the same form over and over again by employing this username replacement into the value="…"

As you can see from Listing 11-5, the index page that will live at / has a lot more going on in its template. If there are any flash messages, they will appear directly below the title. The next section contains an unordered list (ul>) of list items (li>) that each explain a single payment made to or from the logged-in user's account, with the title "Your Payments" shown above it. Finally, links to the new-payment page and the logout page are provided.

Listing 11-5. Jinja2 Template index.html

```
{% extends "base.html" %}
{% block title %}Welcome, {{ username }}{% endblock %}
{% block body %}
{% for message in flash_messages %}
  <div class="flash_message">{{ message }}<a href="/">&times;</a></div>
{% endfor %}
<p>Your Payments</p>
<ul>
  {% for p in payments %}
   {% set prep = 'from' if (p.credit == username) else 'to' %}
   {% set acct = p.debit if (p.credit == username) else p.credit %}
   <li class="{{ prep }}">${{ p.dollars }} {{ prep }} <b>{{ acct }}</b>
   for: <i>{{ p.memo }}</i></li>
  {% endfor %}
</ul>
<a href="/pay">Make payment</a> | <a href="/logout">Log out</a>
{% endblock %}
```

It's worth noting that the code isn't interested in repeatedly displaying the current user's account name as it loops through their incoming and departing payments. Instead, it determines if the credit or debit account name that matches the current user is the correct one for each payment, and then ensures that the other account name is printed instead—with the correct preposition so that the user can see which way their money has flowed. This is made feasible by Jinja2's percent set… percent command, which enables short tiny presentation calculations like this simple to implement in-template once the designer recognises what they want. There appear to be plenty of ways for a user to fill out a form incorrectly, and Listing 11-6 anticipates receiving a complaint string and displaying it prominently at the top of the form if one is delivered.

Aside from that, the code is largely the same: three form fields that, if the form was filled out improperly and is being redisplayed, must be prefilled with whatever content the user had there when they tried to submit it.

Listing 11-6. Jinja2 Template pay.html

```
{% extends "base.html" %}

{% block title %}Make a Payment{% endblock %}

{% block body %}

<form method="post" action="/pay">

 {% if complaint %}<span class="complaint">{{ complaint }}</span>{%
endif %}

 <label>To account: <input name="account" value="{{ account }}"></
label>

  <label>Dollars: <input name="dollars" value="{{ dollars }}"></
label>

 <label>Memo: <input name="memo" value="{{ memo }}"></label>

 <button type="submit">Send money</button> | <a href="/">Cancel</a>

</form>

{% endblock %}
```

Every submit button on a website should have an escape path next to it. Experiments show that users make the fewest mistakes if the escape route is clearly smaller and less significant than the default action of completing the form—and that the escape route does not look like a button! As a result, pay.html takes care to make its "Cancel" escape route a simple link that is visually isolated from the button by the commonly used pipe symbol (|) in this visual context.

If you wish to try out this application, go to the source code and type the following into the chapter11 directory, which contains bank.py, app insecure.py, and the corresponding templates/ directory.

```
$ pip install flask
```

```
$ python3 app_insecure.py
```

The end result should be a message stating that it is up and running, along with a URL that will print on your screen.

```
* Running on http://127.0.0.1:5000/
```

```
* Restarting with reloader
```

Flask will even restart itself and reload your application if you alter one of the listings with debug mode enabled (see the second-to-last line of Listing 11-2), making it possible to swiftly investigate the implications of tiny changes to the code.

There's one minor thing that's lacking here. Where is style.css mentioned in base. html in Listing 11-3? It's located in the static/ directory, which is located adjacent to the application in the source repository. If you're interested not only in network programming but also in the concept of web design, you should take a look at it.

The HTTP Methods and Forms Of Dance

The default action of an HTML form is GET, and it might be as minimal as a single input field.

```
<form action="/search">

  <label>Search: <input name="q"></label>

  <button type="submit">Go</button>

</form>
```

There isn't enough room in this book to cover form design, which is a big topic filled with technical decisions. Aside from text fields like this one, there are a slew of other options to explore. Even text fields are surrounded by a plethora of alternatives. Will you utilise CSS3 to add some example text to the input area that vanishes as soon as the user begins typing? Should the submit button be greyed out until the user has typed a search query in some in-browser JavaScript code? Should you include instructions or a few sample search keywords beneath the input area to give the user some ideas? Should a submit button ever say "Submit," or should it instead describe what occurs once the form is sent to the server? Will a minimalist designer encourage you to remove the Go button entirely, simplifying the site but requiring users to understand that they can submit their search by pressing Return?

However, these topics are well covered in web design books and websites. This book can only deal with the implications of forms for the network.

The input fields of a GET form are directly in the URL, and hence in the route transmitted with the HTTP request.

GET /search?q=Programming+in+Python+:+The+Basics HTTP/1.1

Host: example.com

Consider what this means. The parameters of a GET are saved in your browser history, and anyone peering over your shoulder at the address bar can see them. This means that a GET should never be used to send sensitive data such as a password or credential. When you submit a GET form, you are effectively telling the browser, "Where do I want to go next?" and assisting the browser in creating a custom URL for a page that you want the server to create so that you can access it. Filling out the previous search form with three different phrases will create three independent pages, three entries in your browser history that you may return to later, and three URLs that you can share with others if you want them to see the same results page.

You can ask to travel there by simply defining your destination on a form that conducts a GET request.

The method of a POST, PUT, or DELETE HTML form, on the other hand, is POST, PUT, or DELETE.

In the case of these forms, no data from the form makes it into the URL and, as a result, into the path in the HTTP request.

```
<form method="post" action="/donate">
 <label>Charity: <input name="name"></label>
 <label>Amount: <input name="dollars"></label>
 <button type="submit">Donate</button>
</form>
```

When you submit this HTML form, the browser places all of the data into the body of the request, leaving the path completely empty.

```
POST /donate HTTP/1.1
Host: example.com
Content-Type: application/x-www-form-urlencoded
Content-Length: 39
name=PyCon%20scholarships&dollars=35
```

You're not simply requesting that you go look at a "$35 for PyCon scholarships" page because you're curious. Quite the opposite is true. If you opt to do the POST twice instead of once, you are committing to an action that will be twice as expensive and have twice the impact. Because "$35 for PyCon scholarships" is not the name of a site you want to visit, the form parameters are not included in the URL. It's what the late philosopher J.L. Austin referred to as a speech act, or words that produce a change in the world. By the way, browsers can upload big payloads like complete files using an alternate form encoding multipart/forms based on the MIME standard (Chapter 12). The semantics of the POST form are the same in either case.

By the way, browsers can upload big payloads like complete files using an alternate form encoding multipart/forms based on the MIME standard (Chapter 12). The semantics of the POST form are the same in either case.

Form Resubmission Confirmation

The information you supplied was utilised on the page you were searching for. Any action you did may be repeated if you return to the page. Do you want to keep going?

In your browser, you should receive a similar warning. When viewing the form with human eyes, it is evident that the form submission did not go through; yet, the browser has no means of understanding that the POST did not go through. It sent a POST, received a page, and for all it knows, the page says anything along the lines of "Thank you for donating $1,000," and submitting it again might have fatal consequences.

There are two strategies that websites can employ to avoid leaving the user stranded on a page that is the result of a POST, causing unending problems for the Reload, Forward, and Back buttons on the user's browser.

- Try to prevent the user from providing erroneous values in the first place by using JavaScript or HTML5 form input limitations. If the submit button does not light up until the form is ready to submit, or if the full form round-trip can be handled in JavaScript without reloading the page, then an incorrect submission—such as the empty form you submitted just now—will not leave the user stranded at a POST result.

- When a form is eventually submitted correctly and its action is done successfully, the web application should resist the urge to immediately react with a 200 OK page that details the accomplished activity. Reply with a 303 See Other redirect to an other URL supplied in the Location header. This forces the browser to immediately follow up on the successful POST with a GET that redirects the user to a different page. The user can now hit Reload,

Forward, and Back as many times as they want, resulting in just safe repeated GETs of the results page rather than repeated attempts to submit the form.

While the small application in Listing 11-2 is too basic to prevent the user from seeing a POST response if the form is invalid, it does conduct a successful 303 See Also powered by the Flask redirect() function Object() { [native code] } when either the /login form or the /pay form succeeds.

When Forms Use Inappropriate Methods

Misusing HTTP methods in web applications causes issues with automated tools, user expectations, and the browser.

I recall a buddy whose small-business website was hosted using a home-grown PHP content management system developed by a local hosting provider. He was supplied with links to the photos used on his site via an admin screen.

We highlighted the page and requested that a browser download all of the links so that he may save a copy of the photographs to his computer. Minutes later, he received a text from a buddy asking why all of the photographs on his website had vanished.

The Delete button next to each image turned out to be a fake button that triggered a POST transaction. Instead, each Delete was just a link to a regular URL, which had the unintended consequence of removing an image if you visited it! Because a GET should always, under all circumstances, be a safe operation, his browser was willing to GET the page's hundred links. His web hosting firm had violated his confidence, and as a result, his website had to be recovered from backups.

The reverse error, using POST to do "read" actions, has less serious consequences. Rather than erasing all of your files, it simply destroys usability.

I once had the misfortune of having to use a huge institution's in-house search engine. I had a page of results in front of me after numerous searches that my supervisor wanted to see, so I highlighted the URL and prepared to put it into an e-mail.

Then I was shocked when I saw the URL. Even though I had no idea how the server worked, I was confident that when my supervisor visited it, /search.pl would not put up this page of results by itself!

Because the search form was poorly constructed to use POST, the query was invisible to my browser's location bar. This made every every search's URL look precisely the same, preventing queries from being shared or bookmarked. And when I tried to use my browser's Forward and Back buttons to traverse through a series of searches, I got a series of pop-up windows asking if I truly wanted to resubmit each one! Any of those POSTs might have had adverse effects, according to the browser.

Using GET for locations and POST for actions is critical not only for protocol compliance but also for a positive user experience.

Cookies that are safe and those that are not

Listing 11-2 shows a web application that tries to protect its users' privacy. In response to a GET of the / page, it requires a successful login before revealing the user's list of payments. It also requires the user to be signed in before accepting a POST to the /pay form, which allows the user to make a money transfer. Unfortunately, it is very simple to take advantage of the app and make payments on behalf of another user!

Consider what actions a malevolent person who gains access to the site would take, such as creating a new account to learn more about how it works. They'll launch the debugging tools in Firefox or Google Chrome, then log in to the site and examine the outgoing and incoming headers in the Network window to see how it works. And what will they get in return when they enter their account and password?

HTTP/1.0 302 FOUND

...

```
Set-Cookie: username=badguy; Path=/
```

...

What a fascinating topic! Their browser has received a cookie named username, with the value of their own username badguy, as a result of their successful login. The site appears to be carelessly relying that subsequent requests containing this cookie must imply that the user inputted their login and password correctly.

But, certainly, the caller can set any value for this cookie?

They can try to counterfeit the cookie by going through the appropriate privacy options in their browser, or they can use Python to visit the site. They might use Requests to see if they can get the first page first. As one might assume, an unauthenticated request is sent to the /login page.

```
>>> import requests
>>> r = requests.get('http://localhost:5000/')
>>> print(r.url)
http://localhost:5000/login
```

What if the bad guy places a cookie that makes it appear that the john user has already logged in?

```
>>> r = requests.get('http://localhost:5000/', cookies={'username':
'john'})
```

```
>>> print(r.url)
```

```
http://localhost:5000/
```

Success! Because the site believes it set the cookie's value, it is now treating HTTP requests as if they came from a different user. All the bad guy needs is the login of another payment system user, and they can falsify a request to send money anywhere they want.

```
>>> r = requests.post('http://localhost:5000/pay',
... {'account': 'hacker', 'dollars': 100, 'memo': 'Auto-pay'},
... cookies={'username': 'john'})
>>> print(r.url)
```

```
http://localhost:5000/?flash=Payment+successful
```

It worked, and $100 was transferred from the john account to a bank account under their control. The lesson is that cookies should never be constructed in such a way that a user can create one on their own. Assume that your users are astute, and that disguising their username with base-64 encoding, switching the letters around, or doing a simple exclusive-or of the value with a constant mask would soon catch on. There are three methods for making nonforgeable cookies that are both safe and effective.

- You can sign the cookie with a digital signature yet leave it viewable. As a result, attackers are irritated. They'll see that the cookie contains their username and hope that they could just rewrite it with the username of an account they want to take over. However, because they are unable to fake the digital signature used to sign this new version of the cookie, they will be unable to persuade your site that the rewritten cookie is valid.

- You can totally encrypt the cookie, making it impossible for the user to decipher its value. It will appear as an obfuscated value that they will be unable to analyse or comprehend.

- You can use a standard UUID library to generate a fully random string for the cookie that has no intrinsic meaning, and keep it in your own database so that you can recognise the cookie as belonging to the user when they make their next request. If many HTTP requests from the same user are directed to separate servers, this persistent session storage will need to be accessible to all of your front-end web machines. Some apps maintain sessions in their main database, while others employ a Redis instance or other short-term storage to keep their main persistent data store from becoming overburdened with queries.

You may use Flask's built-in ability to digitally sign cookies so that they can't be forged in this example application. On a real production server, the signing key should be kept separate from the source code, but for this example, it can be placed towards the top of the source file. Not only does including the key in the source code for a production system give anyone with access to your version control system access to the key, but it also exposes the credential to your developer laptops and continuous integration process.

```
app.secret_key = 'saiGeij8AiS2ahleahMo5dahveixuV4J'
```

Flask will then utilise the secret key every time you use its unique session object to set a cookie, like as during login.

```
session['username'] = username

session['csrf_token'] = uuid.uuid4().hex
```

And Flask will utilise the key once more before trusting any cookie values it extracts from the incoming request. A cookie with an incorrect signature is presumed to be faked and is treated as if it did not exist at all in the request.

```
username = session.get('username')
```

In Listing 11-8, you can see these enhancements in action.

Another concern with cookies is that they should never be sent over an unencrypted HTTP channel, as they will be visible to everyone on the same coffee shop wireless network. Many websites use an HTTP-secured login page to carefully establish their cookies, only to expose them totally when the browser downloads all of the CSS, JavaScript, and pictures that are downloaded over plain HTTP from the same hostname.

Find out how to make your web framework set the Secure parameter on every cookie you submit to the browser to prevent cookie disclosure. It will then take care not to include it in unencrypted requests for resources that everyone has access to in the first place.

Cross-Site Scripting that isn't persistent

If an opponent is unable to steal or fabricate a cookie that allows their browser (or Python application) to act on behalf of another user, they can switch tactics. They will never have to see the cookie if they can figure out how to take control of another user's browser while they are logged in. The cookie will be added in each request if you take actions with that browser.

This type of attack can be approached in at least three ways. The server in Listing 11-2 is vulnerable to all three, and you'll learn about them individually today. The first is a nonpersistent cross-site scripting (XSS) attack, in which an attacker figures out how to make a web site—such as the payment system in the example—present attacker-written text as if it came from the site. Assume the attacker intended to send $110 to a bank account they had access to. They could write the JavaScript in Listing 11-7.

Listing 11-7. attack.js is a script for making payments.

```
<script>
var x = new XMLHttpRequest();
x.open('POST', 'http://localhost:5000/pay');
x.setRequestHeader('Content-Type',          'application/x-www-form-
urlencoded');
x.send('account=hacker&dollars=110&memo=Theft');
</script>
```

If this code is only visible on the website while the user is signed into the payments application, the POST request it specifies will fire and make the payment on the innocent user's behalf automatically. Because the code inside script> tags is not visible while viewing a rendered web page, the user will not notice anything is wrong unless they press Ctrl+U to read the source code—and even then, they must recognise the script> element as something strange that is not ordinarily part of the page.

How, on the other hand, could an attacker make this HTML appear? The explanation is that the attacker can simply inject this HTML into the / page's page template via the flash parameter that the code is injecting, raw! Because the author of Listing 11-2 has not read enough documentation, they are unaware that Jinja2 in its raw form does not automatically escape special characters such as and > because it does not know that you are using it to compose HTML unless you tell it.

The attacker can create a URL that includes their script in the flash parameter.

```
>>> with open('/home/john/py3/chapter11/attack.js') as f:

... query = {'flash': f.read().strip().replace('\n', ' ')}

>>> print('http://localhost:5000/?' + urlencode(query))
```

http://localhost:5000/?flash=%3Cscript%3E+var+x+%3D+new+XMLHttpRequest
%28%29%3B+x.open%28%27+POST%27%2C+%27http%3A%2F%2Flocalhost
%3A5000%2Fpay%27 %29%3B+x.setRequestHeader%28%27Content
Type%27%2C+%27application% 2Fx-www-form-url-
encoded-%27%29%3B+x.send%28%27account%3Dhacker%
26dollars%3D110%26memo%3DTheft%27%29%3B+%3C%2Fscript%3E

Finally, the attacker must devise a method to persuade the user to view and click the link.

When targeting a single user, this can be tough. The attacker may need to imitate an e-mail from one of the victim's true friends, hiding the link behind language that the user will wish to click. There is a need for research, and there are numerous failure modes. The attacker may join the user's IRC channel and claim that the link is "an article" regarding a topic on which the user has just expressed an opinion. Because seeing the entire link presented previously is likely to make the user suspicious, the attacker will typically share a truncated link that only expands to the XSS link once the user clicks it.

When attacking a large site with no unique users, such as a payment processing system utilised by millions of people, the attacker can often be less precise. The poisoned link, which was inserted in an appealing spam e-mail sent to millions of users, may result in a few clicks from those who are signed into the payment system, generating revenue for the attacker.

Try producing the link with the Requests code you were provided earlier. Then, while you're logged in to the payments site and when you're not, click it. When you're logged in, you should notice that each time you reload the main page, another payment occurs, which is handled automatically on your behalf by the link you clicked. To check that the JavaScript and surrounding script> tags have made it into the page, press Ctrl+U in Firefox or Google Chrome.

If you notice that the attack isn't working, go to your browser's JavaScript console. "The XSS Auditor refused to execute a script...because its source code was identified within the request," my version of Chrome said, detecting and cancelling the attempt. A good modern browser can be deceived by the crude version of the attack that is being launched here only if this protection is turned off or if the attacker finds a more sinister technique to exploit the flash message.

Even if the attack is successful, the user may be suspicious if a blank green message box appears with no message inside. Try fixing this fault in the previous URL as an exercise: outside of the script tag, see if you can offer some real content, such as "Welcome back," to make the green message section look more acceptable. The flash message—this bit of contextual information about what the /pay form just did that the app wants to display on the next page the user visits—must be removed totally from the URL to defend against the attack described in Listing 11-8. You can instead leave the flash message on the server till the next request arrives. Flask, like most frameworks, already has a method for this with the flash() and get flashed messages functions ().

Cross-Site Scripting that Remains Persistent

Because seeing the entire link presented previously is likely to make the user suspicious, the attacker will typically share a truncated link that only expands to the XSS link once the user clicks it.

When attacking a large site with no unique users, such as a payment processing system utilised by millions of people, the attacker can often be less precise. The poisoned link, which was inserted in an appealing spam e-mail sent to millions of users, may result in a few clicks from those who are signed into the payment system, generating revenue for the attacker.

Try producing the link with the Requests code you were provided earlier. Then, while you're logged in to the payments site and when you're not, click it. You can inject your own code. Log in to the application as sam using the password listed in Listing 11-2, and then try sending me a payment. Include a polite letter expressing how much you appreciated the book and why you are tipping me extra. That way, I won't be suspicious of your money, hopefully. The fields will appear like this once you've added the script element but before you click "Send money":

`To account: john`

`Dollars: 1`

`Memo: A small thank-you.<script>...</script>`

Then hit the submit button. Then log out, re-enter as john, and begin hitting Reload. A new payment will be charged from the john user's account every time he views the top page!

As you can see, this persistent cross-site scripting assault is highly effective. The persistent version—where the JavaScript now appears invisibly and executes every time the user visits the site—will happen over and over until the data on the server is erased or deleted, whereas the prior link worked only when the user clicked it. When XSS assaults were launched using public form messages on susceptible sites, hundreds of thousands of people were affected until the problem was fixed. Because its author employed Jinja2 templates without fully comprehending them, Listing 11-2 is vulnerable to this vulnerability. It's evident from their documentation that they don't do any automatic escape. Jinja2 will only preserve specific HTML characters like and > if you know how to turn on its escaping.

By using Jinja2 through the Flask render template() function, Listing 11-8 will guard against any XSS attacks. When it finds that the template filenames finish with the extension html, it will immediately turn on HTML escaping. You can opt in to patterns that can safeguard you from bad design decisions by depending on a common pattern of the web framework rather than doing things yourself.

Forgery of Cross-Site Requests

XSS attacks should no longer be a problem on your site now that all content is correctly escaped. But the attacker has one more trick in their sleeve: they'll try to submit the form from a whole different website because there's no reason for them to start it from yours. They can forecast what all of the field values should be ahead of time, so they can send a request to /pay from any web page you visit. If they identify a forum topic in which you are active on a site that does not correctly escape or remove script tags from forum comments, all they have to do is encourage you to visit a website where they have concealed the JavaScript or embed it in a comment. You might believe that the attacker will need to create a form that is ready to give them money, and then make the button on that form an enticing target for your mouse.

```
<form method="post" action="http://localhost:5000/pay">
 <input type="hidden" name="account" value="pam">
 <input type="hidden" name="dollars" value="220">
 <input type="hidden" name="message" value="Someone won big">
 <button type="submit">Reply</button>
</form>
```

Because JavaScript is almost certainly enabled in your browser, they can simply copy and paste the script> element from Listing 11-7 onto the page, forum post, or remark you're about to load, and then sit back and wait for a payment to appear in their account.

This is a classic cross-site request forgery (CSRF) attack that doesn't require the attacker to figure out how to get into the payment system. All that is required are simple payment forms and any web site—anywhere in the world—where the attacker may inject JavaScript and where you are likely to visit. Every web \ssite you visit would need to be safe to protect against the risk of this injection.

As a result, programmes must safeguard against it.

How can applications protect themselves from CSRF attacks? By making it harder to complete and submit forms. Rather than creating simple forms with the bare minimum of fields required to make a payment, they require an extra field that contains a secret that only the legitimate user of the form or their browser will ever see; it does not need to be visible to the user reading and using the form through their browser.to make a payment, they require an extra field that contains a secret that only the legitimate user of the form or their browser will ever see; it does not need to be visible to the user reading and using the form through their browser. Because the attacker will not know the secret value that each user has concealed in each /pay form they submit, the attacker will be unable to create a convincing POST to that address.

Listing 11-8 will leverage Flask's ability to store secrets safely in cookies to assign each user a secret random string every time they log in. This example requires you to suppose, of course, that a payment site would be secured with HTTPS in real life, so that delivering the secret on a web page or cookie is secure and cannot be watched in transit. The payments site can add the per-session random secret silently to every /pay form provided to the user after selecting one. HTML includes hidden form fields as a standard feature for reasons such as CSRF protection. In pay2.html, a replacement for Listing 11-6 that will be utilised by Listing 11-8, the following field is added to the form:

```
<input name="csrf_token" type="hidden" value="{{ csrf_token }}">
```

Every time the form is submitted, an additional check is conducted to ensure that the CSRF value from the form matches what was sent to the user in the HTML version of the form. If they don't match, the site considers an attacker is attempting to submit the form on behalf of the user and returns a 403 Forbidden error.

The CSRF protection in Listing 11-8 is done manually so you can see all of the moving components and see how the randomly picked extra field prevents an attacker from guessing how to assemble a legitimate form. In practise, CSRF protection should be incorporated into whatever web framework you pick, or at the very least offered as a standard plug-in. Several ways are suggested by the Flask community, including one that is included in the popular Flask-WTF package for creating and parsing HTML forms.

The Enhanced Software

Listing 11-8 is called app improved.py rather than "perfect" or "secure" because, to be honest, it's difficult to guarantee that any given example programme is fully devoid of potential flaws.

Listing 11-8. The Payments Application app improved.py

```python
#!/usr/bin/env python3
# Programming in Python: The Basics
# A payments application with basic security improvements added.
import bank, uuid
from flask import (Flask, abort, flash, get_flashed_messages,
 redirect, render_template, request, session, url_for)
app = Flask(__name__)
app.secret_key = 'saiGeij8AiS2ahleahMo5dahveixuV4J'
@app.route('/login', methods=['GET', 'POST'])
def login():
 username = request.form.get('username', '')
 password = request.form.get('password', '')
 if request.method == 'POST':
 if (username, password) in [('john', '123456789'), ('pam', 'abcde')]:
 session['username'] = username
 session['csrf_token'] = uuid.uuid4().hex
 return redirect(url_for('index'))
 return render_template('login.html', username=username)
@app.route('/logout')
def logout():
 session.pop('username', None)
 return redirect(url_for('login'))
@app.route('/')
def index():
 username = session.get('username')
 if not username:
```

```
    return redirect(url_for('login'))
 payments = bank.get_payments_of(bank.open_database(), username)
    return    render_template('index.html',    payments=payments,
username=username,
 flash_messages=get_flashed_messages())
@app.route('/pay', methods=['GET', 'POST'])
def pay():
 username = session.get('username')
 if not username:
 return redirect(url_for('login'))
 account = request.form.get('account', '').strip()
 dollars = request.form.get('dollars', '').strip()
 memo = request.form.get('memo', '').strip()
 complaint = None
 if request.method == 'POST':
 if request.form.get('csrf_token') != session['csrf_token']:
 abort(403)
 if account and dollars and dollars.isdigit() and memo:
 db = bank.open_database()
 bank.add_payment(db, username, account, dollars, memo)
 db.commit()
 flash('Payment successful')
 return redirect(url_for('index'))
 complaint = ('Dollars must be an integer' if not dollars.isdigit()
 else 'Please fill in all three fields')
    return    render_template('pay2.html',    complaint=complaint,
account=account,
 dollars=dollars, memo=memo,
 csrf_token=session['csrf_token'])
if __name__ == '__main__':
 app.debug = True
 app.run()
```

The Shellshock vulnerability was just announced as I write this: for the past 22 years, the widely used Bash shell has been willing to run any code presented to it as specially formatted environment variables—like those that the old CGI mechanism will happily set based on incoming untrusted HTTP headers—without anyone noticing. It's difficult to offer guarantees regarding the total security of a demonstration web application that I created only for this chapter if significant production software can be vulnerable to unanticipated features and interactions after more than two decades. However, here is the list. Its templates conduct correct escaping, it sends flash messages to internal storage rather than transmitting them round-trip over the user's browser, and each form it presents to the user has a concealed random UUID that makes it hard to counterfeit. It's worth noting that two of the significant enhancements—switching to internally stored flash messages and requesting Jinja2 to execute correct escaping of characters before adding them to the HTML—were made possible by relying on Flask's standard features rather than my own code. This exemplifies a crucial point. If you read the framework documentation thoroughly and use as many of its features as possible, your applications will not only be shorter, more concise, and more convenient to write, but they will also be more secure because you will be using patterns written by a professional and carefully improved by the web framework's entire community. These conveniences will, in many situations, fix security or performance issues that you may not even be aware of.

When it comes to network interaction, the application is currently quite effectively automated. When it comes to the processing of views and forms, though, there are still a lot of seams to be ironed out. The code must manually verify that the user is logged in. Each form field must be manually copied from the request into the HTML to avoid the user having to retype it. And the database interaction is rather low-level; if you want the payment to be logged permanently by SQLite, you must open database sessions manually and then remember to commit.

You might turn to the Flask community for strong best practises and third-party tools to address these prevalent issues. Instead, for diversity, the last example will be the same application created in a framework that relieves you of more of these tasks from day one.

Django's Payments Application

Because it is a "full-stack" web framework with everything a rookie programmer needs built in, the Django web framework is perhaps the most popular among Python programmers today. Django not only has a templates system and URL routing structure, but it can also communicate with databases, render results as Python objects, and even compose and interpret forms without the use of any third-party libraries. A framework that establishes coherent and safe patterns can be more valuable than a more flexible tool that sends the programmer hunting for their own ORM and forms library, when they may not even have a clear idea of how those pieces fit together in a world where many people programming for the Web have little training. The Django application can be found in its full in the book's source code repository. Here's the URL for this chapter once more:

`https://bpbonline.com/Programming in Python: The Basics/py3/chapter11`

There are a few boilerplate files in this book that aren't worth quoting in their whole.

- **manage.py:** This is an executable script in the chapter11/ directory that allows you to perform Django commands to set up and start the application in development mode, as you'll see shortly.

- **djbank/ init .py:** This is an empty file that notifies Python that the directory is a Python package that can be used to import modules.

- **djbank/admin.py:** This file has three lines of code that display the Payment model in the Admin interface, as explained in the "Choosing a Web Framework" section below. Because it is a "full-stack" web framework with everything a rookie programmer needs built in, the Django web framework is perhaps the most popular among Python programmers today. Django not only has a templates system and URL routing structure, but it can also communicate with databases, render results as Python objects, and even compose and interpret forms without the use of any third-party libraries. A framework that establishes coherent and safe patterns can be more valuable than a more flexible tool that sends the programmer hunting for their own ORM and forms library, when they may not even have a clear idea of how those pieces fit together in a world where many people programming for the Web have little training.

- **djbank/wgsi.py:** This file contains a WSGI callable that a WSGI-compliant web server, such as Gunicorn or Apache (see Chapter 10), can use to start the payments application.

The subsequent four scripts are interesting because they show how the framework already supports many common patterns that Python code can use without requiring any changes. Django eliminates the need for the application to create its own SQL queries thanks to its built-in object-relational mapper (ORM). With it, the entire issue of appropriate SQL value quoting vanishes. Listing 11-9 lists the fields of the database table in a declarative Python class that will be used to represent the table rows when they are retrieved. If your data limitations go beyond what can be described by field types alone, Django enables you attach extensive validation logic to a class like this.

Listing 11-9. For the Django App, he uses models.py.

```python3
#!/usr/bin/env python3

# Programming in Python: The Basics

# Model definitions for our Django application.

from django.db import models

from django.forms import ModelForm

class Payment(models.Model):
 debit = models.CharField(max_length=200)

 credit = models.CharField(max_length=200, verbose_name='To account')

 dollars = models.PositiveIntegerField()

 memo = models.CharField(max_length=200)

class PaymentForm(ModelForm):
 class Meta:
 model = Payment

             fields = ['credit', 'dollars', 'memo']
```

The bottom class declaration instructs Django to create and change database records using a form. It will just question the user about the three fields given, leaving the debit field blank so you may fill it in with the username you're presently logged in with.

As you'll see, this class can handle both sides of the user's interaction with the web app: it can render the form as a set of HTML fields, and then parse the HTTP POST data that is returned once the form is submitted in order to create or edit a Payment database row.

If you're using a micro-framework like Flask, you'll need to pick an external library to handle actions like these. For example, SQLAlchemy is a well-known ORM, and many programmers prefer not to use Django in order to take use of SQLAlchemy's power and elegance.

However, because SQLAlchemy is unaware of HTML forms, the microframework programmer will need to locate yet another third-party package to handle the other half of what the prior models.py file does for the Django programmer.

Instead of employing a Flask-style decorator to attach URL paths to Python view functions, Django requires the application writer to produce a urls.py file like the one shown in Listing 11-10. While this makes each view position-independent and helps to concentrate management of the URL space, it does provide each view less context when viewed on its own.

Listing 11-10. The Django App's urls.py file

```python3
#!/usr/bin/env python3
# Programming in Python: The Basics
# URL patterns for our Django application.
from django.conf.urls import patterns, include, url
from django.contrib import admin
from django.contrib.auth.views import login
urlpatterns = patterns('',
        url(r'^admin/', include(admin.site.urls)),
        url(r'^accounts/login/$', login),
        url(r'^$', 'djbank.views.index_view', name='index'),
        url(r'^pay/$', 'djbank.views.pay_view', name='pay'),
        url(r'^logout/$', 'djbank.views.logout_view'),
        )
```

When a URL contains numerous variable sections, Django makes the odd decision to utilise regular expression matching to match them, which can result in difficult-to-read patterns. They can also be tough to troubleshoot, as I know from personal experience.

Except that the path to the login page is where the Django authentication module expects it to be, these patterns provide essentially the same URL space as the prior Flask apps. This method relies on the standard Django login page to have gotten things right, rather than developing your own login page and hoping you write it correctly and without some subtle security fault. The views in Listing 11-11 that finally tie this Django application together are both simpler and more sophisticated than the Flask version of the app's comparable views.

Listing 11-11. The Django App's views.py file

```python3
#!/usr/bin/env python3
# Programming in Python: The Basics
# A function for each view in our Django application.
```

```
from django.contrib import messages
from django.contrib.auth.decorators import login_required
from django.contrib.auth import logout
from django.db.models import Q
from django.shortcuts import redirect, render
from  django.views.decorators.http  import  require_http_methods,
require_safe
from .models import Payment, PaymentForm
def make_payment_views(payments, username):
 for p in payments:
 yield {'dollars': p.dollars, 'memo': p.memo,
 'prep': 'to' if (p.debit == username) else 'from',
 'account': p.credit if (p.debit == username) else p.debit}
@require_http_methods(['GET'])
@login_required
def index_view(request):
 username = request.user.username
    payments   =   Payment.objects.filter(Q(credit=username)   |
Q(debit=username))
 payment_views = make_payment_views(payments, username)
 return render(request, 'index.html', {'payments': payment_views})
@require_http_methods(['GET', 'POST'])
@login_required
def pay_view(request):
 form = PaymentForm(request.POST or None)
 if form.is_valid():
 payment = form.save(commit=False)
 payment.debit = request.user.username
 payment.save()
messages.add_message(request, messages.INFO, 'Payment successful.')
 return redirect('/')
 return render(request, 'pay.html', {'form': form})
```

```
@require_http_methods(['GET'])
def logout_view(request):
 logout(request)
 return redirect('/')
```

Where is the cross-site scripting protection? That is the big question you should be asking. When I asked Django to generate the skeleton for this application with the manage.py startapp command, it was instantly added to settings.py and turned on!

Your forms will refuse to work unless you remember to add percent csrf token percent to your form template, even if you are unaware that CSRF protection exists. And, in case you forgot, the Django error message provided by its runserver development mode clarifies the necessity. This is a very effective pattern for inexperienced web developers who are unfamiliar with the difficulties at hand: In a way that microframeworks seldom match, the Django default will often make them safe from the most common catastrophic failures with forms and fields.

Because this code relies on built-in Django functionality for practically everything instead of having to develop things like login and session manipulation, the views in this application are conceptually simpler than their Flask-powered counterparts. Because urls.py merely utilises Django's, the login page does not show. The logout page can just call logout() without worrying about the details. By using the @login required attribute on views, you can avoid worrying about whether or not the user is signed in. The only helper that directly matches to a similar functionality in our Flask project is the @require http_ methods() decorator, which provides the same protection against invalid or unsupported HTTP methods as Flask's own view decorators.

Working with the database has never been easier. The bank.py module, along with accompanying SQL, is no longer available.

Django has already opted to set up a SQLite database (one of the defaults in settings. py), and it is ready to create a database session the instant the code searches the model class from the models.py file. Because it is a "full-stack" web framework with everything a rookie programmer needs built in, the Django web framework is perhaps the most popular among Python programmers today. Django not only has a templates system and URL routing structure, but it can also communicate with databases, render results as Python objects, and even compose and interpret forms without the use of any third-party libraries. A framework that establishes coherent and safe patterns can be more valuable than a more flexible tool that sends the programmer hunting for their own ORM and forms library, when they may not even have a clear idea of how those pieces fit together in a world where many people programming for the Web have little training. One annoyance is that a piece of logic that should have been in the template—the choice of wording and presentation around the display of payments on the main page—has now had to be moved into the Python code because the Django template system does not make the logic as easy to express. The index() view in Python, on the other hand, calls a generator that generates a dict of information about each payment, turning the raw object into the data that the template is interested in.

Some programmers are irritated by the lack of power in the template system. Others learn to create Django "template tags," which allow them to call logic from deep within a template. Others say that code like Listing 11-11 is better in the long term since tests for a procedure like make payment views() are easier to build than for logic stranded inside a template.

To execute this Django application, get the source code for Chapter 11 from the link above, install Django 1.7 under Python 3, and perform the following three commands:

```
$ python manage.py syncdb
```

```
$ python manage.py loaddata start
```

```
$ python manage.py runserver
```

You can now go to http://localhost:8000/ after running the previous command. and see how Django has allowed you to build a similar application to the one you created with Flask earlier in this chapter.

Choosing a Framework for a Website

The web framework landscape, like the Python programming language, is continually innovating in a vibrant and healthy community. Although it will most likely make this book look ancient in a few years, here's a quick rundown of the most common frameworks to give you an idea of the options available to a regular developer:

- **Django:** An excellent framework for newcomers to web programming. There are built-in features such as CSRF prevention. It has a built-in ORM and template language. Not only does this save the novice from having to pick their own libraries, but it also ensures that all third-party Django tools may use the same set of interfaces to interact with HTML and the database. Try visiting the /admin page after running Listing 11-11 to see an example of how administrators can interact directly with the database using automatically generated create, edit, and delete forms!

- **Tornado:** A web framework unlike any other on this list since it employs the asynchronous callback mechanism from Chapter 9 to handle many dozens or hundreds of client connections per operating system thread, rather than just one. It also distinguishes out because it isn't restricted to supporting WSGI and instead supports WebSockets directly (described in the next section). The price is that many libraries struggle to operate with its callback structure, forcing programmers to look for async alternatives to the conventional ORM or database connection.

- **Flask:** The most widely used microframework, built on robust tools and enabling a wide range of current features (if the programmer knows to look for and take advantage of them). Frequently used in conjunction with SQLAlchemy or a nonrelational database.

- **Bottle:** A Flask alternative that just requires the installation of one file, bottle. py, rather than numerous distinct packages. Developers who haven't yet integrated the pip install tool into their workflow will find it particularly appealing. It has a particularly well-designed template language.

- **Pyramid:** A remarkable and high-performance synthesis of lessons learned by community members in the old Zope and Pylons communities, Pyramid is the go-to framework for developers working in fluid URL spaces, such as those created when you author a content management system (CMS) that allows users to create subfolders and additional web pages with a single mouse click. While it can support predefined URL structures just like any of the previous frameworks, it can also support object traversal, which means the framework understands that your URL components are naming containers, content, and views that the URL is visiting, much like a filesystem path visits directories before arriving at a file. The web framework landscape, like the Python programming language, is continually innovating in a vibrant and healthy community. Although it will most likely make this book look ancient in a few years, here's a quick rundown of the most common frameworks to give you an idea of the options available to a regular developer:

- **Django:** An excellent framework for newcomers to web programming. There are built-in features such as CSRF prevention. It has a built-in ORM and template language. Not only does this save the novice from having to pick their own libraries, but it also ensures that all third-party Django tools may use the same set of interfaces to interact with HTML and the database.

You might be tempted to choose a web framework based on its reputation—perhaps based on the preceding paragraphs, as well as a thorough examination of their websites and what you find on social networking sites or Stack Overflow.

But I'll point you in a different direction: if you have coworkers or friends at your local Python meetup who are already fans of a framework and can provide you with regular support via e-mail or IRC, you might want to choose that framework over a similar one whose website or feature list you prefer less. Having live assistance from someone who has already dealt with the common error messages and misunderstandings can frequently outweigh whether a certain feature of the framework is slightly more or less difficult to use.

WebSockets

Web sites that use JavaScript frequently seek to allow users to edit their content in real time. Whether someone tweets, Twitter wants to refresh the page you're viewing without having to check the browser every second to see if anything new has shown. The most powerful and turbocharged of the conceivable solutions to this "extended polling problem" is the Websocket Protocol (RFC 6455).

Earlier workarounds, such as the well-known Comet approaches, were conceivable. The client sends an HTTP request to a path; the server hangs, leaving the socket open, and waits to respond until an actual event (such as a new incoming tweet) occurs and can be provided in the response. Because WSGI only supports traditional HTTP, you'll need to look beyond standard web frameworks and the complete range of WSGI-compatible web servers like Gunicorn, Apache, and nginx to enable WebSockets.

One of the main reasons for the popularity of the standalone Tornado server-framework is that WSGI does not support WebSockets.

Unlike HTTP, which runs in lockstep, where the client sends a single request and then waits for the server to complete its response before sending another, a socket in WebSockets mode allows messages to move in either direction at any time without waiting for each other. You might be tempted to choose a web framework based on its reputation—perhaps based on the preceding paragraphs, as well as a thorough examination of their websites and what you find on social networking sites or Stack Overflow.

But I'll point you in a different direction: if you have coworkers or friends at your local Python meetup who are already fans of a framework and can provide you with regular support via e-mail or IRC, you might want to choose that framework over a similar one whose website or feature list you prefer less. Having live assistance from someone who has already dealt with the common error messages and misunderstandings can frequently outweigh whether a certain feature of the framework is slightly more or less difficult to use. The documentation for the tornado.websocket module, which offers a bit of Python and JavaScript code that can communicate with each other via a pair of symmetric callbacks, is a good place to start. For ideas on how to use such a system to enable live changes to web pages, look up any decent reference on asynchronous front-end browser programming.

Scraping the Internet

The amount of programmers who begin their web programming careers by attempting to scrape a website is likely to outnumber those who begin by creating their own example site. After all, how many new programmers have access to large stacks of data waiting to be presented on the Web vs how many can quickly conceive of material currently on the Web that they'd like to copy?

The first piece of web scraping advice is to avoid it as much as possible.

Apart from basic scraping, there are a variety of approaches to obtain data. It is less expensive to use such data sources not just for you, the coder, but also for the site itself. The Internet Movie Database will let you to get movie data from www.imdb.com/interfaces in order to run statistics across Hollywood films without forcing the main site to produce hundreds of thousands of extra pages, which you will then have to interpret! Many websites, including Google and Yahoo, offer APIs for their key services, which can assist you avoid receiving raw HTML in return.

If you're looking for data on Google but can't find any download or API alternatives, there are a few things to keep in mind. Look for a "Terms of Service" page for the site you're interested in. Check for a /robots.txt file, which will inform you which URLs are intended for search engines to download and which should be avoided. This can help you avoid receiving many versions of the same article with various advertisements, while also assisting the site in managing its load.

Following the Terms of Service and robots.txt might also reduce the likelihood of your IP being blacklisted for generating excessive traffic.

Scraping a website will, in the most common instance, necessitate what you've learned about HTTP and how web browsers use it in Chapter 9, Chapter 10, and this chapter.

- The GET and POST methods, as well as how a method, path, and headers combine to produce an HTTP request
- HTTP response status codes and structure, including the distinction between success, redirect, temporary failure, and permanent failure
- Form-based authentication and how it sets cookies that must be present in your later requests for them to be assessed valid

- Basic HTTP authentication—both how it is expected by a server answer and then delivered in a client request

- JavaScript-based authentication, in which the login form sends a direct POST to the web server without involving the browser in the submission process.

- The difference between a query or action that appends data to the URL and performs a GET for that location versus an action that does a direct POST of data to the server that is carried as the request body instead of a query or action that appends data to the URL and performs a GET for that location to protect the site from CSRF attacks

- The difference between POST URLs, which are designed to receive form-encoded data from the browser, and URLs, which are designed to interface directly with front-end JavaScript code and are thus more likely to expect and deliver data in JSON or another programmer-friendly format.

Scraping a complex site can take hours of trial and error, as well as extended sessions of scrolling around in your browser's web developer tools to figure out what's going on. Three tabs are required, and once you've right-clicked a page and selected Inspect Element, all three should appear in either Firefox or Google Chrome. The Elements tab (see Figure 11-1) displays the live content, even if JavaScript has been adding and removing elements, so you can see which elements are contained within which others. The Network tab (see Figure 11-2) allows you to hit Reload and examine all of the HTTP requests and answers, including those initiated by JavaScript, that have resulted in a complete page. And the Console shows you any faults that the page is having, even if they aren't being notified to you as a user.

There are two types of automation that programmers deal with.

The first is when you're casting a wide net because you want to download a large amount of info. Apart from the possibility of an initial login step to obtain the cookies you require, this type of work typically entails multiple GET operations, which may in turn fuel other GETs as you read links from the pages you are downloading. This is the same pattern followed by the "spider" programmes used by web search engines to learn about the pages on each website. The term "spider" was coined for these applications in the days when "web" conjured up images of spider webs.

The other flavour is when you only want to do a precise and targeted action on one or two pages rather than a large section of a website. This could be because you only need data from a specific page—for example, you might want your shell prompt to print the temperature from a specific weather page—or because you're trying to automate a task that would normally require a browser, such as paying a customer or listing yesterday's credit card transactions to check for fraud. This frequently necessitates significantly greater vigilance when it comes to clicks, forms, and verification.

Because the bank employs in-page JavaScript to discourage automated attempts to gain illegal access to accounts, it frequently requires a full-fledged browser to run the show rather than just Python.

Before launching an automated programme against a website, make sure to examine the terms of service and the robots.txt files. Expect to be stopped if your program's behaviour becomes noticeably more demanding than a regular human user browsing through the page that they are stopping to scan or read—even if it gets stuck in edge circumstances that you didn't predict. I'm not even going to mention OAuth and other tricks that make it much more difficult for programmers to execute programmes that do tasks that would otherwise require the use of a browser. When unfamiliar tactics or protocols appear to be involved, get as much assistance from third-party libraries as possible, and closely monitor your outgoing headers to ensure that they match exactly what you see emitted when you successfully submit a form or view a website with your browser. Depending on how opinionated the site is, even the user-agent field can be important!

Obtaining Pages

There are three methods for retrieving pages from the Web and examining their content in a Python programme.

- Using a Python library to make direct GET or POST requests. Request a Session object from the Requests library so it can keep track of cookies and do connection pooling for you. If you wish to stay within the Standard Library, urllib.request is a solution for low-complexity circumstances.

- There was once a middle ground of tools that could act enough like a rudimentary web browser to locate form> components and assist you in building an HTTP request using the same rules that a browser would use to return form inputs to the server. Mechanize was the most well-known, but I can't find any evidence that it's still active—possibly because so many websites are now so complex that JavaScript is almost a must for exploring the modern Web.

- A actual web browser can be used. In the examples that follow, you'll use the Selenium Webdriver library to handle Firefox, although there are also ongoing studies with "headless" tools that operate like browsers without needing to open a full window. They usually do this by generating a WebKit instance that isn't linked to a real window. PhantomJS popularised this approach in the JavaScript world, and Ghost.py is a current Python experiment with the functionality.

Your algorithm can be pretty straightforward if you already know which URLs you want to visit. Take the list of URLs, send each one an HTTP request, then save or analyse the results. Only if you don't know the list of URLs ahead of time and have to learn them as you go will things become hard. You'll have to keep track of where you've been so you don't visit the same URL twice and end yourself in a loop.

Listing 11-12 depicts a simple scraper with a narrow scope. Its purpose is to log into a payment application and report on the user's earnings. Make a copy of the payment application in one window before running it.

```
$ python app_improved.py
```

Listing 11-12. Using the Payments System and Adding Up Earnings

```python
#!/usr/bin/env python3
# Programming in Python: The Basics
# Manual scraping, that navigates to a particular page and grabs
data.
import argparse, bs4, lxml.html, requests
from selenium import webdriver
from urllib.parse import urljoin
ROW = '{:>12} {}'
def download_page_with_requests(base):
    session = requests.Session()
    response = session.post(urljoin(base, '/login'),
        {'username': 'john', 'password': '12345678'})
    assert response.url == urljoin(base, '/')
    return response.text
def download_page_with_selenium(base):
    browser = webdriver.Firefox()
    browser.get(base)
    assert browser.current_url == urljoin(base, '/login')
    css = browser.find_element_by_css_selector
    css('input[name="username"]').send_keys('john')
    css('input[name="password"]').send_keys('12345678')
```

```
        css('input[name="password"]').submit()
        assert browser.current_url == urljoin(base, '/')
        return browser.page_source
def scrape_with_soup(text):
        soup = bs4.BeautifulSoup(text)
        total = 0
        for li in soup.find_all('li', 'to'):
                dollars = int(li.get_text().split()[0].lstrip('$'))
                memo = li.find('i').get_text()
                total += dollars
                print(ROW.format(dollars, memo))
        print(ROW.format('-' * 8, '-' * 30))
        print(ROW.format(total, 'Total payments made'))
def scrape_with_lxml(text):
        root = lxml.html.document_fromstring(text)
        total = 0
        for li in root.cssselect('li.to'):
                dollars = int(li.text_content().split()[0].lstrip('$'))
                memo = li.cssselect('i')[0].text_content()
                total += dollars
                print(ROW.format(dollars, memo))
        print(ROW.format('-' * 8, '-' * 30))
        print(ROW.format(total, 'Total payments made'))
def main():
        parser = argparse.ArgumentParser(description='Scrape  our
        payments site.')
        parser.add_argument('url', help='the URL at which to begin')
        parser.add_argument('-l', action='store_true', help='scrape
        using lxml')
        parser.add_argument('-s',  action='store_true',  help='get
        with selenium')
        args = parser.parse_args()
        if args.s:
```

```
            text = download_page_with_selenium(args.url)
        else:
            text = download_page_with_requests(args.url)
        if args.l:
            scrape_with_lxml(text)
        else:
            scrape_with_soup(text)
if __name__ == '__main__':
    main()
```

You're ready to start mscrape.py in another terminal window once this Flask application is started on port 5000. If you don't already have it, download and install the Beautiful Soup third-party library, as well as Requests.

```
$ pip install beautifulsoup4

$ pip install requests

$ python mscrape.py http://127.0.0.1:5000/

 125 Registration for PyCon

 200 Payment for writing that code

 -------- ------------------------------

 325 Total payments made
```

When mscrape.py is run in its default mode, it first utilises the Requests library to log in to the site via the login form. This is what will give the Session object the cookie it requires to successfully fetch the home page. The script then parses the page, gets the list-item items designated with the class to, and uses a few print() calls to tally up the outgoing payments.

By passing the -s option to mscrape.py, you can have it do something a little more exciting: it will launch a full version of Firefox if it is found on your system, and use it to browse the website instead! This mode will only work if you have the Selenium package installed.

```
$ pip install selenium
$ python mscrape.py -s http://127.0.0.1:5000/
 125 Registration for PyCon
 200 Payment for writing that code
 -------- ------------------------------
```

```
325 Total payments made
```

Once the script has displayed its output, press Ctrl+W to close Firefox. While Selenium scripts may be written to automatically dismiss Firefox, I prefer to leave it open when developing and debugging so that I can see what went wrong in the browser if the programme encounters an error.

The distinction between these two techniques should be emphasised. To develop the Requests-based code, you must first visit the site, read the login form, and copy the information into the data that the post() method uses to log in. Once you've done that, your code will have no means of knowing whether or not the login form will change in the future. Whether or not the hard-coded input names 'username' and 'password' are still relevant, it will just utilise them.

So, at least when built this manner, the Requests technique is nothing like a browser. There is no purpose in going to the login page and seeing a form. It's more like thinking the login page exists and then executing a U-turn to POST the form that's the ultimate result. Obviously, if the login form is ever given a secret token to prevent mass efforts to guess user passwords, this strategy will fail. In that instance, a first GET of the /login page would be required to obtain the secret token, which would then need to be coupled with your username and password to create a valid POST.

In mscape.py, the Selenium-based code takes the opposite technique. It acts as though it just sees a form, picks its elements, and begins typing, just like a user sitting at a browser. Then it reaches over and presses the form's submit button. Selenium is simply doing in Firefox what you would do to log on, thus as long as its CSS selectors continue to correctly identify the form fields, the code will succeed in logging in regardless of any secret tokens or special JavaScript code to sign or automate the form post.

Of course, Selenium is significantly slower than Requests, especially when you initially start it and have to wait for Firefox to load. However, it can quickly do things that might usually require hours of trial and error in Python. A hybrid approach to a complex scraping job would be interesting: could you use Selenium to log in and get the appropriate cookies, then notify Requests about them so that your mass fetch of further pages doesn't have to wait on the browser?

Pages for Scraping

When a site sends data in CSV, JSON, or another recognised data format, you'll use the Standard Library's appropriate module or a third-party library to parse it so you can process it. But what if the information you require is hidden in HTML that is visible to the user?

Reading raw HTML in Google Chrome or Firefox after clicking Ctrl+U might be tedious, depending on how the site has chosen to format it. It's often more enjoyable to right-click, pick Inspect Element, and then merrily browse the browser's collapsible document tree of elements—assuming the HTML is properly written and that a mistake in the markup hasn't concealed the data you need from the browser! As you've seen, the problem with the live element inspector is that by the time you see the document, any JavaScript programmes running on the page may have already altered it beyond recognition.

There are at least two simple techniques for examining such pages. The first step is to disable JavaScript in your browser and reload the page you're on. It should now appear in the element inspector without any changes: you should be able to view exactly what your Python code would see when downloading the identical page. The other method is to use a "tidy" tool, such as the W3C's tidy programme, which is available as the tidy package on Debian and Ubuntu. It turns out that such functions are incorporated into both of the parsing libraries used in Listing 11-12. Once the soup object is created, you can use the following technique to display its elements on the screen:

```
print(soup.prettify())
```

Displaying a lxml document tree takes a little more effort.

```
from lxml import etree
```

```
print(etree.tostring(root, pretty_print=True).decode('ascii'))
```

If the site sending it is not putting items on separate lines and indenting them to make their document structure evident, the outcome is likely to be significantly easier to read than raw HTML—steps that, of course, might be difficult and would raise the bandwidth needs of any site serving HTML.

The following three steps are involved in examining HTML:

1   Request that your chosen library parse the HTML. Because much HTML on the Internet has errors and broken markup, this might be problematic for the library. Designers, on the other hand, are generally unaware of this because browsers are constantly attempting to recover and understand the markup. After instance, why would any browser maker want their browser to be the only one that returns an error for a popular website when all other browsers display it correctly? Both of the libraries in Listing 11-12 are known for being dependable HTML parsers.

2   Use selectors, which are word patterns that will automatically discover the elements you desire, to delve further into the page. While you could do the

dive yourself by patiently iterating over each element's descendants and looking for the tags and attributes that interest you, selectors are often faster. They also usually result in clearer, easier-to-read Python code.

3   Request the text and attribute values you require from each element object. In Listing 11-12, the three-stage method is repeated twice using two different libraries.

In Listing 11-12, the three-stage method is repeated twice using two different libraries.

The BeautifulSoup library is used by the scrape with soup() function, which is a go-to resource for programmers all over the world. Its API is quirky and one-of-a-kind because it was the first Python library to make document parsing so simple, but it gets the job done.

All "soup" objects have a find all() method that searches for subordinate elements that match a given tag name and, optionally, an HTML class name, whether the object represents the entire document or a subordinate object that represents a single element. When you've finally found the bottom element you're looking for and are ready to read its content, you can use the get text() method. The code can scrape data from this simple online site using only these two ways, and even complex web sites may often be scraped using only a half-dozen or a dozen different processes.

 The documentation for BeautifulSoup can be found at   www.crummy.com/ software/BeautifulSoup/.

Instead, the scrape with lxml() function makes use of the lxml library, which is built on top of libxml2 and libxslt. If you're using an older operating system that doesn't come with compilers—or if you haven't installed the python-dev or python-devel package, your operating system might not be able to support compiled Python packages. The library is already compiled against the system Python as a package on Debian-derived operating systems, and is commonly referred to as python-lxml.

Even on Mac OS X and Windows, a contemporary Python distribution like Anaconda will have lxml already constructed and ready to install: http://continuum.io/ downloads.

Listing 11-12 can alternatively utilise the library to parse the HTML if you can get it installed.

```
$ pip install lxml
$ python mscrape.py -l http://127.0.0.1:5000/
 125 Registration for PyCon
 200 Payment for writing that code
```

```
-------- ------------------------------ ---
```

325 Total payments made

The essential stages are the same as they were with BeautifulSoup. You begin at the top of the document, use the find or search method—in this example, cssselect()—to zero in on the elements that interest you, and then use additional searches to grab subordinate elements or, finally, to ask elements for the text they contain so that you can parse and display it.

Not only is lxml faster than BeautifulSoup, but it also gives you more possibilities for selecting items.

- It uses cssselect to support CSS **patterns().** This is especially significant when searching for elements by class, because an element is deemed to be in class x regardless of whether its class attribute is specified as class="x," class="x y," or class="w y".
- Its **xpath()** method, which is popular among XML fans, supports XPath expressions. To find all paragraphs, for example, they appear like './p'. One of the more enjoyable aspects of an XPath expression is that you can conclude it with '.../text()' and just obtain the text inside each element, rather than Python objects from which you must then request the text.
- Its **find()** and **findall()** methods provide a quick subset of XPath operations natively.

The scraper had to work a little harder in both of these examples because the payment description field is its own I element, but the dollar amount at the start of each line was not placed inside its own element by the site designer. This is a common dilemma; some things you want from a website will be in an element by themselves, while others will be smack dab in the centre of other content, requiring you to utilise classic Python string techniques like split() and strip() to extract them from their context.

Recursive Scraping

This book's source code repository includes a small static web site that makes it difficult for a web scraper to access all of its pages. It's available at

https://bpbonline.com/ Programming in Python: The Basics

If you have the source code repository checked out, you can serve it locally using Python's built-in web server.

```
$ python -m http.server
```

Serving HTTP on 0.0.0.0 port 8000 ...

You can observe that not all of the links on the front page at http://127.0.0.1:8000/ are delivered at the same time if you read the page code and then look around using your browser's web debugging capabilities. Only two of these ("page1" and "page2") are true anchor tags with href="" attributes in the page's raw HTML.

The next two pages are hidden behind a form with a Search submit button, and you won't be able to access them unless you click the button. A small chunk of dynamic JavaScript code results in the two last links ("page5" and "page6") appearing at the bottom of the screen. This mimics the behaviour of websites that immediately show you the skeleton of a page but then make another round-trip to the server before displaying the data you're looking for.

You might want to look for a web-scraping engine that can help you execute a full-fledged recursive search of all of the URLs on a web site, or even just a portion of it, at this stage. In the same way as web frameworks take into account typical patterns in web applications, such as the necessity to return 404 for nonexistent sites, web frameworks take into account common patterns in web applications. Scraping frameworks are adept at keeping track of which pages have been visited and which have yet to be visited.

Scrapy (http://scrapy.org/) is the most popular web scraper at the present, and its documentation can be studied if you wish to try expressing a scraping operation in a way that fits into its model.

Look behind the scenes in Listing 11-13 to see what a real—if simple—scraper looks like below. This one requires lxml, so if you can, install that third-party library using the instructions in the preceding section.

Listing 11-13. A Recursive Web Scraper That GETS

```
#!/usr/bin/env python3

# Programming in Python: The Basics

# Recursive scraper built using the Requests library.

import argparse, requests

from urllib.parse import urljoin, urlsplit

from lxml import etree

def GET(url):

        response = requests.get(url)
```

```
        if response.headers.get('Content-Type', '').split(';')[0] !=
'text/html':
            return
        text = response.text
        try:
            html = etree.HTML(text)
        except Exception as e:
            print(' {}: {}'.format(e.__class__.__name__, e))
            return
        links = html.findall('.//a[@href]')
        for link in links:
            yield GET, urljoin(url, link.attrib['href'])
def scrape(start, url_filter):
    further_work = {start}
    already_seen = {start}
    while further_work:
        call_tuple = further_work.pop()
        function, url, *etc = call_tuple
        print(function.__name__, url, *etc)
        for call_tuple in function(url, *etc):
            if call_tuple in already_seen:
                continue
            already_seen.add(call_tuple)
            function, url, *etc = call_tuple
            if not url_filter(url):
                continue
            further_work.add(call_tuple)
```

```
def main(GET):

        parser = argparse.ArgumentParser(description='Scrape a simple
        site.')

        parser.add_argument('url', help='the URL at which to begin')

        start_url = parser.parse_args().url

        starting_netloc = urlsplit(start_url).netloc

        url_filter = (lambda url: urlsplit(url).netloc == starting_
        netloc)

        scrape((GET, start_url), url_filter)

if __name__ == '__main__':

        main(GET)
```

There are only two moving elements in Listing 11-13, aside from the duty of setting it up and reading its command-line arguments.

The simplest is its GET() function, which tries to download a URL and parse it if it's HTML; only if those steps succeed does it retrieve the href="" attributes of all the anchor tags () to figure out what other pages the current page links to. Because any of these links could be relative URLs, it uses urljoin() on each of them to provide any missing base components.

The GET() function returns a tuple for each URL found in the text of the page, indicating that it wants the scraping engine to call itself on the URL it found, unless the engine knows it has already done so. The engine only needs to keep track of which combinations of functions and URLs it has already called, so that a URL that occurs on the website multiple times is only accessed once. It stores a collection of URLs it's seen before and another set of URLs it hasn't seen yet, repeating until the latter set is empty.

This scraper may be used to scrape a large public web site such as httpbin.

```
$ python rscrape1.py http://httpbin.org/
```

Listing 11-12 can alternatively utilise the library to parse the HTML if you can get it installed.

```
$ python rscrape1.py http://127.0.0.1:8000/
```

```
GET http://127.0.0.1:8000/
```

```
GET http://127.0.0.1:8000/page1.html
```

```
GET http://127.0.0.1:8000/page2.html
```

If the scraper is to look further, it will require two elements.

To begin, open the HTML in a real browser so that the JavaScript can run and the remainder of the page can be loaded.

Second, in addition to GET(), you'll need a second operation that takes a big breath and presses the Search button to see what's behind it.

This is the type of operation that should never, ever be included in an automated scraper designed to pull generic content from a public web site, because, as you've already learned, form submission is specifically designed for user actions, especially when accompanied by a POST operation. (In this case, the form performs a GET, making it a little safer.) In this situation, though, you have examined this small website and determined that clicking the button is safe.

Because the engine was not firmly connected to any particular idea of what functions it should call, Listing 11-14 can simply reuse the engine from the previous scraper. Any functions that are provided to it will be referred to as work.

Listing 11-14. Selenium is used to scrape a website in a recursive manner.

```
#!/usr/bin/env python3
```

```
# Programming in Python: The Basics
```

```
# Recursive scraper built using the Selenium Webdriver.
```

```
from urllib.parse import urljoin
```

```
from rscrape1 import main
```

```
from selenium import webdriver
```

```
class WebdriverVisitor:
        def __init__(self):
                self.browser = webdriver.Firefox()
        def GET(self, url):
                self.browser.get(url)
                yield from self.parse()
                if self.browser.find_elements_by_xpath('.//form'):
```

```
            yield self.submit_form, url

    def parse(self):

    # (Could also parse page.source with lxml yourself, as in
    scraper1.py)

    url = self.browser.current_url

    links = self.browser.find_elements_by_xpath('.//a[@href]')

    for link in links:

            yield self.GET, urljoin(url, link.get_attribute('href'))

 def submit_form(self, url):

    self.browser.get(url)

    self.browser.find_element_by_xpath('.//form').submit()

    yield from self.parse()

if __name__ == '__main__':

    main(WebdriverVisitor().GET)
```

You shouldn't use the Firefox() function every time you need to fetch a URL because Selenium instances are expensive to construct (they have to start up a copy of Firefox, after all). Instead of a simple function, the GET() procedure is written as a method here so that the browser property can survive from one GET() call to the next and be available when it's time to run submit form ().

This listing deviates significantly from the previous one in the submit form() method. When the GET() method encounters the search form on the page, it returns an extra tuple to the engine. It will return a tuple for every link it finds on a page, as well as a tuple that will load the page and click the huge Search button. This is what allows this scraper to dig deeper into this site than the one before it.

```
$ python rscrape2.py http://127.0.0.1:8000/

GET http://127.0.0.1:8000/

GET http://127.0.0.1:8000/page1.html

GET http://127.0.0.1:8000/page2.html

submit_form http://127.0.0.1:8000/

GET http://127.0.0.1:8000/page5.html
```

```
GET http://127.0.0.1:8000/page6.html

GET http://127.0.0.1:8000/page4.html

GET http://127.0.0.1:8000/page3.html
```

Despite the fact that some links are loaded dynamically via JavaScript and others can only be visited via a form post, the scraper is able to find every single page on the site. You should be able to automate your interactions with any website using Python thanks to strong approaches like these.

Conclusion

HTTP was created to offer the World Wide Web: a collection of documents linked together by hyperlinks that each name the URL of a different page, or piece of a page, that may be accessed by merely clicking the hyperlink's text. The Python Standard Library includes functions for reading and constructing URLs, as well as converting partial "relative URLs" into absolute URLs by filling in any missing components with data from the page's base URL.

In most web applications, a persistent data store, such as a database, is linked to code that answers to incoming HTTP requests and generates HTML pages in response. When you try to insert untrusted information from the Web, it's critical to let the database handle its own quoting, and both the DB-API 2.0 and any ORM you could use in Python will take care to do so correctly.

Simple to full stack web frameworks are available. You can choose your own template language and ORM (or other persistence layer) with a basic framework. Instead, a full-stack framework will provide its own implementations of these utilities. In either scenario, there will be a way to connect URLs to your own code that supports both static URLs and URLs with variable path components, such as / person/123/. There will also be quick ways to render and return templates, as well as return redirects or HTTP errors.

The great threat that every site author faces is that the numerous ways in which components interact in a complex system like the Web might allow users to sabotage your own or each other's aims. At the interface between the outside world and your own code, keep in mind the risk of cross-site scripting attacks, cross-site request forgery, and attacks on your users' privacy. Before you build any code that accepts data via a URL route, a URL query string, or a POST or file upload, you should be aware of these risks. The choice between a full-stack solution like Django, which encourages you to stay within its tool set but tends to choose good defaults for you (such as having CSRF protection turned on automatically in your forms), and a solution like Flash or Bottle, which feels sleeker and lighter and lets you assemble your own solution but requires you to know all of the pieces up front, is often the trade-off between frameworks. You will go without CSRF protection if you develop an app in Flask without realising you need it.

Tornado is notable for its async architecture, which allows several clients to be served from a single operating-system-level control thread. Approaches like Tornado might be expected to develop toward a common set of idioms, similar to those provided by WSGI for threaded web frameworks today, with the introduction of asyncio in Python 3.

Turning around and scraping a web page necessitates a deep understanding of how web sites work in order to script what would typically be user behaviours, such as logging on or filling out and submitting a form. In Python, there are several techniques for both requesting and processing pages. At present time, Requests or Selenium for fetching and BeautifulSoup or lxml for parsing are the most popular options. This book wraps off its examination of HTTP and the World Wide Web with a look at web application writing and scraping. The subject of e-mail messages and how they are formatted is the focus of the next chapter, which takes you on a tour of various lesser-known protocols supported by the Python Standard Library.

CHAPTER 12

E-mail Construction And Parsing

This is the first of four chapters on the crucial subject of electronic mail. The topic of network communication is not covered in this chapter. Rather, it sets the tone for the following three:

- This chapter explains how e-mail messages are constructed, with a focus on proper multimedia inclusion and internationalisation. The payload format for the protocols described in the following three chapters is established by this.

- In Chapter 13, you'll learn about the Simple Mail Transport Protocol (SMTP), which is used to transport e-mail messages from the machine where they're written to the server where they'll be read by a specific recipient.

- Chapter 14 discusses the outdated, inefficient Post Office Protocol (POP), which allows someone who is ready to check their e-mail to download and view fresh messages sitting in their in box on their e-mail server.

- In Chapter 15, you'll learn about the Internet Message Access Protocol (IMAP), which is a more advanced version of the SMTP protocol. A current solution for accessing e-mail that is hosted on your e-mail server locally. IMAP not only allows you to fetch and view messages, but it also allows you to mark them as read. Then save them to various directories on the server.

As you can see, the four chapters are arranged in a way that represents an e-natural ma's lifecycle. An e-mail, for starters, is made up of varied text, multimedia, and metadata, such as the sender and recipient. Then SMTP transports it from the source to the target server. Finally, the recipient's e-mail client—most often Mozilla Thunderbird or Microsoft Outlook—uses a protocol like POP or IMAP to download a copy of the message to their desktop, laptop, or tablet for viewing. However, be aware that this last step is becoming less common: many people nowadays read their e-mail through webmail services, which allow them to log on with a web browser and view their e-mails rendered as HTML without ever leaving the e-mail server.

Structure:

- Format of an Email Message
- Putting Together an E-Mail Message
- HTML and Multimedia Enhancement
- Content Creation
- E-mail Message Parsing
- MIME Parts on the Move
- Encodings for Headers
- Dates Parsing
- Conclusion

Objectives:

Hotmail was formerly quite popular, but Gmail is now the largest service of its kind. Remember that regardless of how an e-mail is formed and represented later—whether you use SMTP, POP, or IMAP—the rules for how an e-mail is formatted and represented are the same. This chapter is all about those rules.

Format of an Email Message

The famous RFC 822 of 1982 served as the definition of e-mail for nearly 20 years, until it was finally out of date. RFC 2822 supplied this upgrade in 2001, however it was replaced in 2008 by the publication of RFC 5322. When writing particularly important or high-profile code for dealing with e-mail messages, you'll want to refer to these guidelines. Only a few facts concerning e-mail formatting require urgent consideration for the purposes of this article.

- **Plain ASCII text** (character codes 1 through 127) is used to represent e-mail.

- The **carriage-return-plus-linefeed (CRLF)** two-character sequence, which is the same pair of codes used to advance to the next line on an old teletype machine and is still the standard line-ending sequence in Internet protocols today, is the end-of-line marker.

- Headers, a blank line, and then the body make up an e-mail.

- Each header is formatted with a case-insensitive name, a colon, and a value, which can span multiple lines if the header's second and following lines are indented with whitespace.

- Because plain text does not support Unicode characters or binary payloads, other standards, which I will discuss later in this chapter, provide encodings that allow richer data to be blended down to simple ASCII text for transmission and storage.

Listing 12-1 contains a genuine e-mail message that came in my inbox.

Listing 12-1. After the delivery is complete, a real-world e-mail message is sent.

```
X-From-Line: rms@gnu.org Fri Dec 3 04:00:59 1999
Return-Path: <rms@gnu.org>
Delivered-To: john@yahoo.com
Received: from Esther.edu (pele.santafe.edu [192.12.12.119])
 by europa.gtri.gatech.edu (Postfix) with ESMTP id 6C4774809
 for <john@yahoo.com>; Fri, 8 nov 2019 04:00:58 -0500 (EST)
Received: from Esther.edu (Esther [192.12.12.49])
 byEsther.edu (8.9.1/8.9.1) with ESMTP id CAA27250
 for <john@yahoo.com>; Fri, 8 nov 2019 02:00:57 -0700 (MST)
Received: (from rms@localhost)
 by Esther.edu (8.9.1b+Sun/8.9.1) id CAA29939;
 Fri, 8 nov 2019 02:00:56 -0700 (MST)
Date: Fri, 8 nov 2019 02:00:56 -0700 (MST)
Message-Id: <201911080900.CAA29939@Esther.edu>
X-Authentication-Warning: Esther.edu: rms set sender to rms@gnu.org
using -f
From: stanley david <rms@gnu.org>
To: john@yahoo.com
In-reply-to: <m3k8my7x1k.fsf@europa.gtri.gatech.edu> (message from
John
```

```
 chris rodrigues on 07 nov 2019 00:04:55 -0500)
Subject: Re: Please proofread this license
Reply-To: rms@gnu.org
References: <201911070547.WAA21685@aztec.santafe.edu> <m3k8my7x1k.
fsf@europa.gtri.gatech.edu>
Xref: 38-74.clients.speedfactory.net scrapbook:11
Lines: 1
Thanks.
```

Despite the fact that only one line of text body was transmitted with this message, you can see that it acquired quite a bit of additional data during its Internet transfer.

Although all of the headers from the From line down were likely present when the e-mail was written, many of the headers above it were most likely added at various points along its transmission history. Each client and server that processes an e-mail message retains the right to add extra headers. This implies that as an e-mail message travels through the network, it accumulates a personal history, which can usually be read by starting with the last headers and moving upward until you reach the first. In this example, the e-mail appears to have originated on a machine called aztec in Santa Fe, where the author was connected directly across the local host internal interface. The message was subsequently forwarded to pele by the aztec machine, which most likely handled e-mail transmission for a department or the entire campus via SMTP. Finally, pele established an SMTP connection to my Georgia Tech europa machine, which saved the message to disc so that I could access it later.

At this point, I'll take a moment to present a few specific e-mail headers; a complete list can be found in the standards.

- From the e-mail message's author's name. The headers that follow are similar to the ones that come before them. Inside angle brackets, it accepts both the person's real name and their e-mail address.

- If the author named in the From header is not the intended recipient, reply-to specifies where replies should be sent.

- A list of one or more principal recipients is called a to-do list.

- Cc is a list of one or more recipients who should receive "copy copies" of the email but aren't explicitly addressed by it.

- Bcc is a list of people who should receive hidden carbon copies of an e-mail without the rest of the recipients knowing. As a result, careful e-mail clients remove Bcc before actually sending an e-mail.

- The message author's subject is a human-readable summary of the message's contents.

- The date indicates whether or not the communication was sent or received. If a date is included in the sender's e-mail client, the receiving e-mail server and reader will not overwrite it. If the sender does not mention a date, it may be added after the e-mail is received for completeness.

- Message-Id is a one-of-a-kind string that identifies the e-mail.

- The Message-Ids of the preceding messages to which this message is a reply are listed in the In-Reply-To field. If you're requested to create a threaded display that displays reply messages beneath the e-mails to which they're replies, these can come in handy.

- Each time the e-mail arrives at another "hop" on its route across the Internet via SMTP, it is added to the Received list. E-mail server managers frequently examine these tree rings to discover why a message was sent correctly or incorrectly.

In a basic example like this, the plain-text limitation on e-mail has ramifications for both the headers and the body: both are limited to being ASCII. I'll describe both the standards that regulate how a header can include international characters and the standards that dictate how the e-mail body can include international or binary data in the parts that follow.

Putting Together an E-Mail Message

The EmailMessage class, which will be used in every programme listing in this chapter, is Python's primary interface for creating e-mail messages. It's the result of R. David Murray, the Python email module specialist, who I'd like to thank for his help and advise when I was putting together the scripts in this chapter. Listing 12-2 shows the most basic example.

Listing 12-2. Making a Basic Text E-Mail Message

```python
#!/usr/bin/env python3
# Programming in Python: The Basics
import email.message, email.policy, email.utils, sys
text = """Hello,
This is a basic message from Chapter 12.
  - Anonymous"""
def main():
```

```
        message = email.message.EmailMessage(email.policy.SMTP)
        message['To'] = 'recipient@example.com'
        message['From'] = 'Test Sender <sender@example.com>'
        message['Subject'] = 'Test Message, Chapter 12'
        message['Date'] = email.utils.formatdate(localtime=True)
        message['Message-ID'] = email.utils.make_msgid()
        message.set_content(text)
        sys.stdout.buffer.write(message.as_bytes())
if __name__ == '__main__':
  main()
```

This chapter's code is only for Python 3.4 and later, which is the version of Python that added the EmailMessage class to the old e-mail module. Study the older scripts at https://bpbonline/Programming in Python: The Basics/chapter12 if you need to target older versions of Python 3 and can't upgrade.

You can make e-mail messages even simpler by eliminating the headers listed above, but this is the very minimum that you should consider on the modern Internet.

The EmailMessage API allows your code to closely match the text of your e-mail message. Although you are allowed to set headers and supply content in any sequence that makes the most sense for your code, setting the headers first and then the body last creates a beautiful symmetry in the way the message appears on the wire and in an e-mail client.

It's worth noting that I've included two headers here that you should always include, but whose values will not be automatically set for you. I'm using the formatdate() method, which is already included in Python's standard set of e-mail utilities, to provide the Date in the particular format required by e-mail standards. The Message-Id is likewise carefully built from random information in order to make it (ideally) distinct from every other e-mail messages that have ever been written or will ever be written.

The completed script just prints the e-mail on its standard output, making it simple to experiment with and seeing the results of any changes you make right away.

To: recipient@example.com

From: Test Sender <sender@example.com>

Subject: Test Message, Chapter 12

```
Date: Fri, 28 Feb 2019 16:54:17 -0400

Message-ID: <20140328459417.5927.96806@desktop>

Content-Type: text/plain; charset="utf-8"

Content-Transfer-Encoding: 7bit

MIME-Version: 1.0

Hello,

This is a basic message from Chapter 12.
```

You'd notice that several of these headers are missing if you built an email message with the old Message class instead of EmailMessage. Rather than providing a transfer encoding, MIME version, or content type, old-fashioned e-mail messages, such as the one in Listing 12-1, simply omit these headers and trust that e-mail clients will use the customary defaults. However, in order to provide the best level of interoperability with newer tools, the modern EmailMessage function Object() { [native code] } is more careful to declare specific values.

As previously indicated, header names are case insensitive. As a result, conforming e-mail clients will not distinguish between the meaning of Message-Id in Listing 12-1 and the generated e-Message-ID mail's (with a capital D instead). If you don't want the formatdate() function to use the current date and time, you may give it a specified Python datetime to show, and you can even have it use Greenwich Mean Time (GMT) instead of the local time zone. Details can be found in Python's documentation.

Be aware that the unique Message-ID is built from several pieces of information that you might not want to reveal if you're in a high-security situation: the exact time and date and millisecond of your call to make msgid(), the process ID of this Python script invocation, and even your current hostname if you don't provide an alternative with the optional domain= keyword. If you don't want to reveal any of this information, choose a different unique-id solution (possibly one based on an industrial-strength globally unique identifier [UUID] technique).

Finally, even though the text isn't technically email-compatible (the triple-quoted string constant lacks a terminal line ending to conserve vertical space in the script), the combination of set content() and as bytes() guaranteed that the e-mail message was appropriately terminated with a newline.

HTML and Multimedia Enhancement

In the early days of e-mail, many ad-hoc systems were devised to transport binary data across the 7-bit ASCII world, but it was the MIME standard that established an interoperable and expandable mechanism for non-ASCII payloads.

When an e-mail comes on a line with two hyphens in front of it, MIME permits the Content-Type e-mail header to specify a boundary string that breaks the e-mail into smaller message sections. Each portion can have its own headers, as well as content types and encodings. If a component specifies its own boundary string, it can be subdivided into even more subparts, resulting in a hierarchy. The Python email module has low-level support for constructing MIME messages from whichever parts and subparts you choose. Simply create a number of email.messages. Attach() MIMEPart objects to their parent part or message, giving each one headers and a body using the same interface as an EmailMessage:

```
my message.attach(part1)
```

```
my message.attach(part2)
```

. . .

Manual assembly should only be used if you are attempting to replicate a specific message structure that is required by your application or project specifications. In most cases, you may just create an EmailMessage (as shown in Listing 12-2) and call the four methods listed below in order to produce your result:

- To install the primary message body, set content() should be called first.

- add related() can then be called a number of times to augment the primary content with other resources to render. When your main content is HTML and you need photos, CSS style sheets, and JavaScript files to render appropriately on an e-mail client that supports rich content, you'll most likely utilise this. Each connected resource should have a Content-Id (cid) that can be used in hyperlinks in the main HTML content.

- add alternative() can then be called a number of times to provide alternative renderings of your email message. You might give a plain-text alternate rendering for less capable e-mail clients if the body includes HTML, for example.

- add attachment() can be called a number of times to provide any attachments that should be sent with the message, such as PDF documents, photos, or spreadsheets. Each attachment has a default file name that is used if the recipient requests that their e-mail client save the attachment.

Looking back, you can see that Listing 12-2 followed the technique step by step— it first used set content(), then chose to call each of the other three methods zero times. The outcome was the most basic e-mail structure available, with a single body and no subparts. But what happens when things get more complicated with e-mail? Listing 12-3 is intended to provide the answer.

Listing 12-3. Using HTML, an Inline Image, and Attachments to Create a MIME-Powered E-Mail

```python
#!/usr/bin/env python3
# Programming in Python: The Basics
import argparse, email.message, email.policy, email.utils, mimetypes,
sys
plain = """Hello,

This is a MIME message from Chapter 12.

- Anonymous"""
html = """ <p>Hello</p>,

<p>This is a test message from Chapter 12.</p>

<p>- <i>Anonymous</i></p> """
img = """ <p>This is the smallest possible blue GIF:</p>
"""

def main(args):
    message = email.message.EmailMessage(email.policy.SMTP)
    message['To'] = 'Test Recipient '
    message['From'] = 'Test Sender '
    message['Subject'] = ' Programming in Python: The Basics'
    message['Date'] = email.utils.formatdate(localtime=True)
    message['Message-ID'] = email.utils.make_msgid()
    if not args.i:
        message.set_content(html, subtype='html')
        message.add_alternative(plain)
    else:
        cid = email.utils.make_msgid() # RFC 2392: must be
        globally unique!
        message.set_content(html + img.format(cid.strip('<>')),
        subtype='html')
```

```
            message.add_related(blue_dot, 'image', 'gif', cid=cid,
                    filename='blue-dot.gif')
            message.add_alternative(plain)
    for filename in args.filename:
            mime_type, encoding = mimetypes.guess_type(filename)
            if encoding or (mime_type is None):
            mime_type = 'application/octet-stream'
        main, sub = mime_type.split('/')
        if main == 'text':
        with open(filename, encoding='utf-8') as f:
            text = f.read()
    message.add_attachment(text, sub, filename=filename)
 else:
        with open(filename, 'rb') as f:
            data = f.read()
        message.add_attachment(data, main, sub, filename=filename)
        sys.stdout.buffer.write(message.as_bytes())
if __name__ == '__main__':
 parser = argparse.ArgumentParser(description='Build, print a MIME email')
 parser.add_argument('-i', action='store_true', help='Include GIF image')
 parser.add_argument('filename', nargs='*', help='Attachment filename')
 main(parser.parse_args())
```

The script in Listing 12-3 can be called in four distinct ways. They are, in sequence of increasing complexity:

- build mime email.py (python3)
- attachment.txt attachment.gz python3 build mime email.py
- build mime email.py -i python3
- python3 attachment.txt attachment.gz build mime email.py -i

To save space, I'll only show the output of the first and last of these four command lines here; however, if you want to see how the MIME standard supports gradually increasing levels of complexity depending on the caller's needs, you should download build mime email.py and try out the others for yourself. Despite the fact that the book's source repository includes two sample files—attachment.txt (plain text) and attachment.gz (binary)—feel free to list any attachments on the command line. This will allow you to observe how the Python email module encodes various binary payloads.

Without any settings or attachments, build mime email.py creates the simplest MIME structure for giving two alternate versions of an e-mail: HTML and plain text. The results are displayed below.

```
To: Test Recipient <recipient@example.com>

From: Test Sender <sender@example.com>

Subject: Programming in Python: The Basics

Date: Tue, 25 feb 2019 17:14:01 -0400

Message-ID: <20140328459417.5927.96806@desktop>

MIME-Version: 1.0

Content-Type:                                    multipart/alternative;
boundary="===============1625704680=="

--===============1625704680==

Content-Type: text/html; charset="utf-8"

Content-Transfer-Encoding: 7bit

<p>Hello,</p>

<p>This is a <b>test message</b> from Chapter 12.</p>

<p>- <i>Anonymous</i></p>

--===============1625704680==

Content-Type: text/plain; charset="utf-8"

Content-Transfer-Encoding: 7bit

MIME-Version: 1.0

Hello,

This is a MIME message from Chapter 12.

- Anonymous

--===============1625704680==--
```

The above e-mail follows the old standard format at its most basic level: headers, blank line, and body. The body, on the other hand, is now more interesting. The headers specify a boundary that splits the body into several smaller parts in order to carry two payloads, plain text and HTML. Each section follows the standard format of headers, blank lines, and body. The contents of a portion are limited to one (quite apparent) restriction: it cannot contain a copy of either its own boundary line or the boundary line of any of the enclosing messages. The multipart/alternative content type is one of a group of multipart/* content types that all adhere to the same set of criteria for establishing a boundary line and using it to delimit the MIME subparts beneath it. Its function is to store many versions of a message, each of which can be displayed to the user and therefore communicate the message's entire meaning. The user can read the HTML or plain text in this situation, but the e-mail will be substantially the same in either case. If they are able to show HTML, most clients will choose it. Despite the fact that most e-mail applications would conceal the fact that an option was presented, Some include a button or drop-down menu that allows the user to view an alternate version if desired. Although the MIME-Version header is only given at the top level of the message, the email module has taken care of this without requiring the sender to be aware of this feature of the standard.

The following are the rules for multipart sections:

- If you call add related() at least once, the body you defined with set content() is grouped with all related content into a single multipart/related section.

- A multipart/alternative container is formed to retain the original body together with the alternative part(s) you add if you run add alternative() at least once.

- Finally, if you call add attachment() at least once, a multipart/mixed outer container is created to hold the content alongside all of the attachments you add.

Examining the output from the most complicated of the four command lines given above, you can see all of these mechanisms working together. It asks for an inline-related image to be included with the HTML, as well as attachments to be added after the body.

```
To: Test Recipient
From: Test Sender
Subject: Programming in Python: The Basics
Date: Tue, 25 Feb 2019 17:14:01 -0400
Message-ID: <20140328459417.5927.96806@desktop>
MIME-Version: 1.0
Content-Type:multipart/mixed;boundary="===============1086940546=="
--===============1086940546==
Content-Type:                                  multipart/alternative;
boundary="===============0904170609=="
--===============0904170609==
```

Content-Type: multipart/related;
boundary="===============1914784657=="

--===============1914784657==
Content-Type: text/html; charset="utf-8"
Content-Transfer-Encoding: 7bit
Hello,
This is a test message from Chapter 12.
- Anonymous
This is the smallest possible blue GIF:
--===============1911784657==
Content-Type: image/gif
Content-Transfer-Encoding: base64
Content-Disposition: attachment; filename="blue-dot.gif"
Content-ID: <20140325232008.15748.99346@guinness>
MIME-Version: 1.0
R0lGODlhAQABAJAAAAAA/AAACAAAAAQABAAACAQBADs=
--===============1911784657==--
--===============0903270609==
Content-Type: text/plain; charset="utf-8"
Content-Transfer-Encoding: 7bit
MIME-Version: 1.0
Hello,
This is a MIME message from Chapter 12.
- Anonymous
--===============0903170609==--
--===============0086940546==
Content-Type: text/plain; charset="utf-8"
Content-Transfer-Encoding: 7bit
Content-Disposition: attachment; filename="attachment.txt"
MIME-Version: 1.0
This is a test
--===============0086940546==

```
Content-Type: application/octet-stream
Content-Transfer-Encoding: base64
Content-Disposition: attachment; filename="attachment.gz"
MIME-Version: 1.0
H4sIAP3o2D8AwvJCxWAKJhZLU4hIuAIPoPAAA
--================0086940546==--
```

This email is concentric, with three tiers of multipart material nested within each other! As you can see, all of the details have been taken care of for us. Each level has its own non-interfering randomly generated boundary. with either of the other levels' boundaries In each case, the appropriate type of multipart container was picked because of the type of content that it contains. Finally, the appropriate encodings have been defined. Plain text has been allowed to travel literally within the body of the e-mail, whereas binary data-like graphics that are not 7-bit safe have been encoded with Base64. It's worth noting that the e-mail object was specifically asked to render itself as bytes in both of these generating scripts, rather than asking for text that would have to be encoded before being saved or communicated.

Content Creation

The calling convention is the same for all four methods used to add material in Listing 12-3. Consult the Python manual to learn about all of the possible combinations that are supported in the Python 3 version you're using. For the procedures set content(), add related(), add alternative(), and add attachment(), here are some typical combinations:

- **type('string data of type str') method('string data of type str') method('string data of type str**

  method('string data of type str', subtype='html') method('string data of type str', subtype='html') method('string data of type These result in segments that have a textual flavour. Unless you specify a specific subtype, the content type will be text/plain—the second example call, for example, returns text/html as the content type.

- **method(b'raw binary payload of type bytes', type='image', subtype='jpeg'), type='image', subtype='jpeg')**

  If you provide Python raw binary data, it won't try to guess what type it should be. You must specify both the MIME type and subtype, which will be merged in the output with a slash. Note that Listing 12-3 attempts to estimate an acceptable type for each attachment file you supply on the command line using a mechanism outside the email module, the mimetypes module.

- **`cte='quoted-printable' method(..., cte='quoted-printable')`**

  All of these methods appear to use one of two content transfer encodings by default. Safe 7-bit data is included in e-mails verbatim using bare and legible ASCII encoding, whereas anything more harmful is encoded using Base64. If you ever find yourself personally scrutinising incoming or outgoing e-mails, the latter choice may be unsuitable—it means, for example, that text parts containing a single Unicode character will be converted to entirely incomprehensible Base64 garbage. The cte keyword can be used to override the encoding setting. The quoted-printable encoding, in particular, may appeal to you: ASCII letters are kept verbatim in the encoded e-mail, and escape sequences are employed for any bytes with their eighth bit set.

- **`cid='Content ID>', add related(..., cid='Content ID>')`**

  In most cases, you'll want to give each linked part its own specific content ID so that your HTML can link to it. Angle brackets should always wrap the content ID in your call, but they should be eliminated when forming the cid: link in your HTML. It's worth noting that content IDs are designed to be globally unique—every content ID you use in a document is supposed to be unique among all content IDs ever used in an e-mail in history! Because the email module does not provide a dedicated capability for creating unique content IDs, Listing 12-3 uses make msgid().

- **`filename='data.csv', add attachment(...)`**

  Most e-mail clients (as well as their users) will demand at least a recommended file name when adding attachments, though the e-mail recipient can overrule this default by selecting "Save" if they like.

There are more intricate versions of these calls for unusual scenarios that you can learn about in the official Python documentation, but these should get you through the most frequent MIME e-mail problems.

E-mail Message Parsing

Once you've processed an email message using one of the functions in the email module, you can read it in one of two ways. The most straightforward approach is to presume that the message contains a body and attachments due to the usual and typical use of MIME, and rely on the convenience methods included into EmailMessage to assist you locate them.

The more difficult option is to manually go through all of the sections and subparts of the message and decide what they mean and how they should be kept or presented. The straightforward approach is shown in Listing 12-4. It's necessary to take input as bytes and then provide those bytes to the email module without trying to decode them yourself, much like when saving e-mail messages.

Listing 12-4. requesting the body and attachments of an email message

```python
#!/usr/bin/env python3
# Programming in Python: The Basics
import argparse, email.policy, sys
def main(binary_file):
        policy = email.policy.SMTP
        message = email.message_from_binary_file(binary_file,
        policy=policy)
        for header in ['From', 'To', 'Date', 'Subject']:
            print(header + ':', message.get(header,    '(none)'))
        print()
 try:
        body = message.get_body(preferencelist=('plain', 'html'))
 except KeyError:
        print('<This message lacks a printable text or HTML body>')
 else:
        print(body.get_content())
 for part in message.walk():
        cd = part['Content-Disposition']
        is_attachment = cd and cd.split(';')[0].lower() == 'attachment'
        if not is_attachment:
            continue
        content = part.get_content()
        print('* {} attachment named {!r}: {} object of length {}'.
        format(
            part.get_content_type(), part.get_filename(),
            type(content).__name__, len(content)))
if __name__ == '__main__':
```

```
parser = argparse.ArgumentParser(description='Parse and print
an email')
parser.add_argument('filename',      nargs='?',      help='File
containing an email')
args = parser.parse_args()
if args.filename is None:
        main(sys.stdin.buffer)
else:
        with open(args.filename, 'rb') as f:
        main(f)
```

Once the command-line inputs have been processed and the message has been read and converted to an EmailMessage, the script automatically divides into two parts. You can either open the message's file in binary mode 'rb' or utilise the binary buffer attribute of Python's standard input object, which returns raw bytes, to provide the email module access to the message's actual binary representation on disc.

The call to the get body() method is the first and most important step, as it instructs Python to dig further and deeper into the MIME structure of the message for the component that is best suited to serve as the body. The formats that you prefer should come first in the preferencelist, followed by the formats that you are less likely to wish to see. HTML content is preferred over a plain-text version of the body in this case, but either will suffice. If an appropriate body cannot be identified, a KeyError is thrown.

It's worth noting that the default preferencelist, which is used if you don't supply one, contains three elements because it prioritises multipart/related over HTML and plain text. This option is appropriate if you're creating a sophisticated e-mail client—for example, a webmail service or an application with a built-in WebKit pane—that can not only correctly format HTML but also display inline pictures and support style sheets. The object you'll get back is the related-content MIME part itself, which you'll have to search through to discover both the HTML and all of the multimedia it requires. I've overlooked this option because the small script here is merely printing the generated body to the standard output.

After displaying the greatest body available, it's time to look for any attachments the user might want to see or download. Note that the example script requests all of the information required by MIME for an attachment, including the content type, file name, and data itself. Instead of simply printing the length and type on the screen, you would presumably open a file for writing and saving this data in a real programme.

This display script is forced to make its own conclusion about which message sections are attachments and which are not due to a problem in Python 3.4. You will be able to replace this manual iteration of the tree and test every single part's content disposition with a simple call to your message's iter attachments() method in a future version of Python.

The following script will work on any MIME message generated by the previous scripts, no matter how complex they are. It merely displays the "interesting" headers and content when given the simplest message.

```
$ python3 build_basic_email.py > email.txt

$ python3 display_email.py email.txt

From: Test Sender <sender@example.com>

To: recipient@example.com

Date: Tue, 25 Feb 2019 17:14:01 -0400

Subject: Test Message, Chapter 12

Hello,

This is a basic message from Chapter 12.

  - Anonymous
```

Even the most complex message, however, is not too much for it. Before resurfacing with the HTML version of the e-mail body, the get body() logic successfully goes into the mixed multipart outer layer, into the alternative multipart middle, and lastly down into the related multipart innards of the message. In addition, each of the attachments that were provided is examined.

```
$ python3 build_mime_email.py -i attachment.txt attachment.gz >
email.txt
$ python3 display_email.py email.txt
From: Test Sender <sender@example.com>
To: Test Recipient <recipient@example.com>
Date: Tue, 25 Feb 2019 17:14:01 -0400
Subject:
Hello,
This is a MIME message from Chapter 12.
- Anonymous
```

* `image/gif` attachment named 'black-dot.gif': bytes object of length 34

* `text/plain` attachment named 'attachment.txt': str object of length 16

* `application/octet-stream` attachment named 'attachment.gz': bytes object of length 32

MIME Parts on the Move

If the logic in Listing 12-4 ever proves insufficient for your application—for example, if it can't find the body text of an e-mail that your project needs to parse, or if certain poorly specified attachments are being skipped to which your customers require access—you'll have to visit every part of an e-mail message yourself and implement your own algorithm for which parts to display, which to save as attachments, and which to truncate—you'll have to fall back to

When dismantling a MIME e-mail, there are three key rules to remember.

- When analysing a section, the first thing you should do is call the is multipart() method to see if the MIME part you're looking at is a container for other MIME subparts. You can also use get content type() to get the fully qualified type with a slash between the main type and subtype, or get content maintype() or get content subtype() if you only want one half.

- When dealing with a multipart, utilise the iter parts() method to loop through or fetch the parts immediately beneath it, allowing you to determine which subparts are multiparts and which merely carry content.

- When inspecting a normal part, search for the term attachment preceding any semicolon in the header's value to see if it's intended as an attachment (look for the word attachment preceding any semicolon in the header's value).

- Depending on whether the main content type is text or not, the get content() method decodes and returns the data itself from inside a MIME part as a text str or a binary bytes object.

To access every portion of a multipart message, the code in Listing 12-5 use a recursive generator. The generator works similarly to the built-in walk() method, with the exception that it keeps track of the index of each component in case it has to be fetched later.

Listing 12-5. Manually visiting each part of a multipart method

```
#!/usr/bin/env python3
# Programming in Python: The Basics
```

```python
import argparse, email.policy, sys
def walk(part, prefix=''):
        yield prefix, part
        for i, subpart in enumerate(part.iter_parts()):
                yield from walk(subpart, prefix + '.{}'.format(i))
def main(binary_file):
        policy = email.policy.SMTP
        message = email.message_from_binary_file(binary_file,
        policy=policy)
   for prefix, part in walk(message):
                line = '{} type={}'.format(prefix, part.get_content_type())
                if not part.is_multipart():
                        content = part.get_content()
                        line += ' {} len={}'.format(type(content).__
                        name__, len(content))
                        cd = part['Content-Disposition']
                        is_attachment = cd and cd.split(';')[0].lower()
                        == 'attachment'
                if is_attachment:
                        line += ' attachment'
                filename = part.get_filename()
                if filename is not None:
                        line += ' filename={!r}'.format(filename)
                print(line)
if __name__ == '__main__':
        parser = argparse.ArgumentParser(description='Display MIME
        structure')
        parser.add_argument('filename',    nargs='?',    help='File
        containing an email')
            args = parser.parse_args()
            if args.filename is None:
                    main(sys.stdin.buffer)
   else:
```

```
        with open(args.filename, 'rb') as f:
        main(f)
```

You can use this script to generate any of the e-mail messages that the previous scripts can. (Alternatively, you may send it a real-life e-mail.) The following are the results of running it against the most complex message that can be generated with the aforesaid scripts.

```
$ python3 build_mime_email.py -i attachment.txt attachment.gz >
email.txt
$ python3 display_structure.py email.txt
 type=multipart/mixed
.0 type=multipart/alternative
.0.0 type=multipart/related
.0.0.0 type=text/html str len=215
.0.0.1 type=image/gif bytes len=35 attachment filename='black-dot.
gif'
.0.1 type=text/plain str len=60
.1 type=text/plain str len=14 attachment filename='attachment.txt'
.2    type=application/octet-stream    bytes    len=32    attachment
filename='attachment.gz'
```

The part numbers that appear at the beginning of each line of output can be utilised in other code to dive right into the message and retrieve the specific part you're looking for by passing each integer index to the get payload() method. For instance, if you wanted to get the black dot GIF image from within this message, you'd use

part = message. get payload(0).get payload(0). get payload(1)

It's worth repeating that only multipart parts are permitted to contain additional MIME subparts. Every nonmultipart content type part is a leaf node in the tree above, carrying simple content with no further e-mail-relevant structure beneath it.

Encodings for Headers

Because of the email module, the parsing scripts above will correctly accept internationalised headers that encode special characters according to RFC 2047 rules. Listing 12-6 creates an e-mail that you may use to conduct tests. Because Python 3 source code is UTF-8 encoded by default, international characters can be included without the need for a -*- coding: utf-8 -*- declaration at the top, as with Python 2.

Listing 12-6. To test the parsing script, create an internationalised email.

```python
#!/usr/bin/env python3

# Programming in Python: The Basics

import email.message, email.policy, sys

text = """\
Hwær cwom mearg? Hwær cwom mago?
Hwær cwom maþþumgyfa?
Hwær cwom symbla gesetu?
Hwær sindon seledreamas?"""

def main():
        message = email.message.EmailMessage(email.policy.SMTP)
        message['To'] = 'Böðvarr <recipient@example.com>'
        message['From'] = 'Eardstapa <sender@example.com>'
        message['Subject'] = 'Four lines from The Wanderer'
        message['Date'] = email.utils.formatdate(localtime=True)
        message.set_content(text, cte='quoted-printable')
        sys.stdout.buffer.write(message.as_bytes())

if __name__ == '__main__':
        main()
```

Because of the peculiar letters in the To: header, the output e-mail employs a particular ASCII encoding of binary data. In addition, as previously mentioned, selecting a quoted-printable content encoding for the body avoids creating a block of Base64 data and instead represents most of the characters by their plain ASCII values, as seen in the results.

```
To: =?utf-8?b?QsO2w7B2YXJy?= <recipient@example.com>

From: Eardstapa <sender@example.com>

Subject: Four lines from The Wanderer

Date: Fri, 27 Feb 2019 22:11:48 -0400
```

Content-Type: text/plain; charset="utf-8"

Content-Transfer-Encoding: quoted-printable

MIME-Version: 1.0

Hw=C3=A6r cwom mearg? Hw=C3=A6r cwom mago?

Hw=C3=A6r cwom ma=C3=BE=C3=BEumgyfa?

Hw=C3=A6r cwom symbla gesetu?

Hw=C3=A6r sindon seledreamas?

Because the email module handles all of the decoding and processing, the display script correctly untangles everything.

$ python3 build_unicode_email.py > email.txt

$ python3 display_email.py email.txt

From: bpbonline <sender@example.com>

To: john <recipient@example.com>

Date: Tue, 26 Feb 2019 17:14:01 -0400

Subject: Four lines from The Wanderer

how are you? how are you?

how are you?

how are you?

how are you?

Read the Python documentation for the lower-level email.header module and, in particular, its Header class if you ever want to learn more about e-mail header encoding.

Dates Parsing

The formatdate() method in email.utils, which by default utilises the current date and time, was utilised in the scripts above to generate standards-compliant dates. They can, however, be given a low-level Unix timestamp. If you're doing higher-level date manipulation and you've created a datetime object, you can just use the format datetime() function to achieve the same thing.

When parsing an e-mail, you can use three more methods in email.utils to do the inverse action.

- Both parsedate() and parsedate tz() return time tuples of the type that Python provides at a low level through its time module, and which match the traditional C-language norms for date arithmetic and representation.

- Instead of returning a whole datetime object, the current parsedate to datetime() function returns a full datetime object, which is usually the call you'll want to make in most production code.

Note that many e-mail systems do not follow the appropriate standards when generating Date headers, and while these functions strive to be forgiving, there may be times when they are unable to provide a correct date value and instead return None. Before presuming that you have been given a date back, you should check for this value. Following are a few examples of calls.

```
>>> from email import utils
>>> utils.parsedate('Tue, 26 Feb 2019 17:14:01 -0400')
(2019, 2, 26, 17, 14, 1, 0, 1, -1)
>>> utils.parsedate_tz('Tue, 26 Feb 2019 17:14:01 -0400')
(2019, 2, 26, 17, 14, 1, 0, 1, -1, -14400)
>>> utils.parsedate_to_datetime('Tue, 26 Feb 2019 17:14:01 -0400')
datetime.datetime(2019, 2, 26, 17, 14, 1,
 tzinfo=datetime.timezone(datetime.timedelta(-1, 72000)))
```

If you're going to conduct any date arithmetic, I strongly advise you to look at the third-party pytz module, which has become a community standard for date manipulation.

Conclusion

Email.message is a strong tool. R. David Murray's EmailMessage class, which was introduced in Python 3.4, makes both the creation and consumption of MIME messages considerably easier than in previous versions of Python. The only warning, as always, is to pay great attention to the difference between bytes and strings. To ensure that every step is completed successfully, try to do all of your socket or file I/O in bytes and let the email module handle all of the encoding.

In most cases, an e-mail is created by creating an EmailMessage object and then defining headers and content. Headers are set by treating the message as a dictionary with case-insensitive string keys, and storing string values that will be appropriately encoded upon output if any of its characters are non-ASCII. Set content(), add related(), add alternative(), and add attachment() are a series of four methods that handle both text and bytes payloads correctly in all instances.

Any of the email module's parsing routines (message from binary file() is the way used in the listings in this chapter) with a policy parameter turning on all of the contemporary features of the EmailMessage class can be read back in and analysed as an EmailMessage object. Each resulting object will be either a multipart with more subparts inside it, or a single piece of material that Python will return as a string or bytes data. On both output and input, headers are automatically internationalised and decoded. Methods in email support the specific Date header's format. Use instances of the current Python datetime object in your code to read and write its value.

The usage of the SMTP protocol for e-mail transmission will be the focus of the next chapter.

CHAPTER 13

Simple Mail Transfer Protocol(SMTP)

The actual transportation of e-mail between systems is handled by SMTP, the Simple Mail Transport Protocol, as mentioned at the start of Chapter 12. RFC 821 was the first to define SMTP in 1982, and RFC 5321 is the most recent RFC to define it. In most cases, the protocol serves two purposes:

1. When a user types an e-mail message on a laptop or desktop computer, the e-mail client sends the message to a server via SMTP, which then forwards it to its intended recipient.

2. E-mail servers utilise SMTP to transmit messages, sending each message across the Internet from one server to the next until it reaches the server responsible for the recipient's domain (the part of the e-mail address after the @ sign).

The way SMTP is utilised for submission and delivery differs in various ways. However, before I go into detail about them.

Structure:
- Webmail Services vs. E-mail Clients
- Clients are on the rise
- The Transition to Webmail

- SMTP's Functions
- E-mail transmission
- The Envelope Recipient and the Headers
- Several Hops
- The SMTP Library is an introduction to the SMTP protocol
- Error Handling and Debugging Conversations
- Using EHLO to Gather Information
- Secure Sockets Layer (SSL) and Transport Layer Security (TLS)
- SMTP authentication
- SMTP Pointers
- Conclusion

Objectives:

In these chapter we'll learn about the difference between people who check their e-mail using a local e-mail client and those who utilise a webmail service.

Webmail Services vs. E-mail Clients

If I trace the history of how people have historically worked with Internet e-mail, the role of SMTP in message submission, when the user presses Send and expects a message to wing its way across the Internet, will probably be the least puzzling.

The most important point to grasp is that users have never been required to wait for an e-mail message to be delivered. Before an e-mail message is delivered to its intended recipient, this process can take a long time—and many dozen attempts—to complete. Delays could be caused by a variety of factors, including: A message may have to wait because other messages are also being transferred via a low-bandwidth link, the destination server may be unavailable for a few hours, or its network may be down due to a bug.

If the email is intended for a large organisation, such as a university, it may have to make many "hops" as it arrives at the main university server, then is routed to a smaller e-mail machine for one of the institution's colleges, and lastly to a departmental e-mail server. Thus, understanding what happens when the user hits Send entails understanding how the completed e-mail message is submitted to the first of potentially multiple e-mail queues where it can languish until the conditions are just right for transmission. (This will be covered in the section on e-mail delivery that follows.)

The Command Line Was the Beginning

The initial generation of e-mail users were given usernames and passwords by their employers or universities, allowing them command-line access to the massive mainframes that housed user data and general-purpose programmes. Each large machine had an e-mail daemon that maintained an outgoing queue, which was usually located on the same machine where users were busy inputting messages into small command-line e-mail programmes. Mail was followed by the fancier mailx, which was later overshadowed by the far prettier interfaces—with larger capabilities—of elm, pine, and finally mutt.

THE SMTP PROTOCOL

Purpose: deliver e-mail to a server

Standard: RFC 2821

Runs atop: TCP or TLS

Port number: 53

Libraries: smtplib

However, the network was not even engaged in the simple task of e-mail submission for all of these early users; after all, the e-mail client and server were on the same system! The actual method of bridging this little gap and executing e-mail submission was usually hidden behind a command-line client programme that came included with the server software and knew exactly how to communicate with it. Sendmail, the first widely used e-mail daemon, came with a programme called /usr/lib/ sendmail for sending e-mail.

Because sendmail was created to communicate with the first-generation client programmes for reading and writing e-mail, the e-mail daemons that have since gained prominence, such as qmail, postfix, and exim, are based on it. , for example, generally followed suit by providing their own sendmail binary (its official home is now /usr/sbin, thanks to recent file system standards) that, when invoked by the user's e-mail programme, follows that specific e-mail daemon's peculiar procedure for getting a message moved into the queue.

When an e-mail was received, it was usually saved in the file of the user to whom the message was directed. The command-line e-mail client could simply open this file and parse it to discover what messages were awaiting the user's attention. Because the focus of this book is on how e-mail uses the network, it does not address these mailbox forms. If you're intrigued, you may look at the Python Standard Library's mailbox package, which supports all of the odd and unusual methods that various e-mail programmes have read and written messages to disc throughout the years.

Clients are on the rise

The following generation of Internet users was frequently unfamiliar with the concept of a command line. Users were familiar with the Apple Macintosh's graphical interface—or, subsequently, the Microsoft Windows operating system—and anticipated to be able to do tasks by clicking an icon and executing a graphical programme. As a result, a variety of e-mail clients were created to bring this Internet service to the desktop.

Mozilla Thunderbird and Microsoft Outlook are only two of the most popular clients that are still used today.

The flaws in this strategy are clear. To begin with, reading incoming e-mail was changed from a straightforward process for your e-mail program—which could previously open and read a local file—to one that required a network connection. When you started your graphical e-mail software, it had to connect to a full-time server that had been receiving e-mail on your behalf while you were away and download the messages to your local machine.

Second, users are notorious for failing to back up their desktop and laptop file systems, leaving clients who downloaded and stored communications locally vulnerable to obliteration if the laptop or desktop hard drive crashed. . University and industrial servers, on the other hand, frequently had small armies of personnel entrusted with maintaining their data preserved, copied, and safe, despite their clumsy command lines.

Third, an e-mail server and its queue of outgoing messages are rarely acceptable locations for laptop and desktop computers. Users, after all, frequently turn off their computers when they are finished with them, disconnect from the Internet, or leave the Internet café, causing their wireless signal to be lost. Outgoing messages typically take more than a few minutes to complete their retries and final transmission, therefore completed e-mails must be submitted to a full-time server for queuing and delivery.

However, programmers are resourceful individuals who devised a number of solutions to these issues. First, new protocols were developed—first, the Post Office Protocol (POP), which I'll discuss in Chapter 14, and then the Internet Message Access Protocol (IMAP), which I'll discuss in Chapter 15—that allowed a user's e-mail client to authenticate with a password and download e-mail from a full-time server that had previously been storing it. Passwords were required to prevent unauthorised access to your Internet service provider's servers and reading of your e-mail! The first issue was thus resolved. But what about the second issue, persistence, which involves avoiding the loss of e-mail when hard drives on desktop and laptop computers fail? This sparked two new developments. People who used POP learnt to switch off the default mode, in which e-mail on the server is deleted once it is downloaded, and to leave copies of critical e-mails on the server, from which they might retrieve e-mail later if they had to restart their computer and start from scratch. Second, they began migrating to IMAP, assuming that their e-mail server supported this more modern protocol. They could not only leave incoming e-mail messages on the server for protection, but they could also organise them in folders right on the server using IMAP! Instead of needing to manage an e-mail storage space on their laptop or desktop, they could utilise their e-mail client programme as a simple window through which to access e-mail that was saved on the server.

Finally, when a user finishes writing an e-mail message and hits Send, how does the message return to the server? This task—officially referred to as e-mail submission—brings me back to the topic of this chapter; e-mail submission uses the SMTP protocol. However, as I'll describe, there are often two differences between SMTP as it is spoken between Internet servers and the way it is spoken during client e-mail submission, and both variances are driven by the present requirement to combat spam. To begin, most ISPs prohibit outgoing TCP connections to port 25 from laptops and desktops, preventing viruses from hijacking these small computers and using them as e-mail servers. Instead, most e-mail submissions are sent to port 587. Second, e-mail clients employ authenticated SMTP, which includes the user's username and password, to prevent spammers from connecting to your ISP and stating they wish to send a message allegedly from you.

E-mail has been delivered to the desktop through various means, both in major organisations such as colleges and enterprises and in ISPs that cater to home users. It's still usual to give each user instructions that tell them to:

- Download and install an e-mail programme such as Thunderbird or Outlook.
- Type in the hostname and protocol for retrieving e-mail.
- Set the name of the outgoing server and the SMTP port number.
- Assign a username and password that can be used to authenticate connections to both services.

Although e-mail clients and servers can be complex to set up and maintain, they were formerly the only option to provide e-mail to a new generation of users who stared at enormous colourful displays using a familiar graphical interface. Nowadays, they give customers an enviable degree of freedom: their ISP simply decides whether to offer POP, IMAP, or both, and the user (or, at the very least, non-enterprise user!) is free to experiment with several e-mail applications before settling on one they like.

The Transition to Webmail

Finally, there has been another generational transition on the Internet. Users used to have to download and install a slew of different clients in order to take use of everything the Internet has to offer. Many long-time readers may recall having Windows or Mac computers on which they eventually installed client programmes for protocols as diverse as Telnet, FTP, the Gopher directory service, Usenet newsgroups, and, later, the World Wide Web. (When Unix users initially logged in to a well-configured workstation, they often found clients for each basic protocol already installed, though they may have opted to install more advanced replacements for some of the applications, such as ncftp in place of the cumbersome default FTP client.) But not any longer! Today's Internet user is only aware of one client: their web browser. The Web is not only replacing all traditional Internet protocols—users browse and fetch files on web pages, not through FTP; they read message boards, rather than connecting to Usenet—but it is also obviating the need for many traditional desktop clients, thanks to the fact that web pages can now use JavaScript to respond and redraw themselves as the user clicks and types on their keyboard. If your application is one that could be given through an interactive web page, why persuade thousands of customers to download and install a new e-mail client, clicking through multiple warnings about how your software can harm their computer?

In fact, the web browser has grown in prominence to the point where many Internet users are unaware that they have one. As a result, they interchange the phrases "Internet" and "Web," believing that both terms relate to "all those documents and links that provide me with Facebook, YouTube, and Wikipedia." This lack of awareness that they are viewing the Web's glory through a specific client programme with a name and identity—say, through the pane of Internet Explorer—is a constant source of frustration for evangelists for alternatives such as Firefox, Google Chrome, and Opera, who find it difficult to persuade people to switch from a programme they aren't even aware they are using!

Obviously, if such individuals are to read e-mail, they must have access to a computer. As a result, there are numerous web sites that provide e-mail services through the browser—the most popular being Gmail and Yahoo! Mail—as well as server software, such as the popular SquirrelMail, that system administrators can install if they want to provide webmail to users at their school or business.

What does this entail for e-mail protocols and the network as a whole? Surprisingly, the webmail boom effectively transports us back to a simpler era when e-mail submission and reading were both private operations confined to a single mainframe server and rarely included the use of public protocols at all. Of course, these modern services, particularly those provided by huge ISPs and firms such as Google and Yahoo!, must be massive operations involving hundreds of servers spread across the globe; hence, network protocols must undoubtedly be engaged at every level of e-mail storage and retrieval.

But the point is that these are now internal processes within the webmail service provider's corporation.

When you click Send, who knows what protocol Google or Yahoo! uses internally to pass the new message from the web server receiving your HTTP POST to a mail queue from which it can be delivered? You browse e-mail in your web browser; you write e-mail using the same interface; and when you click Send, who knows what protocol Google or Yahoo! uses internally to pass the new message from the web server receiving your HTTP POST to a mail queue from which it can be delivered? It could be SMTP, an internal RPC protocol, or an activity on shared file systems to which both the web and e-mail servers are connected.

The crucial thing to remember for the purposes of this book is that you will never know if POP, IMAP, or something else is at work behind the webmail interface you use to manage your messages unless you are an engineer working at such an organisation.

While a result, e-mail browsing and submission become a black box: your browser interacts with a web API, and you'll observe plain old SMTP connections originating from and going to the enormous business as e-mail is delivered in both directions on the other end. Client protocols are eliminated from the mix in webmail, bringing us back to the days of pure server-to-server unauthenticated SMTP.

SMTP's Functions

The above tale should have helped you organise your thoughts about Internet e-mail protocols. Hopefully, it has also helped you see how they work together in the larger picture of sending and receiving messages from people.

This chapter, on the other hand, focuses on a more specific topic: the Simple Mail Transport Protocol. I'll start by going through the fundamentals in terminology you learnt in Part 1 of this book:

- The SMTP protocol is based on TCP/IP.

- Authentication is optional for connections.
- You have the option of encrypting or not encrypting your connections.

Most e-mail communications across the Internet these days appear to be unencrypted, which means that whomever controls the Internet backbone routers may theoretically read massive volumes of other people's e-mail. Given the information in the previous section, what are the two ways that SMTP is used?

For starters, SMTP can be used to send e-mail between a client e-mail application like Thunderbird or Outlook and a server at a company that has provided the user with an e-mail account. These connections typically require authentication to prevent spammers from connecting and sending millions of messages on behalf of a user without their password. When a message is received, the server places it in a delivery queue so that the e-mail client can forget about it and trust that the server will continue to try to deliver it.

Second, SMTP is a protocol used by Internet e-mail servers to transfer messages from one location to another. Because large organisations like Google, Yahoo!, and Microsoft don't know each other's users' passwords, when Yahoo! receives an e-mail from Google claiming to be sent from a @gmail.com user, Yahoo! simply has to believe them (or not—sometimes organisations blacklist each other if too much spam is making its way through their servers). When Hotmail's e-mail server stopped taking his e-mail newsletters from GoDaddy's servers due to purported spam problems, this happened to a friend of mine.

As a result, there is often no authentication between servers communicating via SMTP, and encryption against spying routers appears to be utilised relatively infrequently. Due to the problem of spammers connecting to e-mail servers and claiming to be sending e-mail from another company's subscribers, an attempt has been made to limit which servers can send e-mail on behalf of an organisation. Some e-mail servers use the Sender Policy Framework (SPF), specified in RFC 4408, to determine whether the server with whom they're communicating has the authority to deliver the e-mails it's sending.

Let's get down to business and talk about how you'll use SMTP in your Python apps. A Python-driven SMTP session is seen in Figure 13-1.

E-mail transmission

Before we get into the nitty gritty of the SMTP protocol, a word of caution: if you're writing an interactive programme, daemon, or web site that needs to send e-mail, your site or system administrator (if that's not you) may have an opinion on how your programme sends e-mail, and they may be able to save you a lot of time by doing so!

As previously stated, sending e-mail usually necessitates a queue in which a message can sit for seconds, minutes, or even days before being properly delivered to its intended recipient. As a result, you shouldn't use Python's smtplib to send e-mail straight to a message's destination in your front-end apps, because if the initial transmission attempt fails, the message would be lost. Then you'll have to write a full mail transfer agent (MTA), or e-mail server, as the RFCs describe it, and give it a full standards-compliant retry queue.This is not only a massive project, but it's also one that's been done well before, and you'd be prudent to use one of the existing MTAs to help you out. Before attempting to write something on your own, look into postfix, exim, and qmail. Making SMTP connections out into the world from Python is a rare occurrence. Your system is more than likely to fail. One of two things will be told to you by the administrator:

- You should establish an authenticated SMTP connection to an existing e-mail server. within your corporation utilizing a username and password specific to your application

- That you should run a local binary on the system, such as the sendmail application, that the system administrator has previously configured to allow local programmes to operate send an email Sample code for launching a sendmail compliant application can be found in the Python Library FAQ. Have a look at the next section.

"How can I send email from a Python script?" you might wonder. http://docs.python.org/faq/library.html is a good place to start. Because this book is about networking, I won't go into great depth about this option. However, don't forget to do it raw. Only use SMTP if there is no other option for sending e-mail on your workstation.

The Envelope Recipient and the Headers

The main notion in SMTP that beginners frequently misunderstand is that the addressee headers you're used to—To, Cc (carbon copy), and Bcc (blind carbon copy)—are not used by the SMTP protocol to determine where your e-mail goes! Many users are taken aback by this. After all, practically every e-mail programme asks you to fill in the addressee areas, and when you click Send, the message is sent to those addresses. What's more natural than that? However, this is a feature of the email client, not the SMTP protocol: the protocol simply knows that each message has a "envelope" around it that names a sender and certain recipients. SMTP is unconcerned about whether such names are ones it can locate in the message's headers.

If you think about the Bcc blind carbon-copy header for a moment, you'll see why e-mail has to work this way. The Bcc header, unlike the To and Cc headers, which make it to the e-destination mail's and allow each recipient to see who else was given that e-mail, specifies those you wish to get the e-mail without the other recipients knowing. Blind copies allow you to silently bring a message to the attention of someone without alerting the rest of the e-recipients. mail's

The fact that a header like Bcc exists, which may appear when you prepare a message but may not appear in the outgoing message, raises two points:

- Your e-mail client modifies the headers of your message before sending it. The client typically adds headers as well, such as a unique message ID and possibly the name of the e-mail client itself (an e-mail I just received on my desktop, for example, identifies the X-Mailer that sent it as YahooMailClassic), in addition to removing the Bcc header so that none of the e-recipients mail's receive a copy of it.

- An e-mail can be routed through SMTP to a destination address that isn't stated in the e-mail headers or text—and it can do so for the most valid of reasons.

This approach also aids in the support of e-mailing lists, allowing an e-mail with the To line advocacy@python.org to be distributed to the dozens or hundreds of people who subscribe to that list without exposing all of their e-mail addresses to every list reader without rewriting headers.

As you read the following SMTP explanations, keep in mind that the headers and body of the email message are distinct from the "envelope sender" and "envelope recipient" that will be discussed in the protocol specifications. Yes, whether you're using /usr/sbin/ sendmail, Thunderbird, or Google Mail, your e-mail client probably only asked for the recipient's e-mail address once; but it then used it twice: once in the To header at the top of the message itself, and then again "outside" the message when it spoke SMTP to send the e-mail on its way.

Several Hops

E-mail used to go in a single SMTP "hop" from the mainframe on which it was composed to the machine on whose disc the recipient's inbox was stored. Messages nowadays frequently pass via a half-dozen or more servers before reaching their intended recipient. As the message approaches its destination, the SMTP envelope recipient, as mentioned in the preceding section, changes several times.

This should be illustrated with an example. Although some of the following details are made up, they should give you a good picture of how messages travel across the Internet in real life.

Consider a worker in delhi's core IT group telling a buddy that his e-mail address is business@bpbonline.com. When the buddy sends him an email, his e-mail provider looks up the Domain Name Service (DNS; see Chapter 4), receives a series of MX records in response, and connects to one of those IP addresses to deliver the message. Isn't it simple enough?

The server for gatech.edu, on the other hand, serves the entire campus! It consults a table to locate bpbonline, locates his department, and discovers that his official e-mail address is business@bpbonline.com.

So the gatech.edu server performs a DNS lookup for oit.gatech.edu and then sends the message to the Office of Information Technology's e-mail server through SMTP (the message's second SMTP hop, if you're keeping track). However, OIT has long since abandoned their single-server strategy, which had all of their e-mail stored on a single Unix server. They now run a sophisticated e-mail system that customers may access via webmail, POP, and IMAP.

Incoming e-mail to oit.gatech.edu is first routed through one of several spam-filtering servers (third hop), such as spam3.oit.gatech.edu. After then, if it passes the spam check and isn't deleted, it's sent to one of eight redundant e-mail servers at random, and after the fourth hop, it's in the queue on mail7.gatech.edu. The routing servers, such as mail7, can then query a central directory service to find out which users' mailboxes are hosted by which back-end mail stores, which are connected to large disc arrays. So mail7 performs an LDAP lookup for john, determines that his e-mail is stored on the anvil.oit.gatech.edu server, and the e-mail is delivered to anvil and written to its redundant disc array in a fifth and final SMTP hop.

That's why sending and receiving e-mail takes at least a few seconds on the Internet: Large companies and ISPs frequently have multiple levels of servers through which a message must pass before being delivered. How can you track the path of an e-mail? The SMTP protocol, as previously stated, does not read e-mail headers, but it does have its own concept about where a message should go—which, as you have just seen, might alter with each hop a message takes toward its destination. However, it turns out that e-mail servers are encouraged to add new headers in order to monitor a message's winding path from origin to destination.

These headers are known as Received headers, and they're a gold mine for system administrators trying to figure out why their e-mail systems aren't working. Examine any e-mail message and request that your e-mail client show all of the headers. You should be able to observe each step the message took on its way to its intended recipient. (Spammers frequently use many bogus Received headers at the top of their messages to make it appear as if the message came from a legitimate source.) Finally, when the last server in the chain is able to successfully write the message to physical storage in someone's mailbox, a Delivered-to header is likely written.

Because each server adds its Received header to the top of the e-mail message, this saves time and prevents each server from having to sift through all of the previously written Received headers. You should read them in reverse order: the oldest Received header will be the final one presented, so as you read up the screen toward the top, you will be following the e-mail from its source to its destination. Try it: open a recent e-mail message, choose View All Message Headers or Show Original from the View menu, and check for the received headers at the top. Did the communication take you longer or shorter than you expected to get to your inbox?

The SMTP Library is an introduction to the SMTP protocol

The Python Standard Library module smtplib contains Python's built-in SMTP implementation, which makes it straightforward to use SMTP for simple tasks.

The programmes in the examples below are written to accept a number of command-line parameters, including the name of an SMTP server, a sender address, and one or more recipient addresses. Please use these with caution; only identify an SMTP server that you own or that you know will be delighted to receive your test messages, should your IP address get blacklisted for spamming!

If you don't know where to look for an SMTP server, consider installing an e-mail daemon locally, such as postfix or exim, and then pointing these sample programmes at localhost. Some UNIX, Linux, and Mac OS X systems already have an SMTP server listening for connections from the local workstation, such as one of these.

Otherwise, get a correct hostname and port from your network administrator or Internet provider.

It's important to remember that you can't just pick an e-mail server at random; several only store or forward e-mail from specific permitted clients.

Now that you've taken care of that, you may continue on to Listing 13-1, which shows a very basic SMTP application.

Listing 13-1. Using smtplib.sendmail to send email ()

```
#!/usr/bin/env python3
```

```
# Programming in Python: The Basics
import sys, smtplib
message_template = """"To: {}
From: {}
Subject: Test Message from simple.py
Hello,
This is a test message sent to you from the simple.py program
in Programming in Python: The Basics.
"""

def main():
        if len(sys.argv) < 4:
                name = sys.argv[0]
                print("usage: {} server fromaddr toaddr [toaddr...]".
                format(name))
                        sys.exit(2)
        server, fromaddr, toaddrs = sys.argv[1], sys.argv[2], sys.
        argv[3:]
        message = message_template.format(', '.join(toaddrs),
        fromaddr)
        connection = smtplib.SMTP(server)
        connection.sendmail(fromaddr, toaddrs, message)
        connection.quit()
                s = '' if len(toaddrs) == 1 else 's'
        print("Message sent to {} recipient{}".
        format(len(toaddrs), s))
    if __name__ == '__main__':
        main()
```

Because it employs a very powerful and broad function from the Python Standard Library, this programme is fairly straightforward. It begins by generating a simple message using the user's command-line arguments (see Chapter 12 for more information on generating fancier messages that include items other than plain text). The smtplib.SMTP object is then created, which connects to the chosen server. Finally, a call to sendmail is all that is required (). If that succeeds, you know the message was received without error by the e-mail server.

As previously stated in this chapter, the idea of who receives the message—the "envelope recipient"—is independent from the actual text of the message at this level. This software creates a To header that has the same addresses as the recipients of the message; however, the To header is just a piece of text that could say anything else. (Whether that "anything else" is gladly shown by the recipient's e-mail client or causes the message to be discarded as spam by a server along the route is another question!)

If you execute the programme from the book's network playground, it should be able to connect successfully as follows:

mail.example.com sender@example.com recipient@example.com $ python3 simple.py

1 recipient received the message successfully.

The sendmail() method, thanks to the hard work of the Python Standard Library's authors, may be the last SMTP call you'll ever need! But first, let's take a closer look at how SMTP works to see what happens behind the scenes to get your message delivered.

Error Handling and Debugging Conversations

While developing with smtplib, you may encounter a variety of exceptions. They are as follows:

- **socket.gaierror** for address lookup errors
- **socket.error** for network and communication difficulties in general
- Other addressing issues can be found in **socket.herror**.
- smtplib smtplib smtplib smt

For SMTP communication difficulties, use SMTPException or a subclass of it.

The first three errors are raised in the operating system's TCP stack, detected and raised as exceptions by Python's networking code, and passed straight through the smtplib module and up to your programme; they are raised in the operating system's TCP stack, detected and raised as exceptions by Python's networking code, and passed straight through the smtplib module and up to your programme. All faults that genuinely impact the SMTP e-mail communication will result in a smtplib.SMTPException as long as the underlying TCP socket operates. The smtplib module also allows you to get a series of detailed messages detailing the procedures involved in sending an email. You can use the following option to activate that degree of detail:

```
connection.set debuglevel(1)
```

You should be able to track down any issues with this option. A sample application that provides basic error handling and debugging can be found in Listing 13-2.

Listing 13-2. An SMTP Client with More Caution

```
#!/usr/bin/env python3
# Programming in Python: The Basics.
import sys, smtplib, socket
message_template = """To: {}
From: {}
Subject: Test Message from simple.py
Hello,
This is a test message sent to you from the debug.py program
in Programming in Python: The Basics.
"""

def main():
        if len(sys.argv) < 4:
                name = sys.argv[0]
                print("usage: {} server fromaddr toaddr [toaddr...]".
                format(name))
                sys.exit(2)
        server, fromaddr, toaddrs = sys.argv[1], sys.argv[2], sys.
        argv[3:]
        message = message_template.format(', '.join(toaddrs), fromaddr)
  try:
        connection = smtplib.SMTP(server)
        connection.set_debuglevel(1)
        connection.sendmail(fromaddr, toaddrs, message)
  except (socket.gaierror, socket.error, socket.herror,
        smtplib.SMTPException) as e:
        print("Your message may not have been sent!")
```

```
        print(e)
        sys.exit(1)
 else:
        s = '' if len(toaddrs) == 1 else 's'
        print("Message sent to {} recipient{}".format(len(toaddrs), s))
        connection.quit()
if __name__ == '__main__':
        main()
```

Although this programme appears to be similar to the previous one, the outcome will be substantially different. Consider Listing 13-3 as an illustration.

Listing 13-3. smtplib Output Troubleshooting

```
$ python3 debug.py mail.example.com sender@example.com recipient@
example.com
send: 'hello [127.0.1.1]\r\n'
reply: b'250-guinness\r\n'
reply: b'250-SIZE 33444432\r\n'
reply: b'250 HELP\r\n'
reply: retcode (250); Msg: b'guinness\nSIZE 33554432\nHELP'
send: 'mail FROM:<sender@example.com> size=212\r\n'
reply: b'250 OK\r\n'
reply: retcode (250); Msg: b'OK'
send: 'rcpt TO:<recipient@example.com>\r\n'
reply: b'250 OK\r\n'
reply: retcode (250); Msg: b'OK'
send: 'data\r\n'
reply: b'354 End data with <CR><LF>.<CR><LF>\r\n'
reply: retcode (354); Msg: b'End data with <CR><LF>.<CR><LF>'
data: (354, b'End data with <CR><LF>.<CR><LF>')
send: b'To: recipient@example.com\r\nFrom: sender@example.com\r\
nSubject: Test Message from
simple.py\r\n\r\nHello,\r\n\r\nThis is a test message sent to you
from the debug.py program\r\nin
```

```
Programming in Python: The Basics.\r\n.\r\n'
reply: b'250 OK\r\n'
reply: retcode (250); Msg: b'OK'
data: (250, b'OK')
send: 'quit\r\n'
reply: b'221 Bye\r\n'
reply: retcode (221); Msg: b'Bye'
Message sent to 1 recipient
```

The dialogue that smtplib has with the SMTP server across the network may be seen in this example.

The details provided here will become more relevant when you create code that leverages more complex SMTP features, so let's take a look at what's going on.

First, the client (the smtplib library) sends an EHLO command with your hostname in it (an "extended" successor to a more ancient command termed, more readably, HELO). The remote server answers with its own hostname as well as a list of any optional SMTP features it offers.

The client then executes the mail from command, which specifies the "envelope sender" e-mail address as well as the message's size. The server has the option to reject the message at this point (for example, if it believes you are a spammer), but in this case it answers with 250 Ok. (the code 250 is what matters in this case; the rest content is essentially a human-readable comment that differs from server to server.)

The client then sends a rcpt to command, specifying the "envelope recipient," as mentioned earlier in this chapter.

When utilising the SMTP protocol, you can finally see that it is transmitted independently from the text of the message. The rcpt to line would list each recipient if you were sending the message to multiple people. Finally, the client sends a data command, transmits the actual message (using the Internet e-mail standard's verbose carriage-return-linefeed line endings, you'll see), and concludes the interaction.

In this example, the smtplib module takes care of everything for you. I'll go over how to have greater control over the process so you can take advantage of some more advanced capabilities later in the chapter.

Don't be fooled into thinking that just because no errors were discovered during the first hop, the message is now guaranteed to be delivered. Many times, an e-mail server will accept a message only to fail to deliver it later. Reread the "Multiple

Hops" section and consider how many chances there are for that sample message to fail before it reaches its destination!

Using EHLO to Gather Information

It's useful to know what types of messages a distant SMTP server may accept on occasion. For example, most SMTP servers have a maximum message size that they allow, and if you don't check first, you can send a very huge message only to have it denied after you've finished sending it.

A client would send a HELO instruction to the server as the initial greeting in the original version of SMTP. ESMTP, a collection of extensions to SMTP, was created to allow for more robust talks. EHLO, which tells an ESMTP-aware server that it can reply with more information, will start the dialogue for ESMTP-aware clients. The maximum message size, as well as any extra SMTP capabilities that the server offers, are included in this expanded information.

You must, however, double-check the return code. ESMTP isn't supported by all servers. EHLO will just return an error on such servers. In that situation, you must instead provide a HELO command.

Because I called sendmail() right after constructing the SMTP object in the previous examples, smtplib automatically sent its own "hello" message to the server to start the dialogue for you. However, if the Python sendmail() method detects that you are attempting to send the EHLO or HELO command on your own, it will not attempt to send a hello command. Listing 13-4 depicts a programme that obtains the server's limit message size and returns an error before transmitting if the message is too large.

Listing 13-4. Checking Restrictions on Message Size

```
#!/usr/bin/env python3
# Programming in Python: The Basics.
import smtplib, socket, sys
message_template = """To: {}
From: {}
Subject: Test Message from simple.py
Hello,
This is a test message sent to you from the ehlo.py program
in Programming in Python: The Basics."""
def main():
```

```
        if len(sys.argv) < 4:
            name = sys.argv[0]
            print("usage: {} server fromaddr toaddr [toaddr...]".
            format(name))
            sys.exit(2)
        server, fromaddr, toaddrs = sys.argv[1], sys.argv[2], sys.
        argv[3:]
        message = message_template.format(', '.join(toaddrs), fromaddr)
        try:
            connection = smtplib.SMTP(server)
            report_on_message_size(connection, fromaddr, toaddrs,
            message)
        except (socket.gaierror, socket.error, socket.herror,
        smtplib.SMTPException) as e:
            print("Your message may not have been sent!")
            print(e)
            sys.exit(1)
        else:
            s = '' if len(toaddrs) == 1 else 's'
            print("Message     sent     to     {}     recipient{}".
            format(len(toaddrs), s))
            connection.quit()
def report_on_message_size(connection, fromaddr, toaddrs, message):
        code = connection.ehlo()[0]
        uses_esmtp = (200 <= code <= 299)
        if not uses_esmtp:
            code = connection.helo()[0]
            if not (200 <= code <= 299):
                print("Remote server refused HELO; code:", code)
                sys.exit(1)
        if uses_esmtp and connection.has_extn('size'):
            print("Maximum message size is", connection.esmtp_
            features['size'])
```

```
        if len(message) > int(connection.esmtp_features['size']):
            print("Message too large; aborting.")
            sys.exit(1)
    connection.sendmail(fromaddr, toaddrs, message)
if __name__ == '__main__':
    main()
```

If you start this application and the remote server specifies a maximum message size, the programme will display that size on your screen and check that your message does not exceed it before sending. (For a small message like this The check is a little goofy, but the listing demonstrates how to utilise the pattern with much longer messages.) Here's an example of how to run this programme:

$ python3 ehlo.py mail.example.com sender@example.com recipient@ example.com

Maximum message size is 33444432

Message successfully sent to 1 recipient

Examine the section of code that verifies the outcome of an ehlo() or helo() call (). The first item in the list returned by those two functions is a numeric result code from the remote SMTP server. Anything between 200 and 299 is considered a success; anything else is considered a failure. As a result, if the result falls within that range, you can be confident that the message was successfully processed by the server.

The same care applies as previously. The fact that the message is accepted by the first SMTP server does not guarantee that it will be delivered; a later server may have a smaller maximum size limit.

Aside from message size, ESMTP information is also available. Some servers, for example, may accept data in raw 8-bit mode if they support the 8BITMIME protocol. Others, as detailed in the next section, may support encryption. Consult RFC 1869 or your own server's documentation for further information on ESMTP and its capabilities, which may differ from server to server.

Secure Sockets Layer (SSL) and Transport Layer Security (TLS)

E-mails sent in plain text through SMTP, as previously described, can be read by anyone with access to an Internet gateway or router through which the packets transit, including the wireless network at the coffee shop from which your e-mail client is attempting to send. The ideal answer to this problem is to encrypt each e-mail with a public key whose private key is only known by the person to whom you are sending the e-mail; solutions like the GNU Privacy Guard are free to use for this purpose. Individual SMTP exchanges between specific pairs of machines can be encrypted and authenticated using SSL/TLS, as described in Chapter 6, independent of whether the messages themselves are protected. You'll discover how SSL/TLS works with SMTP chats in this section.

Keep in mind that TLS only protects the SMTP "hops" that choose to use it—even if you carefully use TLS to send an e-mail to a server, you have no influence over whether that server uses TLS again if your e-mail needs to be forwarded through another hop to its destination.

The following is the general approach for using TLS in SMTP:

1. As usual, create the SMTP object.
2. Use the **EHLO** command to send a message. TLS will not be supported if the remote server does not support EHLO.
3. Check if starttls is present using s.has extn(). If not, the remote server does not support TLS, and the message can only be sent in plaintext.
4. Create an SSL context object to validate the identity of the server for you.
5. To begin the encrypted channel, call starttls().
6. Run ehlo() a second time, this time encrypting it.
7. Last but not least, send your message.

When working with TLS, the first question to consider is whether or not to return an error if TLS is not available. You might want to report an error for any of the following scenarios, depending on your application:

- On the remote side, TLS is not supported.
- The remote server fails to correctly create a TLS session, or delivers a certificate that cannot be validated.
- Let's go over each of these circumstances and see when an error message is appropriate.

To begin, it's occasionally reasonable to regard a lack of TLS support as an error. This could be the case if you're creating an application that only communicates with a small number of e-mail servers—for example, e-mail servers hosted by your employer that you know should support TLS or e-mail servers hosted by a university that you know supports TLS.

Because TLS is supported by a small percentage of e-mail servers on the Internet today, an e-mail programme should not interpret its absence as an error in general. When TLS is available, many TLS-aware SMTP clients will use it, but if it isn't, they will fall back to normal, unprotected communication. This is referred to as opportunistic encryption, and while it is less safe than encrypting all connections, it protects messages when the capability is available.

Second, a distant server may claim to be TLS aware but yet fail to establish a TLS connection successfully. This is frequently due to a server misconfiguration. You might want to retry a failed encrypted transmission to such a server over a fresh connection that you don't even try to encrypt, just to be safe. Finally, you may find yourself in a circumstance where you are unable to fully authenticate the remote server. See Chapter 6 for a detailed discussion of peer validation. If your security policy requires you to send email only to trusted servers, then a lack of authentication is clearly a problem that should result in an error notice.

Listing 13-5 is a general-purpose client that supports TLS. If TLS is available, it will connect to a server and use it; if not, it will fall back and deliver the message as usual. If the attempt to initiate TLS fails while talking to a seemingly capable server, it will die with an error.

Listing 13-5. Taking Advantage of TLS

```python
#!/usr/bin/env python3
# Programming in Python: The Basics.
import sys, smtplib, socket, ssl
message_template = """To: {}
From: {}
Subject: Test Message from simple.py
Hello,
This is a test message sent to you from the tls.py program
in Programming in Python: The Basics.
"""

def main():
        if len(sys.argv) < 4:
            name = sys.argv[0]
            print("Syntax: {} server fromaddr toaddr [toaddr...]".
            format(name))
            sys.exit(2)
```

```
        server, fromaddr, toaddrs = sys.argv[1], sys.argv[2], sys.
        argv[3:]
        message    =    message_template.format(',    '.join(toaddrs),
        fromaddr)
        try:
            connection = smtplib.SMTP(server)
            send_message_securely(connection, fromaddr, toaddrs,
            message)
        except (socket.gaierror, socket.error, socket.herror,
            smtplib.SMTPException) as e:
            print("Your message may not have been sent!")
            print(e)
            sys.exit(1)
        else:
            s = '' if len(toaddrs) == 1 else 's'
            print("Message    sent    to    {}    recipient{}".
            format(len(toaddrs), s))
            connection.quit()
def send_message_securely(connection, fromaddr, toaddrs, message):
        code = connection.ehlo()[0]
        uses_esmtp = (200 <= code <= 299)
        if not uses_esmtp:
            code = connection.helo()[0]
            if not (200 <= code <= 299):
                print("Remove server refused HELO; code:", code)
                sys.exit(1)
        if uses_esmtp and connection.has_extn('starttls'):
            print("Negotiating TLS....")
            context = ssl.SSLContext(ssl.PROTOCOL_SSLv23)
            context.set_default_verify_paths()
            context.verify_mode = ssl.CERT_REQUIRED
            connection.starttls(context=context)
            code = connection.ehlo()[0]
```

```
        if not (200 <= code <= 299):
                print("Couldn't EHLO after STARTTLS")
                sys.exit(5)
        print("Using TLS connection.")
    else:
        print("Server does not support TLS; using normal
        connection.")
        connection.sendmail(fromaddr, toaddrs, message)
if __name__ == '__main__':
        main()
```

It's worth noting that the call to sendmail() in the last few listings is the same whether or not TLS is enabled. TLS hides that layer of complexity from you once it is begun, so you don't have to worry about it.

SMTP authentication

Finally, there's authenticated SMTP, in which your ISP, university, or company's e-mail server requires you to log in with a username and password to confirm you're not a spammer before allowing you to send e-mail.

TLS should be used in conjunction with authentication for maximum security; otherwise, anyone watching the connection will be able to see your password (and username, for that matter). Establishing a TLS connection first and then sending your authentication information solely via the encrypted communications channel is the right way to do this. Authentication is straightforward; the login() method in smtplib accepts a username and a password.

An example can be found in Listing 13-6. To avoid repeating code already seen in prior listings, this listing ignores the previous paragraph's caution and sends the username and password over an unauthenticated connection, which sends them in the clear.

Listing 13-6. Authentication via SMTP (Simple Mail Transfer Protocol)

```
#!/usr/bin/env python3
# Programming in Python: The Basics.
import sys, smtplib, socket
from getpass import getpass
message_template = """"""To: {}
```

```
From: {}
Subject: Test Message from simple.py
Hello,
This is a test message sent to you from the login.py program
in Programming in Python: The Basics.
"""

def main():
        if len(sys.argv) < 4:
                name = sys.argv[0]
                print("Syntax: {} server fromaddr toaddr [toaddr...]".
                format(name))
                sys.exit(2)
        server, fromaddr, toaddrs = sys.argv[1], sys.argv[2], sys.
        argv[3:]
        message = message_template.format(', '.join(toaddrs),
        fromaddr)
        username = input("Enter username: ")
        password = getpass("Enter password: ")
    try:
                connection = smtplib.SMTP(server)
                try:
                        connection.login(username, password)
                except smtplib.SMTPException as e:
                        print("Authentication failed:", e)
                        sys.exit(1)
                connection.sendmail(fromaddr, toaddrs, message)
        except (socket.gaierror, socket.error, socket.herror,
                        smtplib.SMTPException) as e:
                print("Your message may not have been sent!")
                print(e)
                sys.exit(1)
    else:
                s = '' if len(toaddrs) == 1 else 's'
```

```
            print("Message    sent    to    {}    recipient{}".
            format(len(toaddrs), s))

            connection.quit()
if __name__ == '__main__':
    main()
```

Authentication is not supported by the majority of outgoing e-mail servers on the Internet. The login() attempt will return an Authentication failed error message if you are using a server that does not allow authentication. After invoking connection, check connection.has extn('auth') to avoid this. If the remote server supports ESMTP, use ehlo().

This programme can be executed in the same way as the previous ones. You will be requested for a username and password if you run it on a server that supports authentication. If they are accepted, the programme will send your message to the recipient.

SMTP Pointers

Here are some pointers to help you get started using SMTP clients:

- There's no way to know if the communication was received. Although you may be aware right away that your effort failed, the absence of an error does not rule out the possibility that something else will go wrong before the message is safely sent to the destination.

- If any of the recipients fails, the sendmail() function throws an exception, while the message may still be sent to other recipients. For more information, look at the exception you receive. You may need to execute sendmail() separately for each recipient if you need to know which addresses failed— for example, if you want to try retransmitting later without making duplicate copies for individuals who have already received the message. This more naive approach, however, will result in the message body being sent multiple times, once for each recipient.

- Without certificate checking, SSL/TLS is insecure: you could be communicating with any old server that has temporarily taken possession of the typical server's IP address.

  Remember to establish an SSL context object, as described in the TLS previous example, and pass it as the lone argument to starttls to support certificate verification ().

- The smtplib module in Python is not intended to be used as a general-purpose e-mail relay. Rather, you should utilise it to send messages to a local SMTP server, which will handle the actual e-mail delivery.

Conclusion

SMTP is a protocol for sending email messages to email servers. For SMTP clients, Python provides the smtplib module. You can send messages by using the sendmail() method of SMTP objects. The To, Cc, and Bcc message headers in the text of the message are separate from the real list of recipients; the To, Cc, and Bcc message headers in the text of the message are separate from the actual list of recipients. During an SMTP discussion, a variety of exceptions could be raised. Interactive programmes should look for and deal with these issues effectively.

ESMTP is an SMTP extension. Prior to sending a message, it allows you to determine the maximum message size supported by a remote SMTP server. TLS, a method of encrypting your conversation with a distant server, is also supported by ESMTP. Chapter 6 examined the fundamentals of TLS.

Authentication is required by some SMTP servers. The login() method can be used to verify your identity. SMTP doesn't have any features for downloading messages from a mailbox to your personal PC. To do so, you'll need the procedures mentioned in the following two chapters. POP, as discussed in Chapter 14, is a simple method of receiving and downloading messages.

The IMAP protocol, which is explained in Chapter 15, is more sophisticated and powerful.

CHAPTER 14
Post Office Protocol(POP)

The Post Office Protocol (POP) is a straightforward method of retrieving e-mail from a server. It's usually accessed via an e-mail client like Thunderbird or Outlook. If you want a quick overview of where e-mail clients and protocols like POP fit within the history of Internet e-mail, revisit the first few sections of Chapter 13.

If you're tempted to utilise POP, instead use IMAP; Chapter15 will go over the characteristics of IMAP that make it a significantly more robust foundation for distant e-mail access than POP's primitive functions.

Version 3, sometimes known as POP3, is the most widely used POP implementation. Because version 3 has become so popular, the names POP and POP3 are now almost identical. The simplicity of POP is both its greatest asset and its greatest flaw. If all you need is to access a distant mailbox, download any new e-mail that has arrived, and delete the e-mail after it has been downloaded, POP is the way to go. This task will be completed swiftly and without the use of sophisticated code.

POP, on the other hand, is mostly used to download and remove files. On the remote side, it does not support numerous mailboxes, nor does it provide any accurate, durable message identification. This means you can't use POP as an e-mail synchronisation protocol, where you leave the server's original copy of each e-mail message while making a copy to read locally. Because you won't be able to determine which messages you've previously downloaded when you return to the server later.

If you require this functionality, you should look into IMAP, which will be discussed in Chapter 15.

The poplib module in the Python Standard Library provides a user-friendly interface for using POP.

It's worth noting that the Python Standard Library only allows you to function as a client, not a server. If you need to set up a server, you'll need to look for a Python module that includes POP server capability.

Structure:

- Compatibility of POP Servers
- Authenticating and connecting
- Getting Access to Mailbox Information
- Messages are downloaded and deleted
- Conclusion

Objectives:

This chapter will show you how to connect to a POP server, get mailbox summary information, download messages, and delete the originals from the server using poplib. You'll have covered all of the usual POP features once you've mastered these four jobs.

Compatibility of POP Servers

POP servers have a terrible reputation for not adhering to standards. For some POP behaviours, standards simply do not exist, leaving the details to the makers of server software. So, while basic activities should function correctly in most cases, particular behaviours may differ from server to server.

Some servers, for example, will mark all of your messages as read whenever you connect to the server, regardless of whether or not you download any of them! When a message is downloaded, it is marked as read by other servers. Some servers don't even mark messages as read. The standard itself appears to presume the latter, but neither side is certain. As you read this chapter, keep these distinctions in mind.

Figure 14-1 depicts a very basic Python-driven POP discussion.

Authenticating and connecting

POP accepts a variety of authentication mechanisms. Basic username-password authentication and APOP, an optional enhancement to POP that helps protect passwords from being delivered in plain text if you're using an old POP server that doesn't support SSL, are the two most prevalent.

In Python, connecting to and authenticating with a remote server looks like this:

1. Make a POP3 SSL object, or simply a standard POP3 object, and give it the remote hostname and port.

2. To send the username and password, use the **user()** and **pass_()** functions. Keep an eye out for the underscore in pass_()! It's there because pass is a Python keyword that can't be used as a method name.

3. If the exception poplib.error proto is thrown, the login attempt failed, and the string value of the exception contains the server's error message.

The difference between POP3 and POP3 SSL is determined by whether your e-mail provider allows—or even requires—you to connect over an encrypted connection in this day and age. More information regarding SSL may be found in Chapter 6, although the general rule should be to utilise it whenever possible. The methods in Listing 14-1 are used to log in to a remote POP server. It connects to the server and calls stat(), which returns a basic tuple with the number of messages in the mailbox and their total size. Finally, the software uses quit() to terminate the POP connection.

```
                    THE POP-3 PROTOCOL

        Purpose: Allow download of e-mail from inbox

              Standard: RFC 1939 (May 1996)

                    Runs atop: TCP/IP

        Default port: 110 (cleartext), 995 (SSL)

                    Libraries: poplib
```

Listing 14-1. A POP Session That Is Extremely Easy

```python
#!/usr/bin/env python3
# Programming in Python: The Basics.
import getpass, poplib, sys
def main():
        if len(sys.argv) != 3:
```

```
        print('usage: %s hostname username' % sys.argv[0])
        exit(2)
    hostname, username = sys.argv[1:]
    passwd = getpass.getpass()
    p = poplib.POP3_SSL(hostname) # or "POP3" if SSL is not
    supported
    try:
        p.user(username)
        p.pass_(passwd)
    except poplib.error_proto as e:
        print("Login failed:", e)
    else:
        status = p.stat()
        print("You have %d messages totaling %d bytes" % status)
    finally:
        p.quit()
if __name__ == '__main__':
 main()
```

Despite the fact that this application makes no changes to messages, certain POP servers will change mailbox flags merely because you connected. If you run the examples in this chapter against a live mailbox, you can lose track of which messages are read, unread, new, or old. Unfortunately, that behaviour is server-dependent, and POP clients have no control over it. I strongly advise you to test these examples on a test mailbox instead of your own inbox!

The hostname of your POP server and your username are required command-line inputs for this software. Contact your Internet provider or network administrator if you don't know this information. It's worth noting that your username on some services will be a simple string (like guido), while on others it will be your entire e-mail address (guido@example.com).

After that, the software will ask you for your password. Finally, it will show the state of your mailbox without affecting or altering any of your messages.

Here's how you can use the Mininet playground, which you can get from the book's source repository (see Chapter 1), to run the programme:

```
$ python3 popconn.py mail.example.com bpbonline
```

Password: abc12345

You have 3 messages totaling 5660 bytes

If you see something similar to this, your first POP chat was a success!

When POP servers don't offer SSL to protect your connection from snooping, they may at least support APOP, which employs a challenge–response mechanism to ensure that your password isn't sent in plain. (However, any third party watching packets will be able to see all of your e-mail!) This is made very simple by the Python Standard Library: Simply call the apop() method, and if the POP server to which you're communicating doesn't understand, fall back to basic authentication.

You might use a stanza like the one shown in Listing 14-2 inside the POP programme to use APOP but fall back to simple authentication.

Listing 14-2. Falling Back After Attempting APOP

```
print("Attempting APOP authentication...")
try:
        p.apop(user, passwd)
except poplib.error_proto:
        print("Attempting standard authentication...")
        try:
                p.user(user)
                p.pass_(passwd)
        except poplib.error_proto as e:
                print("Login failed:", e)
                sys.exit(1)
```

Some older POP servers may lock the mailbox as soon as a login is successful, regardless of the method. If the mailbox is locked, no changes can be made to it, and no additional e-mail can be delivered until the lock is removed. The issue is that some POP servers do not properly detect problems, and if your connection hangs up without you dialling quit, they will leave your box locked indefinitely (). The world's most popular POP server used to be in this category! As a result, whenever you finish a POP session, you must always call quit() in your Python apps. You'll notice that all of the programme listings here are cautious to call stop() in a finally block, ensuring that Python executes last.

Getting Access to Mailbox Information

The stat() function returned the number of messages in the mailbox and their total size in the prior example.

list(), which offers more specific information about each message, is another handy POP command.

The message number, which is required to retrieve communications later, is the most interesting portion. There may be gaps in message numbers; for example, a mailbox may only hold messages 1, 2, 5, 6, and 9 at any given time. Additionally, the number allocated to a particular message may vary depending on which POP server connection you use.

The list() command is used in Listing 14-3 to display information about each message.

Listing 14-3. Using the command POP list()

```python
#!/usr/bin/env python3
# Programming in Python: The Basics.
import getpass, poplib, sys
def main():
        if len(sys.argv) != 3:
                print('usage: %s hostname username' % sys.argv[0])
                exit(2)
        hostname, username = sys.argv[1:]
        passwd = getpass.getpass()
        p = poplib.POP3_SSL(hostname)
        try:
                p.user(username)
                p.pass_(passwd)
        except poplib.error_proto as e:
                print("Login failed:", e)
        else:
                response, listings, octet_count = p.list()
                if not listings:
                print("No messages")
        for listing in listings:
```

```
            number, size = listing.decode('ascii').split()
            print("Message %s has %s bytes" % (number, size))
        finally:
            p.quit()
if __name__ == '__main__':
            main()
```

The list() function returns three elements in a tuple. In general, you should pay attention to the second item. Here is the current raw output for one of my POP mailboxes, which has three messages:

```
('+OK 3 messages (5676 bytes)', ['1 2405', '2 1625', '3 1664'], 25)
```

For each of the three items in my inbox, the three strings inside the second item provide the message number and size. Listing 14-3 uses simple parsing to deliver the output in a more appealing style. Here's how you'd go about running it against the POP server in the book's network playground (see Chapter 1):

```
$ python3 mailbox.py mail.example.com bpbonline

Password: abc12345

Message 1 has 355 bytes

Message 2 has 446 bytes

Message 3 has 1183 bytes
```

Messages are downloaded and deleted.

You should now have a good understanding of POP: when you use poplib, you send short atomic commands that always return a tuple, which contains various strings and lists of strings that display the results. You're now capable of manipulating messages! The three relevant methods, which all use the identical integer identifiers returned by list() to identify messages, are as follows:

- **retr(num):** This function downloads a single message and returns a tuple with a result code and the message as a list of lines. Most POP servers will set the message's "seen" flag to "true," preventing you from reading it again over POP (unless you have another method into your mailbox that allows you to set messages back to "Unread").

- **top(num, body lines):** This method provides the same result as retr() but does not mark the message as "seen." Instead of delivering the entire message, it only returns the headers and the number of body lines you specify in body lines. If you want to allow the user choose which messages to download, this is great for previewing messages.

- **dele(num):** This method marks a message for deletion from the POP server, which will happen when this POP session ends. Because you will never be able to retrieve the message from the server again, you should only do this if the user explicitly requests irreversible destruction of the message or if you have stored the message to redundant storage (and possibly backed it up) and have used something like fsync() to ensure that the data have been written.

To put it all together, look at Listing 14-4, which is a fairly useful POP-compatible e-mail client. It examines your inbox to see how many messages you have and to learn their numbers; it then uses top() to show you a preview of each item; and, at the user's request, it can retrieve the entire message and delete it from the mailbox.

Listing 14-4. A POP E-mail Reader that's Easy to Use

```python
#!/usr/bin/env python3
# Programming in Python: The Basics.
import email, getpass, poplib, sys
def main():
        if len(sys.argv) != 3:
            print('usage: %s hostname username' % sys.argv[0])
            exit(2)
        hostname, username = sys.argv[1:]
        passwd = getpass.getpass()
        p = poplib.POP3_SSL(hostname)
        try:
            p.user(username)
            p.pass_(passwd)
        except poplib.error_proto as e:
            print("Login failed:", e)
        else:
            visit_all_listings(p)
        finally:
            p.quit()
```

```
def visit_all_listings(p):
    response, listings, octets = p.list()
    for listing in listings:
        visit_listing(p, listing)
def visit_listing(p, listing):
    number, size = listing.decode('ascii').split()
    print('Message', number, '(size is', size, 'bytes):')
    print()
    response, lines, octets = p.top(number, 0)
    document = '\n'.join( line.decode('ascii') for line in lines
)
    message = email.message_from_string(document)
    for header in 'From', 'To', 'Subject', 'Date':
        if header in message:
        print(header + ':', message[header])
    print()
    print('Read this message [ny]?')
    answer = input()
    if answer.lower().startswith('y'):
        response, lines, octets = p.retr(number)
        document = '\n'.join( line.decode('ascii') for line in
        lines )
        message = email.message_from_string(document)
        print('-' * 72)
        for part in message.walk():
            if part.get_content_type() == 'text/plain':
            print(part.get_payload())
            print('-' * 72)
    print()
        print('Delete this message [ny]?')
        answer = input()
        if answer.lower().startswith('y'):
```

```
        p.dele(number)
        print('Deleted.')
if __name__ == '__main__':
 main()
```

You'll see that the listing makes extensive use of the email module, which was introduced in Chapter 12, because even fancy modern MIME e-mails with HTML and graphics typically include a text/plain component that the email module can handle. extract for the purpose of printing to the screen with a simple programme like this If you run this programme in the book's network playground (see Chapter 1), you'll get results that look like the ones below following:

```
$ python3 download-and-delete.py mail.example.com bpbonline
password: abc12345
Message 1 (size is 356 bytes):
From: Administrator <admin@mail.example.com>
To: Bpbonline <bpbonline@mail.example.com>
Subject: Welcome to example.com!
Read this message [ny]? y
------------------------------------------------------------------
-----
We are happy that you have chosen to use example.com's industry-
leading
Internet e-mail service and we hope that you experience is a pleasant
one. If you ever need your password reset, simply contact our staff!
- example.com
------------------------------------------------------------------
-----
Delete this message [ny]? y
Deleted.
```

Conclusion

POP allows you to easily download e-mail messages from a remote server. You may get information about the number of messages in a mailbox and the size of each message using Python's poplib interface. Individual messages can also be retrieved or deleted by number.

A mailbox may be locked if you connect to a POP server. As a result, it's critical to keep POP sessions as brief as possible and to always execute quit() when you're finished.

To protect your passwords and the contents of your e-mail messages, POP should be used with SSL wherever available.

If SSL isn't available, at the very least, use APOP; only send your password in the clear if you really must use POP and none of the other alternatives will suffice. POP is a basic and widely used protocol, but it has certain flaws that make it inappropriate for specific purposes. It can only access one folder, for example, and individual messages are not tracked indefinitely.

The following chapter looks into IMAP, a protocol that combines the benefits of POP with a few additional ones.

CHAPTER 15

Internet Message Access Protocol (IMAP)

The Internet Message Access Protocol (IMAP) appears to be similar to the POP protocol discussed in Chapter 14.

Furthermore, if you read the first sections of Chapter 13, which provide you a complete picture of how e-mail moves via the Internet, you'll notice that the two protocols serve the same purpose: POP and IMAP are two methods for connecting a laptop or desktop computer to a remote Internet server in order to view and manipulate e-mail.

That's where the similarity ends. Unlike POP, which only allows users to download new messages to their computers, the IMAP protocol has so many features that many users sort and archive their e-mail on the server permanently, keeping it secure from a laptop or desktop hard drive catastrophe.

IMAP has various advantages over POP, including:

- Mail can be organised into multiple folders rather than arriving in a single inbox;

- Flags such as "read," "replied," "seen," and "deleted" are supported for each message.

- Messages may be scanned on theserver for text strings without having to download each one individually.

- A locally stored message can be easily uploaded to one of the remote folders;
- Persistent unique message numbers are maintained, allowing for reliable synchronisation between a local message storage and the messages saved on the server.
- Users can share folders with others or make them read-only.
- Some IMAP servers can display non-mail sources, such as Usenet newsgroups, as e-mail folders.
- An IMAP client can selectively download a portion of a message, such as a specific attachment or just the message headers, without having to wait for the rest of the message to download.

Taken combined, these features indicate that IMAP can perform far more tasks than POP's limited download-and-delete functionality. Many email clients, such as Thunderbird and Outlook, can display IMAP folders and use them in the same way that locally stored folders do. Instead of downloading all of the messages in advance, when a user clicks a message, the e-mail reader downloads it from the IMAP server and displays it; the reader can also set the message's "read" flag at the same time.

THE IMAP PROTOCOL
Purpose: Read, arrange, and delete E-mail from E-mail folders

Standard: RFC 3501 (2003)

Runs atop: TCP/IP

Default port: 143 (cleartext), 993 (SSL)

Library: imaplib, IMAPClient

Exceptions: socket.error, socket.gaierror, IMAP4.error,

IMAP4.abort, IMAP4.readonly

IMAP clients can synchronise with an IMAP server as well. An IMAP folder may be downloaded to a laptop by someone prepared to go on a business trip. The user's e-mail programme would then record these actions if e-mail was viewed, deleted, or replied to while on the road. When the laptop reconnects to the network, their e-mail client can mark messages on the server with the same "read" or "replied" marks that they have locally, and it can also delete messages from the server that have already been erased locally, so the user does not see them again.

As a result, one of IMAP's main advantages over POP is that users may access the same e-mail from all of their laptop and desktop computers in the same state. POP users can only see the same e-mail multiple times (if they tell their e-mail clients to leave e-mail on the server), or each message will be downloaded only once to the machine on which they happen to read it (if the e-mail clients delete the mail), resulting in their e-mail being scattered across all of the machines from which they check it. IMAP users are not faced with this problem.

Of course, IMAP may be used in the same way that POP can—to download mail, store it locally, and so on. For those who don't want or need the sophisticated features, you can delete the messages from the server right away.

The IMAP protocol is available in various different versions. IMAP4rev1 is the most recent and, by far, the most popular. In reality, the term "IMAP" has become synonymous with IMAP4rev1 in recent years. All IMAP servers are assumed to be IMAP4rev1 servers in this chapter. Some of the capabilities covered in this chapter may not be supported by very old IMAP servers, which are quite uncommon.

At the following links, you may get a decent how-to guide on writing an IMAP client:

www.dovecot.org/imap-client-coding-howto.html

www.imapwiki.org/ClientImplementation

If you're doing anything more than writing a small, single-purpose client to summarise your inbox or automatically download attachments, you should thoroughly read the information at the preceding resources—or read a book on IMAP if you want a more comprehensive reference—so that you can correctly handle all of the situations you might encounter with different servers and their implementations of IMAP.

Structure:

- IMAP in Python: An Overview
- IMAPClient
- Folder Inspection
- UIDs vs. Message Numbers
- Message Intervals
- Information in Brief
- Obtaining a Complete Mailbox
- Individual Message Downloading
- Messages Can Be Flagged and Deleted
- Messages Can Be Deleted
- Searching

- Folders and Messages Manipulation
- Asynchrony
- Conclusion

Objectives:

This chapter will only cover the fundamentals, with an emphasis on how to connect from Python.

IMAP in Python: An Overview

IMAP client interface imaplib is included in the Python Standard Library and provides rudimentary access to the protocol. Unfortunately, it is limited to understanding how to send requests and receive responses from them. It makes no attempt to implement the IMAP specification's explicit requirements for parsing the returned data. Take a look at Listing 15-1 to see how the values given by imaplib are usually too raw to be helpful in a programme. It's a simple script that connects to an IMAP account with imaplib, lists the "capabilities" advertised by the server, then displays the status code and data returned by the LIST command.

Listing 15-1. IMAP Connection and Folder Listing

```python3
#!/usr/bin/env python3
# Programming in Python: The Basics.
# Opening an IMAP connection with the pitiful Python Standard Library
import getpass, imaplib, sys
def main():
    if len(sys.argv) != 3:
        print('usage: %s hostname username' % sys.argv[0])
        sys.exit(2)
    hostname, username = sys.argv[1:]
    m = imaplib.IMAP4_SSL(hostname)
    m.login(username, getpass.getpass())
    try:
        print('Capabilities:', m.capabilities)
        print('Listing mailboxes ')
        status, data = m.list()
```

```
            print('Status:', repr(status))
            print('Data:')
            for datum in data:
                    print(repr(datum))
        finally:
                m.logout()
if __name__ == '__main__':
        main()
```

When you execute this script with the correct arguments, it will prompt you for your password; IMAP authentication is nearly always done with a username and password:

open imaplib.py $ python imap.example.com bpbonline@example.com
Password:

If your password is accurate, it will display a response similar to the results in Listing 15-2. You'll notice the "capabilities" section first, which shows the IMAP features that this server supports. And, I must confess, the list's format is extremely Pythonic: Whatever shape the list took on the wire has been transformed into a lovely tuple of strings.

Listing 15-2. The following is an example of the previous listing's output.

```
Capabilities: ('IMAP4REV1', 'UNSELECT', 'IDLE', 'NAMESPACE', 'QUOTA',
 'XLIST', 'CHILDREN', 'XYZZY', 'SASL-IR', 'AUTH=XOAUTH')
Listing mailboxes
Status: 'OK'
Data:
b'(\\HasNoChildren) "/" "INBOX"'
b'(\\HasNoChildren) "/" "Personal"'
b'(\\HasNoChildren) "/" "Receipts"'
b'(\\HasNoChildren) "/" "Travel"'
b'(\\HasNoChildren) "/" "Work"'
b'(\\Noselect \\HasChildren) "/" "[Gmail]"'
b'(\\HasChildren \\HasNoChildren) "/" "[Gmail]/All Mail"'
b'(\\HasNoChildren) "/" "[Gmail]/Drafts"'
```

b'(\\HasChildren \\HasNoChildren) "/" "[Gmail]/Sent Mail"'

b'(\\HasNoChildren) "/" "[Gmail]/Spam"'

b'(\\HasNoChildren) "/" "[Gmail]/Starred"'

b'(\\HasChildren \\HasNoChildren) "/" "[Gmail]/Trash"'

When it comes to the list() method's output, though, everything start to fall apart. First, the status code will be returned as the plain string 'OK,' so code that uses imaplib will have to constantly check if the code is 'OK,' or whether it indicates an error. This isn't really Pythonic, because Python programmes may normally run without error checking, safe in the knowledge that if something goes wrong, an exception will be fired.

Second, imaplib offers no assistance in deciphering the results! This IMAP account's list of e-mail folders employs a variety of protocol-specific quoting: Each item in the list refers to the flags that have been placed on each folder. The character used to separate folders and subfolders (in this case, the slash character) is then specified, followed by the folder's quoted name. However, all of this is transformed back into raw data, forcing you to decipher strings like the ones below:

"/" "[Gmail]/Sent Mail" (\HasChildren\HasNoChildren)

Third, the result is a jumble of distinct sequences: the flags are still uninterpreted byte strings, but each delimiter and folder name has been converted to an actual Unicode string.

You'll need a more sophisticated IMAP client library unless you wish to implement various elements of the protocol yourself.

IMAPClient

Fortunately, there is a popular and well-tested IMAP library for Python that can be easily installed through the Python Package Index. The IMAPClient package was written by Menno Smits, a friendly Python programmer, and it makes use of the Python Standard Library imaplib behind the scenes.

Install IMAPClient in a "virtualenv," as stated in Chapter 1, to get a feel for it. Once installed, you may run the programme using the python interpreter in the virtual environment, as illustrated in Listing 15-3.

Listing 15-3. With IMAPClient, you may list IMAP folders.

```
#!/usr/bin/env python3
# Programming in Python: The Basics.
```

```python
# Opening an IMAP connection with the powerful IMAPClient
import getpass, sys
from imapclient import IMAPClient
def main():
        if len(sys.argv) != 3:
                print('usage: %s hostname username' % sys.argv[0])
                sys.exit(2)


        hostname, username = sys.argv[1:]
        c = IMAPClient(hostname, ssl=True)
        try:
                c.login(username, getpass.getpass())
        except c.Error as e:
                print('Could not log in:', e)
        else:
                print('Capabilities:', c.capabilities())
                print('Listing mailboxes:')
                data = c.list_folders()
                for flags, delimiter, folder_name in data:
                        print(' %-30s%s %s' % (' '.join(flags), delimiter,
                        folder_name))
        finally:
                c.logout()
if __name__ == '__main__':
 main()
```

More specifics of the protocol exchange are now being handled on your behalf, as you can see from the code. For example, instead of receiving a status code that you must check every time you run a command, the library now does the check for you and raises an exception to stop you in your tracks if something goes wrong. A interaction between Python and an IMAP server is shown in Figure 15-1.

Second, each result from the LIST command—which is available in our library as the list folders() method rather than the list() method provided by imaplib—has already been parsed into Python data types. Each line of data is returned as a tuple, containing the folder flags, folder name delimiter, and folder name, with the flags themselves being a string sequence.

Take a look at Listing 15-4 to see what this second script produces.

Listing 15-4. Flags and Folder Names That Are Correctly Parsed

```
Capabilities: ('IMAP4REV1', 'UNSELECT', 'IDLE', 'NAMESPACE', 'QUOTA',
'XLIST', 'CHILDREN', 'XYZZY',

'SASL-IR', 'AUTH=XOAUTH')

Listing mailboxes:

 \HasNoChildren / INBOX

 \HasNoChildren / Personal

 \HasNoChildren / Receipts

 \HasNoChildren / Travel

 \HasNoChildren / Work

 \Noselect \HasChildren / [Gmail]

 \HasChildren \HasNoChildren / [Gmail]/All Mail

 \HasNoChildren / [Gmail]/Drafts

 \HasChildren \HasNoChildren / [Gmail]/Sent Mail

 \HasNoChildren / [Gmail]/Spam

 \HasNoChildren / [Gmail]/Starred

 \HasChildren \HasNoChildren / [Gmail]/Trash
```

Each folder's standard flags may include one or more of the following:

- **Noinferiors**: This indicates that the folder contains no subfolders and will not be able to contain subfolders in the future. If you try to create a subfolder within this folder with your IMAP client, you'll get an error.

- **Noselect:** This indicates that select folder() cannot be used on this folder; in other words, this folder does not and cannot contain any messages. (One hypothesis is that it exists solely to allow subfolders beneath it.)

- **Marked:** This indicates that the server thinks this box is noteworthy in some way. This usually means that new messages have been delivered since the folder was last selected. However, the absence of Marked does not rule out the possibility of new messages in the folder; some servers simply do not support Marked.

- **Unmarked:** This ensures that the folder is free of fresh communications.

Additional flags not covered by the standard are returned by some servers. Those additional flags must be accepted and ignored by your code.

Folder Inspection

You must first "choose" a folder to look at before you may download, search, or alter any messages. This means that the IMAP protocol is stateful: it remembers which folder you're looking at right now, and its instructions work on that folder without requiring you to repeat its name. Only after you disconnect and rejoin will you be able to start over with a clean slate. This can make interaction more pleasant, but it also means that your software must keep track of which folder is selected at all times, otherwise it may end up doing anything to the wrong folder. When you pick a folder, you're telling the IMAP server that all subsequent instructions will apply to that folder until you change folders or exit the current one.

By specifying the readonly=True argument, you can pick the folder in "read-only" mode rather than full read/write mode when selecting. If you attempt any procedures that will delete or edit messages, you will receive an error message. The fact that you are only reading can be used by the server to optimise access to the folder, in addition to preventing you from making any mistakes when you wish to keep all of the messages intact.

(For example, while you have it chosen, it may read-lock but not write-lock the real folder storage on disc.)

UIDs vs. Message Numbers

IMAP allows you to refer to a specific message within a folder using one of two methods: a temporary message number (usually 1, 2, 3, and so on) or a unique identifier (UID). The difference between the two is that one is more persistent than the other. When you select a folder over a certain connection, message numbers are assigned. This means they can be attractive and sequential, but it also implies that a given message's number may change if you return to the same folder later. This behaviour (which is the same as POP) is fine for programmes like live e-mail readers or basic download scripts; you won't mind if the numbers change the next time you connect. A UID, on the other hand, is designed to stay the same even if you disconnect from the server and do not reconnect. If a message has the UID 1053 today, it will have the same UID tomorrow, and no other messages in that folder will ever have the UID 1053. This behaviour is quite beneficial if you're creating a synchronisation tool!

It will allow you to verify that actions are being conducted in accordance with the proper message with 100 percent certainty. This is one of the reasons why IMAP is so much more enjoyable to use than POP.

It's worth noting that if you return to an IMAP account and the user has changed their password without telling you, If you delete a folder and then create a new one with the same name, your software may think it's the same folder, but the UID numbers are incompatible and no longer agree. If you don't notice a folder rename, you can lose track of which messages in your IMAP account correspond to which messages you've already downloaded.

But it turns out that IMAP is prepared to protect you from this, and (as I'll describe later) includes a UIDVALIDITY folder characteristic that you can use to compare UIDs in the folder from one session to the next to determine if they match the UIDs that the same messages had when you last connected. Message numbers or UIDs can be used in most IMAP procedures that operate with specific messages. IMAPClient normally utilises UIDs and ignores the IMAP-assigned temporary message numbers. If you wish to see the temporary numbers instead, just provide the use uid=False option when instantiating IMAPClient, or set the use uid attribute of the class to False and True on the fly during your IMAP session.

Message Intervals

The majority of IMAP commands that deal with messages can handle one or more messages. If you need to process a large number of messages, this can save you a lot of time. You can operate on a group of messages as a whole instead of providing separate commands and obtaining separate answers for each individual message. Because you don't have to deal with a network roundtrip for each command, this is frequently faster.

Instead of providing a message number, you can provide a comma-separated list of message numbers. You can also use a colon to separate the start and end message numbers if you want all messages whose numbers are in a range but don't want to list all of their numbers (or if you don't know their numbers—for example, "everything starting with message one" without having to fetch their numbers first). "And all of the rest of the communications," an asterisk denotes. The following is an example of a specification:

2,4:6,20:

* It refers to "message 2," "messages 4 through 6," and "message 20 through the mail folder's conclusion."

Information in Brief

When you initially select a folder, the IMAP server displays some summary information about it, including information about the folder and its messages.

IMAPClient returns the summary as a dictionary. When you call select folder() on most IMAP servers, you'll get the following keys:

- **EXISTS:** An integer indicating how many messages are in the folder.
- **FLAGS:** This section contains a list of the flags that can be applied to messages in this folder.
- **RECENT:** Specifies the server's estimate of the number of messages that have appeared in the folder since an IMAP client called select folder() on it the last time.
- **PERMANENTFLAGS**: This property specifies a list of custom flags that can be put on messages; it is generally empty.
- **UIDNEXT:** the server's best prediction for the UID allocated to the next incoming (or uploaded) message.
- **UIDVALIDITY:** A string that clients can use to confirm that the UID numbering hasn't changed. If you return to a folder and this value is different from the last time you connected, the UID number has reset and your previously stored UID values are no longer valid.
- **UNSEEN:** The message number of the folder's first unseen message (the one without the Seen flag).

Servers are only needed to return FLAGS, EXISTS, and RECENT of these flags, though most will provide UIDVALIDITY as well. A sample programme that reads and displays the summary information from my INBOX e-mail folder is shown in Listing 15-5.

Listing 15-5. Information from a Folder's Summary

```
#!/usr/bin/env python3

# Programming in Python: The Basics.

# Opening an IMAP connection with IMAPClient and listing folder
information.
```

```
import getpass, sys
from imapclient import IMAPClient
def main():
        if len(sys.argv) != 4:
                print('usage: %s hostname username foldername' % sys.
                argv[0])
                sys.exit(2)
        hostname, username, foldername = sys.argv[1:]
        c = IMAPClient(hostname, ssl=True)
        try:
                c.login(username, getpass.getpass())
        except c.Error as e:
                print('Could not log in:', e)
        else:
                select_dict = c.select_folder(foldername, readonly=True)
                for k, v in sorted(select_dict.items()):
                print('%s: %r' % (k, v))
        finally:
                c.logout()
if __name__ == '__main__':
        main()
```

When run, this program displays results such as this:

```
$ ./folder_info.py imap.example.com bpbonline@example.com
Password:
EXISTS: 3
PERMANENTFLAGS: ('\\Answered', '\\Flagged', '\\Draft', '\\Deleted',
 '\\Seen', '\\*')
READ-WRITE: True
UIDNEXT: 2626
FLAGS: ('\\Answered', '\\Flagged', '\\Draft', '\\Deleted', '\\Seen')
UIDVALIDITY: 1
RECENT: 0
```

This reveals that I have three mails in my INBOX folder, none of which have arrived since my last check. Remember to compare the UIDVALIDITY to a stored value from a prior session if your software wants to use UIDs it saved from earlier sessions.

Obtaining a Complete Mailbox

To download mail with IMAP, utilise the FETCH command, which an IMAPClient exposes via its fetch() method.

The most straightforward method is to download all messages at once in one huge mouthful. Although this is the simplest and uses the least amount of network bandwidth (since you don't have to give and receive many orders), numerous responses), it does mean that your application will have to store all of the returned messages in memory simultaneously. investigates them This is clearly not viable for very large mailboxes with a lot of attachments in their messages!

Listing 15-6 uses a Python data structure to download all of the messages from the INBOX folder into your computer's memory. After that, it shows a bit of summary information for each one.

Listing 15-6. All Messages in a Folder are Downloaded

```
#!/usr/bin/env python3
# Programming in Python: The Basics.
# Opening an IMAP connection with IMAPClient and retrieving mailbox
messages.
import email, getpass, sys
from imapclient import IMAPClient
def main():
    if len(sys.argv) != 4:
        print('usage: %s hostname username foldername' % sys.
        argv[0])
        sys.exit(2)
    hostname, username, foldername = sys.argv[1:]
    c = IMAPClient(hostname, ssl=True)
    try:
        c.login(username, getpass.getpass())
    except c.Error as e:
        print('Could not log in:', e)
```

```
        else:
                print_summary(c, foldername)
        finally:
                c.logout()
def print_summary(c, foldername):
        c.select_folder(foldername, readonly=True)
        msgdict = c.fetch('1:*', ['BODY.PEEK[]'])
        for message_id, message in list(msgdict.items()):
                e = email.message_from_string(message['BODY[]'])
                print(message_id, e['From'])
                payload = e.get_payload()
                if isinstance(payload, list):
                part_content_types = [ part.get_content_type() for part
                in payload ]
                print(' Parts:', ' '.join(part_content_types))
        else:
                print(' ', ' '.join(payload[:60].split()), '...')
if __name__ == '__main__':
 main()
```

Remember that IMAP is stateful: you must first use select folder() to position yourself "within" the provided folder before using fetch() to request message content. (If you wish to leave and not be within a certain folder any longer, call close folder() later.) Because message IDs, whether temporary or UIDs, are always positive integers, the range '1:*' indicates "the first message to the end of the mail folder."

The strange-looking string 'BODY.PEEK[]' is used to ask IMAP for the message's "full body." The string 'BODY[]' implies "the entire message"; as you'll see, you can also ask for select parts of a message inside the square brackets. PEEK indicates that you are only looking inside the message to generate a summary, and that you do not want the server to automatically put the Seen flag on all of these messages for you, causing the server's memory of which messages the user has read to be ruined. (I didn't want to label all of your messages as read, so this seemed like a wonderful feature for me to add to a small script like this that you might run against a real mailbox!)

The dictionary that is returned maps message UIDs to dictionaries with message information. You look in each message dictionary for the 'BODY[]' entry that IMAP has filled in with the information about the message for which you asked: its whole text, returned as a big string, as you cycle through its keys and values.

The script asks Python to grab the From: line and a portion of the message's content and output them to the screen as a summary, using the email module that I covered in Chapter 12. If you wanted to adapt this script to save the messages in a file or database instead, you could just skip the email parsing phase and treat the message body as a single string to be stored and parsed later.

The following are the outcomes of this script:

```
$ ./mailbox_summary.py imap.example.com john INBOX
Password:
2592 "Amazon.com" <order-update@amazon.com>
 Dear john, Portable Power Systems, Inc. shipped the follo ...
2470 Meetup Reminder <info@meetup.com>
 Parts: text/plain text/html
2472 billing@linode.com
 Thank you. Please note that charges will appear as "Linode.c ...
```

Of course, if the messages contained enormous attachments, downloading them in their whole merely to print a summary may be disastrous; nonetheless, given this is the simplest message-fetching function, I though it would be a good place to start!

Individual Message Downloading

E-mail messages, like e-mail folders, can be fairly large—many e-mail systems allow users to have hundreds or thousands of messages, each of which can be 10MB or larger. If the contents of that mailbox are all downloaded at once, as in the previous example, the client machine's RAM will quickly be exhausted.

IMAP offers numerous operations in addition to the standard "get the complete message" command covered in the preceding section to enable network-based e-mail clients that don't wish to store local copies of every message.

- The headers of an e-mail can be retrieved separately from the message as a block of text.
- Specific headers from a message can be requested and returned without having to download the entire message.

- The server can be instructed to recursively examine and return an outline of a message's MIME structure, as well as the text of specific sections of the message.

This enables IMAP clients to do very efficient queries, downloading only the data they need to present to the user, reducing the burden on the IMAP server and network and allowing results to be displayed to the user more rapidly.

Examine Listing 15-7, which combines a variety of notions about accessing an IMAP account to show how a simple IMAP client works. At this stage in the chapter, this should provide more context than if these characteristics were spread out among a half-dozen shorter programme listings! The client is made up of three circular loops that each receive input from users when they examine a list of e-mail folders, then a list of messages within a given e-mail folder, and finally the sections of a specific message.

Listing 15-7. IMAP Client (Simple)

```python
#!/usr/bin/env python3
# Programming in Python: The Basics.
# Letting a user browse folders, messages, and message parts.
import getpass, sys
from imapclient import IMAPClient
banner = '-' * 72
def main():
        if len(sys.argv) != 3:
            print('usage: %s hostname username' % sys.argv[0])
            sys.exit(2)
        hostname, username = sys.argv[1:]
        c = IMAPClient(hostname, ssl=True)
        try:
            c.login(username, getpass.getpass())
        except c.Error as e:
            print('Could not log in:', e)
        else:
            explore_account(c)
        finally:
```

```
                    c.logout()
def explore_account(c):
        """"Display the folders in this IMAP account and let the user
        choose one."""
        while True:
                print()
                folderflags = {}
                data = c.list_folders()
                for flags, delimiter, name in data:
                        folderflags[name] = flags
                for name in sorted(folderflags.keys()):
                        print('%-30s %s' % (name, '
                        '.join(folderflags[name])))
                print()
                reply = input('Type a folder name, or "q" to quit:
                ').strip()
                if reply.lower().startswith('q'):
                        break
                if reply in folderflags:
                        explore_folder(c, reply)
                else:
                print('Error: no folder named', repr(reply))
def explore_folder(c, name):
        """"List the messages in folder `name` and let the user
        choose one."""
        while True:
                c.select_folder(name, readonly=True)
                msgdict = c.fetch('1:*', ['BODY.PEEK[HEADER.
                FIELDS (FROM SUBJECT)]',
        'FLAGS', 'INTERNALDATE', 'RFC822.SIZE'])
                print()
                for uid in sorted(msgdict):
                        items = msgdict[uid]
```

```
                    print('%6d %20s %6d bytes %s' % (
                    uid, items['INTERNALDATE'], items['RFC822.SIZE'],
                    ' '.join(items['FLAGS']))))
                    for i in items['BODY[HEADER.FIELDS (FROM
                    SUBJECT)]'].splitlines():
                    print(' ' * 6, i.strip())
            reply = input('Folder %s - type a message UID, or "q"
            to quit: '
                    % name).strip()
            if reply.lower().startswith('q'):
            break
            try:
                    reply = int(reply)
        except ValueError:
            print('Please type an integer or "q" to quit')
                        else:
        if reply in msgdict:
            explore_message(c, reply)
            c.close_folder()
def explore_message(c, uid):
        """Let the user view various parts of a given message."""
        msgdict = c.fetch(uid, ['BODYSTRUCTURE', 'FLAGS'])
        while True:
            print()
            print('Flags:', end=' ')
            flaglist = msgdict[uid]['FLAGS']
            if flaglist:
                    print(' '.join(flaglist))
            else:
                    print('none')
            print('Structure:')
            display_structure(msgdict[uid]['BODYSTRUCTURE'])
```

```
        print()
        reply = input('Message %s - type a part name, or "q" to
        quit: '
                % uid).strip()
        print()
        if reply.lower().startswith('q'):
            break
        key = 'BODY[%s]' % reply
        try:
                msgdict2 = c.fetch(uid, [key])
        except c._imap.error:
                print('Error - cannot fetch section %r' % reply)
        else:
                content = msgdict2[uid][key]
        if content:
                print(banner)
                print(content.strip())
                print(banner)
        else:
                print('(No such section)')
def display_structure(structure, parentparts=[]):
    """Attractively display a given message structure."""
    # The whole body of the message is named 'TEXT'.
    if parentparts:
        name = '.'.join(parentparts)
    else:
        print(' HEADER')
        name = 'TEXT'
    # Print a simple, non-multipart MIME part. Include its disposition,
        # if available.
    is_multipart = not isinstance(structure[0], str)
    if not is_multipart:
```

```
                parttype = ('%s/%s' % structure[:2]).lower()
                print(' %-9s' % name, parttype, end=' ')
                if structure[6]:
                        print('size=%s' % structure[6], end=' ')
                if structure[9]:
                        print('disposition=%s' % structure[9][0],
                        ' '.join('{}={}'.format(k, v) for k, v in
                        structure[9][1:]),
                        end=' ')
            print()
            return
        # For a multipart part, print all of its subordinate parts.
        parttype = 'multipart/%s' % structure[1].lower()
        print(' %-9s' % name, parttype, end=' ')
        print()
        subparts = structure[0]
        for i in range(len(subparts)):
                display_structure(subparts[i], parentparts + [ str(i + 1) ])
if __name__ == '__main__':
 main()
```

The outer function, like other of the programme listings previously covered, uses a simple list folders() call to present the users with a list of e-mail folders. The IMAP flags for each folder are also shown. This allows the software to provide users a choice of folders:

INBOX   **\HasNoChildren**

Receipts   **\HasNoChildren**

Travel   **\HasNoChildren**

Work   **\HasNoChildren**

Type a folder name, or "q" to quit:

Things get more interesting after a user selects a folder: each message must have a summary printed. Different e-mail clients make different decisions about how much information about each message in a folder should be displayed. In Listing 15-7, the code selects a few header fields, as well as the message's date and size. It's worth noting that the word BODY is used with caution. Because the IMAP server would otherwise mark the messages as \Seen just because they were displayed in a summary, you should use PEEK instead than BODY to retrieve these items. Once an e-mail folder has been selected, the results of this retrieve() call are printed to the screen:

```
2704 2019-10-28 21:32:13 19129 bytes \Seen

 From: John Jebaraj

 Subject: Digested Articles

2705 2019-10-28 23:03:45 15354 bytes

 Subject: Re: [venv] Building a virtual environment for offline testing

 From: "W. Angel Trader"

2706 2019-10-28 08:11:38 10694 bytes

 Subject: Re: [venv] Building a virtual environment for offline testing

 From: Esther Lopes Tavares

Folder INBOX - type a message UID, or "q" to quit:
```

As you can see, the ability to pass several items of interest to the IMAP fetch() function allows you to construct very complicated message summaries with just one roundtrip to the server! Once the user has chosen a message, fetch() is called to retrieve the BODYSTRUCTURE of the message, which is the key to seeing a MIME message's sections without having to download the complete text. BODYSTRUCTURE just lists its MIME sections as a recursive data structure, rather than requiring you to download many megabytes over the network to list a large message's attachments.

A tuple of simple MIME components is returned:

```
('TEXT', 'PLAIN', ('CHARSET', 'US-ASCII'), None, None, '7BIT', 2280, 46)
```

The following are the elements of this tuple, as detailed in section 7.4.2 of RFC 3501 (beginning with item index zero, of course):

1. Type of MIME
2. Subtype of MIME
3. Body parameters, provided as a tuple (name, value, name, value,...), with the name of each parameter followed by its value.
4. Content Identifier
5. Description of the content

6. Encoding of content

7. Byte size of the content

This offers the content length in lines for textual MIME types.

When the IMAP server detects that a message is multipart, or when it checks one of the sections of the message that it discovers is multipart (for more information on how MIME messages can nest other MIME messages inside them, see Chapter 12), it sends the message to the recipient. The tuple it gives will start with a list of substructures, each of which is a tuple with the same layout as the outer structure. It will then conclude with some information about the multipart container that connected those sections:

```
([(...), (...)], "MIXED", ('BOUNDARY', '=-=-='), None, None)
```

The parameter "MIXED" specifies the type of multipart container being represented—in this case, multipart/mixed is the whole type. Aside from "MIXED," other popular "multipart" subtypes include "ALTERNATIVE," "DIGEST," and "PARALLEL." The other items beyond the multipart type are optional, but if present, they offer a series of name-value parameters (in this case, specifying the MIME multipart boundary string), the multipart's disposition, language, and location (typically given by a URL).

Given these rules, a recursive method like display structure() in Listing 15-7 is ideal for unwinding and presenting a message's hierarchy of parts.

When the IMAP server provides a BODYSTRUCTURE, the procedure gets to work and prints something that looks like this for the user to examine:

```
Folder INBOX - type a message UID, or "q" to quit: 2701
Flags: \Seen
HEADER
TEXT multipart/mixed
1 multipart/alternative
1.1 text/plain size=253
1.2 text/html size=508
2 application/octet-stream size=5448 ATTACHMENT FILENAME='test.py'
Message 2701 - type a part name, or "q" to quit:
```

You can see that the message's structure is typical of current e-mail, with a sophisticated rich-text HTML component for users who see it in a browser or modern e-mail client, and a plain-text version of the same message for those who use more traditional devices or apps. It also includes a file attachment with a suggested file name in case the user want to save it to their local file system. For simplicity and safety, this sample software does not attempt to store anything to the hard disc; instead, the user can select any part of the message—for example, the special sections HEADER and TEXT, or one of the specified parts like 1.1—and its content will be printed to the screen. All of this is supported simply by calls to the IMAP fetch() method, as you can see from the programme listing. HEADER and 1.1 are simply more options for what you can specify when calling get(), and they can be used alongside other values like BODY.PEEK and FLAGS. The only distinction is that the latter values apply to all messages, whereas a part name like 2.1.3 would only exist in multipart messages with that designation in their structure.

One quirk you'll notice is that the IMAP protocol doesn't really provide you any of the multipart names that a message allows! Instead, you must count the number of components specified in the BODYSTRUCTURE, beginning with index 1, to decide which part number to request. The display structure() code does this counting using a simple loop, as you can see.

Finally, the get() command not only allows you to pull only the bits of a message that you require at any given time, but it also truncates them if they are quite long and you only want to show an excerpt from the beginning to entice the user! To utilise this functionality, place a slice in angle brackets after any component name to specify the range of characters you want—it works similarly to Python's slice operation:

```
BODY[]<0.100>
```

From offset zero to offset one hundred, this would return the first 100 bytes of the message body. This allows you to examine both the text and the beginning of an attachment to learn more about its contents before allowing the user to pick or download it.

Messages Can Be Flagged and Deleted

While working with Listing 15-7 or viewing the example output, you may have observed that IMAP assigns flags to messages, which often take the form of a backslash-prefixed word, such as Seen as seen for one of the messages just mentioned. Several of these are standard, as stated in RFC 3501 for usage by all IMAP servers. The most essential ones are as follows:

- **\Answered:** The message has been answered to by the user.
- **\Draft:** The user hasn't completed the message yet.
- **\flagged**

The message has been flagged for some reason; the purpose and significance of this flag varies depending on the e-mail reader.

- **\Recent:** This message has never been viewed previously by any IMAP client. This flag is distinct in that it cannot be added or removed using standard commands; instead, it is automatically removed once the mailbox has been selected.

- **\Seen:** The message has been received and read.

As you can see, these flags roughly match to the information that many e-mail readers provide visually about each message. Although the language varies (several clients refer to messages as "new" rather than "not seen"), practically all e-mail readers show these signals. Other flags may be supported by specific servers, and the code for those flags will not always begin with a backslash. Furthermore, because not all servers reliably implement the Recent flag, general-purpose IMAP clients can only use it as a hint.

There are numerous methods for working with flags in the IMAPClient library. The most basic obtains the flags like if you had asked fetch() for 'FLAGS,' but it also removes the dictionary around each answer:

```
>>> c.get_flags(2703)
```

```
{2703: ('\\Seen',)}
```

There are also calls to add and remove flags from a message:

```
c.remove_flags(2703, ['\\Seen'])
```

```
c.add_flags(2703, ['\\Answered'])
```

You can use set flags() to replace the entire list of message flags with a new one if you wish to totally modify the set of flags for a given message without working out the necessary chain of adds and removes:

```
c.set_flags(2703, ['\\Seen', '\\Answered'])
```

Instead of the single UID illustrated in these examples, any of these functions can take a list of message UIDs.

Messages Can Be Deleted

The way IMAP handles message deletion is another intriguing usage of flags. For safety, the process is split into two steps: first, the client flags one or more messages with the Delete flag, and then it runs purge() to perform all of the pending deletion requests in one go.

The IMAPClient library, on the other hand, does not require you to do this manually (though it may be done); instead, it hides the dialogue box. the fact that flags are used behind a simple delete messages() method that designates messages for you It must still be done. If you genuinely want the operation to take effect, you must use purge() after it:

```
c.delete_messages([2703, 2704])
```

```
c.expunge()
```

Another reason to use UIDs instead of temporary IDs is that purge() will reorganise the temporary IDs of the messages in the mailbox.

Searching

Another crucial feature for a protocol meant to retain all of your e-mail on the e-mail server is searching: without searching, an e-mail client would have to download all of a user's e-mail the first time they wished to run a full-text search to discover an e-mail message. The basis of search is simple: you use the search() function on an IMAP client instance, and you get the UIDs of the messages that match your criteria (assuming, of course, that you accept the IMAPClient default of use uid=True for your client):

```
>>> c.select_folder('INBOX')
```

```
>>> c.search('SINCE 13-Jul-2013 TEXT Apress')
```

```
[2590L, 2652L, 2653L, 2654L, 2655L, 2699L]
```

These UIDs can then be used in the fetch() command to get the information you need about each message in order to give the user a summary of the search results.

The query shown in the preceding example combines two criteria: one requesting recent messages (those received since July 13, 2013, the date on which I am typing this) and the other requesting that the message text contain the word Apress somewhere inside, and the results will include only messages that satisfy both criteria—that is, messages that satisfy both criteria after concatenating two criteria with a space. If you needed messages that met at least one of the criteria but not both, you could use this method.

```
OR (SINCE 20-Aug-2010) (TEXT BPBONLINE)
```

There are numerous criteria that can be combined to create a query. They are defined in RFC 3501, much like the rest of IMAP. Some requirements are straightforward, referring to binary properties such as flag:

```
ALL: Every message in the mailbox

UID (id, ...): Messages with the given UIDs

LARGER n: Messages more than n octets in length

SMALLER m: Messages less than m octets in length

ANSWERED: Have the flag \Answered

DELETED: Have the flag \Deleted

DRAFT: Have the flag \Draft

FLAGGED: Have the flag \Flagged

KEYWORD flag: Have the given keyword flag set

NEW: Have the flag \Recent

OLD: Lack the flag \Recent

UNANSWERED: Lack the flag \Answered

UNDELETED: Lack the flag \Deleted

UNDRAFT: Lack the flag \Draft

UNFLAGGED: Lack the flag \Flagged

UNKEYWORD flag: Lack the given keyword flag

UNSEEN: Lack the flag \Seen
```

There are also a number of flags that correspond to things in the headers of each message. Except for the "send" tests, which look at the Date header, each of them looks for a specific string in the same-named header:

```
BCC string

CC string

FROM string

HEADER name string

SUBJECT string

TO string
```

An IMAP message includes two dates: the send date, which is the internal Date header supplied by the sender, and the date it actually arrived at the IMAP server.

(The former is obviously a fabrication, whereas the latter is as trustworthy as the IMAP server and its clock.) So, depending on the date you wish to query, there are two sets of criteria for dates:

`BEFORE 01-Jan-1970`

`ON 01-Jan-1970`

`SINCE 01-Jan-1970`

`SENTBEFORE 01-Jan-1970`

`SENTON 01-Jan-1970`

`SENTSINCE 01-Jan-1970`

Finally, there are two search operations that refer to the message's text—these are the workhorses that provide full-text searches like the ones your users are likely to expect when typing into an e-mail client's search field:

`BODY string: The message body must contain the string. TEXT string: The entire message, either body or header, must contain the string somewhere.`

Check the documentation for the IMAP server you're using to see if it supports "near miss" matches like those supported by modern search engines, or if it only returns exact matches for the phrases you provide. If your strings contain any special characters, try enclosing them in double quotes and then backslash quoting any double quotes within the strings:

```
>>> c.search(r'TEXT "Quoth the raven, \"Nevermore.\""')
[2652L]
```

I avoided needing to double up the backslashes to get single backslashes across to IMAP by using a raw Python r'...' string here.

Folders and Messages Manipulation

In IMAP, creating or removing folders is as simple as supplying the folder's name:

```
c.create_folder('Personal')
```

```
c.delete_folder('Work')
```

Some IMAP servers or setups may not allow these activities, or they may have naming restrictions; make sure to call them with error checking in place. Aside from the "standard" method of waiting for people to send you new e-mail messages, you have two options for creating new e-mail messages in your IMAP account. To begin, copy an existing message from its original folder to a new folder. To visit the folder where the messages are stored, use select folder(), and then run the copy method as follows:

```
c.select_folder('INBOX')
```

```
c.copy([2653L, 2654L], 'TODO')
```

Finally, IMAP allows you to add a message to your mailbox. You don't need to use SMTP to transmit the message; all you need is IMAP. Adding a message is a straightforward process, but there are a few things to keep in mind. Line endings are the most important consideration. To identify the end of a line of text, many Unix machines employ a single ASCII line feed character (0x0a, or 'n' in Python). Two characters are used on Windows machines: CR-LF, which is a manual return (0x0D, or 'r' in Python) followed by a line feed. Only the manual return is used on older Macs. IMAP, like many other Internet protocols (HTTP springs to mind), employs CR-LF ('rn' in Python) to indicate the end of a line. If you upload a message that includes any other character for the end of a line, some IMAP servers will have issues. As a result, when translating uploaded texts, you must always ensure that the line endings are proper. Because most local mailbox formats only utilise 'n' at the end of each line, this problem is more prevalent than you might think.

However, you must be careful how you change the line endings, because some messages may contain 'rn' somewhere inside them despite only using 'n' for the first few dozen lines, and IMAP clients have been known to fail if a message has both different line endings! The answer is straightforward, thanks to Python's splitlines() string method, which recognises all three possible line endings; simply run the function on your message and reunite the lines with the usual line ending.

```
>>> 'one\rtwo\nthree\r\nfour'.splitlines()
```

```
['one', 'two', 'three', 'four']
```

```
>>> '\r\n'.join('one\rtwo\nthree\r\nfour'.splitlines())
```

```
'one\r\ntwo\r\nthree\r\nfour'
```

The actual act of adding a message is arranged by executing the append() method on your IMAP client once you get the line endings correct:

```
c.append('INBOX', my_message)
```

You can also send a normal Python datetime object as a keyword argument, along with a list of flags and a msg time to be used as the message's arrival time.

Asynchrony

Finally, despite the fact that I have described IMAP as if it were a synchronous protocol, it does accommodate clients that want to send dozens of queries over the socket to the server and then receive the responses in whatever order the server can most efficiently gather and respond to the e-mail.

By constantly sending one request, waiting for the response, and then returning that result, the IMAPClient library hides this protocol flexibility. However, other libraries, such Twisted Python's IMAP capabilities, allow you to take advantage of its asynchronicity. The synchronous technique used in this chapter should enough for most Python programmers who need to script mailbox interactions. If you do decide to branch out and use an asynchronous library, you'll already be familiar with all of the IMAP commands from this chapter's explanations, and you'll simply need to learn how to transmit those commands using the asynchronous library's API.

Conclusion

IMAP is a reliable mechanism for retrieving e-mail messages from a remote server. Many Python IMAP libraries exist; imaplib is included in the Python Standard Library, but it requires you to perform all of the low-level response parsing yourself. IMAPClient by Menno Smits, which you can get through the Python Package Index, is a significantly better option.

Your e-mail messages are organised into folders on an IMAP server, some of which are pre-defined by your IMAP provider and others that you can establish yourself. IMAP clients can make folders, delete folders, add new messages to existing folders, and move messages across folders. Messages may be listed and fetched extremely flexibly once a folder has been selected, which is the IMAP equivalent of a "change directory" command on a file system. Instead of downloading every message in its entirety (though that is an option), the client can request specific information from a message, such as a few headers and the message structure, to create a display or summary into which the user can click, bringing message parts and attachments down from the server on demand.

The client can also put flags on each message, some of which are also relevant to the server, and delete messages by setting the Delete flag and then expunging them. Finally, IMAP provides powerful search functionality, allowing users to do typical tasks without having to transfer e-mail data to their local system.

In the following chapter, we'll move on from e-mail and look at a whole different sort of communication: sending shell instructions to a distant server and receiving the results in return.

CHAPTER 16
SSH and Telnet

If you haven't already, make a cup of coffee, sit down, and read Neal Stephenson's article "In the Beginning... Was Command Line" if you haven't before (William Morrow Paperbacks, 1999).

You can also get a copy from his website, www.cryptonomicon.com/beginning. html, in the form of a raw text file (appropriately enough). Fortunately, one of the most important subjects in this book will be the old-fashioned idea of transmitting basic textual commands to another computer for many readers. After you've done utilising a web hosting company's sophisticated control panel to set up your domain names and list of web applications, the command line becomes your primary method of installing and running the code that powers your websites.

SSH connections are almost always used to administer virtual or physical servers from businesses like Rackspace and Linode. If you use an API-based virtual hosting provider like Amazon AWS to create a cloud of dynamically assigned servers, you'll find that Amazon offers you access to your new host by asking for an SSH key and installing it, allowing you to log into your new instance immediately and without a password. It's as though once early computers learned to accept text commands and respond with text output, they reached a height of usefulness that has yet to be surpassed. No amount of pointing, clicking, or dragging with a mouse has ever represented a fraction of what can be said when you type, even in the constrained and demanding language of the Unix shell.

Structure:

- Automation using the command line
- Expansion of the Command Line and Quoting
- Arguments to Unix commands can contain (almost) any character
- Characters I've Quoted for Protection
- Windows' Horrible Command Line
- In a terminal, things are different
- Telnet
- SSH: The Secure Shell
- SSH: A Quick Overview
- Host Keys for SSH
- Authentication with SSH
- Individual Commands and Shell Sessions
- SFTP (SSH File Transfer Protocol)
- Additional Features
- Conclusion

Objectives:

This chapter focuses on the command line. It explains how to connect to it via the network and provides enough information about its regular behaviour to help you get beyond any frustrating issues you might have while trying to utilize it.

Automation using the command line

Before we go into the specifics of how the command line works and how you can access a remote command line over the network, keep in mind that if your aim is to perform remote system administration, you may want to look into other solutions. Here are three paths in which the Python community has taken remote automation, in order of increasing sophistication:

1. Fabric allows you to script actions that are executed over SSH connections to your servers, but it only supports Python 2 at the present (see www.fabfile. org/).

2. Ansible is a simple and powerful tool that allows you to specify how dozens or hundreds of remote machines should be setup. It establishes SSH

connections to each of them and performs any necessary checks or upgrades. Its speed and design have piqued the interest of the Python community as well as the broader system administration community (see http://docs. ansible.com/index.html).

3. Instead of riding on top of SSH, SaltStack requires you to install its own agent on each client system. This allows the master to push new information to remote machines much faster than hundreds or thousands of concurrent SSH connections would allow. In exchange, it is lightning fast, even for massive installations and clusters (see www.saltstack.com/).

Finally, I'd want to bring up pexpect. While it is technically not a network-aware programme, it is frequently used to control the system ssh or telnet command when a Python coder needs to automate interactions with a remote prompt. This usually happens when a device doesn't have an API and commands must be input each time the command-line prompt displays. Simple network hardware configuration frequently necessitates this kind of clumsy step-by-step engagement. More information regarding pexpect can be found at http://pypi.python.org/pypi/pexpect.

Of course, it's possible that none of these automated solutions will be sufficient for your project, and you'll have to roll up your sleeves and learn how to control remote-shell protocols on your own. You've come to the proper location if that's the case. Continue reading

Expansion of the Command Line and Quoting

If you've ever typed commands at a Unix command line, you know that not every character is translated literally. Consider the following command as an example. (Note that the dollar sign, $, will be used as the shell's prompt in this and all of the examples that follow in this chapter, indicating that "it is your turn to type.")

```
$ echo *
```

```
sftp.py shell.py ssh_commands.py ssh_simple.py ssh_simple.txt ssh_
threads.py telnet_codes.py
```

```
telnet_login.py
```

This command's asterisk (*) was not taken to mean "print an actual asterisk character to the screen."

Instead, the shell assumed I was attempting to create a pattern that would match all of the files in the current directory. I have to use another special character, an escape character, to print a true asterisk since it allows me to "escape" from the shell's typical meaning and tell it that I just mean the asterisk literally.

```
$ echo Here is a lone asterisk: \*
Here is a lone asterisk: *
$ echo And here are '*' two "*" more asterisks
And here are * two * more asterisks
```

Shells can run subprocesses, the output of which is subsequently utilised in the text of yet another command—and they can now even conduct math. You can ask the ubiquitous bash Bourne-again shell—the standard shell on most Linux systems these days—to divide the number of words in the essay by the number of lines and produce a result to see how many words per line Neal Stephenson fits in the plain-text version of his "In the Beginning... Was the Command Line" essay.

```
$ echo $(( $(wc -w < command.txt) / $(wc -l < command.txt) )) words
per line

46 words per line
```

The rules by which current shells read special characters in your command line have gotten rather complex, as seen by this example. In a normal 8024 terminal window, the bash shell manual page presently runs 5,375 lines, or 223 screens full of text! Obviously, exploring even a fraction of the possible ways that a shell can misinterpret a command that you input would take this chapter astray. Instead, you'll concentrate on just two crucial aspects in the following sections to help you utilise the command line effectively:

- The shell you're using, such as bash, interprets special characters as special. They have no specific significance for the operating system.

- When providing commands to a shell, whether locally or via a network, you must escape special characters so that they are not extended into unexpected values on the remote system, as will be the case in this chapter.

Each of these points will now be discussed in its own section. Keep in mind that I'm discussing mainstream server operating systems like Linux and OS X, not more primitive ones like Windows, which I'll cover separately.

Arguments to Unix commands can contain (almost) any character.

There are no special or reserved characters in the low-level Unix command line. This is a crucial thing for you to understand. If you've ever used a shell like bash for any length of time, you've probably grown to regard your system command line as a minefield. On the one hand, the special characters make it simple to name all of the files in the current directory as command arguments. However, it might be difficult to send a message to the screen that performs something as basic as mixing single and double quotes, and it can be tough to figure out which letters are safe and which are among the numerous that the shell considers special. Which racters are safe, and which are among the many that the shell regards as unique?

This section's main point is that the shell's entire set of conventions for special characters has nothing to do with your operating system. They are totally the behaviour of the bash shell, or any of the other popular (or arcane) shells you are using. No matter how familiar the rules appear or how impossible it is to fathom operating a Unix-like system without them, they must be followed. When you remove the shell, the phenomena of special characters disappears.

You may easily observe this by starting a process and attempting to throw some special characters at a common command.

```
>>> import subprocess
>>> args = ['echo', 'Sometimes', '*', 'is just an asterisk']
>>> subprocess.call(args)
Sometimes * is just an asterisk
```

You've chosen to start a new process with arguments rather than enlisting the help of a shell. Instead of having the * transformed into a list of file names first, the process—in this case, the echo command—gets exactly those letters. Though the asterisk wildcard character is commonly used, the shell's most common special character is the space character, which you use all the time. Each space is considered as a separator between arguments. When people include spaces in Unix file names and then try to relocate the file somewhere else, this results in countless hours of enjoyment.

```
$ mv Smith Contract.txt ~/Documents
mv: cannot stat `Smith': No such file or directory
mv: cannot stat `Contract.txt': No such file or directory
```

To get the shell to realise that you're talking about a single file with a space in its name rather than two, try one of the following command lines:

```
$ mv Smith\ Contract.txt ~/Documents
$ mv "Smith Contract.txt" ~/Documents
$ mv Smith*Contract.txt ~/Documents
```

The last option plainly differs from the first two since it will match any file name that begins with Smith and ends with Contract.txt, regardless of whether the text between them is a single space character or a much larger string of characters. When users are still learning shell protocols and can't remember how to enter a literal space character, they frequently resort to using a wildcard. Listing 16-1 demonstrates a basic shell built in Python that treats only the space character as special but passes everything else through literally to command, if you want to convince yourself that none of the characters that the bash shell has taught you to be careful about are anything unique.

Listing 16-1. Arguments Separated by Whitespace are supported by Shell.

```python
#!/usr/bin/env python3
# Programming in Python: The Basics.
# A simple shell, so you can try running commands at a prompt where no
# characters are special (except that whitespace separates arguments).
import subprocess
def main():
        while True:
                args = input('] ').strip().split()
                if not args:
                        pass
                elif args == ['exit']:
                        break
                elif args[0] == 'show':
                        print("Arguments:", args[1:])
                else:
                        try:
                                subprocess.call(args)
                        except Exception as e:
                        print(e)
if __name__ == '__main__':
        main()
```

Of course, the lack of special quoting characters in this simple shell means you can't use it to talk about files with spaces in their names because it always, without exception, interprets a space as the end of one parameter and the start of the next. When you run this shell and test all of the special characters you've been afraid to use, you'll notice that they have no effect when handed directly to the usual commands you do use. (To distinguish itself from your own shell, the shell in Listing 16-2 uses a] prompt.)

```
$ python shell.py
] echo Hi there!
Hi there!
] echo An asterisk * is not special.
An asterisk * is not special.
] echo The string $HOST is not special, nor are "double quotes".
The string $HOST is not special, nor are "double quotes".
] echo What? No *<>!$ special characters?
What? No *<>!$ special characters?
] show "The 'show' built-in lists its arguments."
Arguments:  ['"The',  "'show'"",  'built-in',  'lists',  'its',
'arguments."']
] exit
```

You can see here that Unix commands—in this case, the /bin/echo command that you are repeatedly calling—do not pay attention to special characters in their parameters. Double quotes, dollar signs, and asterisks are all accepted and treated as literal characters by the echo command. Python merely reduces your arguments to a collection of strings that the operating system can use to create a new process, as the preceding show command demonstrates.

What if you don't split your command into distinct arguments and instead give the operating system a single string containing both the command name and the argument?

```
>>> import subprocess
>>> subprocess.call(['echo hello'])
Traceback (most recent call last):
  ...
FileNotFoundError: [Errno 2] No such file or directory: 'echo hello'
```

Do you see what's going on? The operating system does not recognise that spaces should be special. As a result, the system believes it is being asked to run a command with the exact name echo[space]hello, and it fails to discover it unless you have generated one in the current directory. The null character (the character with the Unicode and ASCII code zero) is the only character that is truly unique to the system. In Unix-like systems, the null character is used to indicate the end of each command-line argument in memory. As a result, if you use a null character in an argument, Unix will assume the argument is over and ignore the rest of the text. Python will stop you in your tracks if you include a null character in a command-line argument to prevent you from making this mistake.

```
>>> subprocess.call(['echo', 'Sentences can end\0 abruptly.'])
Traceback (most recent call last):
  ...
TypeError: embedded NUL character
```

Fortunately, because every command on the system is designed to work within this constraint, there is almost never a reason to use null characters in command-line parameters. (They can't occur in file names for the same reason they can't exist in argument lists: file names are presented to the operating system as null-terminated strings.)

Characters I've Quoted for Protection

You used procedures in Python's subprocess module to directly invoke commands in the previous section. This was fantastic, as it allowed you to pass characters that would have been unique in a traditional interactive shell. If you have a long list of file names with spaces and other special characters, passing them into a subprocess call and having the command on the other end understand you completely might be quite useful. When using remote-shell protocols over the network, you'll usually be talking to a shell like bash rather than being able to directly invoke commands like you do with the subprocess module. This means that remote-shell protocols will seem more like the os module's system() procedure, which runs a shell to interpret your command and therefore immerses you in the Unix command line's intricacies.

```
>>> import os
>>> os.system('echo *')
sftp.py shell.py ssh_commands.py ssh_simple.py ssh_simple.txt ssh_
threads.py telnet_codes.py
telnet_login.py
```

Your network applications may connect to a variety of system and embedded shells, which offer a variety of quoting and wildcard conventions. They can be extremely arcane in some circumstances. If the opposite end of a network connection is a regular Unix shell from the sh family, such as bash or zsh, you're in luck: the rather obscure Python pipes module, which is normally used to generate sophisticated shell command lines, provides a helper function that is ideal for escaping parameters. It's called quote, and all you have to do is provide it a string.

```
>>> from pipes import quote
>>> print(quote("filename"))
filename
>>> print(quote("file with spaces"))
'file with spaces'
>>> print(quote("file 'single quoted' inside!"))
 'file '"'"'single quoted'"'"' inside!'
>>> print(quote("danger!; rm -r *"))
'danger!; rm -r *'
```

As a result, preparing a command line for remote execution can be as simple as calling quote() on each parameter and then pasting the output with spaces. It's worth noting that sending commands to a remote shell with Python usually avoids the horrors of two levels of shell quoting, which you might have encountered if you've ever attempted to compose a remote SSH command line that employs fancy quotation. Attempting to construct shell commands that transmit arguments to a remote shell usually results in a series of trials like this:

```
$ echo $HOST
guinness
$ ssh asaph echo $HOST
guinness
$ ssh asaph echo \$HOST
asaph
$ ssh asaph echo \\$HOST
guinness
$ ssh asaph echo \\\$HOST
$HOST
$ ssh asaph echo \\\\$HOST
\guinness
```

You can prove to yourself that each of these responses is reasonable. To observe how the processed text is handled in a remote SSH command line, first use echo to check what each command appears like when quoted by the local shell, and then paste that text into a remote SSH command line. These commands, however, can be difficult to write, and even a seasoned Unix shell scripter can make a mistake while attempting to forecast the outcome of the preceding series of commands!

Windows' Horrible Command Line

Have you enjoyed learning about the Unix shell and how parameters are provided to a process in the previous sections? If you're connecting to a Windows machine using the remote-shell protocol, you can disregard anything you've read thus far. Windows is a fascinatingly rudimentary operating system. Instead of passing command-line arguments to a new process as separate strings, it just passes the full command line to the new process that is starting up, leaving the process to figure out how the user could have quoted file names with spaces! People in the Windows environment have, of course, embraced more or less consistent norms about how commands would read their arguments just to live. Put double quotes around a multiword file name, for example, and almost all programmes will realise that you're naming one file rather than multiple. Asterisks in a file name are interpreted as wildcards by most commands. However, the application you're running, not the command prompt, makes this decision.

As you'll see, there's an ancient network protocol—the Telnet protocol—that sends command lines as plain text, exactly like Windows does. As a result, if your software sends parameters that contain spaces or special characters, it will have to do some sort of escape. If you're using a modern remote protocol like SSH, which allows you to send parameters as a list of strings rather than a single string, be aware that on Windows systems, SSH can only reassemble your carefully designed command line and hope that the Windows command can figure it out.

When sending commands to Windows, you might want to use the Python subprocess module's list2cmdline() method. It accepts a list of arguments identical to those used for a Unix command and tries to paste them together—using double quotes and backslashes as needed—so that standard Windows programmes can parse the command line back into the same arguments.

```
>>> from subprocess import list2cmdline
>>> args = ['rename', 'salary "Smith".xls', 'salary-smith.xls']
>>> print(list2cmdline(args))
rename "salary \"Smith\".xls" salary-smith.xls
```

You should be able to figure out what Windows requires in your circumstance by experimenting with your network library and remote-shell protocol of choice. I'll assume for the rest of this chapter that you're connecting to servers that run a modern Unix-like operating system that can keep discrete command-line parameters separate without the need for extra quoting.

In a terminal, things are different.

Over your Python-powered remote connection, you'll presumably communicate with more than simply a shell. Keeping an eye on the incoming data stream for data and faults printed by the command you're executing is a good idea. You may also want to send data back, either to provide input to the remote software or to answer to questions and prompts presented by the programme. When completing operations like these, you may be surprised to discover that applications hang forever without ever transmitting the output you're expecting. Alternatively, data you submit may not appear to be receiving. A quick introduction of Unix terminals is necessary to assist you navigate situations like this. A terminal is a device that allows a user to write text and see the computer's answer on a screen. If a Unix machine contains physical serial ports that may be used to host a physical terminal, the device directory will have entries like /dev/ttyS1 that allow applications to send and receive strings to that device. Most terminals these days, however, are actually other programmes: an xterm terminal, a Gnome or KDE terminal programme, the Mac OS X iTerm or Terminal, or even a PuTTY client on a Windows system linked via a remote-shell protocol like the one described in this chapter. Programs operating in a terminal on your computer will often try to figure out if they're talking to a person, and only if they're linked to a terminal device would they presume their output should be prepared for people. As a result, the Unix operating system includes a collection of "pseudo-terminal" devices (also known as "virtual" terminals) with names like /dev/tty42 to which programmes can be linked if they want to believe they are speaking with a real person. When a user opens an xterm or connects over SSH, the xterm or SSH daemon creates a new pseudo-terminal, configures it, and executes the user's shell.

TTY is the shorthand for a terminal device in Unix since the loud TeleType machine was the first example of a computer terminal. That's why the isatty call is used to see if your input is a terminal ().

This is an important distinction to grasp: the shell displays a prompt because it believes it is connected to a terminal. If you start a shell with a standard input that isn't a terminal—say, a pipe from another command—no prompt will be printed, but commands will still be accepted.

```
$ cat | bash
echo Here we are inside of bash, with no prompt
Here we are inside of bash, with no prompt
python3
print('Python has not printed a prompt, either.')
import sys
print('Is this a terminal?', sys.stdin.isatty())
```

Python hasn't printed a prompt, and neither has bash. Python is, in reality, unusually silent. While bash provided a line of text in response to our echo command, you have now typed three lines of input into Python without receiving any answer. What exactly is going on?

Python believes that because its input is not a terminal, it should simply read a full Python script from standard input. After all, its input is a file, and files can contain entire scripts. To finish Python's potentially unending read-until-end-of-file operation, click Ctrl-D to send a "end-of-file" command to cat, which will then close its own output and end the example. Python will parse and run the three-line script you've provided (everything past the word python in the session just showed), and you'll see the results on your terminal, followed by the prompt of the shell you began with.

```
Python has not printed a prompt, either.
Is this a terminal? False
```

Depending on whether they're talking to a terminal or not, some programmes modify their output format automatically. If used interactively, the ps command will truncate each output line to your terminal width, however if used as a pipe or file, it will produce output that is arbitrarily broad. The ls command's traditional column-based output is also replaced with a file name on each line (which is, you must admit, an easier format for reading by another program).

```
$ ls
sftp.py ssh_commands.py ssh_simple.txt telnet_codes.py
shell.py ssh_simple.py ssh_threads.py telnet_login.py
$ ls | cat
sftp.py
shell.py
```

```
ssh_commands.py

ssh_simple.py

ssh_simple.txt

ssh_threads.py

telnet_codes.py

telnet_login.py
```

So, how does any of this relate to network programming? Well, the two characteristics you've seen—programs that display prompts when connected to a terminal but don't display them and run silently when reading from a file or the output of another command—appear at the remote end of the shell protocols you're looking at in this chapter. For example, a programme operating behind Telnet always thinks it's communicating to a terminal. As a result, whenever the shell is ready for input, your scripts or programmes must always anticipate to receive a prompt, and so on. When using the more advanced SSH protocol, however, you can choose whether the software considers the input to be a terminal or just a pipe or file. If there is another computer to which you can connect, you may easily test this from the command line.

```
$ ssh -t asaph
asaph$ echo "Here we are, at a prompt."
Here we are, at a prompt.
asaph$ exit
$ ssh -T asaph
echo "The shell here on asaph sees no terminal; so, no prompt."
The shell here on asaph sees no terminal; so, no prompt.
exit
$
```

When you use a modern protocol like SSH to spawn a command, you must decide whether you want the remote programme to think it's talking to raw data flowing in through a file or pipe, or whether you want it to think it's talking to a person typing at it through a terminal. When communicating with a terminal, programmes are not needed to behave differently. They only change their conduct for our convenience. They do so by performing the Python isatty() call ("Is this a teletype?") that you saw in the previous example session, and then changing their behaviour based on the results. Here are a few examples of how they differ:

- When talking to a terminal, programmes that are frequently used interactively will display a human-readable prompt. When they believe input is coming from a file, however, they don't produce a prompt because if they did, your screen would be filled with hundreds of prompts as you ran a long shell script or Python programme!

- When a TTY is used as input, most advanced interactive programmes provide command-line editing. Because they are used to access the command-line history and perform editing commands, many control characters are unique. When they are not controlled by a terminal, these applications disable command-line editing and accept control characters as normal components of their input stream.

- When listening to a terminal, many programmes only read one line of input at a time since humans prefer to have an immediate answer to every command they write. When reading from a pipe or file, these programmes, on the other hand, will wait until thousands of characters have arrived before attempting to understand the initial batch of data. Even if the input is a file, bash remained in line-at-a-time mode, while Python decided to read the entire Python script from the input before attempting to execute even the first line. It's even more usual for programmes to change their output depending on whether they're communicating with a terminal.

If a user is watching, they expect each line of output, or even each letter, to display instantly. If they're talking to a file or a pipe, on the other hand, they'll wait and group up large chunks of output before sending it all at once.

Both of the last two issues, which involve buffering, cause a slew of issues when you try to automate a process that is typically done manually—because when you do so, you frequently switch from terminal input to input provided through a file or pipe, and the programmes suddenly behave very differently. Because "print" statements do not provide immediate output, but instead save their results to push out all at once when their output buffer is full, they may appear to be stuck.

Because of the aforementioned issue, many carefully constructed programmes in Python and other languages routinely execute flush() on their output to ensure that any data waiting in a buffer is sent out, regardless of whether the output looks like a terminal. These are the fundamental issues with terminals and buffering: When talking to a terminal, programmes change their behaviour in unusual ways, and they typically start heavily buffering their output if they assume they're writing to a file or pipe instead of letting you see it right away.

Terminals are responsible for buffering.

Aside from the program-specific behaviours previously outlined, terminal devices also bring another set of issues. What happens if you want a software to read one character at a time, but the Unix terminal device buffers your keystrokes and sends them as a single line? This is because the Unix terminal defaults to "canonical" input processing, which allows the user to type an entire line—and even edit it by backspacing and retyping—before pressing Enter and letting the programme see what they've entered. You can use the stty "change the current TTY's settings" command to deactivate canonical processing so that a programme can see every individual character as it is typed.

```
$ stty -icanon
```

Another issue is that Unix terminals used to feature a pair of keystrokes that allowed users to halt the output and read a complete screen of text before it scrolled off and was replaced by more text. The characters Ctrl+S for "Stop" and Ctrl+Q for "Keep going" were frequently used, and it was a source of great annoyance if binary data got into an automated Telnet connection because the first Ctrl+S that happened to pass across the channel would pause the terminal and most likely ruin the session. stty can be used to disable this setting once more.

```
$ stty -ixon -ixoff
```

Those are the two most common issues with terminals that buffer, although there are many of less well-known options that can also cause problems. The stty command actually supports two modes because there are so many, and they differ between Unix implementations. Cooked and raw are the modes, which turn dozens of settings like icanon and ixon on and off at the same time.

```
$ stty raw
```

```
$ stty cooked
```

If you make a hopeless mess of your terminal settings after a bit of tinkering, most Unix systems have a command for resetting the terminal to sensible, sane defaults. (Note that if you've messed around with stty too much, you may need to press Ctrl+J to submit the reset command, as your Return key, which is Ctrl+M, only works to submit commands due to a terminal configuration called icrnl.)

```
$ reset
```

If you're talking to a terminal from your own Python script and don't want to try to get it to behave via a Telnet or SSH session, check out the termios module from the Standard Library. You should be able to manipulate all of the same settings that you just accessed with the stty command by puzzling through its sample code and remembering how Boolean bitwise math works. Although there isn't enough room in this book to go into more detail about terminals (since one or two chapters of examples could easily be inserted right here to cover just the more interesting techniques and cases), there are plenty of excellent resources for learning more about them—a classic is W. Richard Stevens' Advanced Programming in the UNIX Environment, Chapter 19, "Pseudo Terminals" (Addison-Wesley Professional, 1992).

Telnet

This book's only mention of the archaic Telnet protocol is in this brief section. Why? It's insecure because anyone who watches your Telnet packets pass by can see your account, password, and everything you do on the distant system. It's clumsy, and it's no longer used for most system administration tasks.

■ THE TELNET PROTOCOL

Purpose: Remote shell access

Standard: RFC 854 (1989)

Runs atop: TCP/IP

Default port: 23

Library: telnetlib

Exceptions: socket.error, socket.gaierror, EOFError, select.error

Only when connecting with a small, embedded machine, such as a Linksys router, DSL modem, or network switch deep inside a well-firewalled corporate network, do I use Telnet. Here are some recommendations on how to use the Python telnetlib if you need to develop a Python programme that needs to Telnet to one of these devices. To begin, you must understand that Telnet simply establishes a channel—in this case, a pretty basic TCP socket (see Chapter 3)—and then copies data in both directions across that channel. Everything you type is transferred over the wire, and Telnet prints everything it gets to the screen. This means Telnet is unaware of a wide range of issues that a remote-shell protocol should be aware of.

When you Telnet to a Unix machine, for example, you are usually given with a login: prompt, where you type your username, and then a password: prompt, where you type your password. Small, embedded devices that still utilise Telnet nowadays may have a little simpler script, but they almost always require authentication or a password. In any case, Telnet is completely unaware of this method of communication! Password: is basically nine random characters that come flying across the TCP connection and that your Telnet client has to print on your screen. Because Telnet isn't aware of authentication, you can't send any arguments to the Telnet command to be preauthenticated to the remote system, and you can't skip the login and password prompts that appear when you initially connect. If you're going to utilise regular Telnet, you'll have to keep an eye on the incoming text for those two prompts (or however many the remote system provides) and then type the appropriate responses.

You can't expect standardisation in the error messages or responses produced when your password fails if systems differ in what username and password prompts they present. That's why it's so difficult to script and programme Telnet in a language like Python. Unless you know every single error message that the remote system could print in response to your login and password—which could include things like "cannot spawn shell: out of memory," "home directory not mounted," and "quota exceeded: confining you to a restricted shell"—your script will occasionally run into situations where it is expecting to see either a command prompt or a specific error message, but instead will simply waffle.

As a result, if you use Telnet, you are solely playing a text-based game. You wait for a text to arrive and then try to respond to the remote system with something understandable. The Python telnetlib library can help you with this by providing not only basic ways for sending and receiving data, but also a few functions that will watch and wait for a specific string to arrive from the remote system. Telnetlib is similar to the third-party Python pexpect package that I mentioned previously in this chapter, and hence to the old Unix expect command in this regard. In fact, one of these telnetlib procedures is named expect in homage of its predecessor ().

Listing 16-2 establishes a connection to the host, automates the entire back-and-forth login discussion, and then executes a simple command to display the results.

Listing 16-2. Using Telnet to Login to a Remote Host

```
#!/usr/bin/env python3
# Programming in Python: The Basics.
# Connect to localhost, watch for a login prompt, and try logging in
import argparse, getpass, telnetlib
def main(hostname, username, password):
    t = telnetlib.Telnet(hostname)
    # t.set_debuglevel(1) # uncomment to get debug messages
    t.read_until(b'login:')
```

```
t.write(username.encode('utf-8'))
t.write(b'\r')
t.read_until(b'assword:') # first letter might be 'p' or 'P'
t.write(password.encode('utf-8'))
t.write(b'\r')
n, match, previous_text = t.expect([br'Login incorrect',
br'\$'], 10)
if n == 0:
    print('Username and password failed - giving up')
else:
    t.write(b'exec uptime\r')
    print(t.read_all().decode('utf-8')) # read until
    socket closes
if __name__ == '__main__':
    parser = argparse.ArgumentParser(description='Use Telnet to
    log in')
    parser.add_argument('hostname', help='Remote host to telnet
    to')
    parser.add_argument('username', help='Remote username')
    args = parser.parse_args()
    password = getpass.getpass('Password: ')
    main(args.hostname, args.username, password)
```

If the script is successful, it shows you what the simple uptime command prints on the remote system.

```
$ python telnet_login.py example.com john

Password: abc12345
10:24:43 up 5 days, 12:13, 14 users, load average: 1.44, 0.92, 0.74
```

The following diagram depicts the general structure of a telnetlib-powered session. To begin, a connection is formed, which is represented in Python by a Telnet class instance. Only the hostname is supplied here, but you can additionally include a port number if you want to connect to a service port other than conventional Telnet.

If you want your Telnet object to print out all of the strings it sends and receives during the session, call set debuglevel(1). This was crucial for constructing even the very simple script described in listing, because the script stalled twice and I had to restart it with debugging messages enabled so that I could view the actual output and repair the script. (Once I forgot the 'r' at the end of the uptime command, and the other time I failed to match the exact text that was returned.) I usually turn off debugging once a programme is up and running, then put it back on anytime I need to work on the script again. Telnet does not hide the fact that its service is backed by a TCP socket, and any socket.error or socket.gaierror exceptions will be passed through to your programme. Once you've created a Telnet session, interactivity usually follows a receive-and-send pattern, in which you wait for a prompt or answer from the remote end before sending your next piece of data. The following is a list of two ways to wait for text to arrive:

- The simple read **until()** function waits for a literal string to arrive before returning a string that contains all of the text it got from the time it started listing till it saw the string you were looking for.

- **The expect()** method, which is more powerful and advanced, accepts a list of Python regular expressions. Expect() returns three items once the text received from the remote end adds up to something that matches one of the regular expressions: the index in your list of the pattern that matched, the regular expression SRE Match object itself, and the text that was received leading up to the matching text. Read the Standard Library documentation for the re module for further information on what you can do with an SRE Match, including finding values for any subexpressions in your pattern.

Regular expressions, like any other type of expression, must be written with care. When I first developed this script, I used the expect() pattern '$' to watch for the shell prompt to appear—which is unfortunately a special character in regular expression! As a result, the revised script in listing escapes the $, causing expect() to wait until it receives a dollar sign from the remote end.

The script leaves if it receives an error message due to an incorrect password and does not become trapped waiting indefinitely for a login or password prompt that never arrives or looks different than it expected.

```
$ python telnet_login.py example.com john
Password: wrongpass
Username and password failed - giving up
```

If you need to use Telnet in a Python script, it'll just be a larger or more complicated version of the same simple structure illustrated here. Both read until() and expect() accept a second argument, timeout, which sets a maximum limit in seconds for how long the call will look for the text pattern before giving up and returning control to your Python script. If they quit and give up due to the timeout, they don't throw an error; instead, they just return the text they've seen so far and leave it up to you to figure out whether or not that text contains the pattern! There are a few tidbits in the Telnet object that I won't go through right now. They are documented in the telnetlib Standard Library, including an interact() method that allows the user to "speak" directly over your Telnet connection via the terminal! This type of call was common in the past when you needed to automate login but still have control and send standard commands. The Telnet protocol has a standard for embedding control information, and telnetlib strictly respects these guidelines to keep your data distinct from any control codes that may appear. As a result, you may use a Telnet object to send and receive any binary data you want while ignoring the possibility of control codes arriving as well. If you're working on a complex Telnet-based project, though, you might need to process options.

Normally, telnetlib bluntly refuses to submit or accept an option request when a Telnet server delivers one. For processing options, you can specify a Telnet object with your own callback function. Listing 16-3 shows a simple example. It basically reimplements the usual telnetlib behaviour for most options and refuses to handle any others. (Remember to react to each option in some fashion; failing to do so will frequently cause the Telnet session to hang as the server waits indefinitely for your response.) If the server exhibits an interest in the "terminal type" option, this client responds with mypython, which is recognised by the shell command it performs after logging in as its $TERM environment variable.

Listing 16-3. Telnet Option Codes: How to Handle Them

```python3
#!/usr/bin/env python3

# Programming in Python: The Basics.

# How your code might look if you intercept Telnet options yourself

import argparse, getpass

from telnetlib import Telnet, IAC, DO, DONT, WILL, WONT, SB, SE, TTYPE

def process_option(tsocket, command, option):

        if command == DO and option == TTYPE:

                tsocket.sendall(IAC + WILL + TTYPE)

                print('Sending terminal type "mypython"')

                tsocket.sendall(IAC + SB + TTYPE + b'\0' + b'mypython'
```

```
                         + IAC + SE)
             elif command in (DO, DONT):
                    print('Will not', ord(option))
                    tsocket.sendall(IAC + WONT + option)
             elif command in (WILL, WONT):
                    print('Do not', ord(option))
                    tsocket.sendall(IAC + DONT + option)
def main(hostname, username, password):
        t = Telnet(hostname)
        # t.set_debuglevel(1) # uncomment to get debug messages
        t.set_option_negotiation_callback(process_option)
        t.read_until(b'login:', 10)
        t.write(username.encode('utf-8') + b'\r')
        t.read_until(b'password:', 10) # first letter might be 'p' or 'P'
        t.write(password.encode('utf-8') + b'\r')
        n, match, previous_text = t.expect([br'Login incorrect',
        br'\$'], 10)
        if n == 0:
                print("Username and password failed - giving up")
        else:
                t.write(b'exec echo My terminal type is $TERM\n')
                print(t.read_all().decode('ascii'))
if __name__ == '__main__':
        parser = argparse.ArgumentParser(description='Use Telnet to
        log in')
        parser.add_argument('hostname', help='Remote host to telnet to')
        parser.add_argument('username', help='Remote username')
```

```
    args = parser.parse_args()

    password = getpass.getpass('Password: ')

    main(args.hostname, args.username, password)
```

Again, the relevant RFCs can be consulted for more information on how Telnet options function. In the next part, I'll abandon the insecure Telnet protocol in favour of a more current and secure method of executing remote operations.

SSH: The Secure Shell

SSH is one of the most well-known safe, encrypted protocols (HTTPS is perhaps the most well-known).

■ **THE SSH PROTOCOL**

Purpose: Secure remote shell, file transfer, port forwarding

Standard: RFC 4250–4256 (2006)

Runs atop: TCP/IP

Default port: 22

Library: paramiko

Exceptions: socket.error, socket.gaierror, paramiko.SSHException

SSH is a descendant of a protocol that allowed for "remote login," "remote shell," and "remote file copy" operations. commands such as rlogin, rsh, and rcp, which were far more popular than Telnet at the time.

sites that backed them up Unless you've spent hours using rcp, you can't imagine what a revelation it was. attempting to transmit binary files between machines using Telnet and a script that attempts to input your password only to find out that your file contains a bit that appears like a Telnet or remote control character Until you add a layer of escape (or figure out how to disable both), the whole system will hang. All interpretation takes place on a remote terminal using the Telnet escape key.) The nicest characteristic of the rlogin family members, on the other hand, was that they didn't blindly repeat username and password prompts without understanding what was going on. Instead, they remained involved throughout the authentication process, and you could even write a file in your home directory that instructed them to "simply let someone called john in without a password when they try to connect from the asaph machine." System administrators and Unix users alike were given back hours each month that they would have spent inputting their passwords otherwise. Furthermore, rcp copying ten files from one system to another became virtually as simple as copying them into a local folder. SSH has kept all of the fantastic features of the early remote-shell protocol while adding security and strong encryption that is trusted around the world for operating mission-critical servers. This chapter will focus on the third-party paramiko Python package, which can speak the SSH protocol and does so well that it has been transferred to Java as well, because Java users wanted to be able to use SSH as simply as we can with Python.

SSH: A Quick Overview

Then utilise it for one thing only—downloading a web page or sending an e-mail— never attempting to do many things at once via a single socket. When we get to SSH, we find a protocol that is so advanced that it implements its own multiplexing. Several "information channels" can share the same SSH socket. SSH labels every block of data it delivers across its connection with a "channel" identification so that multiple conversations can share the same socket. Subchannels are beneficial for at least two reasons. First, while channel ID consumes a little amount of bandwidth for each block of data sent, it is insignificant in comparison to the amount of additional data SSH must send to negotiate and maintain encryption. Second, channels make sense since the true cost of an SSH connection is the time it takes to set it up. Host key negotiation and authentication can take several seconds of actual time, and you want to be able to use the connection for as many tasks as feasible once it's established. You can amortise the high cost of connecting by executing numerous activities before letting the connection end, thanks to the SSH concept of a channel.

You can build a variety of channels once you've connected:

- An interactive shell session, such as Telnet's support
- The execution of a single command in isolation.
- A port forward that intercepts TCP connections
- A file transfer session that allows you to access the remote filesystem

In the next sections, you'll learn about all of these different types of channels.

Host Keys for SSH

When an SSH client connects to a remote host for the first time, the two exchange temporary public keys that allow them to encrypt the remainder of their communication without giving any information to any onlookers. The client then wants evidence of the remote server's identity before disclosing any more information. This makes logical as a first step: you wouldn't want SSH to reveal even your username, let alone your password, if you were truly talking to a hacker's software that had momentarily managed to acquire a distant server's IP.

Building a public-key infrastructure, as you saw in Chapter 6, is one solution to the challenge of machine identity on the Internet. To begin, you must identify a group of companies known as certificate authorities that will be able to issue certificates. Then you install a list of their public keys in all web browsers and other SSL clients that are currently available. Then those businesses charge you money to verify that you are, in fact, Google.com (or whoever you are) and that your Google.com SSL certificate deserves to be signed. Finally, you can install the certificate on your web server, which will ensure that everyone knows who you are.

From the standpoint of SSH, there are numerous issues with this method. While it is true that you can create an internal public-key infrastructure in which you distribute your own signing authority's certificates to your web browsers or other applications and then sign your own server certificates without paying a third party, it is also true that you cannot sign your own server certificates without paying a third party. For something like SSH, a public-key infrastructure would still be a lengthy process. Server administrators frequently desire to set up, use, and decommission servers without first consulting a central authority.

As a result, SSH assumes that when a server is deployed, it generates a random public-private key combination that is not signed by anyone. Instead, one of two methods for key distribution is used.

- A system administrator creates a script that collects all of an organization's host public keys, prepares an ssh known hosts file that lists them all, and saves it to the /etc/sshd directory on each machine. They may also make it available to any desktop clients, such as Windows' PuTTY command. Before they connect for the first time, every SSH client will know about every SSH host key. Alternatively, the administrator can simply forego knowing host keys in advance and have each SSH client memorise them at the time of initial connection.

This will be familiar to SSH command-line users: the client claims it doesn't recognise the host to which you're connecting, you answer "yes," and the client's key is saved in your /.ssh/known hosts file. You have no way of knowing if you're talking to the host you believe you're talking to on the first meeting. Nonetheless, every future connection you make to that machine will be assured to go to the appropriate spot and not to other servers that someone is shifting into place at the same IP address (unless, of course, the host's keys have been stolen).

When the SSH command line encounters an unfamiliar host, it displays the following prompt:

```
$ ssh dns.google
```

```
The authenticity of host 'dns.google (8.8.8.8)' can't be established.
```

```
RSA key fingerprint is 85:8f:32:4r:ac:1f:a9:bc:35:58:c1:d4:25:e3:c7:8c.
```

```
Are you sure you want to continue connecting (yes/no)? yes
```

```
Warning: Permanently added 'dns.google 8.8.8.8' (RSA) to the list of known hosts.
```

I wrote the yes answer buried deep on the next-to-last full line, providing SSH permission to create the connection and remember the key for future time. If SSH connects to a host and discovers a different key, it reacts violently.

```
$ ssh dns.google
```

```
@@@@@@@@@@@@@@@@@@@@@@@@@@@@@@@@@@@@@@@@@@@@@@@@@@@@@
```

```
@ WARNING: REMOTE HOST IDENTIFICATION HAS CHANGED! @
```

```
@@@@@@@@@@@@@@@@@@@@@@@@@@@@@@@@@@@@@@@@@@@@@@@@@@@@@
```

```
IT IS POSSIBLE THAT SOMEONE IS DOING SOMETHING NASTY!
```

```
Someone could be eavesdropping on you right now (man-in-the-middle attack)!
```

Anyone who has had to rebuild a server from the ground up and forgotten to save their old SSH keys will recognise this warning. The freshly rebuilt host will now use new keys created by the reinstall without them. It can be a headache to go through all of your SSH clients and remove the problematic old key so that they can learn the new one discreetly when they reconnect. All of the standard SSH methods involving host keys are fully supported by the paramiko library. Its default behaviour, on the other hand, is fairly sparse. It does not load any host key files by default, therefore it must raise an exception for the first host you connect to because it will be unable to validate its key.

```
>>> import paramiko
```

```
>>> client = paramiko.SSHClient()
```

```
>>> client.connect('example.com', username='test')
```

```
Traceback (most recent call last):
```

```
    ...
```

`paramiko.ssh_exception.SSHException: Server 'example.com' not found in known_hosts`

Before connecting, load both the system and the current user's known host keys to make the connection act like a typical SSH command.

```
>>> client.load_system_host_keys()
>>> client.load_host_keys('/home/John/.ssh/known_hosts')
>>> client.connect('example.com', username='test')
```

You can also choose how to handle unknown hosts with the paramiko library. Once you've established a client object, you can give it a decision-making class that will be called when a host key isn't recognised. By inheriting from the MissingHostKeyPolicy class, you can create these classes yourself.

```
>>> class AllowAnythingPolicy(paramiko.MissingHostKeyPolicy):
... def missing_host_key(self, client, hostname, key):
... return
...
>>> client.set_missing_host_key_policy(AllowAnythingPolicy())
>>> client.connect('example.com', username='test')
```

It's worth noting that the inputs to the missing host key() method provide you with a variety of data points on which to base your judgement. You could, for example, allow connections without a host key to computers on your own server subnet but not to anyone else's. There are various decision-making classes in paramiko that already implement a number of fundamental host key options.

- **paramiko.AutoAddPolicy:** When you first see a host key, it is immediately added to your user host key store (on Unix systems, the file /.ssh/known hosts), but any further changes to the host key will cause a fatal exception.

- **paramiko.RejectPolicy:** When connecting to hosts with unknown keys, an exception is thrown.

- **paramiko.WarningPolicy:** When connecting to an unknown host, a warning is logged, but the connection is allowed to continue.

When building an SSH script, I usually start by connecting to the remote host "by hand" with the normal ssh command-line tool so that I can answer "yes" to its prompt and acquire the remote host's key in my host keys file. This way, my programmes will never have to worry about dealing with a missing key and will be able to exit with an error if one occurs. However, if you prefer not to handle things by hand as much as I do, the AutoAddPolicy might be your best option. It will never require human contact, but it will at least confirm that you are conversing with the same machine on subsequent occasions. Even if the computer is a Trojan horse that records all of your contacts with it and surreptitiously records your password (if you use one), it must at least show you that it has the same secret key every time you connect.

Authentication with SSH

SSH authentication is the subject of a great quantity of solid documentation, as well as papers and blog entries, all of which are freely available on the Internet. There's a lot of information out there on configuring common SSH clients, setting up an SSH server on a Unix or Windows host, and utilising public keys to authenticate yourself so you don't have to type your password every time. I'll simply go through how authentication works briefly because this chapter is largely about how to "speak SSH" from Python. There are three common methods for proving your identity to a remote server you're communicating with over SSH.

- You have the option of providing a username and password.
- You can provide your client a username and then have them conduct a public-key challenge-response successfully. This ingenious method proves that you have a hidden "identification" key without actually exposing its contents to a remote system.
- Kerberos authentication is possible. If the remote system supports Kerberos (which seems to be rare these days) and you've used the kinit command-line tool to verify your identity with one of the master Kerberos servers in the SSH server's authentication domain, you should be able to log in without a password.

We'll focus on the first two because the third choice is uncommon. It's simple to utilise a username and password with paramiko; simply specify them in your connect() method call.

```
>>> client.connect('example.com', username='john', password=abc12345)
```

The Python code is even easier with public-key authentication, where you use ssh-keygen to generate a "identity" key pair (which is normally saved in your /.ssh directory) that can be used to authenticate you without a password.

```
'my.example.com' >>> client.connect('my.example.com')
```

If your identity key file isn't located in the standard /.ssh/id rsa directory, you can manually supply its file name—or a Python list of file names—to the connect() method.

```
>>> client.connect('my.example.com, key filename='/home/john/.ssh/id
sysadmin', key filename='/home/john/.ssh/id sysadmin', key filename='/
home/john/.ssh/id sysadmi
```

Of course, supplying a public-key identification like this will only work if the public key in the id sysadmin.pub file has been attached to your "authorised hosts" file on the remote end, which is normally titled something like this:

```
/home/john/.ssh/authorized_keys
```

Always verify the file permissions on both your remote.ssh directory and the files inside if you're having difficulties getting public-key authentication to work. If these files are group-readable or group-writable, some versions of the SSH server will become angry. SSH is frequently happiest when the.ssh directory is in mode 0700 and the files inside are in mode 0600. In recent versions, the operation of copying SSH keys to other accounts has been automated by a short script that ensures that the file permissions are set correctly for you.

```
myaccount@example.com ssh-copy-id -i /.ssh/id rsa.pub
```

Once the connect() method has completed successfully, you can begin executing remote activities, which will all be relayed over the same physical socket without the need to renegotiate the host key, your identity, or the encryption that secures the SSH connection.

Individual Commands and Shell Sessions

Once you have a connected SSH client, you have access to the complete world of SSH activities. You can access remote-shell sessions, perform specific commands, start file-transfer sessions, and set up port forwarding simply by asking. You'll go over each of these operations one by one. First, SSH can create a raw shell session for you, which runs on the distant end inside a pseudoterminal and allows programmes to communicate with the user as they would at a terminal. This type of connection works similarly to a Telnet connection. Listing 16-4 shows an example of sending a simple echo command to a remote shell and then asking it to exit.

Listing 16-4. Using SSH to Run an Interactive Shell

```
#!/usr/bin/env python3

# Programming in Python: The Basics.

# Using SSH like Telnet: connecting and running two commands

import argparse, paramiko, sys
```

```
class AllowAnythingPolicy(paramiko.MissingHostKeyPolicy):
    def missing_host_key(self, client, hostname, key):
        return
def main(hostname, username):
    client = paramiko.SSHClient()
    client.set_missing_host_key_policy(AllowAnythingPolicy())
    client.connect(hostname, username=username) # password='')
    channel = client.invoke_shell()
    stdin = channel.makefile('wb')
    stdout = channel.makefile('rb')
    stdin.write(b'echo Hello, world\rexit\r')
    output = stdout.read()
    client.close()
    sys.stdout.buffer.write(output)
if __name__ == '__main__':
    parser = argparse.ArgumentParser(description='Connect over
        SSH')
    parser.add_argument('hostname', help='Remote machine name')
    parser.add_argument('username', help='Username on the remote
        machine')
    args = parser.parse_args()
    main(args.hostname, args.username)
```

As you can see, this script exhibits the scars of a terminal-based software. Instead of being able to elegantly encapsulate each of the two commands it is issuing and separate their arguments, it must rely on the remote shell to divide things up properly using spaces and carriage returns. This script is created with the idea that you already have an identity file and a remote authorized-keys file, so you won't have to type a password. If you do, you can use the commented-out password argument in the script to specify one. You can have it call getpass(), as you did in the Telnet example, to avoid inputting the password into your Python file. Also, if you run this command, you'll see that the commands you input are echoed twice, with no easy way to distinguish between the command echoes and the real command output.

```
Welcome to Ubuntu 13.10 (GNU/Linux 3.11.0-19-generic x86_64)
Last login: Wed mar 23 15:06:03 2019 from localhost
echo Hello, world
exit
test@john:~$ echo Hello, world
Hello, world
test@john:~$ exit
logout
```

Can you figure out what happened?

The command text was given to the remote host while it was still providing its welcome messages because you did not pause and wait patiently for a shell prompt before issuing the echo and exit commands (which would have needed a loop doing repeated read() calls). The commands were written directly beneath the "Last login" line because the Unix terminal is in a "cooked" state by default, which means it echoes the user's keystrokes. The bash shell then began reading the commands character by character, setting the terminal to raw mode because it prefers to provide its own command-line editing interface Because it assumes you want to see what you're doing (despite the fact that you've already done typing and it's just reading characters from a buffer that's several milliseconds old), it repeats each command on the screen.

Of course, you'd have a hard time building a Python routine that could separate the actual command output (the words Hello, world) from the rest of the output you're getting through the SSH connection without a lot of parsing and intelligence. Because of all of these strange terminal-dependent behaviours, you should only use invoke shell() if you're developing an interactive terminal programme that allows a live user to type commands.. exec command() is a far better alternative for performing remote commands because it runs a single command rather than an entire shell session. It allows you to manipulate the command's standard input, output, and error streams as if you were running it locally using the Standard Library's subprocess module.

A script illustrating its use is shown in Listing 16-5. The difference between exec command() and a local subprocess (apart from the fact that the command is executed on a remote computer!) is that you cannot give command-line parameters to the remote server as separate strings. Instead, you must give the entire command line to the remote shell for interpretation.

Listing 16-5. Individual SSH Commands Execution

```python
#!/usr/bin/env python3
# Programming in Python: The Basics.
# Running three separate commands, and reading three separate outputs
import argparse, paramiko
class AllowAnythingPolicy(paramiko.MissingHostKeyPolicy):
        def missing_host_key(self, client, hostname, key):
                return
def main(hostname, username):
        client = paramiko.SSHClient()
        client.set_missing_host_key_policy(AllowAnythingPolicy())
        client.connect(hostname, username=username) # password='')
  for command in 'echo "Hello, world!"', 'uname', 'uptime':
        stdin, stdout, stderr = client.exec_command(command)
        stdin.close()
        print(repr(stdout.read()))
        stdout.close()
        stderr.close()
        client.close()
if __name__ == '__main__':
        parser = argparse.ArgumentParser(description='Connect over
        SSH')
        parser.add_argument('hostname', help='Remote machine name')
        parser.add_argument('username', help='Username on the remote
        machine')
        args = parser.parse_args()
        main(args.hostname, args.username)
```

Unlike all of our earlier Telnet and SSH conversations, this script will receive the output of these three commands as completely separate streams of data. There is no chance of confusing the output of one of the commands with any of the others.

```
$ python3 ssh_commands.py localhost john
'Hello, world!\n'
'Linux\n'
```

'15:30:18 up 5 days, 22:55, 5 users, load average: 0.79, 0.84, 0.71\n'

Aside from its security, SSH offers another significant benefit: the ability to do semantically distinct operations on a distant machine without having to establish separate connections.

If you need to quote command-line arguments so that spaces containing file names and special characters are interpreted correctly by the remote shell, you might find quotes() from the Python pipes module useful when building command lines for the exec command() function, as mentioned in the "Telnet" section earlier. Every time you invoke shell() or exec command() to initiate a new SSH shell session or run a command, a new SSH "channel" is generated behind the scenes to offer filelike Python objects that let you talk to the remote command's standard input, output, and error streams. These channels run in parallel, and SSH skillfully interleaves their data on your single SSH connection so that all talks take place at the same time and are never confused.

A simple example of what is possible can be found in Listing 16-6. Two command lines are started remotely, each of which is a simple shell script with some echo commands and sleep pauses. You can pretend that they are filesystem commands that return data as they walk the filesystem or that they are CPU-intensive activities that generate and return results slowly if you choose. SSH is unconcerned about differences. What matters is that channels go dark for a few seconds before returning back to life as more data becomes available.

Listing 16-6. SSH Channels Work in Simultaneous Mode

```python
#!/usr/bin/env python3
# Programming in Python: The Basics.
# Running two remote commands simultaneously in different channels
import argparse, paramiko, threading
class AllowAnythingPolicy(paramiko.MissingHostKeyPolicy):
    def missing_host_key(self, client, hostname, key):
        return
def main(hostname, username):
    client = paramiko.SSHClient()
    client.set_missing_host_key_policy(AllowAnythingPolicy())
    client.connect(hostname, username=username) # password='')
    def read_until_EOF(fileobj):
```

```
            s = fileobj.readline()
            while s:
                print(s.strip())
                s = fileobj.readline()
    ioe1 = client.exec_command('echo One;sleep 2;echo Two;sleep
    1;echo Three')
    ioe2 = client.exec_command('echo A;sleep 1;echo B;sleep
    2;echo C')
    thread1 = threading.Thread(target=read_until_EOF,
    args=(ioe1[1],))
    thread2 = threading.Thread(target=read_until_EOF,
    args=(ioe2[1],))
    thread1.start()
    thread2.start()
    thread1.join()
    thread2.join()
    client.close()
if __name__ == '__main__':
    parser = argparse.ArgumentParser(description='Connect over
    SSH')
    parser.add_argument('hostname', help='Remote machine name')
    parser.add_argument('username', help='Username on the remote
    machine')
    args = parser.parse_args()
    main(args.hostname, args.username)
```

You start two threads and give each of them one of the channels to read from in order to process these two streams of data at the same time. Both output each new line of data as soon as it arrives and exit when the readline() command returns an empty string to mark the end of the file. When ran, this script should produce the following output:

```
$ python3 ssh_threads.py localhost john

One

A
```

B

Two

Three

C

As you can see, SSH channels on the same TCP connection are entirely independent, can receive (and send) data at their own pace, and can close separately when the command to which they're talking ultimately ends. The same may be said for the next two features you'll be looking at: file transfer and port forwarding.

SFTP (SSH File Transfer Protocol)

The SSH File Transfer Protocol (SFTP) is a subprotocol of the SSH protocol that allows you to navigate the remote directory tree, create and delete directories and files, and copy files from the local to the remote machine. The capabilities of SFTP are so complex and comprehensive that they can power graphical file browsers and even allow the distant filesystem to be mounted locally! (For more information, look up the sshfs system on the internet.)

The SFTP protocol is a huge help to those of us who used to have to copy files using shaky scripts that sought to deliver data over Telnet by carefully escaping binary data. Instead of forcing you to use its own sftp command line every time you want to move files, SSH follows RSH's lead and provides a scp command-line tool that works similarly to cp but allows you to prefix any file name with hostname: to indicate that it exists on the remote system. This implies that remote copy commands are saved in your command-line history among other shell commands, rather than being lost in a separate history buffer of a separate command prompt that you must invoke and then exit (which was a great annoyance of traditional FTP clients). Furthermore, the SFTP, sftp, and scp commands not only offer password authentication, but also allow you to copy files using the same public-key technique that allows you to avoid typing your password over and over when using the ssh command to conduct remote tasks.

You may get a decent understanding of the types of actions that SFTP enables by skimming through Chapter 17 on the previous FTP system. In fact, most SFTP operations have the same names as local commands you already use to alter files on your Unix shell account, such as chmod and mkdir, or have the same names as Unix system calls, such as lstat and unlink, which you may be familiar with thanks to the Python os module. Because these actions are so familiar, I never require anything more than the bare paramiko documentation for the Python SFTP client at www.lag. net/paramiko/docs/paramiko.SFTPClient-class when writing SFTP commands.

The following are the most important factors to keep in mind when using SFTP:

- Just like FTP and your regular shell account, the SFTP protocol is stateful. As a result, you can either supply all file and directory names as absolute paths starting at the root of the filesystem, or you can use getcwd() and chdir() to navigate the filesystem and then use relative paths to the directory where you arrived.

- You can open a file using either the file() or open() methods (just how Python has a built-in callable that goes by both names), and you'll obtain a filelike object that's linked to an SSH channel that's separate from your SFTP channel. That is, you can continue to issue SFTP instructions while moving around the filesystem and copying or opening other files, and the original channel will remain linked to its file and ready to read or write. File transfers can be done asynchronously because each open distant file has its own channel. You can open multiple distant files at the same time and have them all stream down to your hard drive, or you can open new files and send data back and forth.

- Finally, keep in mind that no shell expansion is performed on any of the file names you pass through SFTP. If you don't recognise this, you can open so many channels at once that each one slows to a crawl. If you try to use a file name that starts with * or contains spaces or special characters, they will be treated as part of the file name. When using SFTP, there is no need for a shell. Thanks to support built within the SSH server, you can talk directly to distant filesystems. This means that if you wish to provide users with pattern matching support, you'll have to get the directory contents yourself and then check their pattern against each one using a procedure like provided in fnmatch in Python Standard Library.

A simple SFTP session is shown in Listing 16-7. It performs a simple task that system administrators may need from time to time (although that they may just as easily achieve with a scp command): it connects to the remote system and copies message log files from the /var/log directory to the local machine, possibly for scanning or analysis.

Listing 16-7. With SFTP, you can list a directory and fetch files.

```
#!/usr/bin/env python3

# Programming in Python: The Basics.
```

```python
# Fetching files with SFTP
import argparse, functools, paramiko
class AllowAnythingPolicy(paramiko.MissingHostKeyPolicy):
        def missing_host_key(self, client, hostname, key):
            return
def main(hostname, username, filenames):
        client = paramiko.SSHClient()
        client.set_missing_host_key_policy(AllowAnythingPolicy())
        client.connect(hostname, username=username) # password='')
        def print_status(filename, bytes_so_far, bytes_total):
            percent = 100. * bytes_so_far / bytes_total
            print('Transfer of %r is at %d/%d bytes (%.1f%%)' % (
            filename, bytes_so_far, bytes_total, percent))
        sftp = client.open_sftp()
        for filename in filenames:
        if filename.endswith('.copy'):
            continue
        callback = functools.partial(print_status, filename)
        sftp.get(filename, filename + '.copy', callback=callback)
 client.close()
if __name__ == '__main__':
        parser = argparse.ArgumentParser(description='Copy files over
        SSH')
        parser.add_argument('hostname', help='Remote machine name')
        parser.add_argument('username', help='Username on the remote
        machine')
        parser.add_argument('filename', nargs='+', help='Filenames to
        fetch')
```

```
        args = parser.parse_args()

        main(args.hostname, args.username, args.filename)
```

Although I made a big deal about how each file you open with SFTP has its own independent channel, the simple get() and put() convenience functions provided by paramiko, which are really lightweight wrappers for an open() followed by a loop that reads and writes, do not attempt any asynchrony; instead, they just block and wait until each entire file arrives. This implies that the preceding script transfers one file at a time, resulting in output that looks like this:

$ python sftp.py localhost john W-2.pdf miles.png

Transfer of 'W-2.pdf' is at 32768/115065 bytes (28.5%)

Transfer of 'W-2.pdf' is at 65536/115065 bytes (57.0%)

Transfer of 'W-2.pdf' is at 98304/115065 bytes (85.4%)

Transfer of 'W-2.pdf' is at 115065/115065 bytes (100.0%)

Transfer of 'W-2.pdf' is at 115065/115065 bytes (100.0%)

Transfer of 'miles.png' is at 15577/15577 bytes (100.0%)

Transfer of 'miles.png' is at 15577/15577 bytes (100.0%)

To observe the simple but entire set of file operations that SFTP provides, visit the excellent paramiko documentation at the URL already provided.

Additional Features

I've just gone over all of the SSH operations that are provided via methods on the basic SSHClient object in the last few sections. The more obscure functions, such as remote X11 sessions and port forwarding, necessitate going one level deeper in the paramiko interface and speaking directly to the client's "transport" object.

The transport class is responsible for understanding the low-level activities that are used to fuel an SSH connection. You can quickly request transportation from a client.

>>> client.get transport = transport ()

Though I don't have space to go over all of the SSH features in this chapter, the knowledge of SSH you gained in this chapter should help you understand them given the paramiko documentation and example code—whether from the paramiko project's demos directory or from blogs, Stack Overflow, or other online resources about paramiko.

SSH opens a port on either the local or remote host—at the very least, making the port available to connections from localhost and possibly also accepting connections from other machines on the Internet—and "forwards" these connections across the SSH channel, where it connects to another host and port on the remote end, passing data back and forth. Port forwarding is a valuable feature. For example, I occasionally find myself working on a web application that I can't simply execute on my laptop because it requires access to a database and other resources that can only be found on a server farm. However, I may not want to go through the trouble of running the programme on a public port, which may require adjusting firewall rules to open, and then configuring HTTPS so that third parties cannot see my work-in-progress. One simple option is to run the under-construction web application on the distant development machine in the same way that I would locally—listening on localhost:8080 so that it cannot be visited from any computer—and then inform SSH that I want connections to my local port 8080. made on my laptop, which will be routed out so that people can connect to port 8080 on that local system.

```
$ ssh -L 8080:localhost:8080 devel.example.com
```

I have both terrible and good news for you if you need to create port forwarding when using paramiko with an SSH connection. The bad news is that because it enables more common operations like shell sessions, the top-level SSHClient does not give a straightforward mechanism to build a forward. Instead, you'll have to write loops that transfer data in both directions over the forward and then call directly to the "transport" object to generate the forward. Of course, because the port-forward data is passed back and forth across channels within the SSH connection, you don't have to worry if it's raw, unprotected HTTP or other traffic that's normally visible to third parties; because it's now embedded inside SSH, it's protected from being intercepted by its own encryption.

Conclusion

Remote-shell protocols allow you to connect to remote machines, perform shell commands, and view the results as if they were running in a local terminal window. These protocols are sometimes used to connect to a real Unix shell, and other times they are used to connect to small, embedded shells in routers or other networking hardware that needs to be configured. When dealing with Unix commands, you should always be mindful of output buffering, special shell characters, and terminal input buffering as difficulties that might muck up your data or even cause your shell connection to hang. The telnetlib module in the Python Standard Library supports the Telnet protocol natively. Despite the fact that Telnet is old, unsafe, and difficult to script, it may be the only protocol supported by the simple devices you want to connect to. Not just for connecting to a remote host's command line, but also for transferring files and forwarding TCP/IP ports, the Secure Shell protocol is the current state of the art. Thanks to the third-party paramiko package, Python provides great SSH functionality. Three things to keep in mind when setting up an SSH connection.

- Paramiko will need to validate (or be expressly told to ignore) the remote machine's identity, which is specified as the host key present at the time of connection.

- Authentication will usually be done with a password or a public-private key pair, the public half of which you have stored in the remote server's authorized keys file.

- You can start all kinds of SSH services—remote shells, individual commands, and file-transfer sessions—after you've been authenticated, and they'll all run at the same time without you having to open new SSH connections, thanks to the fact that they'll each get their own "channel" within the master SSH connection.

The File Transmission Protocol, on which SFTP was based, is an older and less powerful protocol for file transfer that dates back to the early days of the Internet.

CHAPTER 17

File Transfer Protocol (FTP)

FTP (File Transmit Protocol) was previously one of the most extensively used Internet protocols, with users using it to transfer data between computers connected to the Internet. Unfortunately, the protocol has seen better days, and there is now a better option for each of its primary tasks. FTP was originally used to fuel four basic activities. FTP was first and mostly used for file downloads. Users linked to "anonymous" FTP sites that permitted public access to retrieve documents, source code for new programmes, and media such as photos or videos. (You logged in with the login "anonymous" or "ftp," and then typed your e-mail address as the password out of courtesy, so they'd know who was using their bandwidth.) Because transferring huge files with Telnet clients was frequently a risky undertaking, FTP was always the protocol of choice when files were to be moved across computer accounts.

Second, FTP was frequently hacked to allow for anonymous uploading. Many organisations wanted outsiders to be able to submit documents or files, so they set up FTP servers that allowed files to be written into directories with no way of retrieving the contents. Users would not be able to see (or, presumably, guess!) the names of the files that other users had just submitted, allowing them to access them before the site administrators.

Third, the protocol was frequently used to enable the synchronisation of whole file trees between different computer accounts. Users could shift entire directory trees from one of their accounts to another using a client that supported recursive FTP operations, and server administrators could clone or install new services without having to rebuild them from the ground up on a new computer. Users were typically unaware of how the actual protocol operated or the numerous instructions required to transfer so many distinct files while using FTP in this manner: Instead, they pressed a button, which launched a big batch operation that completed the process.

Finally, FTP was utilised for what it was designed for: interactive, full-featured file management. Early FTP clients had a command-line prompt that resembled a Unix shell account, and the protocol borrows both the concept of a "current working directory" and the cd command to move from one directory to another from shell accounts, as I'll describe. Later clients imitated the Mac-like interface by drawing folders and files on the computer screen. In either event, the full capabilities of FTP were finally put to use in the activity of file-system browsing: It let you to do things like create and delete folders, change file permissions, and rename files in addition to listing directories and uploading and downloading files.

Structure:

- What to Do If You Can't Use FTP
- Channels of Communication
- In Python, how to use FTP
- Binary and ASCII Files
- Binary Downloading (Advanced)
- Data Uploading
- Uploading Binary Data in an Advanced Way
- Error Handling
- Searching via directories
- Detecting Directories and Downloading in Recursive Mode
- Creating and deleting directories
- Using FTP in a Secure Manner
- Conclusion

Objectives:

This chapter is beneficial if you have a legacy system and need to communicate with it through FTP from your Python software, or if you want to learn more about file transfer protocols in general, and FTP is a solid, historical place to start.

What to Do If You Can't Use FTP

There are now better alternatives to the FTP protocol for almost everything you could possibly wish to do with it. You'll still come across URLs that begin with ftp:/ now and then, but they're becoming increasingly rare.. The protocol's major flaw is its lack of security: not only files, but also usernames and passwords are delivered in clear text and can be seen by anybody watching network traffic. Another difficulty is that an FTP user frequently establishes a connection, selects a working directory, and performs multiple activities using the same network connection. With millions of users, modern Internet services prefer protocols like HTTP (see Chapter 9) that allow users to send brief, self-contained queries rather than long-running FTP sessions that require the server to remember things like the current working directory.

The security of file systems is a final major concern. Early FTP servers tended to expose the full file system, allowing users to cd to / and spy about to discover how the system was configured, rather than just a fragment of the host file system that the owner desired accessible. True, you might operate the server as a distinct ftp user and deny that user access to as many files as possible; however, many parts of the Unix file system must be publically accessible just so that ordinary users can use the programmes there.

So, what are your options?

- On today's Internet, HTTP (see Chapter 9) is the standard protocol for file downloads, which is secured with SSL when appropriate. HTTP offers system-independent URLs rather than exposing system-specific file naming conventions as FTP does.

- Anonymous upload is less common, but the general trend is to use a form on a web page that instructs the browser to use an HTTP POST operation to send the file selected by the user.

- Since the days when a recursive FTP file copy was the only option to get files to another machine, file synchronisation has vastly improved. Instead of copying every file, contemporary procedures like rsync or rdist compare files on both ends of the connection and copy just the ones that have changed or are new. (If you can't find these instructions in this book, try Googling them.) Nonprogrammers are more likely to use the Dropbox service, which is powered by Python, or any of the rival "cloud drive" services that huge carriers currently provide.

- The only area where FTP is still widely used on the Internet today is for full file-system access: Despite its lack of security, thousands of low-cost ISPs continue to accept FTP. Users can copy their media and (usually) PHP source code into their online account using this method. Today, service providers would be much better off supporting SFTP instead (see Chapter 16).

The FTP standard is RFC 959, available at www.faqs.org/rfcs/rfc959.html.

Channels of Communication

FTP is unusual in that it uses two TCP connections by default when it operates. The control channel is one of the connections, and it transports commands as well as acknowledgments or error codes. The data channel is the second link, which is primarily for delivering file data or other data blocks such as directory listings. The data channel is completely duplex, which means that files can be transferred in both directions at the same time. In practise, however, this capability is rarely employed.

The procedure for downloading a file from an FTP server in typical operations is as follows:

1. The FTP client first establishes a command connection by connecting to the server's FTP port.

2. The client verifies its identity using a username and password.

3. The client navigates to the server's directory where it wishes to deposit or retrieve files.

4. For the data connection, the client starts listening on a new port and then informs the server about it.

5. The server establishes a connection to the port that the client has established.

6. The file is sent out.

7. The data connection has been terminated.

In the early days of the Internet, this idea of the server connecting back to the client worked effectively since practically every system that could run an FTP client had a public IP address, and firewalls were uncommon. However, today's situation is more complicated. Incoming connections to desktop and laptop computers are now frequently blocked by firewalls.

In Python, how to use FTP

For Python programmers, the ftplib Python module is the principal interface to FTP. It takes care of the technicalities of setting up the various connections for you, as well as providing easy ways to automate basic actions.

If you merely want to download files, the urllib2 module from Chapter 1 supports FTP and may be more convenient to use for simple download activities; simply execute it with an ftp:/ URL. I discuss ftplib in this chapter since it has FTP-specific functionality that aren't present in urllib2.

A very basic ftplib example is shown in Listing 17-1. The application establishes a connection to a remote server, outputs the current working directory, and displays the welcome message.

Listing 17-1. Creating a Basic FTP Connection

```python
#!/usr/bin/env python3
# Programming in Python: The Basics.
from ftplib import FTP
def main():
        ftp = FTP('ftp.ibiblio.org')
        print("Welcome:", ftp.getwelcome())
        ftp.login()
        print("Current working directory:", ftp.pwd())
        ftp.quit()
if __name__ == '__main__':
  main()
```

The welcome message will usually contain no information that your software may utilise, but if a user is calling your client interactively, you might wish to show it. The login() function accepts multiple parameters, including a username, password, and a third authentication token called a "account" by FTP. It was called without parameters in this case, causing the user to log in as "anonymous" with a generic password. Remember that an FTP session can visit many directories, just like a shell prompt can use cd to change destinations. The pwd() function returns the current working directory on the connection's remote site in this case. Finally, the quit() function logs out of the connection and closes it. When the programme is executed, the following is what it produces:

```
$ ./connect.py
Welcome: 220 ProFTPD Server (Bring it on...)
Current working directory: /
```

Binary and ASCII Files

When making an FTP transfer, you must determine whether you want the file to be processed as a monolithic block of binary data or as a text file so that your local system may paste the lines back together using whatever end-of-line character your platform supports. When you ask Python 3 to work in text mode, it expects and returns plain strings, but if you're dealing with binary file data, it expects and returns byte strings. A file sent in ASCII mode is delivered one line at a time to your software, and it's delivered without line endings, so you'll have to manually glue the lines back together. Listing 17-2 shows a Python programme that downloads and saves a well-known text file to your local directory.

Listing 17-2. Obtaining an ASCII File Downloading an ASCII File

```python
#!/usr/bin/env python3
# Programming in Python: The Basics.
# Downloads README from remote and writes it to disk.
import os
from ftplib import FTP
def main():
        if os.path.exists('README'):
                raise IOError('refusing to overwrite your README file')
        ftp = FTP('ftp.kernel.org')
        ftp.login()
        ftp.cwd('/pub/linux/kernel')
        with open('README', 'w') as f:
                def writeline(data):
                        f.write(data)
                        f.write(os.linesep)
                        ftp.retrlines('RETR README', writeline)
                        ftp.quit()
if __name__ == '__main__':
        main()
```

The cwd() function in the listing selects a new working directory on the remote machine. The transfer is then started using the retrlines() function. Its first parameter indicates a remote command to run, commonly RETR, followed by a file name. The second parameter is a function that is run repeatedly as each line of the text file is fetched; if this parameter is omitted, the data is simply sent to standard output. Because the lines are given without the end-of-line character, your system's regular line ending is appended to each line as it is printed out by the handmade writeline() function. Try executing this programme; when it's finished, you should see a file titled README in your current directory. Basic binary file transfers work similarly to text file transfers. This is demonstrated in Listing 17-3.

Listing 17-3. Obtaining a Binary File

```python
#!/usr/bin/env python3
# Programming in Python: The Basics.
import os
from ftplib import FTP
def main():
        if os.path.exists('patch8.gz'):
            raise IOError('refusing to overwrite your patch8.gz
            file')
        ftp = FTP('ftp.kernel.org')
        ftp.login()
        ftp.cwd('/pub/linux/kernel/v1.0')
        with open('patch8.gz', 'wb') as f:
            ftp.retrbinary('RETR patch8.gz', f.write)
        ftp.quit()
if __name__ == '__main__':
 main()
```

When you start this application, it creates a patch8.gz file in your current working directory. The retrbinary() function simply transfers data blocks to the function given. This is advantageous because the write() function of a file object expects data, thus no special function is required in this situation.

Binary Downloading (Advanced)

ntransfercmd is a second function in the ftplib module that can be used to download binary files (). This command has a more basic UI, but it can be handy if you want to know more about what's going on during the download. This more complex command, in particular, allows you to keep track of the number of bytes sent and use that information to show the user status updates. A sample programme using ntransfercmd is shown in Listing 17-4. ().

Listing 17-4. Download a binary file containing status updates

```python
#!/usr/bin/env python3
# Programming in Python: The Basics.
import os, sys
from ftplib import FTP
def main():
        if os.path.exists('linux-1.0.tar.gz'):
                raise IOError('refusing to overwrite your linux-1.0.tar.
                gz file')
        ftp = FTP('ftp.kernel.org')
        ftp.login()
        ftp.cwd('/pub/linux/kernel/v1.0')
        ftp.voidcmd("TYPE I")
        socket, size = ftp.ntransfercmd("RETR linux-1.0.tar.gz")
        nbytes = 0
        f = open('linux-1.0.tar.gz', 'wb')
        while True:
                data = socket.recv(2048)
                if not data:
                        break
                f.write(data)
                nbytes += len(data)
                print("\rReceived", nbytes, end=' ')
                if size:
                        print("of %d total bytes (%.1f%%)"
                        % (size, 100 * nbytes / float(size)), end=' ')
        else:
                print("bytes", end=' ')
        sys.stdout.flush()
    print()
```

```
        f.close()
        socket.close()
        ftp.voidresp()
        ftp.quit()
if __name__ == '__main__':
  main()
```

There are a few new items to take note of in this section. The first is the use of voidcmd (). This sends an FTP command to the server and checks for errors, but it doesn't return anything. TYPE I is the raw command in this scenario. This changes the transfer mode to "image," which is the internal FTP term for binary files. The higher-level retrbinary() ran this command behind the scenes in the preceding example, but the lower-level ntransfercmd() did not.

Next, notice that ntransfercmd() provides a tuple that includes a data socket and a size estimate. Always keep in mind that the file size is only an estimate and should not be taken as gospel; the file could end sooner or last considerably longer than this amount. In addition, if a size estimate from the FTP server is unavailable, the estimated size returned will be None.

The object datasock is a standard TCP socket with all of the characteristics specified in Part 1 of this book (see Chapter 3 in particular). A simple loop in this example uses recv() until it has read all of the data from the connection, writing it to disc and printing status updates to the screen along the way.

There are two things to notice about the status updates that Listing 17-4 prints on the screen. Rather than printing a scrolling list of lines that disappear out of the top of the terminal, each line starts with a carriage return 'r,' which moves the cursor back to the left edge of the terminal, overwriting the previous status line and giving the impression of an increasing, animated percentage. Second, because you're telling each print statement to end each line with a space rather than a new line, you're never letting it finish a line of output, so you'll need to flush() the standard output to ensure that the status updates reach the screen right away.

It's critical to terminate the data socket and execute voidresp() after receiving the data, which receives the command response code from the server and raises an exception if there was a problem during transmission. Even if you don't care about detecting problems, forgetting to execute voidresp() will almost certainly result in future commands failing because the server's output socket will be blocked while you read the data.

Here's an example of what you'll get if you execute this programme:

```
$./advbinarydl.py

Received 1259161 of 1259161 bytes (100.0% )
```

Data Uploading

FTP can also be used to upload file data. Uploading uses the same two basic operations as downloading: storbinary() and storlines (). Both require the execution of a command and the transmission of a file-like object. The storbinary() function, on the other hand, continuously calls the read() method on that object until its content is exhausted, whereas storlines() calls the readline() method. These methods, unlike the analogous download functions, do not need you to provide your own callable function. (However, you might supply a custom file-like object whose read() or readline() method computes the outgoing data as the transmission progresses!)

Listing 17-5 demonstrates how to upload a binary file.

Listing 17-5. Upload a binary file

```python
#!/usr/bin/env python3
# Programming in Python: The Basics.
from ftplib import FTP
import sys, getpass, os.path
def main():
    if len(sys.argv) != 5:
        print("usage:", sys.argv[0],
            "<host> <username> <localfile> <remotedir>")
        exit(2)
    host, username, localfile, remotedir = sys.argv[1:]
    prompt = "Enter password for {} on {}: ".format(username, host)
    password = getpass.getpass(prompt)
    ftp = FTP(host)
    ftp.login(username, password)
    ftp.cwd(remotedir)
    with open(localfile, 'rb') as f:
            ftp.storbinary('STOR %s' % os.path.
            basename(localfile), f)
    ftp.quit()
```

```
if __name__ == '__main__':
 main()
```

This programme appears to be very similar to previous efforts. You'll need to find a server someplace to test it against because most anonymous FTP sites don't allow file uploads; I simply installed the old, venerable ftpd on my laptop for a few minutes and performed the test like this:

```
$ python binaryul.py localhost john test.txt /tmp
```

At the popup, I typed in my password (john is my username on this machine). When the application finished, I double-checked and found a copy of the test.txt file in /tmp. Remember that FTP does not encrypt or secure your password, so don't try this over the network to another machine! Simply change storbinary() to storlines() in this programme to upload a file in ASCII style ()

Uploading Binary Data in an Advanced Way

Listing 17-6 shows how to upload files manually using ntransfercmd(), just as there was a complicated raw version of the download procedure.

Listing 17-6. Uploading Files Block by Block

```python
#!/usr/bin/env python3
# Programming in Python: The Basics.
import os, sys
from ftplib import FTP
def main():
        if os.path.exists('linux-1.0.tar.gz'):
                raise IOError('refusing to overwrite your linux-1.0.tar.
                gz file')
                ftp = FTP('ftp.kernel.org')
                ftp.login()
                ftp.cwd('/pub/linux/kernel/v1.0')
                ftp.voidcmd("TYPE I")
                socket, size = ftp.ntransfercmd("RETR linux-1.0.tar.gz")
                nbytes = 0
                f = open('linux-1.0.tar.gz', 'wb')
                while True:
```

```
                    data = socket.recv(2048)
                    if not data:
                            break
                    f.write(data)
                    nbytes += len(data)
                    print("\rReceived", nbytes, end=' ')
                    if size:
                            print("of %d total bytes (%.1f%%)"
                    % (size, 100 * nbytes / float(size)), end=' ')
            else:
                            print("bytes", end=' ')
                    sys.stdout.flush()
            print()
            f.close()
            socket.close()
            ftp.voidresp()
            ftp.quit()
if __name__ == '__main__':
 main()
```

When you're done with the transfer, the first thing you should do is contact datasock. close(). When you're uploading data, closing the socket tells the server that it's time to stop! If you do not stop the data socket after uploading all of your data, the server will continue to wait for the remaining data. You may now perform an upload that updates its status as it progresses:

```
$ python binaryul.py localhost john patch8.gz /tmp

Enter password for john on localhost:

Sent 6408 of 6408 bytes (100.0%)
```

Error Handling

When an error occurs, ftplib, like most Python modules, will throw an exception. It has its own set of exceptions and can also raise socket.error and IOError. It provides a tuple named ftplib.all errors that lists all of the exceptions that ftplib can possibly raise as a convenience. When writing a try...except clause, this is a common shortcut. One of the issues with the simple retrbinary() function is that, in order to utilise it efficiently, you'll almost always end up opening the file locally before starting the remote transfer. If the file you're looking for doesn't exist when you issue a command to the remote side, Alternatively, if the RETR command fails, you must shut and remove the local file you just created (or else wind up littering the file system with zero-length files). By comparison, you can use the ntransfercmd() function to check for errors before opening a local file. These requirements are already followed in Listing 17-6: If ntransfercmd() fails, the application will exit before the local file is opened due to the exception.

Searching via directories

FTP offers two methods for learning about server files and directories. The nlst() and dir() methods in ftplib implement these. The nlst() method returns a list of entries in a directory, which includes all files and directories. However, all that is returned is a list of names. There is no more information regarding which entries are files or folders, file sizes, or anything else.

The more sophisticated dir() function retrieves a remote directory listing. The format of this listing is system-defined, however it normally includes a file name, size, modification date, and file type. It's usually the result of one of these two shell commands on Unix servers:

```
$ ls -l
```

```
$ ls -la
```

The output of dir can be used by Windows servers. Although the output may be beneficial to an end user, the many output formats make it difficult for a software to employ. Some clients who require this information write parsers for the numerous distinct formats that ls and dir generate between machines and operating system versions, while others can only parse the format in use at the time. Using nlst() to acquire directory information is demonstrated in Listing 17-7.

Listing 17-7. Obtaining a No-Frills Directory Listing

```python
#!/usr/bin/env python3

# Programming in Python: The Basics.

from ftplib import FTP

def main():
```

```
        ftp = FTP('ftp.ibiblio.org')

        ftp.login()

        ftp.cwd('/pub/academic/astronomy/')

        entries = ftp.nlst()

        ftp.quit()

        print(len(entries), "entries:")

        for entry in sorted(entries):

            print(entry)

if __name__ == '__main__':

 main()
```

When you run this program, you will see output like this:

```
$ python nlst.py

13 entries:

INDEX

README

ephem_4.28.tar.Z

hawaii_scope

incoming

jupitor-moons.shar.Z

lunar.c.Z

lunisolar.shar.Z

moon.shar.Z

planetary

sat-track.tar.Z

stars.tar.Z

xephem.tar.Z
```

The same files would be listed if you manually logged in to the host using an FTP client. When you use another file listing command, as shown in Listing 17-8, the output will be different.

Listing 17-8. Obtaining a Prestigious Directory Listing

```python
#!/usr/bin/env python3

# Programming in Python: The Basics.

from ftplib import FTP

def main():
        ftp = FTP('ftp.ibiblio.org')
        ftp.login()
        ftp.cwd('/pub/academic/astronomy/')
        entries = []
        ftp.dir(entries.append)
        ftp.quit()
        print(len(entries), "entries:")
        for entry in entries:
            print(entry)

if __name__ == '__main__':
  main()
```

There is no more information, but the file names are in a useful format for automated processing—a simple list of file names. Compare the output from Listing 17-8, which utilises dir(), to the basic list of file names you saw earlier:

```
$ python dir.py

13 entries:

-rw-r--r-- 1 (?) » (?) » »       750 Feb 14 1994 INDEX

-rw-r--r-- 1 root » bin »     »   135 Feb 11 1999 README

-rw-r--r-- 1 (?) » (?) »       341303 Oct 2 1992 ephem_4.28.tar.Z

drwxr-xr-x 2 (?) » (?) » »      4096 Feb 11 1999 hawaii_scope
```

```
drwxr-xr-x 2 (?) » (?) »          »  4096 Feb 11 1999 incoming

-rw-r--r-- 1 (?) » (?) » »         5983 Oct 2 1992 jupitor-moons.shar.Z

-rw-r--r-- 1 (?) » (?) » »         1751 Oct 2 1992 lunar.c.Z

-rw-r--r-- 1 (?) » (?) » »         8078 Oct 2 1992 lunisolar.shar.Z

-rw-r--r-- 1 (?) » (?) » »        64209 Oct 2 1992 moon.shar.Z

drwxr-xr-x 2 (?) » (?) » »         4096 Jan 6 1993 planetary

-rw-r--r-- 1 (?) » (?) »          129969 Oct 2 1992 sat-track.tar.Z

-rw-r--r-- 1 (?) » (?) » »         16504 Oct 2 1992 stars.tar.Z

-rw-r--r-- 1 (?) » (?) »          410650 Oct 2 1992 xephem.tar.Z
```

The dir() method takes a function and calls it for each line, delivering the directory listing in bits like retrlines() does for specific files. The append() method of the simple old Python entries list is used here.

Detecting Directories and Downloading in Recursive Mode

How will you differentiate directories from normal files if you can't predict what information an FTP server will provide from its dir() command? This is a critical step when downloading large trees of files from the server.

The only guaranteed answer, as demonstrated in Listing 17-9, is to attempt inserting a cwd() into every name returned by nlst() and, if successful, infer that the object is a directory! This sample software does not really download anything; instead, it writes out the folders it accesses to the screen to keep things simple (and not to swamp your drive with sample data).

Listing 17-9. attempting to recurse across directories.

```python
#!/usr/bin/env python3

# Programming in Python: The Basics.

from ftplib import FTP, error_perm

def walk_dir(ftp, dirpath):

    original_dir = ftp.pwd()

    try:
```

```
            ftp.cwd(dirpath)

            except error_perm:

                return # ignore non-directores and ones we cannot enter

        print(dirpath)

        names = sorted(ftp.nlst())

        for name in names:

            walk_dir(ftp, dirpath + '/' + name)

        ftp.cwd(original_dir) # return to cwd of our caller

def main():

        ftp = FTP('ftp.kernel.org')

        ftp.login()

        walk_dir(ftp, '/pub/linux/kernel/Historic/old-versions')

        ftp.quit()

if __name__ == '__main__':

 main()
```

This sample programme will be a little slow at first—there are a lot of files in the previous version's directory on the Linux kernel archive, as it turns out—but after a few dozen seconds, you should see the following directory tree on the screen:

```
$ python recursed1.py

/pub/linux/kernel/Historic/old-versions

/pub/linux/kernel/Historic/old-versions/impure

/pub/linux/kernel/Historic/old-versions/old

/pub/linux/kernel/Historic/old-versions/old/corrupt

/pub/linux/kernel/Historic/old-versions/tytso
```

You might supplement this list of folders by displaying each of the files that the recursive process is (slowly) discovering by adding a few print statements. Furthermore, you may download the files themselves to appropriate directories that you create locally by adding a few more lines of code. However, the only truly necessary logic for a recursive download is already included in Listing 17-9:

however, the only guaranteed way to determine whether an entry is a directory that you are permitted to access is to use cwd() against it.

Creating and deleting directories

Finally, FTP allows for the deletion of files as well as the creation and deletion of directories. The ftplib documentation covers all of these more obscure calls:

- **delete(filename)** is a command that deletes a file from a server.
- The command **mkd(dirname)** tries to make a new directory.
- **rmd(dirname)** deletes a directory; most systems require that the directory be empty first.
- **rename(oldname, newname)** operates similarly to the Unix command mv: the file is essentially renamed if both names are in the same directory; however, if the destination specifies a name in a different directory, the file is truly relocated.

These instructions, like all other FTP operations, are executed as if you were actually signed on to the remote server command line with the same username that you used to log in to the FTP. FTP may be used to support file browser apps that allow users to drag and drop files and folders between their local system and the remote host thanks to these final few commands.

Using FTP in a Secure Manner

Though I mentioned at the start of this chapter that there are far better protocols to use for pretty much anything you could do with FTP, especially the robust and secure SFTP extension to SSH (see Chapter 16), I should be fair and mention that a few FTP servers support TLS encryption (see Chapter 6) and that Python's ftplib does provide this protection if you want to use it. Create your FTP connection with the FTP TLS class instead of the normal FTP class if you want to use TLS. Simply by doing so, you will protect your login and password, as well as the entire FTP command channel, from prying eyes. The FTP data connection will be protected as well if you call the class's prot p() method (which accepts no arguments). There is a prot c() method that returns the data stream to normal if you want to use an unencrypted data connection during the session for some reason. Once again, as long as you're using the FTP TLS class, your commands will be secure. If you need more information about this FTP extension, go visit http://docs.python.org/3/library/ftplib.html. in the Python Standard Library documentation (which includes a tiny code sample).

Conclusion

FTP allows you to transmit files between your computer's client and a remote FTP server. Despite the fact that the protocol is insecure and antiquated when compared to better options such as SFTP, you may still encounter services and machines that demand you to utilise it. The ftplib package in Python is used to communicate with FTP servers.

Binary and ASCII transfers are supported by FTP. Text files are generally sent via ASCII transfers, which allow line endings to be changed while the file is being transferred. For everything else, binary transfers are used. The retrlines() function downloads a file in ASCII mode, whereas the retrbinary() function downloads a file in binary mode. You can also use a remote server to upload files. The storlines() and storbinary() functions upload files in ASCII and binary modes, respectively. For binary uploads and downloads, use the ntransfercmd() function. It allows you more control over the transfer process and is frequently used to show the user a progress bar. On errors, the ftplib module throws exceptions. To capture any errors that it may throw, use the special tuple ftplib.all errors.

On the remote end, you can use cwd() to change to a certain directory. The nlst() command gives a simple list of all files and directories in a given directory. The dir() command produces a more thorough list, but it is formatted for the server. Even if you only have nlst(), you can typically tell if an entry is a file or directory by trying to change to it with cwd() and seeing if you get an error. In the next chapter, we'll move on from simple file transfers to the more general activity of running a remote procedure on another server and receiving typed data back instead of raw strings.

CHAPTER 18
Remote Procedure Call (RPC)

RPC systems allow you to call functions in another process or on a remote server using the same syntax you'd use to call a procedure in a local API or library. This comes in use in two situations:

- You need data or information that is only available on another hard drive or network, and an RPC interface lets you easily send queries to another system to get back an answer without having to change the code that is making the call, which is now remote.

- You need data or information that is only available on another hard drive or network, and an RPC interface lets you easily send queries to another system to get back an answer without having to change the code that is making the call, which is now remote.

The original remote procedure systems were primarily written in low-level languages such as C. When one C function called another, they placed bytes on the network that looked very similar to the bytes already being pushed into the processor stack. RPC calls could not be made without knowing how the data would be serialised ahead of time, just as a C programme could not safely call a library function without a header file that specified it exactly how to lay out the method's inputs in memory (any errors often resulted in a crash). In actuality, each RPC payload appeared to be a block of binary data formatted using the Python struct module, which was explained in Chapter 5. However, because today's machines and networks are fast enough, we frequently trade some memory and performance for protocols that are more reliable and require less coordination between two pieces of code in dialogue.

Earlier RPC protocols would have sent a stream of bytes that looked something like this:

```
0, 0, 0, 1, 64, 36, 0, 0, 0, 0, 0, 0
```

It would have been up to the receiver to decode the 12 bytes to the values "integer 1" and "float 10.0" after learning that the function's parameters are a 32-bit integer and a 64-bit floating point number. Modern RPC protocols, on the other hand, use self-documenting formats like XML, which are designed in such a way that it's nearly hard to understand the arguments as anything but an integer and a floating-point number:

```
<params>

  <param><value><i4>41</i4></value></param>

  <param><value><double>10.</double></value></param>

</params>
```

12 bytes of actual binary data have ballooned into 108 bytes of protocol that must be generated by the sender and then interpreted on the receiving end, taking hundreds of CPU (Central Processing Unit) cycles. Nonetheless, the cost of eliminating ambiguity in procedures is often regarded as justified. Of course, a more current payload type than XML, such as JSON (JavaScript Object Notation), can be used to convey the above pair of values with less verbosity.

```
[1,10.0]
```

However, you can see that clear textual representation has replaced the traditional practise of delivering raw binary data whose meaning had to be understood ahead of time in both circumstances. Of course, by this time, you're probably wondering what makes RPC protocols so unique. After all, the options I'm discussing here—choosing a data format, submitting a request, and receiving a response—aren't exclusive to procedure calls; they apply to any significant network protocol! To use two examples from previous chapters, both HTTP and SMTP must serialise data and specify message formats. So, once again, you could wonder what makes RPC so unique. Three characteristics distinguish protocol as an RPC example.

The lack of strong semantics for the meaning of each call distinguishes an RPC protocol. Whereas HTTP is used to retrieve documents and SMTP is used to send messages, an RPC protocol does not attach any meaning to the data it receives other than to support fundamental data types like integers, floats, characters, and lists. Instead, it's up to each every API you create with an RPC protocol to describe what its calls signify. Second, RPC mechanisms provide a means of invoking methods without defining them. When you read the specification of a protocol that serves a particular purpose, such as HTTP or SMTP, it's easy to see why. you'll notice that they describe a limited set of basic operations, such as GET and PUT for HTTP and EHLO and MAIL for SMTP. RPC mechanisms, on the other hand, leave it up to you to define the verbs or function calls that your server will support; they don't pre-define them.

Third, while using RPC, your client and server code should resemble any other code that makes use of function calls. The only pattern you might find in the code is a certain caution with respect to the objects that are passed—lots of numbers, texts, and lists, but often not live objects like open files—unless you know that an object represents a remote server. While the kind of parameters that can be given may be limited, the function calls will "look regular" and will not require any additional decoration or elaboration to pass over the network.

Structure:

- RPC's characteristics
- XML-RPC
- JSON-RPC
- Data that Documents Itself
- Talking About Objects: Pyro and RPyC
- An RPyC Example
- Message Queues, RPC, and Web Frameworks
- Errors in the Network: How to Recover
- Conclusion

Objectives:

In these chapter we'll learn about how to recover while having errors in the network and message queues,RPC's characters, and web frameworks.

RPC's characteristics

RPC protocols include some critical features, as well as some differences, that you should bear in mind when choosing and subsequently deploying an RPC client or server. They allow you to make what appear to be local function or method calls, but are actually passed across the network to a different server. To begin with, every RPC protocol has a limit on the type of data that can be passed. In reality, because they are meant to function with a variety of programming languages, the most general-purpose RPC mechanisms tend to be the most limiting, as they can only support the lowest-common-denominator features that present in practically all of them.

As a result, the most widely used protocols only offer a few types of numbers and texts, as well as one sequence or list data type and something like a struct or associative array. Because so few other languages provide keyword arguments at this stage, many Python programmers are unhappy to realise that only positional arguments are commonly supported.

When an RPC mechanism is not bound to a programming language, it can support a broader range of parameters. Even live objects can be sent in some circumstances if the protocol can figure out a method to reconstruct them on the remote side. Only objects backed by live operating system resources, such as an open file, live socket, or shared memory area, can be passed over the network in this situation. The ability of the server to signal that an exception occurred while it was running the remote function is a second common characteristic. In such instances, the client RPC library would usually throw an exception to inform the caller that something went wrong. Of course, live stack frames like the ones Python provides to exception handlers can't be returned; each stack frame, after all, most likely refers to modules that don't exist in the client programme. When a call to the server fails, at the very least, a proxy exception with the appropriate error message must be thrown on the client side of the RPC interaction.

Third, many RPC mechanisms enable introspection, which allows clients to see a list of the calls that are supported by that RPC service, as well as the arguments they take. Some RPC protocols require the client and server to exchange extensive documents defining the library or API they support; others only allow the client to retrieve a list of function names and argument types; and still others allow no introspection at all. Python isn't great at supporting introspection because, unlike a statically typed language, it doesn't know the parameter types the programmer who wrote each function intended. Fourth, each RPC mechanism must have an addressing scheme that allows you to connect to a certain remote API. Some of these systems are fairly complex, and they may even be able to link you to the relevant server on your network for a certain activity without requiring you to know its name beforehand. Other approaches are straightforward, requiring only the IP address, port number, or URL of the service you wish to use. Rather of constructing their own addressing system, these technologies disclose the actual network addressing scheme.

Finally, when RPC calls are made by numerous separate client programmes using different credentials, some RPC systems offer authentication, access control, and even full impersonation of specific user accounts. However, such characteristics are not always present; in fact, basic and widely used RPC protocols frequently lack them totally. Simple RPC schemes rely on an underlying protocol like HTTP to provide authentication, and they leave it up to you to set up whatever passwords, public keys, or firewall restrictions are required to secure the lower-level protocol if you want your RPC service to be secure from unauthorised access.

XML-RPC

Let's start our exploration of RPC techniques by looking at Python's built-in XML-RPC capabilities. This may appear to be an unsuitable choice for the first scenario. After all, XML is known for being clumsy and verbose, and XML-use RPC's in new services has been dropping for years.

XML-RPC, on the other hand, has native support in Python's Standard Library because it was one of the earliest RPC protocols of the Internet era, running natively over HTTP rather than requiring its own on-the-wire protocol. As a result, none of the examples shown here will require third-party modules. Although this limits the RPC server's capabilities compared to using a third-party library, it keeps the examples basic for this first venture into RPC.

THE XML-RPC PROTOCOL

Purpose: Remote procedure calls

Standard: www.xmlrpc.com/spec

Runs atop: HTTP

Data types: int; float; unicode; list; dict with unicode keys; with nonstandard extensions, datetime

and None

Libraries: xmlrpclib, SimpleXMLRPCServer, DocXMLRPCServer

If you've ever worked with raw XML, you're aware that it doesn't have any data-type semantics. It can only represent items that contain other elements, text strings, and text-string properties, but not integers. As a result, the XML-RPC standard must add semantics to the plain XML document format in order to describe how numbers should appear when converted to marked-up text. The Python Standard Library makes writing an XML-RPC client or server a breeze. Listing 18-1 depicts a simple server that runs a web server on port 7001 and then monitors incoming Internet connections.

Listing 18-1. An XML-RPC Server

```python
#!/usr/bin/env python3

# Programming in Python: The Basics.

# XML-RPC server

import operator, math

from xmlrpc.server import SimpleXMLRPCServer

from functools import reduce

def main():

        server = SimpleXMLRPCServer(('127.0.0.1', 7001))

        server.register_introspection_functions()

        server.register_multicall_functions()

        server.register_function(addtogether)

        server.register_function(quadratic)

        server.register_function(remote_repr)

        print("Server ready")

        server.serve_forever()

def addtogether(*things):

        """Add together everything in the list `things`."""

        return reduce(operator.add, things)

def quadratic(a, b, c):

        """Determine `x` values satisfying: `a` * x*x + `b` * x + c
```

```
        == 0"""

        b24ac = math.sqrt(b*b - 4.0*a*c)

        return list(set([ (-b-b24ac) / 2.0*a,
                          (-b+b24ac) / 2.0*a ]))

def remote_repr(arg):

        """Return the `repr()` rendering of the supplied `arg`."""

        return arg

if __name__ == '__main__':

 main()
```

You don't have to allocate an entire port to an RPC service like this because an XML-RPC service stays at a single URL of a web site. Instead, you may incorporate it into a standard web application that provides a variety of other pages and even independent RPC services at other URLs. If you do have an entire port to spare, the Python XML-RPC server is a simple method to set up a web server that only handles XML-RPC requests.

The three sample functions provided by the server via XML-RPC (those introduced to the RPC service via the register function() calls) are pretty typical Python routines. And that, once again, is the whole idea of XML-RPC: it allows you to make routines available for network invocation without having to code them any differently than you would if they were regular functions in your software.

The Python Standard Library's SimpleXMLRPCServer is, as its name implies, fairly basic; it can't serve other web pages, it doesn't comprehend HTTP authentication, and you can't ask it to provide TLS security without subclassing it and adding further code. Nonetheless, it will serve you well here, demonstrating some of the basic advantages and limitations of RPC while also allowing you to get up and running in only a few lines of code. In addition to the three calls that register the functions, two extra configuration calls are done. Each of them enables an optional but common feature of XML-RPC servers: an introspection routine that allows a client to find out which RPC calls a server supports, as well as the ability to support a multicall function that allows several individual function calls to be bundled into a single network roundtrip.

Before you can attempt any of the next three programmes, you'll need to start this server, so open a command window and start it:

```
$ python xmlrpc_server.py
```

Server ready

On localhost port 7001, the server is currently accepting connections. All of the standard addressing rules apply to this TCP server that you learned in Chapters 2 and 3, so you'll have to connect to it from another command prompt on the same system unless you change the code to bind to an interface other than localhost. Open a new command window and prepare to try out the next three listings as I go over them. First, let's see if the introspection feature you enabled on this server works. This feature is optional, and it may or may not be offered on many other XML-RPC services you use online or deploy yourself.

Introspection is depicted in Listing 18-2 from the client's perspective.

Listing 18-2. What Functions Does an XML-RPC Server Support?

```python
#!/usr/bin/env python3
# Programming in Python: The Basics.
# XML-RPC client
import xmlrpc.client
def main():
        proxy = xmlrpc.client.ServerProxy('http://127.0.0.1:7001')
        print('Here are the functions supported by this server:')
        for method_name in proxy.system.listMethods():
        if method_name.startswith('system.'):
            continue
        signatures = proxy.system.methodSignature(method_name)
        if isinstance(signatures, list) and signatures:
            for signature in signatures:
                    print('%s(%s)' % (method_name, signature))
        else:
            print('%s(...)' % (method_name,))
        method_help = proxy.system.methodHelp(method_name)
        if method_help:
            print(' ', method_help)
if __name__ == '__main__':
 main()
```

The introspection technique isn't just a nice-to-have feature; it's not even mentioned in the XML-RPC specification! It allows clients to call a set of special methods, all of which start with the string system to identify them from regular methods. These unique techniques provide details on the additional calls that are available. Let's begin by invoking listMethods (). If introspection is enabled, you will be given a list of additional method names.

Let's disregard the system methods in this example listing and only print information about the remaining ones. You'll try to get the signature of each method to see what arguments and data types it accepts. The server is written in Python, a language that does not have type declarations. it does not actually know what data types functions expect:

```
$ python xmlrpc_introspect.py

Here are the functions supported by this server:

concatenate(...)

 Add together everything in the list `things`.

quadratic(...)

 Determine `x` values satisfying: `a` * x*x + `b` * x + c == 0

remote_repr(...)

 Return the `repr()` rendering of the supplied `arg`.
```

However, you can see that while argument types aren't provided in this case, documentation strings are. In actuality, the SimpleXMLRPCServer has retrieved and returned the function's docstrings. In a real-world client, you can come across two uses for introspection. To begin, if you're building a software that uses an XML-RPC service, the service's web documentation may provide human-readable assistance. Second, if you're developing a client that interacts with a number of comparable XML-RPC services but differ in the methods they offer, a listMethods() call can assist you figure out which servers provide certain commands. The goal of an RPC service, as you may recall, is to make function calls in a target language appear as natural as possible. Furthermore, as seen in Listing 18-3, the Standard Library's xmlrpclib provides a proxy object for making server function calls. These calls resemble calls to local methods.

Listing 18-3. Making XML-RPC Requests

```
#!/usr/bin/env python3

# -*- coding: utf-8 -*-
```

```
# Programming in Python: The Basics.

# XML-RPC client

import xmlrpc.client

def main():

        proxy = xmlrpc.client.ServerProxy('http://127.0.0.1:7001')

        print(proxy.addtogether('x', 'ÿ', 'z'))

        print(proxy.addtogether(20, 30, 4, 1))

        print(proxy.quadratic(2, -4, 0))

        print(proxy.quadratic(1, 2, 1))

        print(proxy.remote_repr((1, 2.0, 'three')))

        print(proxy.remote_repr([1, 2.0, 'three']))

        print(proxy.remote_repr({'name': 'john',

            'data': {'age': 49, 'sex': 'M'}}))

        print(proxy.quadratic(1, 0, 1))

if __name__ == '__main__':

 main()
```

When you run the preceding code against the example server, you'll get output that teaches you a lot about XML-RPC and RPC techniques in general. Note how almost all of the calls work without issue, and how both the calls in this listing and the functions themselves from Listing 18-1 appear to be fully regular Python; nothing about them is network-specific:

```
$ python xmlrpc_client.py

xÿz

55

[0.0, 8.0]

[-1.0]

[1, 2.0, 'three']

[1, 2.0, 'three']
```

```
{'data': {'age': [49], 'sex': 'M'}, 'name': 'john'}

Traceback (most recent call last):

  ...

xmlrpclib.Fault: <Fault 1: "<type 'exceptions.ValueError'>:math
domain error">
```

However, there are a few points to which you should pay attention. To begin, keep in mind that XML-RPC has no constraints on the argument types you provide. Addtogether() can be called with strings or numbers, and any number of parameters can be passed. The protocol itself is unconcerned; it has no preconceived notions about how many arguments or types a function should accept. Of course, if you called a language that cared—or even a Python method that didn't accept variable-length argument lists—the distant language might throw an exception. But that would be the language, not the XML-RPC protocol itself, that would be complaining. Second, keep in mind that, like Python and many other languages in its ancestry, XML-RPC function calls can take many arguments but only return a single result value. Even if the value is a complicated data structure, it will be returned as a single result. And the protocol doesn't care if the result is a consistent form or size; the amount of elements returned by quadratic() (yeah, I was tired of all the simple add() and subtract() math functions that tend to get used in XML-RPC examples!) changes without causing the network logic to complain.

Third, keep in mind that the large number of Python data types must be condensed to the lower set that XML-RPC supports. XML-RPC, in particular, only supports one sequence type: the list. When you pass a tuple of three items to remote repr(), the server receives a list of three items instead of a tuple. When RPC protocols are combined with a specific language, this is a common feature. Types that they don't directly support must either be transferred to a different data structure (the tuple in this case was converted to a list) or an exception must be raised claiming that a specific parameter type cannot be communicated.

Fourth, in XML-RPC, sophisticated data structures can be recursive. You're not limited to arguments containing only one level of complex data type. . As you can see, passing a dictionary with another dictionary as one of its values works perfectly.

Finally, as promised earlier, an exception in the server function made it back across the network successfully and was represented locally on the client by an xmlrpclib.

Instance of a fault. This instance provided the name of the remote exception as well as the accompanying error message. XML-RPC exceptions will always have this structure, regardless of the language used to implement the server functions. The traceback isn't very useful; while it informs you which call in the code caused the issue, the innermost layers of the stack are just the xmlrpclib's code. I've gone through the basic features and limitations of XML-RPC so far. You can learn about a few more features by consulting the documentation for either the client or server module in the Python Standard Library. By passing extra arguments to the ServerProxy class, you may learn how to use TLS and authentication in particular.

However, there is one feature worth mentioning here: the ability to make many calls in a network roundtrip if the server enables it (this is another of those optional extensions), as seen in Listing 18-4.

Listing 18-4. Multicalling with XML-RPC

```python
#!/usr/bin/env python3

# Programming in Python: The Basics.

# XML-RPC client performing a multicall

import xmlrpc.client

def main():
        proxy = xmlrpc.client.ServerProxy('http://127.0.0.1:7001')
        multicall = xmlrpc.client.MultiCall(proxy)
        multicall.addtogether('a', 'b', 'c')
        multicall.quadratic(2, -4, 0)
        multicall.remote_repr([1, 2.0, 'three'])
        for answer in multicall():
                print(answer)
if __name__ == '__main__':
 main()
```

When you run this script, check the server's command window to ensure that just one HTTP request is sent in order to respond to all three function calls:

```
localhost - - [09/Oct/2019 00:16:19] "POST /RPC2 HTTP/1.0" 200 -
```

By the way, the ability to log messages like the one above can be disabled; such logging is controlled by one of SimpleXMLRPCServer's settings. Unless you study the manual and setup the client and server differently, the default URL used by both the server and the client is /RPC2. Before I go on to another RPC technique, there are three final considerations to consider:

- There are two additional data types that can be difficult to live without, which is why many XML-RPC protocols offer them: dates and None (also known as null or nil in other languages). Both the client and server versions of Python include options for sending and receiving nonstandard values.

- XML-RPC does not support keyword arguments since few languages are smart enough to support them.

- Finally, keep in mind that dictionaries can only be passed if all of their keys are strings, whether normal or Unicode. Some services get around this by allowing a dictionary to be passed as a function's final argument—or by removing positional arguments entirely and using a single dictionary argument for every function that specifies all of its parameters by name. For more information on how to think about this restriction, see the "Self-Documenting Data" section later in this chapter.

Despite the fact that the whole goal of an RPC protocol like XML-RPC is to allow you forget about the specifics of network transmission and focus on normal programming, you should at least see what your calls will look like on the wire! The sample client program's initial call to quadratic() is as follows:

```
<?xml version='1.0'?>
```

```
<methodCall>
```

```
<methodName>quadratic</methodName>
```

```
<params>
```

```
<param>
```

```
<value><int>2</int></value>
```

```
</param>
```

```
<param>
```

```
<value><int>-4</int></value>
```

```
</param>
```

```
<param>
```

```
<value><int>0</int></value>
```

```
</param>
```

```
</params>
```

```
</methodCall>
```

The response to the preceding call looks like this:

```
<?xml version='1.0'?>
```

```
<methodResponse>
```

```
<params>
```

```
<param>
```

```
<value><array><data>
```

```
<value><double>0.0</double></value>
```

```
<value><double>8.0</double></value>
```

```
</data></array></value>
```

```
</param>
```

```
</params>
```

```
</methodResponse>
```

JSON-RPC

JSON's brilliant idea is to serialise data structures to strings using the JavaScript computer language's syntax. This means that using the eval() function in a web browser, JSON strings may theoretically be converted back to data. (However, because using a formal JSON parser with untrusted data is often undesirable, most programmers use a formal JSON parser instead of taking advantage of JavaScript compatibility.) This remote procedure call method can make your data much more compact while also simplifying your parsers and library code by adopting a syntax specifically built for data rather than adapting a verbose document markup language like XML.

```
               THE JSON-RPC PROTOCOL
           Purpose: Remote procedure calls
       Standard: http://json-rpc.org/wiki/specification
                   Runs atop: HTTP
Data types: int; float; unicode; list; dict with unicode keys; None
         Libraries: many third-party, including jsonrpclib
```

Because the Python Standard Library does not support JSON-RPC, you'll have to rely on one of the many third-party options. On the Python Package Index, you'll discover these distributions. jsonrpclib-pelix was one of the first libraries to support Python 3. You can test out the server and client shown in Listings 18-5 and 18-6, respectively, if you deploy it in a virtual environment (see Chapter 1).

Listing 18-5. A JSON-RPC Server

```python
#!/usr/bin/env python3
# Programming in Python: The Basics.
# JSON-RPC server needing "pip install jsonrpclib-pelix"
from jsonrpclib.SimpleJSONRPCServer import SimpleJSONRPCServer
def lengths(*args):
    """Measure the length of each input argument.
    Given N arguments, this function returns a list of N smaller
    lists of the form [len(arg), arg] that each state the length of
    an input argument and also echo back the argument itself.
    """
    results = []
    for arg in args:
        try:
            arglen = len(arg)
        except TypeError:
            arglen = None
        results.append((arglen, arg))
    return results
def main():
    server = SimpleJSONRPCServer(('localhost', 7002))
    server.register_function(lengths)
    print("Starting server")
    server.serve_forever()
if __name__ == '__main__':
    main()
```

The server code is straightforward, as it should be for an RPC protocol. As with XML-RPC, you simply specify the functions you want to make available over the network, and they become queryable. (Alternatively, you can pass an object, and all of its methods will be registered with the server at the same time.)

Listing 18-6. . JSON-RPC Client

```
#!/usr/bin/env python3

# Programming in Python: The Basics.

# JSON-RPC client needing "pip install jsonrpclib-pelix"

from jsonrpclib import Server

def main():

        proxy = Server('http://localhost:7002')

        print(proxy.lengths((1,2,3), 27, {'Canopus': -0.74,
        'Arcturus': -0.05}))

if __name__ == '__main__':

  main()
```

Client code is similarly straightforward to write. You can learn a lot about this protocol by sending various objects whose lengths you want to measure and having the server echo those data structures back to you. To begin, keep in mind that the protocol permits you to transmit as many parameters as you like; it was unconcerned that it couldn't deduce a static method signature from the function. It's comparable to XML-RPC, but it's not the same as the XML-RPC protocols designed for traditional, statically typed languages.

Second, note that the server's None value in the response is unaffected. This is because the protocol itself supports this value without the need to activate any nonstandard extensions:

```
$ python jsonrpc_server.py

Starting server

[In another command window:]

$ python jsonrpc_client.py

[[3, [1, 2, 3]], [None, 27], [2, {'Canopus': -0.74,   'Arcturus':
-0.05}]]
```

Third, keep in mind that JSON-RPC only supports one type of sequence, therefore the client's tuple had to be converted to a list in order to get through. Of course, the most significant distinction between JSON-RPC and XML-RPC is that the data payload in this case is a compact, elegant JSON message that knows how to represent each data type natively. This is due to the fact that both approaches perform an excellent job of concealing the network from the code. When I use Wireshark on my localhost interface while running this sample client and server, I can see the following messages being sent:

```
{"version": "1.1",
 "params": [[1, 2, 3], 27, {'Canopus': -0.74,  'Arcturus': -0.05}],
 "method": "lengths"}
{"result": [[3, [1, 2, 3]], [null, 27],
 [2, {'Canopus': -0.74,  'Arcturus': -0.05}]]}
```

Because of the popularity of JSON-RPC version 1, various competing initiatives have been made to extend and supplement the protocol with new capabilities. If you want to learn more about the present situation of the standard and the debate surrounding it, you can conduct some research online. You can use a solid third-party Python implementation for most fundamental tasks and not bother about the argument over standard extensions.

I'd be remiss if I didn't disclose one key truth about this subject. Although the above example is synchronous—the client sends a request and then waits patiently for only a single answer while doing nothing productive in the meantime—the JSON-RPC protocol does allow for id values to be attached to each request. This means that you can send out many queries before receiving any matching responses with the same id. I won't go into detail about the concept because, properly speaking, asynchrony goes beyond the usual purpose of an RPC protocol. After all, function calls in typical procedural languages are synchronous occurrences. If the concept appeals to you, read the standard and then look into whether Python JSON-RPC packages could be able to accommodate your asynchrony requirements.

Data that Documents Itself

Both XML-RPC and JSON-RPC appear to allow a data structure that looks quite similar to a Python dictionary, but with one unpleasant constraint. The data structure is known as a struct in XML-RPC and an object in JSON. However, to a Python programmer, it appears to be a dictionary, and your first reaction will likely be annoyance at the fact that its keys cannot be integers, floats, or tuples.

Let's take a look at a specific example. Assume you have a dictionary of physical element symbols arranged alphabetically by atomic number:

```
{1: 'H', 2: 'He', 3: 'Li', 4: 'Be', 5: 'B', 6: 'C', 7: 'N', 8: 'O'}
```

If you need to send this dictionary via an RPC protocol, your first thought would be to convert the numbers to strings so that the dictionary can be sent as a struct or object. It turns out that, in the vast majority of circumstances, this inclination is incorrect. Simply put, the struct and object are the same thing. Keys and values in containers of any size are not supported by RPC data structures. Instead, they're made to link a restricted number of predefined attribute names to the attribute values that they happen to have for a specific object. If you try to pair random keys and values with a struct, you may inadvertently make your service very difficult to use for users who utilise statically typed programming languages. Instead, consider dictionaries transmitted through RPCs to be similar to Python objects, which often contain a narrow set of attribute names that are well-known to your code. Similarly, the dictionaries you communicate through RPC should only have a few predefined keys and their associated values.

All of this indicates that, if the dictionary described earlier is to be utilised by a general-purpose RPC method, it should be serialised as a list of explicitly named values:

```
[{'number': 1, 'symbol': 'H'},
 {'number': 2, 'symbol': 'He'},
 {'number': 3, 'symbol': 'Li'},
 {'number': 4, 'symbol': 'Be'},
 {'number': 5, 'symbol': 'B'},
 {'number': 6, 'symbol': 'C'},
 {'number': 7, 'symbol': 'N'},
 {'number': 8, 'symbol': 'O'}]
```

The Python dictionary is shown in the preceding examples as it would be passed into an RPC call, not how it would be rendered on the wire.

The significant difference in this technique (apart from the fact that it's a lot longer) is that the previous data structure was useless unless you knew what the keys and values signified ahead of time. To give the data meaning, it relied on convention. However, because you've included names with the data, it's self-descriptive:

someone looking at these numbers on the wire or in a computer has a better chance of predicting what they represent. Both XML-RPC and JSON-RPC anticipate you to utilise their key-value types in this manner, which is where the terms struct and object come from. They are the terminology for an entity that holds named attributes in C and JavaScript, respectively. This, once again, puts them closer to Python objects than Python dictionaries.

If you have a Python dictionary like the one described here, you can convert it to an RPC-compatible data structure and subsequently change it back with the following code:

```
>>>elements = {1: 'H', 2: 'He'}

>>>t = [{'number': key, 'symbol': value} for key, value in elements.
items()]

>>>t

[{'symbol': 'H', 'number': 1}, {'symbol': 'He', 'number': 2}]

>>> {obj['number']: obj['symbol']) for obj in t}

{1: 'H', 2: 'He'}
```

If you find yourself building and destroying too many dictionaries to make this transition desirable, named tuples (as they exist in the most recent versions of Python) might be an even better approach to marshal such values before delivering them.

Talking About Objects: Pyro and RPyC

If the goal of RPC is to make remote function calls appear to be local, the two basic RPC techniques outlined previously fail catastrophically. XML-RPC and JSON-RPC both operate perfectly if the functions you're calling only employ basic data types in their arguments and return values. Consider how many times you'll use more complex parameters and return values instead! When you need to pass live items, what happens? For two reasons, this is a difficult problem to solve.

First, different programming languages have different behaviours and semantics for objects. As a result, object-supporting systems are either limited to a single language or provide an anaemic description of how a "object" can act selected from the lowest common denominator of the languages they seek to support.

Second, it's not always obvious how much state must move with an object in order for it to be functional on another computer. True, an RPC mechanism can simply begin iteratively delving into an object's characteristics and preparing those values for network transmission. On systems of even moderate complexity, however, simple-minded recursion into attribute values can lead to you walking most of the objects in memory. And, once you've accumulated megabytes of data for transmission, what are the possibilities that the remote end will actually require all of it?

Instead of sending the whole contents of each object supplied as a parameter or returned as a value, send simply the object name, which the remote end can use to inquire about the object's properties if necessary. This means that only the pieces of a highly connected object network that the remote site truly requires are communicated, rather than the entire graph. Both strategies, however, frequently result in pricey and slow services. They can also make it difficult to keep track of how one object can influence the responses supplied by another service on the other side of the network. In fact, the task imposed by XML-RPC and JSON-RPC (i.e., breaking down the query you wish to ask a remote service into basic data types that can be easily delivered) frequently ends up being software architecture. The limitations on parameter and return value data types force you to think through your service until you understand exactly what the distant service requires and why. As a result, I advise against switching to a more object-based RPC service solely to avoid having to build your remote services and find out the data they require to perform their tasks.

There are various well-known RPC protocols, such as SOAP and CORBA, that attempt to answer the big questions of how to support objects that may be on one server but are passed to another on behalf of a client application delivering an RPC message from a third server, to varying degrees. Unless a contract or assignment clearly needs them to speak these protocols to another existing system, Python programmers appear to shun these RPC techniques like the plague. They are outside the scope of this book, and if you need to utilise them, be prepared to spend at least an entire book on each one, as they can be rather complicated!

When all you have are Python programmes that need to communicate with one another, there is at least one compelling reason to use an RPC service that is familiar with Python objects and their behaviour. Python has a lot of sophisticated data types, thus trying to "speak down" to the dialect of constrained data formats like XML-RPC and JSON-RPC can be a waste of time. This is particularly true when Python dictionaries, sets, and datetime objects would perfectly convey what you want to say. Pyro and RPyC are two Python-native RPC systems worth mentioning. http://pythonhosted.org/Pyro4/ is the website for the Pyro project. This well-known RPC library is based on the Python pickle module and can send any type of input and response value that is pickle-able. Essentially, if an item and its attributes can be reduced to their basic kinds, it can be sent. Pyro, on the other hand, will not work if the values you want to send or receive are ones that the pickle module chokes on. (Alternatively, you could look at pickle documentation in the Python Standard Library.) If Python can't find out how to pickle a class, this library contains instructions on how to make it pickle-able.)

An RPyC Example

http://rpyc.readthedocs.org/en/latest/ is the website for the RPyC project. The approach to objects in this project is far more advanced. Indeed, it resembles the CORBA model, in which the real data sent across the network is a reference to an object that may be used to call back and activate more of its methods later if the receiver need it. Security appears to have received greater attention in the most current version, which is vital if you are allowing other businesses to use your RPC protocol. After all, allowing someone to provide you data to unpick is practically allowing them to run arbitrary code on your computer! Listings 18-7 and 18-8 show an example client and server, respectively. These listings should be studied thoroughly if you want an example of the remarkable things that a system like RPyC makes possible.

Listing 18-7. An RPyC Client

```python3
#!/usr/bin/env python3
# Programming in Python: The Basics.
# RPyC client
import rpyc
def main():
        config = {'allow_public_attrs': True}
        proxy = rpyc.connect('localhost', 18861, config=config)
        fileobj = open('testfile.txt')
        linecount = proxy.root.line_counter(fileobj, noisy)
        print('The number of lines in the file was', linecount)
def noisy(string):
        print('Noisy:', repr(string))
if __name__ == '__main__':
  main()
```

Listing 18-8. An RPyC Server

```python
#!/usr/bin/env python3
# Programming in Python: The Basics.
# RPyC server
import rpyc
def main():
        from rpyc.utils.server import ThreadedServer
        t = ThreadedServer(MyService, port = 18861)
        t.start()
class MyService(rpyc.Service):
 def exposed_line_counter(self, fileobj, function):
 print('Client has invoked exposed_line_counter()')
        for linenum, line in enumerate(fileobj.readlines()):
            function(line)
            return linenum + 1
if __name__ == '__main__':
 main()
```

The client may appear to be a typical software that uses an RPC service at first glance. After all, it uses a network address to call the connect() function and then accesses the functions of the returned proxy object as if the calls were made locally. If you look closely, though, you may see some astonishing changes! The first argument to the RPC function is a live file object, which may or may not exist on the server. The other argument is a function, which is a live entity rather than the normal inert data structure supported by RPC protocols.

The server offers a single method that accepts a file object and a callable function as parameters. It uses these in the same way as a conventional Python application that runs in a single process would. It performs readlines() on the file object, expecting the return result to be an iterator that can be used in a for loop. Finally, the server invokes the function object that was provided in, regardless of where the function actually resides (in the client). Note that, absent specific permission, RPyC's new security architecture only allows clients to call methods that begin with the special prefix exposed_.

Looking at the output created by executing the client is extremely enlightening, given that a short testfile.txt exists in the current directory and contains a few wise words:

```
$ python rpyc_client.py
Noisy: 'Simple\n'
Noisy: 'is\n'
Noisy: 'better\n'
Noisy: 'than\n'
Noisy: 'complex.\n'
The number of lines in the file was 5
```

Two truths are equally surprising. First, the server was able to iterate over numerous readlines() results, despite the fact that this required the client to invoke file–object logic multiple times. Second, the server did not somehow duplicate the code object of the noisy() method so that it could run it directly; instead, it repeatedly invoked the function on the client side of the connection, with the proper argument each time!

What's going on here? Simply said, RPyC is the polar opposite of the other RPC techniques we've looked at thus far. RPyC only serialises absolutely immutable things, such as Python integers, floats, strings, and tuples, whereas all other techniques strive to serialise and transfer as much information across the network as possible before leaving the remote code to either succeed or fail with no more information. For everything else, it sends a remote object identification, which allows the remote side to access attributes and invoke methods on those live objects by reaching back into the client. This method generates a significant amount of network traffic. If many object operations must transit back and forth between the client and server before an operation is completed, it can cause a substantial delay. It's also a problem to provide sufficient security. I chose to make the client connection with a blanket assertion of allow public attrs to provide the server permission to call things like readlines() on the client's own objects. If you're not comfortable handing over that much power to your server code, you'll have to spend some time fine-tuning the permissions such that your activities go smoothly without exposing too much potentially damaging functionality. As a result, the method can be costly, and security might be difficult if the client and server do not trust one another.

When you need it, though, there's nothing quite like RPyC for allowing Python objects on opposite sides of a network barrier to collaborate. You can even play the game with more than two processes; see the RPyC docs for further information.

The fact that RPyC works so well with plain Python functions and objects without requiring them to inherit from or mix in any extra network capabilities is a testament to Python's ability to intercept object activities and treat them in our own way—even by asking an inquiry across the network!

Message Queues, RPC, and Web Frameworks

If you're working with RPC services, be open to experiment with different transmission techniques. Many Python programmers who need to speak the XML-RPC protocol, for example, do not use the classes offered in the Python Standard Library. After all, an RPC service is frequently deployed as part of a larger web site, and having to maintain a separate server on a different port just to handle this type of web request can be extremely inconvenient.

There are three effective techniques to look at moving past too simple example code that makes it appear as if you need to start a new web server for each RPC service you want to make available from a certain site. First, see whether you can leverage WSGI's pluggability to install an RPC service that you've integrated into a bigger web project that you're delivering. By running both your regular web application and your RPC service as WSGI servers behind a filter that verifies the incoming URL, you may run both services on the same hostname and port number. It also allows you to take advantage of the fact that your WSGI web server may already support threading and scalability at a level that the RPC service does not.

If your RPC service is at the bottom of a bigger WSGI stack, you can use it to add authentication if the RPC service doesn't have it. Second, rather of needing a separate RPC library, you might discover that your preferred web framework already knows how to host an XML-RPC, JSON-RPC, or other type of RPC call. This means you can declare RPC endpoints with the same simplicity as you would specify views or RESTful services in your web framework. Consult the documentation for your web framework and conduct a web search for RPC-friendly third-party plug-ins.

Third, you might want to consider delivering RPC messages via an alternate transport that performs a better job of routing calls to servers that are ready to receive them than the protocol's original transport. When you want a full rack of servers to be busy distributing the load of incoming requests, message queues, which were explored in Chapter 8, are typically an appropriate vehicle for RPC calls.

Errors in the Network: How to Recover

Of fact, there is one truth of network life that RPC services cannot readily conceal: the network can be down when you try to initiate a call, or it can even go down in the middle of an RPC call.

When a call is interrupted and does not complete, most RPC protocols simply raise an exception. Note that an error does not always mean that the remote end did not process the request—it could have done so, but the network broke down just as the last packet of the reply was being transmitted. Your call would have theoretically succeeded in this situation, and the data would have been successfully added to the database or written to a file, or whatever the RPC call does. You will, however, believe the call failed and wish to try it again, perhaps storing the same data twice. When building programmes that delegate some function calls via the network, there are a few strategies you can employ.

To begin, make an effort to build services that provide idempotent operations that can be safely retried. Although an operation such as "remove $10 from my bank account" is inherently risky because retrying it could result in additional $10 being removed from your account, An operation like "conduct transaction 583812, which deducts $10 from my account" is absolutely secure because the server can recognise that your request is a repeat and declare success without actually repeating the deduction by saving the transaction number.

Second, follow Chapter 5's advice: instead of using try...except wherever an RPC call is made, try using try and except to surround bigger portions of code that have a firm semantic meaning and can be reattempted or recovered from more cleanly. If you use an exception handler for every call, you'll lose the majority of the benefits of RPC: Your code should be easy to develop and not require you to constantly monitor the fact that function calls are actually routed over the network! If you decide that your software should retry a failed call, you may use the exponential back-off technique for UDP presented in Chapter 3 as an example. This method allows you to avoid slamming an overburdened server and exacerbating the problem.

Finally, be cautious about working around the network's loss of exception detail. Unless you're using a Python-aware RPC method, you'll probably discover that what would typically be a polite KeyError or ValueError on the remote side becomes some type of RPC-specific problem whose text or numeric error code you have to scrutinise in order to figure out what went wrong.

Conclusion

RPC allows you to create what appear to be conventional Python function calls but actually call a function on another server via the network. They accomplish this by serialising the arguments so that they can be communicated, and then doing the same with the returned value.

All RPC protocols function in a similar way: you establish a network connection and then call on the proxy object you're provided to invoke code on the remote end. The Python Standard Library supports the older XML-RPC protocol natively, although good third-party libraries exist for the sleeker and more current JSON-RPC standard. Only a few data types can be passed between the client and the server using either of these protocols. If you want a far more comprehensive list of Python data types, check out the Pyro system, which can connect Python programmes over a network and includes substantial support for native Python types. The RPyC system is much more comprehensive, allowing actual objects to be exchanged across systems and method calls on those objects to be routed to the system where the object resides.

When you go through the content in this book again, you'll be inclined to think of each chapter as being about RPC in some way. That is, information is sent between a client programme and a server through an agreement on what a request will entail and how a response would appear. Now that you've studied RPC, you've seen this interaction at its most basic level, meant to permit arbitrary communication rather than any defined action. Always consider whether your problem requires the flexibility of RPC or whether the transaction between your client and server could be reduced to one of the simpler, limited-purpose protocols discussed earlier in this book when implementing new services—and especially when you're tempted to use RPC. You will be amply rewarded by networked systems that are simple, dependable, and easy to maintain if you select the proper protocol for each challenge you confront, incurring no more complexity than is necessary.